W9-AXB-580

◆ ◆Hall of Fame

08-169

"Angell's perceptions are fresh, vivid and uncannily accurate. . . . A gentleman, Angell does not harangue or vent his frustration on players or owners. He is, however, opinionated. Drugs, player-owner conflicts, artificial turf, the designated hitter, 'the wave' and superegos such as Pete Rose, George Steinbrenner and even baseball commissioner Peter Ueberroth come under close scrutiny. . . . Only a fan who cares this much could observe so carefully and write so eloquently. The late Bill Veeck once said that baseball is a game to be savored. The same could be said for *Season Ticket*."

Linda Perkins
San Francisco Chronicle

"He sounds like no other baseball journalist. . . . He writes with respect of every player he mentions, making the game larger than winning and losing, bigger than persons or teams, a triumph of art and grace. . . . Angell's artistry is significantly free of statistical trivia, but rich with statistics where statistics are interesting, amusing, or touching."

Mark Harris
Chicago Tribune Book World

"Angell has done for spring training what Ansel Adams did for the Western landscape."

Jerry Shriver
USA Today

Property of
Canadian Baseball
Hall of Fame

◆ ◆ ◆

"Mr. Angell explores the art of catching, pitching, playing the infield and reviving a decrepit franchise, and discovers subtleties that will prove useful whether readers want to play or watch the game, or even own a team. There are baseball's personalities to illuminate. . . . And, of course, there is [the] language to be wrought."

Christopher Lehmann-Haupt
The New York Times

"*Season Ticket* constitutes a historical document, capturing all of the priceless moments of [the last five] years. . . . Angell has been called, among other things, the poet laureate of baseball. Others may have written as well about the game, but none has done it as consistently well or with as much passion. . . . An invaluable baseball companion for the true baseball fan, those men and women whose calendars are marked by the comings and goings of the four seasons—Spring Training, Opening Day, the World Series and the Winter Meetings."

Dave Mawson
Worcester Sunday Telegram

"As always, Angell's prose is crystal clear, his observations are right on the mark, and his book is a joy to read."

Library Journal

"A must for fans. . . . Here is superlative clubhouse, field, dugout and even spring-training reportage that not only describes the stars of our time . . . but also examines in detail (based on extensive conversations with the leading practitioners) the intricacies of catching, infield play and pitching, the problems of running a club and the mysteries of managing, and the appeal of baseball's hall of fame in Cooperstown, N.Y. . . . Once again, Angell affirms that he is the bard of the diamond."

Publishers Weekly

"Taking up where he left off in 1982's *Late Innings*, Angell offers another welcome collection of leisurely elegant essays, mainly from *The New Yorker*, which log the high and low points of professional baseball's five . . . recent seasons. . . . An unabashed fan, he takes obvious delight in examining and explaining aspects of the game's evolution. . . . Insights as well as intelligence from a nonpareil among baseball journalists."

The Kirkus Reviews

"Predictably eloquent. . . . Angell's great appeal as a baseball writer is . . . he's one of us, just another guy at the ball park."

Booklist

Also by Roger Angell:

THE STONE ARBOR

A DAY IN THE LIFE OF ROGER ANGELL

THE SUMMER GAME*

FIVE SEASONS

LATE INNINGS*

Published by Ballantine Books

SEASON TICKET

A Baseball Companion

Roger Angell

BALLANTINE BOOKS • NEW YORK

Copyright © 1988 by Roger Angell

All rights reserved under International and Pan-American Copyright Conventions. Published in the United States of America by Ballantine Books, a division of Random House, Inc., New York, and simultaneously in Canada by Random House of Canada Limited, Toronto.

For information about permission to reproduce selections
from this book, write to Permissions,
Houghton Mifflin Company, 2 Park Street,
Boston, Massachusetts 02108.

The material in this book first appeared in
The New Yorker, some of it in different form.

Library of Congress Catalog Card Number: 87-29399

ISBN 0-345-35814-7

First published by Houghton Mifflin Company. Reprinted by permission of Houghton Mifflin Company.

Printed in Canada

First Ballantine Books Edition: March 1989

"Don't you know how hard this all is?"

TED WILLIAMS,
*on batting in particular
and baseball in general*

Contents

• ◆ •

Preface

IT IS MY HOPE THAT OLD AND NEW BASEBALL FANS WILL FIND
in this book a rough replica of their own actual or imaginary
explorations of the game over the past five years—a journey
through the seasons, with stopovers at the spring camps; notes
and exclamations about the midsummer campaigns; conversations with vivid players or movers of the pastime; excursions
and distractions (including a consideration of the most distracting issue of drugs); and the intensive pursuit of the late pennant
races, the championship playoffs, and the World Series. As before, I have covered this beat in haphazard fashion, following
my own inclinations and interests. Friends and critics have
sometimes called me a historian of the game or a baseball es-
sayist or even a baseball poet, but I decline the honors. It seems
to me that what I have been putting down for a quarter century
now is autobiography: the story of myself as a fan. I have tried
to do this seriously, because fans matter, but with a light hand,
for baseball has brought me much pleasure.

This is my fourth baseball book, and if there has been a
shift of gaze, it is because I have at last sensed that there is more
losing than winning in our sport, and that a fan's best defense
against inexorable heartbreak is probably to learn more about
how the game is really played. I care a lot about the games and

the moments and the men on the field—the 1986 Mets–Red Sox World Series still seems a cruelly unfair test of my deepest loyalties—but in recent years I have become engrossed in the craft and techniques of the game: not just how the runs were scored but why. I have talked for hours on end with catchers and pitchers (famous starters and young blazers, and an exceptional relief artist), and infielders, hitters, coaches, managers, scouts, executives, and owners, and most of the time I started with the same question: "How do you do what you do?" They responded with floods of information and instruction, example and anecdote, all put forth with an intensity that confirmed my belief that this placid, easy game is in fact a thing of such difficulty that it easily holds off our wish to master it and bend it to our desires. No team in this decade has established itself as a dynastic power—it is quite the contrary, in fact—despite the best corporate and strategic efforts of twenty-six major-league duchies to achieve that end: a macrocosm of the resistance presented by every game, almost every inning, on the long summer schedule. Since I am a fan, I will always be an amateur of baseball, but I no longer feel like an outsider; none of the old pros I talked to on the field or in the dugout or up in the stands gave me the impression that he had subdued the game, either. We are baffled but still learning, and we keep coming back for more.

—R.A.

◆ ◆ ◆

TWO CHAPTERS HAVE BEEN SHUFFLED OUT OF CALENDAR ORDER in the book, in the interest of better flow. In the interest of sanity, I have omitted mention (for the most part) of the trades or other shifts of affiliation that have moved some players and managers along to other teams since their appearance in these pages.

ONE

◆ ◆ ◆

La Vida

SUMMER 1987

BASEBALL OPENS YOUR EYES. EACH NEW SEASON, IT TAKES me four or five games before I begin to see what's really happening on the field—how the pitcher is working to this particular batter; the little shifts in the infield defense, with men on base, as the count progresses; how bold or how cautious this manager will be with his fresh assemblage of hitters and base runners. Over the winter I also seem to forget another part of baseball—the stuff away from, or off to one side of, the teams and the standings and the vivid events on the diamond, which can reward the experienced and reawakened fan. But that, too, comes back in time. At Tiger Stadium, early in June–June, 1984: the Year of the Tiger, it turned out—I watched the Toronto Blue Jays valiantly trying to chip away at Detroit's mountainous early-season lead in the American League East in a contest that the visitors eventually won, 6–3, thus narrowing the Detroit margin to three and a half games. (The Jays never came as close again.) There was a big, apprehensive crowd and plenty of action—back-to-back doubles by the Jays' Dave Collins and Lloyd Moseby and an inside-the-park homer by George Bell—but between all the action and the cheering and the rest of it my attention was taken by a spider I happened to notice up in one corner of the frame of the open press-box window before me. It was a

1

very small spider—a dot, really—but a busy one. It was working on a web. Inning by inning, the creature persisted, laying out struts and cables, catwalks and connectors, and the stadium floodlights illuminating the green field below us also lit up the little construction project as it grew in size and beautiful design. The white light struck each fresh thread with silver as it appeared, magically, where there had been none before, and was stretched to its planned and perfect mooring. I pointed out the web to my seatmate in the press box, and he studied it, too, and in time I noticed that each of us was following the game in the same way—watching the pitch or the play below and sometimes making an entry in his scorecard, but then returning at once to the smaller event above us in the window. I ran into that writer, an old friend, in October at the World Series in Detroit, and after we'd exchanged some remarks about the players and the pitching and the coming game he said, "Say, do you remember that night back here in the summer, with that little spider? Wasn't that *something*? You know, I woke up the other night and I was thinking that again. Funny . . ."

Then I might add that the thing we remember at my house about a Fourth of July Mets–Astros game at Shea (four of us had gone to it: a family party) isn't the terrific postgame fireworks or a little bloodletting of Astro runs in the first inning but our getaway from the parking lot afterward. (I hope soon to complete my small monography on stadium-quitting.) Actually, by the time we turned up at Shea the lot was full, with the gates and pay booths closed, and we had to make do with a narrow, muddy little junkyard off some street out beyond the center-field parking sectors, where a local entrepreneur took our seven bucks and then absolutely buried us in a welter of other late-comers. No hope, but when we found our way back there, hours later, beyond the motionless thousands of overheating cars and captive fans and patriots self-blocked in the main lot, someone in our group spotted a little alley at the back of the yard, and we took a chance and swung that way, against the flow of cars inching out, and found a miracle there: an empty street. I zipped through a couple of blocks, hung a right away from the honking tangle, extemporized a dazzling U-turn under the Whitestone Express-way, guessed and grabbed another right, spotted the good old boat basin off to my right, and laid a little left onto the Grand Central Parkway: home free, homeward bound, with the cheers of my fans loud in the car and cascades of Queens-side Roman candles on either hand celebrating our brilliant departure.

Nor is there anything in my baseball notebooks about the second game of a Saturday doubleheader in the middle of August—the Twins against the Red Sox at Fenway in the latter stretches of one of those long, nearly eventless games when the sawdust slowly begins to leak out of the pastime. Why do I remember it so well? The pitcher out there has run the count to 3–1. There is a foul, then another foul. The pitcher doesn't want the new ball the umpire has thrown in and asks for another one. He gets it and rubs it slowly in his hands. He winds and throws: another foul. The outfielders shift from foot to foot and stare deeply into the grass before them. A base runner leads cautiously away from first, then trots back as the pitcher steps off the rubber. The third-base ump walks seven steps out toward left field, turns, and strolls back again. Another foul ball, bounced softly past first base. "Throw it *straight*," somebody in the press box mutters. There are spatters of applause in the stands, but they die away for lack of hope. The lights are on, for evening has crept closer, and here and there in the lower decks I can see some fans getting up, in twos and threes, and heading up the aisles for home and dinner. The park is half empty by now. Out in the sloping right-field sector of the seats, there is a thin, a-cappella rendering of "Happy Birthday," for somebody—her name is Ella, it turns out—and other fans around the park join in on the last "happy birthday to you-ooo!" and Ella gets a little round of applause, too. But that ends as well (a coach is out talking to the pitcher now), and even the everyday noises of the baseball park—the hum of voices, the undercurrent of talk and cheers and laughter and vender cries—drop and fade, and Fenway Park is almost silent, just for a minute. The flag in center field hangs motionless in the last late sunlight, its pole a startling pink. The rightfield bleachers are bathed in pastel, and a first breath of evening cool floats up from the lighted field below. I sigh and stretch, wanting the game to get on with itself, but in no hurry, really. No place to go, no place I need to be. Midsummer.

BASEBALL IS NOT LIFE ITSELF, ALTHOUGH THE RESEMBLANCE keeps coming up. It's probably a good idea to keep the two sorted out, but old fans, if they're anything like me, can't help noticing how cunningly our game replicates the larger schedule, with its beguiling April optimism; the cheerful roughhouse of June; the grinding, serious, unending (surely) business of midsummer; the September settling of accounts, when hopes must be traded in for philosophies or brave smiles; and then the abrupt running-down of autumn, when we wish for—almost demand— a prolonged and glittering final adventure just before the curtain. But nowhere is this metaphor more insistent than in baseball's sense of slippage; our rueful, fleeting awareness that we tend to pay attention to the wrong things—to last night's rally and to-morrow's pitching match-up—while lesser and sweeter moments slide by unperceived. Players notice this, too. Bob Gibson, the most competitive man I have ever seen on a ballfield, once told me that what he missed most after he had retired wasn't the competition at all. "I don't miss the pitching but I can't say I don't miss the game," the Cardinal Hall of Famer said. "I miss it a *little*. There's a lot I don't want to get back to. . . . I think it's the life I miss—all the activity that's around baseball. I don't miss playing baseball but I miss . . . baseball. *Baseball*. Does that sound like a crazy man?"

I told him he wasn't crazy, and I think I also said that I'd heard some other players and managers use the same phrase in the same way: *the life*. It was a little while, however, before I began to appreciate that this other side of the game was there for me, as well. *La vida* is not the same for a middle-aged baseball writer as it is for the players (scribes—even the beat men—never wholly belong in the clubhouse, the way the players do), but there are some compensations; for one thing, the life is easy for me to bring back, because I wrote down so much of it. For another, I was encouraged to write about myself, myself as a fan, which is a kind of reporting that other lucky baseball writers should be given as their beat. I could be lighthearted or even trivial, if it suited me, and I could revisit old baseball friends whenever I wished.

Earl Weaver, for one. Here he is, as jaunty as ever, even when seen in serious circumstances—just before his last game in base-ball (or so he thought and we all thought), on the first Sunday in October, 1982. He lost that day, and the Brewers, not his Orioles, progressed to the playoffs and then on into a bruising seven-game World Series with the Cardinals. When the Orioles' season came to its end that afternoon in Baltimore, the downcast but grateful multitudes in Memorial Stadium repeatedly sum-moned Weaver back to the field with their applause. He waved his cap again and again, and then led the funny local letter-cheer for the fans one more time, stubbily spelling out the name of their team, with tears glistening on his face. But never mind that; here is the beginning:

This is the final day of the regular season, the last tick on the great summerlong, hundred-and-sixty-two-game clock, and the two teams here in Memorial Stadium—the Orioles and the visiting Milwaukee Brewers—are tied for first place in the American League East. The winners of this game will finish up with ninety-five victories and sixty-seven losses (the best record in either league in 1982) and will catch an evening flight to the Coast to begin preparations for the league-championship series that opens on Tuesday against the California Angels. There is such a thing as caring too much, and here on the sun-warmed field, chattering with writer friends and watching the batters in the cage, I realize that I almost don't want this game played, for one of these two sterling, embattled clubs—equal favorites of mine, if that is possible—must lose before the day is done. But play they must, and, deep down, I want the Orioles to win, because of Earl. He is retiring after fourteen and a half seasons at the helm, during which span his teams have twelve times won ninety games or more, with six divisional championships, four pennants, and one World Championship. Only the late Joe Mc-Carthy had a better managerial record in this century. Retiring now is Weaver's idea, announced more than a year ago; he wants less time in airplanes and hotel lobbies, more time to give to his vegetable garden, to the dog track, to visiting his grandchildren. "Anybody has to be stupid to work when he doesn't have to," he has said, but he is only fifty-two years old, and the betting is that he will be back in a year or two, managing somewhere, at a very large salary, and talking baseball better than anyone else.*
Here, sitting at ease in his dugout, his cap pushed back, one leg comfortably crossed, ankle on knee, over the other, and with the press kneeling and sitting and leaning in about him in a three-deep semicircle, he is hoarse and cheerful and profane, and so eager in response that he makes each reporter's questions sound simply conversational. He is himself, that is, and the

---

*Quite right, and the job, it turned out, was managing the Orioles. Earl took up the reins again in midseason of 1985, and helped steer his old club to a second-place finish. The next year, however, everything went sour—most of all, the pitching—as the team slipped into the cellar of the American League East, and when it was over Earl stepped down for good. In retrospect, I think I should have known that the first retirement wouldn't work. Earlier in 1982, I recall, I asked him in a casual sort of way if he was truly ready to leave—and in particular if he'd be able to stick to his promise to stay out of baseball altogether. Wasn't it possible that he'd end up coaching a college team or even a high-school team somewhere, the way so many other retired skippers had done? "I *hate* kids and I hate fucking kid baseball!" he barked, startling us both into laughter. He wanted the real thing, nothing less.

burdens of this special day have not dimmed him. No, he tells us, making out the lineup card this morning didn't require any more care than usual. "I think hard about all my lineup cards," he says, "so this was no harder than the other hundred and sixty-one." No, he hadn't worried about the games ahead when he was out in Detroit the other day and down by four. "What happened in *that* game and what was happening to Milwaukee in the game over in Boston was what mattered. It's always one game at a time. You can't do nothing about the other ones." The talk shifts to Jim Palmer, who will start today, and to his opponent, the veteran Don Sutton. "I'll get goose bumps when Jimmy walks in from the bullpen before the game," Weaver says. "I always do. He's a lot responsible for us being here today, you know." Palmer, at 15–4 for the year, has lost only one game in his last twenty-four starts. "There've been times when he did it with just this"—he taps his forehead—"and the other man out there today can do the same thing if he has to. It's always easy for the scouts to say 'Pitch a good fastball up and in on this batter,' but maybe the guy on that little hill can't always *do* it."

There is more, and in the next few minutes Earl stands up (not an extended process for him, at five feet six and a half inches) to illustrate a right-handed batter leaning out over the plate in pursuit of an outside slider and to show how good infielders all reflexively lean to their left in response; sits down again and recalls the pain he experienced in the spring of 1948, when he was an aspiring seventeen-year-old second baseman and was suddenly cut from the roster of the Class B Lynchburg, Virginia, club and had to watch his teammates depart on a train while he and another unfortunate waited for the bus that would take them to join the Class D West Frankfort, Illinois, team ("The guy to feel sorry for," Earl says, "is the kid with West Frankfort who thought he had the second-base job nailed down until I turned up"); and gets up again to illustrate a play in 1964, when he was managing the Elmira (N.Y.) Pioneers. Coaching at third base, he watched a wild pitch that struck the corner of the plate and bounced crazily into the air. "I go halfway down the line to see if the catcher can make the play," he says, "and when he does I try to stop my base runner, Paul Blair, who is coming in all the way from second, but by the time I spin around, Paulie is *there*"—he puts the palm of his hand an inch in front of his nose—"and when I pick myself up I've got footprints here and here and here. Yes, he scored."

In time, he goes off to talk for the television cameras, and when he steps up out of the dugout there is an instant response from the early crowd—a fervent little scattering of "Wea-ver! Wea-ver!"—which he acknowledges with a shy half wave. Like the fans, I want more Earl, but I can console myself by remembering how many dugout monologues and postgame interviews and springtime dissertations and late-night World Series battle summations I have heard from him over the years—all of them, without exception, a lesson and a treat. Back in August, almost two months earlier, I interrupted a seaside vacation in eastern Maine to catch a couple of Orioles–Red Sox games at Fenway Park—to see the teams and hear the crowds and revisit my true favorites, the Bosox, in their jewel-green home park, but mostly to call on Earl Weaver in his last summer of baseball. I had no idea then, of course, that his club would make it back from its third-place spot in the standings, and neither did he, I think. In the dugout just before that series began, Weaver said, "This is a big game for us—I hate to say it. We've lost eleven of sixteen, and our ass is about to hit the water. We just died in Chicago." Rick Dempsey, his veteran catcher, came by at that instant and murmured, "Outmanaged again," and Earl laughed. Clif Keane, the emeritus professor of insults of the Boston press, asked Dempsey about his .129 lifetime batting average (he is in fact a career .235 hitter), and Dempsey said, "Yes, I got to admit it. I got fourteen years in and I've never been hot." Earl lit another Raleigh and politely asked a hovering young woman sportswriter from a suburban Massachusetts paper if she knew any two-syllable words, and when she said yes, she did, he said, "Then you'll go far. This man"—he nodded toward Keane—"got by all these years on just one syllable at a time: 'They-played-a-game-on-this-day-and-our-team-beat-their-team-by-a-score-of-two-to-one.' " "That was for *you*!" Keane cried. "I always did that when I knew you were in town and might buy the paper!" And so on. But there was some real baseball in it, too, and soon Earl was on his feet to show us how he and his coaches had been working with the brilliant young Baltimore rookie Cal Ripken, who was making the difficult transition from third base to shortstop in midseason and had just begun to learn not to take the tiny half step toward the plate which every third sacker makes with the pitch—because he must be so quick to respond to a bunt or a bulletlike line drive—but which the shortstop must avoid, since it can cost him a full stride to one side or the other in the much wider area of the field he must cover. "Wherever he plays, you can write him in for the next fifteen years, because that's how good he is," Earl said of Ripken. "He's got fifteen home runs already, and he ain't missed a ground ball yet, and that's amazing."

The following day at the Fens, Earl was sitting beside Jim Palmer during the dugout levee and, in response to some question or other, unwarily said, "I watch a game with my mind completely blank. Most of the time, I'm only thinking that I'm glad I don't have to make a decision." Palmer, nodding his head happily, said, "Me, too, Earl. I'm always glad about that." The next exchanges have slipped my mind, but when Palmer picked up his glove and went up onto the field I noticed how Weaver followed him with his gaze. The little manager and the tall pitcher have been together on the Orioles ever since the summer of 1969—over two thousand games now—and they have had some celebrated disagreements. Most of the time, though, they remind me of a father and son who have been forced to spend too many days and hours together behind the counter in the family stationery store or delicatessen. There are hundreds of shared anecdotes that they tell differently and squabble over, and a few serious, semi-public differences of opinion between them about business strategy and comportment, but mostly they convey the pleasingly complicated impression that while they can hardly bear each other's company for a single day longer, they care about and count on each other more than either one can admit. The moment one of them is out of earshot of the other, what you hear is a compliment. This time, Earl turned to one of the Baltimore writers and said, "Do you remember Jim pitching that day against Oakland—the old Oakland team, when they were so tough—when he started rearranging our outfielders, the way he does? Bando is coming up, with men on base, and he's a right-handed hitter, of course, and Jimmy begins to move our *right* fielder—I think it's Rettenmund—in, and then over a step, and then *back* a half step, like a goddam photographer arranging a picture, and then he holds up his hands—Hold it! Right there!—and the next pitch, the very next goddam pitch, Bando hits a *shot* out to right, and the fielder goes like this and like this, bending in and leaning back while he's watching the ball, but he never has to take a single goddam step, and he makes the catch. Jim Frey was coaching with us then, and he turns to me on the bench and says, 'Well, now I've seen everything.' " Weaver laughed and coughed, and shook his head at the memory of it. "Nobody like Jim Palmer," he said.

• ◆ •

ONE SPRING IN MESA, ARIZONA, I RAN INTO GENE AUTRY, the owner of the California Angels, who was chatting with some of his players in the visiting-team dugout. He was wearing cowboy boots and a narrow string tie. He looked gentle and old and agreeable, the way he always does. When the Angels lost the American League playoff in 1982 by dropping three games in a row to the Brewers (after winning the first two games), and then threw away another championship series in 1986 under even more unlikely and scarifying circumstances, everybody in baseball felt bad, I think, because they so wanted a Gene Autry team in a World Series. We chatted a little, and he told me about his baseball beginnings. "I was always a Cardinals fan then," he said, "because I came from Oklahoma, and they had the Dean brothers and Pepper Martin and all those other Okies playing for them. Then I followed the Cubs, because I'd started in singing over Station WLS, in Chicago. The Gabby Hartnett–Charlie Grimm Cubs, I mean. Oh, I had a lot of baseball friends. I have a photo at home of me and Casey Stengel and Mantle and Whitey Ford. I wouldn't take anything in the world for that photo. You know, I was thinking just the other day about the old days down home, when we'd listen to Bob Kelley, who did those game re-creations from the Coast over the radio, from a telegraph ticker. You don't remember that, I imagine. There'd be nothing, and then you'd hear the ticker begin to go and you'd know something was happening in the game, and then he'd describe it. He could bring it all alive for you."

But I did remember. I still do—me, at ten or eleven, with my ear next to the illuminated, innerly-warmed gold celluloid dial of the chunky, polished-wood family radio, from which there emerges, after an anxious silence, the clickety, train-depot sounds of a telegraph instrument suddenly bursting with news. Then a quick, closer *tock*!—the announcer or some studio hand rapping on the mike with a pencil, I suppose—and the re-creator, perched in his imaginary press box, says, "Uh-oh. . . . Hafey really got hold of that delivery from Fat Freddie. The ball is rolling all the way to the wall in left, and here come two more Cardinal runs across the plate. . . ." The front door slams—my father home from work, with the New York *Sun* under his arm (and the early-inning zeros of that same Giants road game on the front page, with the little white boxes for the rest of the line score still blank), and I get up to meet him with the bad news.

◆ ◆ ◆

SPRING TRAINING IS THE LIFE. ONE MARCH DAY IN PHOENIX Municipal Stadium, I strolled slowly away from the batting cage in the dazzling desert sunlight and climbed the shallow grandstand steps behind the Oakland home dugout, on my way to grab a pre-game hamburger and a cold Coors at the little freeload picnic grounds for the media out by left field. The fans were coming in—old folks carrying seat cushions and scorecards, college kids in T-shirts and cutoff jeans, young women in sandals with serious tans and white "A's"-emblazoned painter's caps, kids balancing mammoth cups of popcorn—and unhurriedly scouting around for good seats in the unreserved rows. A last fly ball rose and dropped untouched behind second, where an Oakland coach and a batboy were picking up the batting-practice balls and dropping them into a green plastic laundry basket. The first visiting ballplayers, fresh off their bus, were playing catch over in front of their dugout; it was the Giants this time, and I was looking forward to seeing Al Oliver again and to watching this kid pitcher Garrelts (if he did work on this day, as promised) and a couple of others, but there was no hurry about the game's starting, of course, and nothing to worry about even if I did miss a few pitches and plays while I lingered over my lunch. A friend of mine, a beat man with the San Francisco *Chronicle*, came along and fell into step beside me. Smiling a little behind his shades, he nodded toward the field and the players and the filling-up stands and murmured, "You know, it's a shame to have to mess all this up with the regular season."

Teams in Arizona and Florida play with identical rules and before the same sort of audiences, but the two spring flavors are quite different. I don't understand it. Florida ball seems more citified, hurried, and temporary; no matter how rustic the setting, I always have the sense that the regular season impends, and that these humid, sunny afternoons are just postcards, to be glanced at later on and then thrown away. Arizona baseball is slower, sweeter, and somehow better fixed in memory. For one thing, there seem to be more young children in attendance at the western parks; the stands are stuffed with babies and toddlers— or else I just notice them more. In Phoenix one afternoon, a small barefoot creature came slowly and gravely up the aisle behind the home dugout wearing nothing but a Pamper. Six- or seven-year-old home-team batboys are already veterans of two or three Arizona seasons. In one game at Scottsdale, matters were suspended briefly when a very young rookie bat-person in pigtails went out on the field after a base on balls, picked up the bat (they were both the same length: the thirty-three-inch model), and paused, staring slowly back and fourth, until she remembered which dugout she had come from, and then returned there, smiling in triumph. The home-plate umpire, I noticed, made a good call, holding up one hand and watching over his shoulder until we were ready for baseball once again. It wouldn't have happened in Florida.

For me, Arizona baseball is personified by a young woman vender at Phoenix Stadium I came to recognize, after several springs, by her call. She would slowly make her way down an aisle carrying her basket and then sing out a gentle, musical "*Hot* dog! . . . *Hot* dog!"—a half note and then down four steps to a whole note. She'd go away, and later you heard the same pausing, repeated cry at a different distance, like the cry of a single bird working the edge of a meadow on a warm summer afternoon. "*Hot* dog!"

Old fans and senior scribes want the spring camps to remain exactly the same; they should be like our vacation cottages at the lake or the shore—a fusty and familiar vicinity in which we discover, every year, the sparkle and renewing freshness of another summer. The wish is doomed, of course. Each succeeding March, the small ballparks are visibly more crowded and the audiences younger and more upscale, with affluent, Hertz-borne suburban families on the kids' spring break lately beginning to outnumber the cushion-carrying retirees in the stands. Authors and television crews cram the sidelines at the morning workouts, and by game time the venders at the souvenir stands look like Bloomingdale's salesgirls during Christmas week. Spring training is "in," worse luck, and even the most remote baseball bivouacs are incipient Nantuckets. Out in Mesa, descending hordes of Cubs fans absolutely swamp little HoHoKam Park every game day, lining up at breakfast time to buy up the twenty-three hundred unreserved seats that go on sale at ten o'clock; the park put in new bleacher seats in 1985, enlarging its capacity to eight thousand, but this was insufficient to handle the numbers of the new faithful. A friend of mine—a retired Chicago baseball writer who lives in Arizona now—told me that he drove over to the Cubs training complex on the very first day of spring training that same year, when only the pitchers and catchers had reported, and counted license plates from twenty-six states in the parking lot. "There were maybe a thousand fans at the workout," he said. "A thousand, easy, just watching the pitchers doing sit-ups."

Chain O'Lakes Park, the Red Sox training site in Winter Haven, is less frantic, but it has changed, too. It was an inning or two into my first game there in 1985 when I saw the difference: the old, fragrant orange grove out beyond the right-field and center-field fences was gone, replaced by a cluster of low, not quite finished white buildings, with a drooping banner out front that said "LAKEFRONT CONDOMINIUMS." I gestured miserably at this phenomenon, and my seatmate, a Boston writer, said, "Yes, I know. Remember when we used to write 'and Yaz hit it into the orchard'? Now what do we say?"

Trying to perk me up, he pointed out that the two nesting ospreys I had seen here on prior spring trips were still in residence in their big, slovenly nest on top of the light pole in short right-field foul ground; just the day before, he said, a batter with the visiting Reds had skied a foul ball that had landed in the nest—landed and stayed there, that is—but the birds did not seem discomposed. I kept an eye out, and over the next few innings I saw one or perhaps both of them depart and return to their perch, coming in with a last flutter of their great wings and then settling down on whatever they were keeping there above the field. Someday soon, I decided, we would hear about the first confirmed sighting of a young red-stitched osprey (*Pandion ueberrothiensis*) here, hard by the banks of Lake Lulu. I cheered up. A little later in that game, we had a brief shower—the first rain in weeks, I was told—and some of the older fans got up from their unprotected seats along the left- and right-field lines and came and stood in the aisles of the roofed grandstand, out of the wet. The game went on, with the sitting and standing fans quietly taking it in, and I had a sudden, oddly familiar impression (this has hit me before, in this park at this time of year) that I had found my way into a large henhouse somewhere and was surrounded by elderly farmyard fowls. We perched there together, smelling the aroma of mixed dust and rain, and waited for the sun to come out again.

THE LIFE—BASEBALL AS A SIDE ORDER, SO TO SPEAK—IS NOT necessarily slow or reflective. What I remember about an October now seven years gone isn't an unmemorable World Series between the Dodgers and the Yankees (the Dodgers won it) but the crowds at the Stade Olympique, up in Montreal, during the stirring Dodgers–Expos playoff games there. All that is still clear: the middle innings of Game Three, say (the clubs had come back from Los Angeles with the series tied), with the Dodgers' Jerry Reuss and the Expos' Steve Rogers locked in hard combat, and the Dodgers up a run—the only run of the game so far— and the encircling, in-leaning rows upon rows of avid, baseball-mad Canadians, seeming to sway and shudder and groan and cry in the chilly northern night air with every pitch and movement of the fray. And to sing. When I wrote about this, several days later, I still half heard in the dusty back chambers of my head the vapid, endlessly repeated chorus of that damnable Expo marching song—*"Val-de-ri! Val-de-rah!"*—that the locals bellowed together, in enormous and echoing cacophony, at every imaginable stitch and wrinkle of the games' fabric. The song is not some famous indigenous voyageurs' chantey, as one might suppose, but only the old, implacably jolly "Happy Wanderer" hiking ditty that generations of sub-adolescents across the continent have had to warble through ("Val-de-ra-ha-ha-ha-ha-ha!") during mosquitoey marshmallow roasts at Camp Pineaway. But the Montrealers sang it with a will—sang it because they *wanted* to, of all things—and they won my heart. I didn't even mind the weather, which was unsuitable, if never quite unbearable, or the appalling ballpark. The round, thick-lipped, inward-tilted concrete upper wall of the Stade Olympique appears to hang over the stands and the glum, Astro-Turfed field in a glowering, almost threatening way, shutting out the sky, and fastballs and hard-hit grounders are so hard to see from above, for some reason, that the accompanying noise from the crowd is always an instant or two out of sync. This time I didn't care, because the teams and the players and the quality of play were all so good that every part of the games mattered and made you glad you were there and no place else in the world just then.

In the sixth inning of that third game, the Expos tied things up with a single and a walk and a little roller by Larry Parrish, *just* through between Cey and Russell at third and short. Reuss, perhaps ever so slightly distracted by the blizzards of torn-up *journeaux*, and the layered explosions of noise, and the illuminated "PLUS FORT!" up on the scoreboard, and the back-and-forth billowings of an enormous white Québecois flag, and the hundredth or perhaps thousandth bellowed cascade of *"Val-de-ri!"*'s and *"Val-de-rah!"*'s—now got a fastball a millimeter or two higher than he wanted to against the next batter, outfielder Jerry White, who socked the ball up and out into the left-field stands for a homer and three more runs and, it turned out, the game.

I imagine everyone who thinks of himself or herself as an Expo fan still clings to that moment, for the team lost the next two games—lost them late, under grindingly painful circumstances—to miss out on the World Series, and sank into a long baseball torpor. Sometimes it's wiser to remember the byplay of big games—the songs and the rest of it—instead of their outcome, because losing hurts so much. Players understand this all too well. A day or two before the end, Steve Rogers, talking about all the singing and happiness in the Montreal stands, shook his head a little and said, "Yes, it's beautiful, but—well, euphoria is not always the name of the game."

◆ ◆ ◆

PEOPLE WHO DON'T FOLLOW BASEBALL VERY CLOSELY ASSUME that fans care only about their own club. I don't agree. Whenever I happen upon a Little League game or a high-school game or a Sunday game in Central Park between a couple of East Harlem amateur nines, it only takes me an inning or so before I find myself privately rooting for one of the teams out there. I have no idea how this choice is arrived at, but the process is more fun if the two sides offer a visible, almost moral, clash of styles and purpose, and—even better—if each seems to be personified by one of its players. At that 1982 Cardinals–Brewers World Series, York and Lancaster were brilliantly depicted by the rival center fielders; the frail, popeyed, apologetic-looking Cardinal rookie, Willie McGee; and the hulking, raggedy-ass veteran Brewer slugger, Gorman Thomas. McGee had a great series, it turned out, both at the plate and in the field; in the third game, which the Cardinals won, 6–2, he smacked home runs in two successive at-bats, and in the ninth he pulled down a mighty poke by Gorman Thomas (of *course*) after running at full tilt from mid-center field into deep left center and then to the top of the wall there all in one flowing, waterlike motion—a cat up a tree—with no pause or accelerations near the end to adjust for the catch; at the top of his leap, with his back to the field, he put his glove up and bit to his left, and the ball, in the same instant, arrived. The play almost broke my heart, for I had already somehow chosen the Brewers and Gorman Thomas as my own. Thomas, as it happened, did nothing much in the Series—three little singles, and this after a summer in which he had hit a league-leading thirty-nine home runs—so I certainly wasn't front-running. The frowsy Thomas was a walking strip mine; he had worn the same pair of uniform stockings, now as threadbare as the Shroud of Turin, since opening day of 1978. I recall a moment in the Brewer clubhouse during the Series when a group of us were chatting with Thomas's father—he was the retired postmaster of Charleston, South Carolina—and some genius reporter asked what Gorman's room had looked like back when he was a teen-ager. "Turrible!" Thomas *père* said, wincing at the thought. "Why, I could hahdly make myself look in theah!"

◆ ◆ ◆

EVENTS ON THE FIELD QUALIFY IN THE LIFE, AS WELL; THEY only have to be a little special. In September 1986, during an unmomentous Giants–Braves game out at Candlestick Park, Bob Brenly, playing third base for the San Franciscos, made an error on a routine ground ball in the top of the fourth inning. Four batters later, he kicked away another chance and then, scrambling after the ball, threw wildly past home in an attempt to nail a runner there: two errors on the same play. A few moments after *that*, he managed another boot, thus becoming only the fourth player since the turn of the century to rack up four errors in one inning. In the bottom of the fifth, Brenly hit a solo home run. In the seventh, he rapped out a bases-loaded single, driving in two runs and tying the game at 6–6. The score stayed that way until the bottom of the ninth, when our man came up to bat again, with two out, ran the count to 3–2, and then sailed a massive home run deep into the left-field stands. Brenly's accountbook for the day came to three hits in five at-bats, two home runs, four errors, four Atlanta runs allowed, and four Giant runs driven in, including the game-winner. A neater summary was delivered by his manager, Roger Craig, who said, "This man deserves the Comeback Player of the Year Award for this game alone." I wasn't at Candlestick that day, but I don't care; I have this one by heart.

Or consider an earlier concatenation that began when Phil Garner, a stalwart Pirate outfielder, struck a grand slam home run against the Cardinals at Three Rivers Stadium one evening in 1978. Every professional player can recall each grand slam in his career, but this one was a blue-plate special, because Garner, who is not overmuscled, had never hit a bases-loaded home run before—not in Little League play; not in Legion or high-school ball; not in four years with the University of Tennessee nine; not in five years in the minors; not in six hundred and fifty-one prior major-league games, over two leagues and five summers. Never.

We must now try to envisage—perhaps in playlet form—the events at the Garner place when Phil came home that evening:

P.G. (*enters left, with a certain swing in his step*): Hi, honey.

Mrs. P.G.—or C.G. (her name is Carol): Hi. How'd it go?

P.G.: O.K. (pause) Well?

C.G.: Well, what?

P.G.: What! You mean . . .

C.G.: (*alarmed*): *What* what? What's going on?

P.G.: I can't believe it. You missed it. . . .

Yes, she had missed it, although Carol was and is a baseball fan and a fan of Phil's, as well as his wife, and was in the custom of attending most of the Pirates' home games and following the others by radio or television. When he told her the news, she was delighted but appalled.

C.G.: I can't get over not seeing it. You can't imagine how bad I feel.

P.G.: (*grandly*): Oh, that's O.K., honey. I'll hit another one for you tomorrow.

And so he did.

ATTENTION MUST BE PAID. IN MARCH, 1984, I WATCHED A TALented left-handed Blue Jay rookie pitcher named John Cerutti work three middle innings against the Red Sox at Winter Haven; at one point he struck out Jim Rice with a dandy little slider in under his fists. I talked to Cerutti after the game and learned that he was four credits away from his B.A. degree in economics at Amherst (he has since graduated) and that his senior thesis had to do with the role of agents in major-league player salaries. I also discovered that he had a baseball hero: Ron Guidry.

"I don't have many fond memories of baseball until I was about eighteen and pitching for the Christian Brothers Academy, in Albany," he said. "Then I got the notion that I might make it in the game someday. I had a real good year that year—it was 1978—and, of course, that was the same time that Guidry had *his* great year. I was a Yankee fan—always had been—so naturally I followed him and pulled for him, and that spring I began to notice that something weird was happening to us. I mean, I won seven games in a row, and he won his first seven. Then I was 9–0 when he was exactly the same—we were winning together, me and *Ron Guidry*! School ended and I graduated, but I went on pitching in American Legion ball. I was 13–0 when I lost my first game, and I thought, Uh-oh, that's the end of it, but that very same night Guidry lost, too, for the first time—I was watching on TV—so we were still the same. Well, I guess you know he finished up the year with a 25–3 record, and was the Cy Young winner and all, and I ended at 25–2. So you could say we both had pretty good years. That affinity began."

Cerutti said all this a little offhandedly—with a trace of college-cool irony, perhaps—but his face was alight with humor and good cheer.

"So do you want to know my dream now?" he went on. "My dream is that first I make this club some day, and then I end up pitching a game against Ron Guidry. It's a big, big game—a Saturday afternoon at the Stadium, one of those big crowds, with a lot riding on it—and I beat him, 1–0. It could just happen."

"I know," I said.

"Keep watching," he said.

"I'll be there," I said.

Making the Blue Jays took a little longer than Cerutti had expected, but when he was called up from Syracuse in the spring of 1986, it was noticed that he had his stuff together at last; he went 9–4 for the season, with a shutout along the way, and took up his place in the Toronto starting rotation. I was happy about the promotion (I had renewed acquaintance with him briefly a couple of times in the interim, mostly in Florida), and in June this summer I watched him work a game against the Yankees in New York one evening—watched him over the tube, I mean. It was a significant game for both clubs, since the Blue Jays were a half game up on the Yankees at the top of the American League East. There I was, with my dinner and a drink before me and with John Cerutti, big as life, up there on the screen, when several rusty synapses clicked on at last. "My God!" I cried. "It's Guidry, too. It's happened."

I had blown our date, but Cerutti kept his, all right, beating the Yankees by 7–2, it turned out, to solidify his teams's hold on first place. Not Cerutti's plan *exactly*, but close enough.

I considered rushing up to the Stadium to catch the later innings, but I didn't. I got there early the next evening, however, and at batting practice a couple of writer friends said, "You see John Cerutti? He was looking for you last night."

He came in from the field at last—he had been doing his sprints out there—and found me in the dugout. "Hey," he said cheerfully. "Where were you?"

"I blew it," I said. "I'm sorry, John—I stood you up. I feel bad about it. Only you said it would be a *Saturday*."

"Well, I looked for you," he said. "Everyone else was here. I heard a couple of days ago that it might be me and the Gator, so I called my mom and she came down for it. In the end, I had to leave sixteen tickets for people from home. They knew how long I'd been waiting. It was all just the way I'd dreamed about it. In the first couple of innings, I kept thinking, Here I am, with my spikes on the same pitching rubber where Ron Guidry's spikes were a minute ago. It was a thrill."

"I know—I saw it at home," I said miserably. "There's no excuse, only well, you know . . . I didn't believe it. Life isn't *like* this."

"I know," he said. "But this is different."

"This is baseball, you mean."

"That's right," he said. "In baseball—well, stuff can happen."

TWO

◆

In the Fire

CONSIDER THE CATCHER. BULKY, THOUGHT-BURDENED, unclean, he retrieves his cap and mask from the ground (where he has flung them, moments ago, in mid-crisis) and moves slowly again to his workplace. He whacks the cap against his leg, producing a puff of dust, and settles it in place, its bill astern, with an oddly feminine gesture and then, reversing the movement, pulls on the mask and firms it with a soldierly downward tug. Armored, he sinks into his squat, punches his mitt, and becomes wary, balanced, and ominous; his bare right hand rests casually on his thigh while he regards, through the portcullis, the field and deployed fielders, the batter, the base runner, his pitcher, and the state of the world, which he now, for a waiting instant, holds in sway. The hand dips between his thighs, semaphoring a plan, and all of us—players and umpires and we in the stands—lean imperceptibly closer, zoom-lensing to a focus, as the pitcher begins his motion and the catcher half rises and puts up his thick little target, tensing himself to deal with whatever comes next, to end what he has begun. These motions—or most of them, anyway—are repeated a hundred and forty or a hundred and fifty times by each of the catchers in the course of a single game, and are the most familiar and the least noticed gestures in the myriad patterns of baseball. The catcher

19

has more equipment and more attributes than players at the other positions. He must be large, brave, intelligent, alert, stolid, foresighted, resilient, fatherly, quick, efficient, intuitive, and impregnable. These scoutmaster traits are counterbalanced, however, by one additional entry—catching's bottom line. Most of all, the catcher is invisible. He does more things and (except for the batter) more difficult things than anyone else on the field, yet our eyes and our full attention rest upon him only at the moment when he must stand alone, upright and unmoving, on the third-base side of home and prepare to deal simultaneously with the urgently flung or relayed incoming peg and the onthundering base runner—to handle the one with delicate precision and then, at once, the other violently and stubbornly, at whatever risk to himself. But that big play at home is relatively rare. Sometimes three or four games go by without its ever coming up, or coming to completion: the whole thing, the street accident—the slide and the catch, the crash and the tag and the flying bodies, with the peering ump holding back his signal until he determines that the ball has been held or knocked loose there in the dust, and then the wordless exchanged glances ("That all you got?" . . . "You think that *hurt*, man?") between the slowly arising survivors. Even when the catcher has a play on the foul fly—whipping around from the plate and staring up until he locates the ball and then, with the mask flipped carefully behind him, out of harm's way, following its ampersand rise and fall and poising himself for that crazy last little swerve—our eyes inevitably go to the ball at the final instant and thus mostly miss catch and catcher.

But this slight is as nothing compared to the anonymity we have carelessly given to our receiver in the other, and far more lengthy, interludes of the game. Because he faces outward—I *think*: none of this seems certain—and because all our anticipation of the events to come (in this most anticipatory of sports) centers on the wide green-sward before us and on its swift, distant defenders, our awareness of the catcher is glancing and distracted; it is as if he were another spectator, bent low in order not to spoil our view, and although at times he, too, must cover ground quickly, he is more often waiting and seemingly out of it, like the rest of us. We fear or dote upon the batter, depending on which side is up; we laugh at pitchers a little, because of their contortions, but gasp at their speed and stuff; we think of infielders as kids or terriers, and outfielders are gazelles or bombardiers or demigods; but catchers are not so easy to place in our imagination. Without quite intending it, we have probably always patronized them a little. How many of us, I wonder, have entirely forgotten "the tools of ignorance," that old sports-page epithet for the catcher's impedimenta (it was coined in the nineteen-twenties by Muddy Ruel, a catcher with the Senators, who practiced law in the off-season). And think for a moment of the way the umpire watches the catcher as he goes about his housekeeping there behind the plate. Sometimes the arbiter has actually picked up the man's cap and mask from the ground during the play just previous, and now he hands them over with an odd, uncharacteristic touch of politeness. Both of these men wear shin guards and chest protectors and masks, and although theirs is mostly an adversary relationship, they crouch in identical postures, inches apart (some umpires actually rest one hand on the catcher's back or shoulder as the pitch is delivered), and together engage in the dusty and exhausting business down behind the batter, living and scrounging on the hard corners of the sport. For one game, that is. Tomorrow, the umpiring crew will rotate, as it does for each game, and the ump working behind home will be stationed out at third base—almost a day off for him—so that he can recover from such labors, but the same catcher most likely will still be down there bent double behind the batters. *Here y'are*, the ump's courtly little gesture seems to say. *You poor bastard.*

I thought a lot about catchers during the long winter off-season that is just now drawing to a close, and found for the first time that I was able to envision a couple of them at work at their trade, in the same way that, like most fans, I can easily bring back the mannerisms of a favorite batter—George Brett, Lou Piniella, Mike Schmidt—as he steps into the box and prepares for the pitch, or the unique pause and stare and windup motion of some pitcher—Steve Carlton, Rick Sutcliffe, Fernando Valenzuela—whose work I know by heart. Suddenly, this winter, I could envision Rick Dempsey, the dandy midsize Oriole receiver, coming up onto the balls of his feet in the crouch after delivering a sign, with his orange-daubed glove inviting an outside-corner pitch to the batter. A base runner flies away from first with the pitcher's first move, and the delivery is low and away, a very tough chance, but Dempsey is already in motion, to his right and forward—"cheating," in catchers' parlance—and he seizes the pitch with the back of the mitt nearly touching the dirt and his bare right hand almost simultaneously plucking the ball from the pocket. The catch drives the glove backward, but because Dempsey has anticipated so well, the force and direction of the pitch are simply translated into the beginnings of his rising pivot and the upcocking of his arm for the peg—a line has become an upswooping circle—and he steps eagerly but unhurriedly across the plate to start the throw to second.

Finding Dempsey in my mind's eye in January was not quite startling, since he played so well in the course of the Orioles' five-game victory over the Phillies in the World Series last fall (he won the Most Valuable Player award for the classic, in which he batted .385, with five extra-base hits, and, even more important, was the prime receiver during the Baltimore pitching staff's 1.60-E.R.A. stifling of the National League champs), but some other catchers turned up in my hot-stove reveries as well. Bob Boone, for instance. Boone, who is thirty-six, now catches for the Angels, after a decade of notable defensive work with the Phillies. He is six feet two—a large man, although there is nothing hulking or overmuscled about him—but his movements behind the plate are gliding and water-smooth. He sets up with his left foot flat and the right foot back an inch or two, with its heel up, and once the sign is delivered he tucks his right hand behind his thigh—almost standard stuff, but if you keep your eyes on him you begin to pick up the easy body movement that slips him imperceptibly into place behind each arriving pitch and the silky way the ball is taken into the glove, without haste or grabbing. If something goes wrong—a pitch bounced into the dirt off to his right, say—his motion toward the ball is quickly extended, with the whole body swinging in the same arc as the pitch: the right knee goes into the dirt, with the leg tucked along the ground, while the glove is dropped straight down to dam off the opening below the crotch. No attempt is made to catch the pitch—catchers are endlessly trained in this, since it contravenes all baseball instinct—and the ball is simply allowed to bounce off his body. Boone locates it on the ground (his mask has flown off, spun away by an upward flick of his hand) and only then looks up to check the base runner; if he's going, the play is in front of him. It's an anxious, scattery set of moves, or should be by rights, but Boone makes them seem controlled and confident, as if the mistake had been reversed and turned into something risky for the other team. Nothing in these classic maneuvers is unique to Boone, except for the thoughtful elegance of their execution; he helps you appreciate the work.

Talking to catchers is even more fun than watching them, as I discovered last season, when I began to sense how little I knew

about their dusty trade and sought out a few of them for enlightenment. They were surprised to be asked, it turned out, and then
they seemed eager to dispel some of the peculiar anonymity that
has surrounded such a public occupation: if you want an earful,
go to a man in a highly technical profession who feels he is
unappreciated. My instructors—almost a dozen of them in the
end—came in different sizes and ages and uniforms and degrees
of experience, and they were almost a random sample. Inevitably, I missed some of the best-known practitioners (including
the celebrated Johnny Bench, who retired after the 1983 season;
Montreal's Gary Carter, who is paid well over a million dollars
per annum for his work and is perhaps the leading candidate to
succeed Bench as the No. 1 catcher; Lance Parrish, of the Tigers; Jim Sundberg, late of the Texas Rangers and now of the
Brewers; and the testy Jerry Grote, who is out of baseball and
living in Texas, after winding up an extended career with the
Mets and three other clubs, during which he was thought of as
perhaps the best handler of pitchers around), but the catchers I
did talk to were so voluble and expressive in their responses that
I did not come away with the feeling that any major theorems
of their profession were closed to me. Indeed, their replies were
so long and meaty that I realized along the way that I simply
wouldn't have time to take up *every* aspect of catching with
them—blocking the plate, for instance, or the nasty little problem of catching and holding the knuckleball and the spitter, or
the business of learning an extraordinary physical stoicism that
allows the man behind the plate to disregard or play through the
daily bruises and batterings that come with the job (most regular
catchers experience pain of one form or another, and in one or
several places on their bodies, right through the season), or the
relative importance of the pre-game strategic review of the other
team's hitters, or the business of veiling your signals from enemy
base runners, or the prevalence of low tricks like surreptitiously
nicking or scuffing the ball in aid of your pitcher, and more.
These themes would have to wait for remedial sessions. Bob
Boone told me at one point that he thought it took about three
hundred major-league games for a catcher to feel comfortable
back there, and I realized that the best I could hope for as an
outsider was a glimpse at such a body of skills.

I talked to my informants separately, beginning with extended
colloquies around battings cages and in dugouts and clubhouses
during the leisurely 1983 spring term in Arizona and Florida,
and then coming back for some short refreshers whenever I ran

into one of them during the regular season. In time, these interviews ran together in my mind and seemed to turn into one extended, almost non-stop conversation about catching, with the tanned, knotty-armed participants together in the same room, or perhaps ranged comfortably about on the airy porch of some ancient summer hotel, interrupting each other, nodding in recollection, doubling back to some previous tip or topic, laughing together, or shouting in sudden dissent. But they grew more serious as they went along. One of the surprising things about the catchers' catcher-talk, I realized after a while, was how abstract it often was. Old names and games, famous innings and one-liners and celebrated goofs seemed to drop out of their conversation as they got deeper into it, as if the burden of anecdote might distract them (and me) from a proper appraisal of their hard calling. Everything about catching, I decided somewhere along the way, is harder than it looks.

◆ ◆ ◆

TERRY KENNEDY, THE TWENTY-SEVEN-YEAR-OLD RECEIVER FOR the San Diego Padres, is six feet four and weighs two hundred and twenty pounds—almost too big for a catcher. He is prized for his bat and his durability—in the past two seasons he played in a hundred and fifty-three and a hundred and forty-nine games (very high figures for a catcher) and batted in ninety-seven and ninety-eight runs. At one time, there was some thought of moving him out to play first base, until a year ago, when the Padres acquired a fellow named Steve Garvey in the free-agent market. Now Kennedy must stay behind the plate and work on his quickness—work to become smaller, almost.

"Throwing is where mobility matters," he told me in Phoenix one afternoon. "I'm learning to cheat a little back there, with men on base. Once I determine where the pitch is, I'm starting up. You *have* to do that, with all the fast runners we're seeing on the base paths. Coming up right is what throwing is all about. There's a two-step or a one-step release. I start with a little jab-step with my right foot and go right forward. The important thing is to be true with that throw, so you try to keep your fingers on top of the ball. If they're off to one side, the ball will banana on you"—sail or curve, that is—"as it goes out there. You can even throw a little from the side, as long as your fingers are on top."

Kennedy's home pro is Norm Sherry, the Padres' pitching

coach, who put in four years as a backup catcher with the Los Angeles Dodgers and the Mets, sandwiched in the middle of sixteen seasons in the minors; he has managed at both levels (he was the Angels' skipper for a term), but, with his dark glasses, his seamed and mahogany-tanned face, and his quick, thrusting way of talking, he suggests the quintessential infantry sergeant.

"Terry's coming on and coming on," Sherry told me. "It takes a long time to learn to call a game, but Terry was much more of a catcher in the second half of the season last year. He understood situations better. You can't work on that kind of stuff in the spring, but I been pitching forty or fifty pitches to him every day—curves and fastballs and in the dirt—and he has to come up throwing. Young catchers today don't have such good mechanics, because they all rely on this one-handed glove. If you take the pitch with one hand, you don't have your throwin' hand on the ball in good position when you start back. They look up and see the guy running and make any old kind of grab at the ball, and that's where you get those errors. I try to get them to take the ball two-handed, and that also closes up the front shoulder, the way it should be to start your throw. So many of them are in a *panic* when they see somebody movin' and they lose control of everything. Sometimes you see a man even knock his mask so it sort of half slides across his face. Then he can't see anything, because he was in such a hurry. But if you just take that little half step in advance, you've done all the hurrying you need to do. You just have to stand up and take a good stride and throw it.

"So much of this started with Johnny Bench, you know, who became such a good catcher with that one-handed glove. All the young catchers started to follow him, to pick up that style. But not many guys are Johnny Bench. He had great big hands, and wherever he grabbed the ball he got seams. It was like Willie Mays and his basket catch—only a few could do it well."

Months later, Joe Garagiola showed me a trick about seams. We were standing behind the batting cage together before the first World Series game in Baltimore last fall, and when Johnny Bench's name came up—he had just closed out his distinguished seventeen-year career with the Cincinnati Reds: indisputably the greatest catcher of his era—Garagiola, after adding several accolades, suddenly echoed Norm Sherry's little demurrer. In a way, he said, Bench had almost set back the art of catching, because of his own great skills. "You have to get that good grab on the ball," Joe said in his quick, shill-sharp way, "and you can't always do that if you're hot-doggin' with that mitt. You gotta get seams to throw straight. Here—get me a ball, somebody.'' A ball was sneaked from the cage, and Garagiola, blazer and all, half crouched and suddenly became a catcher again. (He had a successful nine-year career at the position, mostly with the Cardinals, before taking up his second life, behind the microphone.) ''Here's what Branch Rickey made us do when we were just young catchers tryin' to come up in the Cardinal system,'' he said. ''Take the pitch in two hands, with your bare hand closing it in there, and then *grab seams*. If you take hold of it this way''—he held the ball on one of its smooth white horseshoe-shaped sectors, with the red stitching on either side of his forefinger and middle finger—'''you got no *idea* where it's going to end up. But you can learn to shift it in your hand while your arm is comin' up to start the peg. Just a little flip in the air and you can get seams. Look.''

He raised his hand quickly three or four times in a row and took a fresh grip on the ball as he did so. Each time, he had seams. He laughed in his famous, engaging way, and said, ''Nights in spring training, Mr. Rickey made us each take a ball with us when we went to the movies and practice that in the theatre. Three or four catchers sittin' in a row, grabbing seams!''

◆ ◆ ◆

THE ''ONE-HANDED GLOVE'' THAT SO MANY OF MY CATCHING informants referred to is the contemporary lightweight mitt that everyone, including Little Leaguers, now employs behind the plate. Thanks to radical excisions of padding around the rim and thumb, it is much smaller than its lumpy, pillowlike progenitor, more resembling a quiche than a deep-dish Brown Betty. The glove comes with a prefab central pocket, but the crucial difference in feel is its amazing flexibility, attributable to a built-in central hinge, which follows the lateral line of one's palm. The glove is still stiffer and more unwieldy than a first baseman's mitt, to be sure, but if you catch a thrown ball in the pocket the glove will try to fold itself around the ball and hold it, thus simply extending the natural catching motion of a man's hand. Catching with the old mitt, by contrast, was more like trying to stop a pitch with a dictionary; it didn't hurt much, but you had to clap your right hand over the pill almost instantly in order to keep it in possession. Indeed, this technique of nab-and-grab was almost the hardest thing for a boy to learn about catching when I first tried it (and instantly gave it up), many years ago, and a mistimed clutch at the ball was often suddenly and horribly painful as well. The new glove turned up in the nineteen-sixties, and its first artisan was Randy Hundley, a smooth, lithe receiver with the Chicago Cubs. Its first and perhaps still its greatest artist, its Michelangelo, was Johnny Bench, whose extraordinary balance and quickness, coupled with the glove, allowed him to take everything one-handed and, moreover, to make every kind of catch back there look as effortless and natural as the gestures of a dancer. He made the lunging, manly old art look easy, which may explain why so many baseball people—including many of the catchers I talked to—seem to find it necessary to set Bench a little to one side when they speak of him: to mount him as a museum exhibit of catching, a paradigm locked away behind glass, and to examine it with appropriate murmurings of wonder and then walk away. "Bench was picture-perfect," Ted Simmons said. "A marvellous mechanical catcher. There's no better. In the light of all that praise, it's very hard for any other catcher to be considered in that way." Carlton Fisk said, "Bench did so many things almost perfectly that it almost seemed robotical. Everything was done so automatically that it didn't seem to have much creativity to it." Sometimes catchers can sound like authors.

◆ ◆ ◆

FOR BOB BOONE, THE CATCHER'S FRONT SHOULDER IS THE KEY to strong throwing. "You have to have that closed front side, just the way you do in hitting," he told me. "When the arm goes through, the front shoulder opens up. Coming up to that position is basically a three-step movement, but some can skip all that and take just one step and throw. That takes a real strong arm. Parrish can do it. I went to it early in my career, because it was simple for me then, but I don't think it's the most effective. If your arm doesn't get all the way through—if it never quite catches up to your body and you let the throw go from out *here*—you get that three-quarters, Thurman Munson throw. Thurman threw that way because he didn't have a strong arm, and I'm sure he weighed that quick release against velocity and accuracy. But he didn't have a choice, really. For me, that shift to get the shoulder into position is where the throw is made. Velocity is a gift—and most catchers in the majors have it—but quickness is in your feet."

Boone speaks in a deliberate, considering sort of way. He is a thoughtful man, with a saturnine look to him that contrasts strikingly with his gentle, almost sleepy smile. He is a graduate of Stanford, where he majored in psychology (not much of a help to him in baseball, he confided—not even in dealing with umpires). During the negotiations arising from the 1981 baseball strike, he represented the National League for the Players Association. Possibly because of this union activity, he was not signed to a new contract by the Phillies the next season, and crossed leagues to join the Angels, where he enjoyed immediate success, winning a Gold Glove award (his third) for his defensive prowess, and handling the theretofore listless California mound staff in a manner that helped bring the club to the championship playoffs that fall. We talked in the visiting-team clubhouse during the middle innings of an Angels–Cubs spring game at Mesa, while he slowly took off his uniform (he had played the first four innings) and showered and dressed, waiting for his teammates to be done, waiting for another team bus. I didn't think we covered much ground in our talk, but I was wrong about that; his modest, off-speed delivery fooled me. In the days and weeks that followed, I heard Boone-echoes in things that other catchers and coaches were telling me, and realized that I had already been put in the game, as it were, by what he had imparted.

One catcher's attribute that Boone always seemed to come back to in our talk was consistency—doing hard things right again and again, doing them as a matter of course. "Everyone at the major-league level has talent," he said at one point, "but the players who last are the ones who are consistent. People who can control themselves over one hundred and sixty-two games are rare, and that's why the old idea of the starting nine has sort of gone out. It seems that a lot of players get into bad spells and have to have a rest. I think you have to prepare your *mind* to play a full season, and of course you have to train for it physically. I work a lot on flexibility. You have to be able to deal with pain, to the point where it doesn't affect how you hit and catch and throw. That comes with time. You experience things and deal with them. I don't look at the catcher's job as one that's going to tire me out more than other players get tired. Getting tired is just part of the season, so you prepare for that, too."*

*On September 16th, 1987, Bob Boone caught his 1919th major-league game, thereby surpassing the all-time receivers' record held by Al Lopez. Although he didn't sign

IN SARASOTA, DAVE DUNCAN WAS TALKING ABOUT THE GREAT recent upsurge of base-stealing in both leagues, and what the coaching staffs were doing to combat it. (Per-team base-stealing totals have risen dramatically in the past two decades, thanks in part to the individual exploits of motorers like Lou Brock, of the Cardinals, who at the age of thirty-five set a new one-season record with a hundred and eighteen stolen bases in 1974, and Rickey Henderson, of the Oakland A's and then the Pittsburgh Pirates, set amazing new *team* stolen-base records in each league, in 1976 and 1977, with three hundred and forty-one and two hundred and sixty thefts, respectively. Back in the nineteen-forties and fifties, the major-league clubs averaged fewer than fifty stolen bases per year, with everyone waiting to stroll around the bases after a home run, but now National League teams average about a hundred and fifty swipes per summer, and the A.L. about forty or fifty fewer, with the difference probably attributable to the quicker, artificial-turf basepath carpets that predominate in the senior circuit.) Duncan, who is the pitching coach for the Chicago White Sox, caught for eleven years with Kansas City, Oakland, Cleveland, and Baltimore. He handled the hairy A's flingers— Catfish Hunter, Vida Blue, Rollie Fingers—during the first of Oakland's three successive world-championship seasons, in the early nineteen-seventies: yes, *that* Dave Duncan. He is a slender, soft spoken gent with wide-spaced pale-blue eyes.

"*Everyone's* running, it seems," he said. "And everything is being timed now. I don't remember anybody putting a clock on a catcher when I was out there. Now there are three or four guys on the bench with stopwatches, and the first-base coach in the spring has a stop-watch, too. It's gotten so you can figure in advance that you've got a chance against a particular base runner if *this* guy is pitching for you and *that* guy is behind the plate. We've all learned the figures. A good time for a catcher, from the moment of his catch until the moment his peg arrives at second, is around two seconds. If you find a catcher who can get it out there in one-nine or one-eight, that's a quick release.

with the Angels until May 1st, he worked behind the plate in more than one hundred games, as usual, and threw out just under fifty percent of enemy base runners. He is forty years old, and his mind is prepared to go right on catching.

Meanwhile, a man who takes an average lead and gets himself down to second in three-three is a good base runner. A tenth off makes him a real rabbit, and if you're going to throw him out you've got to do everything right—hold him pretty close, a quick delivery from the mound, and then a pitch that the catcher can handle easily. A catcher with a good throwing arm—a Rick Dempsey, a Lance Parrish, a Mike Heath—is almost a necessity nowadays. Bob Boone is about the best there is at calling a good game and also throwing well. He's very consistent, with good accuracy and great anticipation."

I remembered at once. "With a Rickey Henderson or a Tim Raines or a Lou Brock on base," Boone had told me, "you work at setting up the same way as always and at knowing what your own maximum speed is. If you try to go beyond that, you become erratic and you're actually slower. It's like a boxer throwing a jab. He wants to do it at his maximum all the time, but if he suddenly wants a little extra he's much less—you can see it. Actually, it's almost easier with a speedster—with a Rickey Henderson leading away out there—because you know he's going to go. The other guys, the ones you don't expect to run, are harder to keep up for, and you have to do that on every pitch, really, with a man on base. You tell yourself, 'I've got a right-handed pitcher and he's throwing a curveball here, so I have to be aware of my right side, 'cause that's where it's going. O.K., *I'm prepared.*' "

In 1982, Boone was the only regular catcher in either league to throw out more than fifty percent of the opposition's would-be base stealers; he got fifty-eight percent of them, and cut down Rickey Henderson six times out of thirteen. This is still not a dazzling success ratio, to be sure, and since it is demonstrable that athletes today are much quicker afoot than their predecessors, it seems certain that not even time-motion studies and smart catchers are going to keep base runners from sprinting off for second in ever-increasing numbers in the seasons just ahead. It has occurred to me that this phenomenon may represent the first breakdown of baseball's old and beautiful distances: if ninety feet from base to base is no longer enough to keep a single or a base on balls from becoming an almost automatic double, then someone may have to go back to the drawing board at last in order to restore caution to the austere sport—and to cheer up catchers a little, too.

"I admire Bob Boone and this kid Tony Peña, with the Pirates," Tim McCarver said from across the room, so to speak;

we were in St. Petersburg, where McCarver, now a Mets broadcaster, was preparing to do a Mets–Red Sox game. He played in four different decades, from the late fifties to the early eighties, mostly for the Cardinals (he was Bob Gibson's favorite receiver), and he is humorous, snub-nosed, and cheerfully opinionated. "Peña does so many things right already that he makes me *salivate*," he said. "The Phillies let Bob Boone go because they said he couldn't throw anymore—a terrible rap. So he goes over to the Angels and leads the league in throwing out runners and takes the Angels right to the doorstep of the World Series. He's conscientious and he's always in great shape, and his throwing is only a little part of it. I never could throw well, so I always thought calling a game was the biggest thing. That will never become a noted part of the game, because there are no stats for it, and the fans don't care about it, and most of the scouts don't know a whole lot about it, either. Even today, scouts and some managers will say, 'He can really catch,' when they mean 'He can really throw.' This is real bullshit, because throwing just isn't a very important part of it, when you think about it. Gene Mauch is one of the few managers who really understood and appreciated catching. I always felt some resentment about not being appreciated, but that was balanced out by pitchers who knew what I was doing back there. Some of them didn't appreciate me until the time came when they had to pitch to somebody else." He laughed.

◆ ◆ ◆

ALL RIGHT, FORGET ABOUT THROWING. THINK ABOUT CATCHing the ball instead—seizing that imminent, inbound, sinking or riding, up-and-in or down-and-away, eighty-to-ninety-five-m.p.h. hardball, and doing it, moreover, in a way that might just turn the umpire's call to your advantage. Terry Kennedy told me that sometimes you can take a pitch close to the inside edge of the plate (inside to a right-handed batter, that is) and slightly rotate your glove to the left at the last instant—he shifted his mitt so that the thumb moved from two o'clock to noon—and thus win a strike call from the ump. "But you can't hold it there, to make the point," he said. "They *hate* it if you keep the glove up there, and it's almost an automatic ball."

Milt May said that just catching the ball cleanly was a big help to the umpires, and led to better calls, while Tom Haller (we will meet these deponents in a minute) told me that Del

Crandall, the celebrated Milwaukee Braves receiver of a quarter of a century ago, had taught him how to catch an away pitch, on the outside corner, with his glove parallel to the ground, and to take the ball in the webbing instead of in the pocket. "The ball could be an inch or two off the strike zone and he still might call it a strike, because the glove itself is still over the plate," Haller said. "And a high pitch you can take with a little downward move sometimes. You teach a young catcher to take most pitches as close to the plate as possible, because the farther back you are, the more it can bend out of the strike zone. If your glove is back to where that pitch looks like a ball now, the crowd may even react to it, and then the ump thinks, Hell, I'm going to call that a ball after all."

Bob Boone again: "There are a few little tricks of framing and catching the ball that might convince an umpire—shifting your body instead of your glove, or maybe the way you collapse your glove as you make the catch. But you don't want to work on that umpire too much. More often, a catcher will take a strike away from the pitcher by catching it improperly—knocking it out of the strike zone, or moving the glove with the pitch so that it carries the ball out of the strike zone after the catch, and even if you roll your glove you might help the umpire to make up his mind the wrong way."

He left the umpires for a moment and segued into the problems of setting up for the pitcher—presenting the best sort of target for each pitch. "Some pitchers want to throw to your whole body, and not just the glove," he said. "Then if you want the pitch outside, on that far corner, you have to get yourself on out there in a way that the batter won't notice. There's an art in that—it takes time to learn it. You slide over at the last second—and it's much harder to do that against a batter with an open stance, of course: somebody like Rod Carew, on our club—and you also try to get a little closer, which makes it that much tougher for him to spot you. There are some guys who can always seem to sense where you are, no matter what you do. And of course there are a few peekers, too."

I said that he sounded disapproving.

"Well, you tell them to cut it out," Boone said. "But if it goes on you can just say a word to your pitcher. Then you set up outside and he throws inside. That usually stops it right away, and if the batter says anything about it you just say, 'Hey, you were *looking*.' "

But let's finish the introductions. I remember Milt May when he was a blond, promising rookie receiver with the Pittsburgh Pirates, almost fifteen years ago. Now much of his hair has gone, and he is on the down side of a respectable, journeyman sort of career that has taken him by turns to the Astros, Tigers, White Sox, Giants, and—early last season—back to the Pirates again, where he is now a backup to the effulgent Peña. I talked to him in Arizona last spring, while he was still a Giant. Milt May, incidentally, is the son of Pinky May, an infielder with the Phillies around the Second World War. Oddly enough, Terry Kennedy is the son of Bob Kennedy, who was a major-league infielder-outfielder and later on served in various capacities, as coach, manager, and front-office executive, with, among other clubs, the Cubs, Cardinals, and Astros; and Bob Boone's pop, Ray Boone, was a well-known American League shortstop and third baseman in his day. Maybe *not* so oddly: perhaps years of serious baseball talk at the family breakfast table adds a secret something—a dab of sagacity, say—to the Wheaties and thus turns out good catchers down the line.

Tom Haller put in a dozen years at catch for the Giants and Dodgers and Tigers. Now he runs the baseball side of things for the Giants, as V.P. for Baseball Operations. The other catchers in our group, who are leaning forward in the chairs a little restlessly over there as they wait to be heard from, are probably more familiar. The long lanky one is Carlton Fisk, and the intense fellow, smoking a cigarette, is Ted Simmons. In a *minute*, you guys—all right?

Surprisingly, there was more agreement about umpires among the panelists than about anything else. Grudging respect was what I heard for the most part, and then, after the conversation had run in that direction for a few minutes, even the grudgingness seemed to drop away. Ted Simmons, the Milwaukee Brewers veteran, described the catcher-umpire relationship in social terms. "It's like meeting people at a cocktail party," he said. "Some you like and some you can't stand, but you know you have to be at least polite with everybody in order to keep things going."

"You can beef about pitches, but you always do it when you're walking back toward the plate from the mound—after a play maybe," Haller put in. "You don't turn around and do it, you know. Young catchers are always being tested by the umps, and they have to learn to take some bad calls and not say anything. Catchers who are moaning and bitching all the time really can hurt their team, but there's such a thing as being too quiet, too.

You hear an umpire say, 'Oh, he's a good catcher—you never hear a word of complaint out of him,' but to me that's a catcher who isn't sticking up for his team out there.''

"I don't mess with umpires," young Terry Kennedy said. "Let 'em sleep. They say, 'The ball missed the corner,' and I say unwaveringly, 'No, it *hit* the corner,' but I'm quiet about it.'' He laughed, almost helplessly.

Carlton Fisk: "Any game where there's a lot of situational friction—all that yelling and screaming—it can suddenly be very hard on your team. Young umps and young catchers are both new kids on the block, trying to establish themselves, but in time the respect appears, and it can grow. After a while, a good umpire knows you're not going to give him a hard time, and you start to feel he won't squeeze you too much back there. I got along real well with Bill Haller''—he's Tom Haller's older brother—"who just retired. The same for Richie Garcia and Dave Phillips and Steve Palermo. I get along with Ken Kaiser, who can't get along with a lot of players. He umpired with me in the minor leagues, so we go back a long way together. With most of them, it's strictly professional—a 'How's it going?' and then you get on with the game.''

Tom Haller: "Al Barlick was the best ball-and-strike umpire I ever worked with. He took a lot of pride in that. Others—well, Dusty Boggess was on the way out, I think, when I was coming up, and one day I'd been getting on him back there and I said something he didn't like. The next pitch was right down the middle and I'd hardly caught it when he yelled 'Baw-ell!' In time, I learned. As I got older, I began to appreciate how good most of them were.''

Bob Boone: "The umpire has to be himself, so I try to be as honest with him as I can. You're not going to fool a major-league umpire for long. If one of them asks me about a borderline pitch that went for us—a called strike, I mean—he may do it a couple of pitches later: 'What did you think about that pitch?' and I'll tell him, even if I'm saying 'Well, I thought it was a little outside' or 'I thought it was a little high.' That way, he knows if I make a gripe on a pitch later on I'm not trying to steal anything from him.''

Milt May: "They respect your opinion because they know you respect them. Some days, *I'm* not seein' the ball too well, and after the hitter's gone I might ask, 'Say, where was that second pitch? Did you think it was high enough?'—or whatever. I think the instant replays have made the umps look good, because it's turned out they're right so much of the time. Only a catcher who's down there with them can know how hard it is. They don't know what pitch is comin'—whether it's meant to be a slider or a sinker, or what. That ball is *travelling* and doin' different things, and maybe one half inch of it is going to catch the black. If there's a hundred and forty pitches in a game, fifty of them are balls and fifty are strikes, and the other forty are so close—well, dad-*gone*, somebody's going to be mad.''

Carlton Fisk: ''If I know an umpire's preferences, that gives me some borders to aim at. Some are notorious high-ball umps, and others have a very low strike zone. If you have a high-strike umpire and your pitcher is a sinkerball specialist, you might remind the umpire early in the game: 'Hey, this guy's keepin' the ball down real good the last few games—he's pitching real well.' That puts him on notice. And if your pitcher is the kind that's around the strike zone all the time he'll always get more calls from the umpire.''

Tom Haller: ''Umpires tend to be good at what a pitcher is good at because they anticipate that pitch.''

Bob Boone: ''When you change leagues, the way I did, you have to learn the new umpires' strike zones, and when you can argue and when you can't. Paul Runge has a low strike zone—he's going to make you swing that bat when you're up there. He's got a little bigger plate than some, but he's very consistent. You certainly can't change him. Lee Weyer has an extremely wide strike zone. Everyone knows it, and the catchers sort of count on it. Others have a smaller strike zone, and they're known as hitters' umpires.'' (Both Runge and Weyer are National League umps, and later on, after this part of our conversation, I realize that Boone, a diplomat, has not discussed his umpire preferences in the American League, where he now goes to work.)

Milt May: ''You come to appreciate a pitcher who's always around the plate, because he's helping himself with that ump so much. He might miss the black by an inch sometimes, but the umpire will ring it up right away, because he's come to expect strikes from him. It's only natural.''

Bob Boone: ''The real negotiation isn't between the catcher and the umpire—it's between the *pitcher* and the umpire. The pitcher has to show that he can put the ball where he wants it and move it around. If he establishes that he knows where the ball is going, and that he's not just lucking out on the corners, the umpires will be a lot more forgiving with him than they will with the man who's all over the place and suddenly comes in with something close. A good pitcher—a Tommy John, who *lives* on the corners—sets up a rhythm with the umpire, and anything he throws will get a good long look. That's what control is all about.''

Milt May: "The only thing that gets me upset is having two or three pitches in the same spot that are called strikes, and then you come back to that spot and the umpire misses it, just when you most needed that strike. But—well, I'd hate to call about twenty of those pitches myself.''

Bob Boone: "When I'm back there, I want my umpire to call his very best game ever. That's the ideal.''

◆ ◆ ◆

EVERY CATCHER EXUDES STABILITY AND COMPETENCE—THERE'S something about putting on the chest protector and strapping on those shin guards that suggests a neighborhood grocer rolling up the steel storefront shutters and then setting out the merchandise to start the day—but Milt May seemed a little different from the other professionals I consulted. For some reason, I kept thinking that he and I could have played on the same team. I am much older than he is, and I never even lettered in baseball, so this was a dream of some sort. May and I talked during a Giants morning practice in Scottsdale, and he apologized to me each time he had to break off and go take his hacks in the batting cage. He was thirty-two, but he looked a bit older—or perhaps only wearier. Established catchers take on a thickness in their thighs and a careworn slope around the shoulders. Or possibly we only imagine that, from thinking about all those bent-over innings and hours—many thousands of them in the end. But May sounded young and even chirpy when he talked baseball, and up close his face was almost boyish. He hadn't shaved yet that day, and the stubble along his chin was red-gold in the morning sunshine. At one point, he said, "I think I'm like some other catchers—if I hadn't been able to catch I probably wouldn't have been able to make it to the big leagues at all. Maybe you can't run, but if you've got good hands and don't mind the work you can play. Not too many people want to do it." A bit later in the day, I noticed that when May flipped off his mask behind the plate his on-backward cap pushed his ears out a little on either side of his head. Then I understood my dream. Milt May is the kind of kid who always got to catch back when I played on pickup teams as a boy. He was big and slow, and he looked sort of funny out there, but he didn't mind the bumps and the work and the dirt, because that way he got to play. None of the rest of us wanted the job, and most of us couldn't have done it anyway.

◆ ◆ ◆

THAT AFTERNOON, TOM HALLER AND I SAT ON FOLDING CHAIRS in a front-row box in the little wooden stadium in Scottsdale and took in an early-March game between his Giants and the Seattle Mariners. Haller is a large, pleasant man, with an Irish-touched face, and a perfect companion at a game—silent for good long stretches but then quick to point out a telling little detail on the field or to bring up some play or player from the past, for comparison. He was watching his own rookies and stars out there, of course, but he had generous things to say about the young Mariner receiver, Orlando Mercado, who somehow folded himself down to about the height of a croquet wicket while taking a pitch.

"These kids we're seeing today—this one, and that Peña that the Pirates have—are lower than anybody I used to play with," he said in his light, faintly hoarse voice. "Maybe they're better athletes than they used to be—more agile, and all. I still wish they'd move the top half of their bodies more when they're after the ball. That glove has made everybody lazy. You just stick out your hand."

There was an infield bouncer to deep short, and Mercado trailed the play, sprinting down behind first base to back up the peg from short. Haller nodded in satisfaction. "It's hard on you physically behind the plate," he said. "All that bending and kneeling. One way to help yourself is to get on down to first base on that play and do it every single time. You let yourself out a little, so you're not cramped up all day."

A bit later, he said, "Mainly, you have to be a student of the game. There are so many little things to the job. You have to look the same when you're setting up for the fastball and the breaking ball, so you don't tip the pitch. A batter steps up, and he may have moved his feet in the box since the last time you saw him play, and that might completely change the way you and your pitcher've decided to pitch to him. You can't stop everything and call a conference to discuss what to do. You have to decide."

Then: "What you do can get sort of subtle sometimes. If you're ahead by a few runs or way behind in a game, you might decide to give a real good hitter the pitch that he's waiting for—his favorite pitch. Say he's a great, great breaking-ball hitter. Normally, you'd absolutely stay away from that pitch with anything over the plate, but in that special situation you might think, Let's let him have it, this once—let him hit it. That way, you put it in his head that he might get it again from you, later on in the game or the next time he faces that same pitcher. He'll be looking for it and waiting for it, and he'll never see it again. You've got a little edge on him."

In the game, the Giants had base runners on second and third, with one out, and the Mariners chose to pitch to the next batter, outfielder Chili Davis, who instantly whacked a double to right, for two runs. "If you've got an open base, you should try to remember to use it," Haller observed. "So often, you have the intention of putting a good hitter on, rather than letting him hurt you. You go to work on his weakness—let's say, something outside and away—and you get lucky and get two strikes on him, and then the pitcher decides, Hey, I can strike this bozo out. So you come in with the fastball and, bam, he kills you. You got greedy and forgot.

"Sometimes the little breaks of the game begin to go against your pitcher, and you can see him start to come apart out there. You have to watch for that and try to say something to him right off, because you can't do much to settle down a pitcher once he really gets upset. If he's sore, it means he's lost his concentration and so he's already in big trouble. You go out and try to get him to think about the next pitch, but you know he's probably not going to be around much longer."

The game flowed along quietly—nothing much, but not without its startlers. Orlando Mercado, batting against a Giants right-hander named Segelke, in the fifth, spun away from a sailing fastball, but too late—the pitch caught him on the back of his batting helmet and he sagged to the ground. It looked bad for a minute—we'd all heard the ugly sound of the ball as it struck and ricocheted away—but in time Mercado got up, albeit a little groggily, and walked with a Mariner trainer back to his dugout, holding a towel to his ear, which had been cut by the edge of the helmet.

In another part of the game, the Seattle second baseman, Danny Tartabull, cued a high, twisting foul up over the Giants dugout. Milt May came back for it, but it was in the stands, close to the front rows somewhere, and as I peered up, squinting in the sun, I realized at last that it was *very* close to the good seats. I cringed away, holding my notebook over my dome, and Tom Haller stood up beside me and easily made the bare-handed catch. Sensation. The Giants dugout emptied as the San Francisco minions gave their boss a standing O and Haller's friends in the stands—hundreds of them, by the sound of it—cheered noisily, and then a couple of former Giant managers, Wes Westrum and Charlie Fox (they are both scouts now), waved and called over to him from their seats nearby to express raucous awe. Haller flipped the ball to Bob Lurie, the Giants' owner, who was in an adjoining box. "I think I just saved you three bucks," he said. He was blushing with pleasure.

It had been a good five years since anything hit into the stands had come anywhere near that close to me—and, of course, it was the most *immediate* lesson in catching I was to get all year. Then I realized I'd missed the play again. "How did you take that ball, Tom?" I said. "I—"

He made a basket of his hands. "I was taught this way," he said. "Then if you bobble it you can still bring it in to your chest."

Haller's paws are thick and gnarled, and there seems to be an extra angle in the little finger of his right hand. He saw me looking at it now, and held out the hand. "Richie Allen hit a foul and tore up that part," he said. "I had a few dislocations and broken fingers along the line, and this split here needed seven stitches. Usually, you looked for blood, and if there wasn't any that meant you were all right. You could pop a dislocation back in and stay in the game. We were trained to tuck your right thumb inside your fingers and curve the fingers around, so if there was a foul tip the ball would bend them back in the right direction. Nowadays, catchers can just hide that hand behind their leg, because of the new glove. So it has its advantages."

Late in the game, the third Mariner catcher of the afternoon— a rookie named Bud Bulling—was struck by a foul that caromed into the dirt and up into his crotch. He remained on his knees in the dirt for a minute or two, waiting for that part of the day to be over, while the Giants players called to him in falsetto voices. "I got hit like that in the spring of my very first year up with the Giants," Haller said. "I tried not to say anything, and when I got back to the clubhouse I took the cup out of my jock all in pieces. Each spring, you wait for that first shot between the legs and you think, *All* right, now I'm ready to start the season.''

The game ended (the Giants won it, and Chili Davis had racked up a homer, two doubles, and a single for the day), and as we stood up for the last time Haller called to a Mariner coach out on the grass. ''I see some of us get old and gray!'' Tom said.

''Yeah, I saw you,'' the coach said. ''Your hands still look pretty good!'' He waved cheerfully.

''That's Frank Funk,'' Haller said to me. ''Frank was my first roommate in organized ball. We were in spring training together in the Giants' minor-league complex in Sanford, Florida, in 1958. He was a pitcher and I was a catcher, and they put us together to see if we could learn something.''

He'd had a great afternoon—you could see that. He was tickled.

◆ ◆ ◆

NO CATCHER OF OUR TIME LOOKS MORE IMPERIOUS THAN CARL-ton Fisk, and none, I think, has so impressed his style and mannerisms on our sporting consciousness: his cutoff, bib-sized chest protector above those elegant Doric legs; his ritual pause in the batter's box to inspect the label on his upright bat before he steps in for good; the tipped back mask balanced on top of his head as he stalks to the mound to consult his pitcher; the glove held akimbo on his left hip during a pause in the game. He is six-three, with a long back, and when he comes straight up out of the chute to make a throw to second base, you some-times have the notion that you're watching an aluminum exten-sion ladder stretching for the house eaves; Bill Dickey, another straightback—he was the eminent receiver for the imperious Yankee teams of the thirties and forties—had that same household-contraption look to him when getting ready to throw. Fisk's longitudinal New England face is eroded by reflection. He is a Vermonter, and although it has been three years now since he went over to the White Sox, he still looks out of the uniform to me without his Fenway habiliments. Pride is what he wears most visibly, though, and it's also what you hear from him.

''I really resent that old phrase about 'the tools of igno-rance,' '' he said to me in the White Sox dugout in Sarasota. ''No catcher is ignorant. I've caught for pitchers who thought that if they won it's because they did such a great job, and if they lost it's because you called the wrong pitch. A lot of pitchers need to be led—taken to the point where they're told what pitch to throw, where to throw it, when to throw it, and what to do after they've thrown it. The good pitcher knows that if you put down the fastball''—the catcher's flashed signal: traditionally one finger for the fastball, two for a breaking ball, three for a changeup, and four for variants and specials—''it's also meant to be down and in or down and away, and if you put down a breaking ball then it's up to him to get that into some low-percentage area of the strike zone. The other kind just glance at the sign and fire the ball over the plate. That's where you get that proverbial high hanger—and it's your fault for calling it. But you know who the best pitchers are, and they know you. I worked with Luis Tiant as well as with anybody, and if he threw a fastball waist-high down the middle—well, it was nobody's fault but his own, and he was the first to say so. Not many fans know the stats about catchers, but smart pitchers notice after a while that they'll have a certain earned-run average with one catcher, and that it'll be a point and a half higher with another catcher on the same club. Then they've begun to see that it isn't just their talent that's carrying them out there.''

There are some figures that even fans can understand, however: in 1980, Fisk's last year in Boston, the Red Sox won sixty-eight games and lost forty-four when he was behind the plate but were fifteen and thirty-three when he was not. His bat helped, then and always (he is a lifetime .281 hitter, with two hundred and nine career homers, and of course he is the man whose twelfth-inning home run won the sixth game of the 1975 World Series—still a high-water mark of the October classic), but Fisk, in conversation, showed a splendid ambivalence about the two sides of his profession. Hitting mattered, but perhaps not as much as the quieter parts of the job.

''Catchers are involved every day,'' he said, ''and that's one of the reasons why, over the years, they've been inconsistent in their productiveness. You can go a month and make a great offensive contribution, and then maybe a month and a half where there's little or none. But because of the ongoing mental involvement in the pitcher-batter struggle you don't have the luxury of being able to worry about your offensive problems. You just haven't got time. I think catchers are better athletes than they used to be. They run better and they throw better, and more of them hit better than catchers once did. I'm not taking anything away from the Yogi Berras and the Elston Howards and the rest, but there never were too many of them. With the turn of the seventies, you began to get catchers like myself and Bench and Munson, and then Parrish and Sundberg and Carter, and then Peña—you go down the rosters and they're all fine athletes. Bench started hitting home runs and Munson started hitting .300, and that old model of the slow, dumb catcher with low production numbers started to go out of date."

Then there was the shift: "It always bothered me that catchers seemed defined by their offensive statistics—as if a catcher had no other value. Famous guys who hit twenty-five or thirty home runs or bat in a hundred runs may not have as much value as somebody hitting .250 or less—a Jerry Grote, say—but his pitchers and his teammates sure know. Look at Bill Freehan, with that good Detroit team back in the sixties and early seventies. He was a very average sort of runner, with an average, quick-release sort of arm, and nothing very startling offensively. But you just can't *measure* what he did for that Tiger pitching staff—people like McLain and Lolich and Joe Coleman."

He had brought up a side issue that has sometimes troubled me. There have been a hundred and seven Most Valuable Player awards since the annual honor was instituted by the Baseball Writers Association of America, in 1931, and thirteen of them have gone to catchers—very close to a one-in-nine proportion, which looks equitable. Catchers who are named M.V.P.s tend to get named again—Roy Campanella and Yogi Berra won the award three times apiece, and Johnny Bench twice—but it is hard not to notice that almost every M.V.P. catcher posted startling offensive figures in his award-winning summers: Gabby Hartnett batted .344 in 1935, Ernie Lombardi batted .342 in 1938, Bench had a hundred and forty-eight runs batted in in 1970. And so forth. Only one M.V.P. catcher—Elston Howard, in 1963—had offensive statistics (.287 and eighty-five R.B.I.s) that suggest that his work behind the plate had also been given full value by the voting scribes. The B.B.W.A.A. is engaged in an interesting ongoing debate about whether pitchers should be eligible for the M.V.P. award (as they are now), given the very special nature of their work. I think we should look at the other end of the battery and consider the possibility that, year in and year out, each of the well-established veteran catchers is almost surely the most valuable player on his club, for the reasons we have been looking at here.

Fisk cheered up a little after his musings. He tucked a nip of Skoal under his lower lip, and told me that catching left-handed pitchers had been the biggest adjustment he'd had to make when he went over to the White Sox. "Except for Bill Lee, we didn't have that many left-handers my twelve years in Boston," he said. "Because of the Wall. But there are good left-handers on this club, and that's taken me a little time. When you're calling a game with a left-handed pitcher against a lot of right-handed batters, you have to do it a little differently. A left-hander's breaking ball always goes to my glove side, and his fastball and sinkerball run the other way. That fastball up over here, from a lefty pitcher, is a little harder for me to handle, for some reason. I'm still conscious of it, but I'm beginning to have a better time of it now."

I thought about Fisk often and with great pleasure last summer, while his White Sox streaked away with the American League West divisional title. He batted .289, with twenty-six homers, for the year, and the Chicago pitchers (including LaMarr Hoyt, whose 24–10 and 3.66 record won him the Cy Young Award) outdid themselves. Fisk's season ended in the White Sox' excruciating 3–0 loss to the Orioles in the fourth game of the American League championship series, at Comiskey Park, in a game in which Britt Burns, the young left-handed Chicago starter, threw nine innings of shutout ball before succumbing in the tenth. Fisk had but one single in five at-bats in that game, but I think he found some rewards just the same. There in Sarasota, he'd said, "When things are working well and the pitcher stays with you the whole way and you're getting guys out and keeping in the game—well, there's just no more satisfying feeling. You want to win it and you want to get some hits, but if your pitcher is doing his best, inning after inning, then you know you've done your job. It doesn't matter if I don't get any hits, but if I was an outfielder in that same game and all I'd done was catch a couple of routine fly balls—why, then I wouldn't have anything to hang my hat on that day."

Tim McCarver also spoke of this sense of deeper involvement. Like many useful long-termers, he was moved to easier positions when the demands of the job began to wear him down, but he didn't like it much not catching. "Joe Torre had been through that same shift," he said to me, "and he told me that when I changed position I'd be amazed how much my mind would begin to wander. When I moved out to first base—I played more than seventy games there in 1973—I couldn't believe it. I had to keep kicking myself to pay attention."

◆ ◆ ◆

CALLING A GAME, OF COURSE, IS THE HEART OF IT, AND WHAT
that requires of a catcher, I came to understand at last, is not
just a perfect memory for the batting strengths and weaknesses
of every hitter on every other club—some hundred and sixty-
five to a hundred and ninety-five batters, that is—but a sure
knowledge of the capabilities of each pitcher on his staff. The
latter is probably more important. Milt May said, "If I had a
chance to play against a team I'd never seen before but with a
pitcher I'd caught fifty times, I'd much rather have that than play
against a team I'd played fifty times but with a pitcher I didn't
know at all."

The other desideratum is a pitcher with good control—far
rarer, even at the major-league level, than one might suppose.
"There are very few guys who can really pitch to a hitter's
weakness," May said. "Most of 'em just want to pitch their
own strength. Young pitchers usually have good stuff—a good
moving fastball—and they pitch to hitters in the same pattern.
Most of their breaking balls are out of the strike zone, so they
go back to the fastball when they're behind, and of course if
you're up at bat you notice something like that."

Here is Bob Boone again: "It's much more fun catching a
guy with excellent control, because then you feel you're part of
the whole jockeying experience. Here's a ball that's just inside—
fine. Now go back outside and put the ball on the corner this
time. You're *orchestrating* that. Catching somebody like Tommy
John is more work mentally, but it's much more pleasurable,
and after it's over you'll both think, Hey, we had a great game.
There's no doubt that a catcher can help a pitcher, but he can't
be a dictator out there. When you've established that rapport
with a pitcher you know, what you put down in a situation is
almost always just about what he's thinking. When that happens,
it gives the pitcher the confidence to throw a good pitch. You
adjust as you go along—to the hitters and to your pitcher's abilities on that given day. If you can do it, you want to save something to use late in the game, because there are always a few
batters you can't get out the same way more than once. If you've
got through the order the first time without using your pitcher's
whole repertoire, you're a little ahead. But pitchers change as a
game goes along, of course, and then you have to adjust to *that*.
Say your pitcher's best pitch is his slider, but then by the way he
warms up for the next inning you think *Uh-oh*, because suddenly
it isn't anymore—not at that moment. But then four pitches later

it may be back again. It's a feel you have, and that's what you really can't teach to young catchers.

"Sometimes you get a sudden notion for an exotic call—something that's really strange in a certain situation that you somehow know is the right thing. You're jamming the man—throwing the ball right by him—and suddenly you call for a changeup. Ordinarily, you don't do that, but even if I'm watching a game from the bench I can sometimes feel when the moment comes: *Now throw him the changeup.* It's strange and it's strictly feel, but when it happens and you have the closeness with the pitcher he'll come in after the inning and say, 'You know, I had exactly the same idea back there!' But in the end, of course, it's how he throws those pitches that matters."

Pitchers can always shake off a catcher's sign, to be sure—some shakeoffs are only meant to set up doubt in the batter's mind—and catcher-pitcher negotiations go on between innings or during a mound conference. These last are not always diplomatic murmurings. "There almost has to be a lot of screaming and yelling between pitchers and catchers if they're going to get along," Tim McCarver told me. "With Gibby"—Bob Gibson, that is—"it sometimes happened right out on the mound. I remember a game against the Pirates when Clemente hit one of his patented shots to right field, and when Gibby came past me to back up the throw in he yelled, 'Goddam it, you've got to put down something more than one finger back there!' "

Ted Simmons said, "Sometimes you have to persuade your pitcher out of a certain pitch in the middle of the game. It's hard for him to remain objective in the heat of battle. If he's had some success, I might go out there and ask what he's thinking, and if he says, 'Over the years, I've gotten this guy out with this pitch in this situation, even though it's dangerous'—let's say there are two on and he's getting ready to throw a changeup—then I say, 'Fine. Let's go.' But if I go out there and he says, 'Well, I just got a *feel*, man,' and he's lookin' at me with cloudy eyes, I say, 'Look, we'll do that next time—O.K.?' It's a matter of being convincing."

Ted Simmons, I should add, is one of the most convincing men in baseball. He is a sixteen-year man in the majors—the last three with the Brewers, the rest with the Cardinals—and is one of the prime switch hitters in the game: in 1975 he batted .332 for the Cards and drove in a hundred runs. He is known for his intelligence and knowledge of the game—splendid assets, but what I most enjoy about Simba is his passionate way of

talking baseball. He talks the way Catfish Hunter used to pitch—
feeling for the corners early on and then with a widening flow
of ideas and confidence and variation in the late going: Cooperstown stuff. When we sat down together at Sun City last
spring, I asked him about the difference between National
League pitching—almost an idle question, I thought, since I was
pretty sure I knew the answer: a lower strike zone in the National
League, and more breaking balls in the A.L.

"I don't know how it began, but it's there, all right," Simmons said. "It's a difference of *approach*. The National League,
in my mind, throws the slow stuff early in the count and then
throws the fastball late, with two strikes on the batter. To me,
that makes more sense, because you're forcing the batter to hit the
ball—that's the objective—and the odds are always against a base
hit, even with the best hitters. The American League approach,
from what I've seen of it in two years, is to throw hard early—
to get two strikes and no balls, or 2–1 or 2–2—and *then* go to
the slow stuff. So if you're 2–1 in the A.L., you're apt to go
to 3–2 every time, because they'll throw a curveball and you'll
foul it. Then a curve or a slider, and you'll take it, for 3–2. Then
another slider or curve, and you'll foul it, then *another* curveball, and you'll swing and miss it for a strikeout or hit a fly ball
for the out. So there are three or four extra pitches on almost
every batter, and that's one reason why the American League
has such long games. The A.L. philosophy is to get two strikes
and then don't let him hit, and the N.L. thinks, Get two strikes
and *make* him hit it."

I asked him which league had the better pitchers, and he
thought about it for a while. "I think the American League
pitchers are *probably* better, on balance," he said at last, "because they have to be refined when the count is against them—
to throw that breaking ball and get it over the plate, throw it in
a way to get the man out. The very best of them may be more
subtle and refined and tough than the N.L. pitchers. I'm talking
about guys like Dave Stieb, of the Toronto Blue Jays, and Pete
Vuckovich here. Vukey was with me on the Cardinals, you know,
but he made the adjustment very fast when he came over to this
league. But there are always exceptions. Somebody like Steve
Rogers"—of the National League Montreal Expos—"could
pitch very well in this league."

Bob Boone and Milt May have also had experience in both
leagues, but they both gave a slight edge to National League
pitching. May said that the N.L.'s preference for the slider—the

faster breaking ball—as against the American League's prejudice for the curve, might make the crucial difference. Boone said, "I think the real difference between the leagues is about six National League pitchers. Soto, Seaver, Carlton, Rogers, maybe Reuss, and any one of three or four others. Put 'em over in the American League, and they're even." (Tom Seaver, who came to the Chicago White Sox over this winter, has already made the switch.) "I would guess there are deeper counts in the A.L., but I wouldn't know for sure. I know there's more confidence in control in the A.L. In either league, it's hard as hell to get a base hit, most days."

Simmons wanted to be sure that I understood the extent of the catcher's involvement with other aspects of the game—with his manager, for instance, and with the deployment of the defense on the field. "With some managers," he said, "you can come to them in the dugout in the middle of the game and say, 'This pitcher has *had* it. I assume you know that. But I want you to know I'm having to struggle with every pitch in every inning. I can't set up a program with this man, because he's faltering. Now I want some notion about your objectives. Do you intend to pitch him one more inning, or three more?' Then if the manager says, 'Wow, let's get somebody up out there,' I can say, 'Well, O.K., I can get him through one more inning,' and you work that inning like it's the ninth, with nothing held back. But there are some managers who can't respond to that assertive approach, because of their personalities—I can think of a half dozen of them that I've been involved with—and with those, well, you have to find some other way to get the message across."

We moved along to defensive alignments, and I noticed that sometimes the intensity of his message made Simmons lift his hands to either side of his face as he talked, as if he were peering out of his mask at the game.

"You have to move your people around," he said. "It's part of your job, and part knowing how your manager wants things done. You've got a left-handed pull hitter up there, and you decide you're going to do one of two things. You're going to throw him low fastballs away and hopes he tries to pull it, or slow stuff inside and *make* him pull it. So you set up your defense accordingly. Your second baseman plays in the hole, your shortstop is back of second base, and everyone in the outfield moves over two steps toward right. But if your second baseman is still playing at double-play depth, then you've got to stop and move him over. You can do that with a little gesture, just before you put down the sign—and I never put down anything until I know I have the second baseman and the shortstop's attention anyway. I just look them right in the eye and go—'' He waggled his glove hand imperceptibly. ''If he still has a question, when you get back to the bench you can say, 'Hey, don't you see how we're pitchin' that guy?' This happens a lot, but people don't always appreciate it. Sometimes you'll see catchers with large reputations who'll stop and turn to the umpire and call time out and turn to the world and walk out a few steps and gesture to the man they want to move over, and everyone in the stands will say, 'Ah, yes, there's a man who knows what he's doing.' But it just isn't essential. It isn't done.''

The ultimate responsibility—for the game itself, Simmons suggested—is more difficult. ''The catcher is the man who has to be able to think, and he has to make the decisions—and to face the consequences when he's wrong,'' he went on. ''Whether it's fun for you or a burden, that's where it's *at*, and the real satisfaction in catching is making that decision for everyone— for your pitcher, your team, your manager, and the home crowd. It's all in your lap. Think of a situation. Think of something that happens all the time. The count is two balls and one strike, they have a man on first base, and you're ahead by one run. There's a pretty good hitter up—he doesn't strike out much. Now, you're the catcher and you've got to decide if they're going to hit-and-run. And with that you've got to decide if you're going to pitch out and negate all that, and what the consequences will be if you're wrong.

''*Now* we've got to where the fun is—where you know your allies, the capabilities of your pitcher and your team, and you also know the opposition, to the point where you're playin' with their heads. Because you know their manager and their way of playing, you know already what they're going to do. You have a gut feeling about it: *God, he's going to run*. You *know*. But instead—it's so easy to do this—you think, Well, I'd better play it safe, because I'm not sure, and we don't want 3–1 on this good hitter. So you call a fastball away to that right-handed batter, and he does hit the ball to right on the hit-and-run—the runner's gone—and now you've got first and third, which is much, much worse. And you say to yourself, God *almighty*, I *knew* they were going to run! Why didn't I pitch out? Well, what you learn later on, when you've grown up as a catcher, is not to fight that urge, because you understand that if you were in their dugout and you were that manager you'd run. So you learn to stop being just a catcher, and to be them as well as yourself. Until you can get to that point, accept that burden, you're not in control. Once you do, you're a successful catcher—the man everyone relies on and looks to for leadership, whether they know it or not.''

• ◆ •

TED SIMMONS HAD A GOOD SEASON LAST YEAR, IN SPITE OF THE sudden late-summer collapse of the defending-champion Brewers, who wound up in fifth place in their division, eleven games behind the Orioles. He kept his stroke when all about him were losing theirs, and wound up with a .308 average and a hundred and eight runs batted in. For all that, it was probably Simmons' last year of regular work behind the plate. During the off-season, Milwaukee traded for Jim Sundberg, and it is expected that he will now take over the day-to-day catching chores for the Brewers. Simmons, who has suffered from a chronic problem in his right shoulder, looked slow and work-worn behind the plate in most of the games in which I watched him last year, and he is at an age when many full-service catchers begin to wear down physically. I think he will find surcease in his new role as a designated hitter—if his pride allows him to accept this limited service. But I still felt bad when I heard the news of the trade, since it seemed to mean that Simmons' passionate involvement in the flow of things would now become distanced and muted. The game is no longer in his lap. His change of fortune made me recall a remark of Dave Duncan's last spring: ''By the time you've learned it all, by the time you're really proficient, you're almost too old to go on catching.''

I cheered up pretty quickly, however, when I recalled one more little talk I'd had with Ted Simmons, which had made me realize that his special feeling for the subtleties and rewards of catching will never be entirely lost to his teammates. On another day in Arizona last spring, I watched a few innings of a morning B-squad game between the Padres and the Brewers. Simmons wasn't playing, but then I spotted him in the Milwaukee dugout, where he was seated between two younger Brewer catchers, Ned Yost and Bill Schroeder; Simmons kept moving and gesturing, and when I changed my seat, moving a little closer to the diamond, I saw, without much surprise, that he was talking excitedly. When the game ended, I sought him out and asked him about it.

"We were just talkin' catching," he said. "I feel that every ballplayer, including myself, has the responsibility of training his replacement. People who are afraid to do that aren't very secure. What we saw was what you saw in that game—do you remember it? There was a time in the fifth when they're up at bat, with a man on first, and the count on the batter went to 2–2. I said to the guys with me, 'You've got two alternatives on the next pitch—what are they?' They both had the answer: fastball in or slider away. I said fine, but how do you decide which to call, and they didn't know. I said, 'Based on your pitcher'—and never mind right now which pitcher we were talkin' about. 'Based on your knowledge of this pitcher, can he throw the 3–2 slider for a strike?' They both said no, and I said, 'Well, then, you have to call for the slider on the 2–2, so that if the pitcher misses with it, then he'll be able to come back with the fastball on 3–2. But if he's a pitcher who *can* throw the slider on 3–2, then you can put down the fastball on 2–2—the fastball inside, to lock him out. If you miss, then you go to the slider on 3–2, and he's dead.'

"Our other catcher, Steve Lake, was in the game, so I didn't talk to him. He was in the fire, and we were lookin' into it. But that's all there is to it, you know. Does the man back there know what's going on? If he does, he can throw bad and he can run bad and block bad, but he's still the single most important player on the field."

THREE

◆ ◆ ◆

The Baltimore Fancy

CARL YASTRZEMSKI, ENCIRCLED FOR THE LAST TIME BY the Fenway Park multitudes, stood at a microphone in the first-base coaching box before the game and waved his cap to the crowd. He turned slowly to face the left-field stands, the cap held high, with the green of the underside of its bill showing, and then slowly back in the other direction, toward right field, and then to face out toward the bleachers, and the waves of clapping and cheers seemed to move and swirl around him, almost visible in the damp afternoon air. He gestured toward the home dugout, and his teammates came up and out onto the field, in their white uniforms and shiny dark warmup jackets, to surround him and shake his hand, and he and Jim Rice embraced; then the Red Sox pitchers and catchers and coaches left the bullpen and came walking and running across the grass to join him and be near him. The cheering rose again (it went on all afternoon, really), and Yaz approached the microphone with a piece of paper in his hand. ''Thank you very much,'' he said, but then he stopped and walked a little distance out onto the diamond and waved his hand, with his head down. He was crying.

This was the last day of the 1983 season and Carl Yastrzemski's last day in uniform; his 3,308th game, more games than

51

anyone else has played in baseball; and the end of his twenty-third year as a player. I am not much for the pomp and cere-monies of the sport, but I had made a promise with myself way back last winter to keep this date, when it was clear that Yaz at last would be stepping down. Flying up on the shuttle in the morning, I thought about all those years of Yaz and all those different lifetime, all-time statistics (third in times at bat, behind Hank Aaron; seventh in hits, behind Honus Wagner; sixth in total bases, behind Babe Ruth; and so forth) and all the scores of times I had seen him play (I have no idea how many), and it came to me that the pervasive, unshakable image of Carl Ya-strzemski that I carry inside me is of his making an out in a game, in some demanding or critical situation—a pop-up instead of a base hit, or perhaps an easy grounder chopped toward a waiting infielder—with Yaz dropping his head in sudden disap-pointment and self-disgust as he flips the bat away and starts up the line, his chance gone once again. Often he did come through, of course—the homers (four hundred and fifty-two of them, all told); the long doubles caromed off the left-center-field part of the wall; the sure and splendid catches; the deadly, rally-destroying pegs from the closed-in left-field corner; the whole sustained, unmatched performance in the late-pennant scramble and then the World Series in 1967—and I have all that in mind as well, but it seems inevitable that I should remember him, rather, in the act of failing, for no other great ballplayer I have seen was more burdened by the difficulties of this most unfor-giving of all sports, and by the ceaseless demands he made on his own skills, and by the expectations that we had of him in every game and almost every at-bat of that long stretch of sea-sons that was now ended. Playing any sport well at the upper levels requires violent concentration, which is why professional athletes display such glum countenances as they go about their work; Yaz wasn't glum, he was funereal. None of it had ever looked easy for him, or even like much fun, and late this sum-mer, when he began to reflect about his career and its meanings, he put aside some of the preoccupied silence that often enwrapped him in the clubhouse and talked a little more freely with reporters about what it had been like for him. He agreed with what we had seen and sensed. "I loved the game, I loved the competition, but I never enjoyed it," he said. "It was all hard work, all the time. I let the game dominate me. It even got harder as I got older, because then I had more to prove." He said this, or some variation of it, many times, and sometimes with an odd lightness, almost an air of relief, but even then he did not let down or enjoy himself much. A *Times* reporter, Steve Cady, called on him in the clubhouse at Fenway Park in late September and saw a recent message that Yaz had written to himself taped on the back of his locker: "In box with left leg and all weight on it. Nothing on front leg. WAIT. Stay back. Relax." Right to the end, he was learning his trade.

There were other notable farewells this year. Jim Kaat stepped down after twenty-five years as a major-league hurler, most recently with the Cardinals—the longest pitching career on the books. Vida Blue, only thirty-four, was dropped by the Royals in midseason and subsequently entered treatment at a drug-rehabilitation center: a different kind of departure, but one that should not make us forget that effulgent first full summer of his, back in 1971, when, just turned twenty-two, Vida Blue stood the baseball world on its ear with a 24–8 and 1.82 record for the Oakland A's, and won the Cy Young Award and the Most Valuable Player Award in his league, all in his first full year. Finally, Johnny Bench hung up his spikes, after seventeen years with the Reds and a hatful of records: twice M.V.P. and the most lifetime home runs hit by a catcher (three hundred and twenty-five, out of his all-positions total of three hundred and eighty-nine). He was the centerpiece of the memorable Cincinnati Big Red Machine of the early nineteen-seventies. He quit catching a couple of years ago, when the wear and tear of the position became too much, and played first base and third base instead, but he will be remembered most, I think, for his skills behind the plate. He came to the fore just when the much smaller hinged catching mitt first became popular, and his shortstop-quick hands and his smoothness and balance and mobility behind the bat instantly caused all the catchers in the land to imitate his one-handed style, but none of them, then or now, could touch him.

Bench and Yastrzemski made their last road trips around their leagues in the styles that suited their personalities, with the extroverted Bench cheerfully accepting gifts and trophies and appearing at center-diamond rituals during "Day"'s in his honor in a great many ballparks. Yaz declined, only at last agreeing to the one home-park official "Yaz Day"—a great outpouring of flowers and gifts and tears and speeches at Fenway Park on the day before that last Sunday. It was like Yaz, I think, to want one more game after that, so that he could go out playing before fans who preferred to come for the baseball rather than for the party. On that last afternoon, he let it be known, he wanted to go back to his old position in left field, where he had not played in the past three years, instead of just appearing once again as the D.H. Before the game, Bosox manager Ralph Houk was talking in his office to a few writers about the kind of player Yaz had been. "Unlike some people we've voted into the Hall of Fame, he could beat you a lot of different ways," Houk said. "He'd move a man from first to third with no outs, make a great play in the outfield, steal a base when he had to, break up the double play out there in the middle of a big game, or throw out a runner who seemed to have the base made—the whole thing. He hit for average, hit for power, ran the bases—whatever. Even now, if you put a man on first, Yaz will make some kind of contact up at the plate. I sure hope he don't hurt himself today, playing out in the field, out there on that wet grass." Houk threw up his hands—his trademark gesture. "Well, if he does, we'll just shoot him and drag him off the field, like an old race horse," he said. "He's come this fucking far, he'll go one more game."

So he did, and the game—a meaningless little engagement between the sixth-place Bosox and the last-place Indians—was all right, too, and even fun after a while, because Jim Rice whacked a three-run homer that drove in all the Boston runs (the home side won, 3-1) and tied him with Cecil Cooper (who was having a great afternoon against the Tigers, it turned out) for the R.B.I. title, and the Fenwayites gave Jim a mighty standing O of his own in his final turn at the plate. Yaz got his hit—a trifling wrong-side single past the third baseman, in the third—and that was all that anyone really cared about, in the end. He came up for the last time in the seventh, and again paused for our pelting cheers and applause, holding his cap aloft and turning to face every part of the stands. He badly wanted a homer, of course, but the Cleveland pitcher, Dan Spillner, was so nervous out there, so intent on not spoiling things with a base on balls, that he very nearly *did* walk him, and Yaz had to take his last flailing cut at a pitch that was up by his ears, and popped it up harmlessly to second. He ran out to left field for the top of the eighth, but came off immediately for a substitute, sent out by Ralph Houk to give us one more chance to say goodbye, and the fans waved their handkerchiefs this time, to "Auld Lang Syne," with tears everywhere now, even in the press box. Later, when the game was over, Yaz, summoned back, came out onto the darkening field once again, and this time he trotted slowly around the perimeter of the field, touching the hands of the fans in the low front rows as he went by. He knew at last—I think the realization must have come to him very late, maybe only days or weeks before, breaking into the web of his concentration and pressured shyness and pride in work: he knew what he had meant to New England fans, and was trying to tell us that the feelings ran deep and in both directions. I did not expect such a thing of him—it did not seem in his nature to have worked this all out the way he did—but the fact that he could do it meant that he was still in the game all the way, even on his last day. He had indicated as much in his little speech at the beginning of the afternoon, when he said (this was the whole speech), "I saw the sign that said 'Say It Ain't So, Yaz,' and I wish it weren't. This is the last day of my career as a player, and I want to thank all of you for being here with me today. It has been a great privilege to wear the Red Sox uniform the past twenty-three years and to have played in Fenway in front of you great fans. I'll miss you and I'll never forget you."

There was a postgame press conference up in the Red Sox press lounge on top of the roof behind home plate, and when Yaz finally turned up there he was applauded by the writers, too. He was in his uniform pants and long-sleeved undershirt now, with a towel around his neck. "I feel super—the best I've felt in a long, long time," he said. "I feel ten years younger than I did fifteen minutes ago. Now I don't have to do all that again." He paused and shook his head, and a sudden, almost boyish smile lit up his face. He looked restored—his own age at last. He is forty-four.

◆ ◆ ◆

MIDSUMMER BASEBALL FEELS AS IF IT WOULD LAST FOREVER; late-season baseball becomes quicker and terser, as if sensing its coming end, and sometimes, if we are lucky, it explodes into thrilling terminal colors, leaving bright pictures in memory to carry us through the miserable months to come. Not this year. This time, the long campaigns closed almost silently, never producing that two-team or three-team, final-weekend rush to the wire that we have come to expect in at least a couple of divisions. In the Championship Series—those brusque, dangerous best-of-five playoffs—the Chicago White Sox scored but one run in their last twenty-seven innings of the year and fell dead before the Baltimore Orioles, while the Dodgers, it will be recalled, performed even more feebly in losing to the Phillies; both winners needed only four games to wrap up their pennants. This sort of preamble sometimes sets the stage for a protracted and melodramatic World Series, as happened in 1979, when the Pirates overcame a two-game deficit to put down the Orioles; in 1975, when we had that incomparable seven-game Series—the "War and Peace" of baseball—between the Red Sox and the ultimately victorious Cincinnati Reds; and last year, when the Cardinals hung on to win a dishevelled seven-game alley-fight with the Milwaukee Brewers. This year, however, the Phillies put up such a minimal offense in the Series—mostly the little popping sounds of solo home runs—that as the games went along our attention shifted away from the events on the field and toward the very different team personae and styles of play of the two clubs: a useful baseball seminar, to be sure, but not quite the entertainment we had wished for. The Orioles, after dropping the opener by 2–1, swept the next four games behind some exemplary sustained staff pitching, concluding with a numbing 5–0 shutout by Scott McGregor, which not only closed the lid on the Phillies but seemed to put away this particular baseball year altogether, quickly and for good. Such a last act does not require a grand retrospective, but these 1983 playoffs and Series do afford us a chance to look at the sport in a more discriminating fashion, undistracted by heroics and mere brilliance, and so perhaps pick up a better sense of how games are really won and lost.

Fans in some unlikely places will have much to savor, once they recover from the sting of their ultimate disappointments of this season. In Toronto, there were those weeks in mid-July when the Blue Jays, who had tied for last place in 1982, were leading the pack in the A.L. East and everyone in town was talking about the young pitchers Dave Stieb, Jim Clancy, and Luis Leal (a new Tiant, it sometimes seemed), and first baseman Willie Upshaw, and the dashing Lloyd Moseby, in center, and the late-blooming slugger Jesse Barfield, and the club's utterly unexpected show of power. (The Blue Jays led their league in batting this year, and fell two homers short of taking the home-run title as well.) The Jays stayed in the thick of things until a road trip in late August, when they were beaten in the tenth inning on three successive nights; the following week, in deep shock, they gave up winning runs in the ninth, ninth, and twelfth innings and dropped out of the race for good. They will be back, surely, and so will their politely exuberant fans, who turned out in amazing numbers (1,930,292) at the little local ball yard, Exhibition Stadium, which was built for football and thus seats its bleacher fans in stands that angle oddly away from the center of the diamond. Baseball attendance over all was at a record high of 45,565,910 this summer—almost a million more than last year. Seven teams set new attendance marks, and ten clubs drew more than two million fans apiece.

Not many warm fan feelings were evident in Montreal, where the Expos' partisans, made wary by the team's late failures in recent summers, took to booing their heroes at every opportunity; prime targets for *la framboise* were fifteen-million-dollar (for eight years) catcher Gary Carter, who had a subpar .270, seventeen-home-run season, and bullpen ace Jeff Reardon, who during one barren stretch was obdurately booed whenever he threw a ball *or* a strike. Reardon's wife, making an invited appearance during a midseason charity affair at Olympic Stadium, was also booed, and left the field in tears. The Expos, fulfilling something or other, still held first place in their division on September 14th and then fell into the well again, finishing third, eight games out.

Who else failed? Why, the Milwaukee Brewers, defending champions in the American League, who somehow remained afloat until Labor Day but went through September like an ember in a snowbank, to finish fifth, eleven games out—exactly the same distance from the top achieved in the other league by their rivals of last October, the World Champion Cardinals. There were other horrid collapses. For the second year running, the Atlanta Braves' front office removed the tacky wigwam of their club mascot, Chief Noc-A-Homa, from its reservation in left field, thereby making room for two hundred and fifty more paying customers, and once again the team suffered immediate disaster, this time losing its muscular third baseman Bob Horner for the rest of the year with a wrist injury, and its entire bullpen to an epidemic seizure of pitching vapors, while the club slipped from its comfy five-and-a-half-game lead in the N.L. West to a three-game deficit, behind the Dodgers, all in the space of a month. The tepee, which perhaps should be traded in for a Winnebago, was hastily re-reërected, but too late. Maybe next year the Great Spirit of Baseball, if left alone, will bring the Braves what they really need, which is some bench strength.

On an up note, the most vivid statistic of the year was perhaps the .361 batting mark of the Red Sox' resourceful and patient left-side swinger Wade Boggs, whose .357 average for his first two years' work in the majors has not been exceeded (according to baseball historian Bob Davids) since Lefty O'Doul's .358

(figured on a slightly different basis) in 1928–29. His teammate Jim Rice led the American League in homers (thirty-nine) and, as previously noted, tied for runs batted in (a hundred and twenty-six) with the Brewers' Cecil Cooper; other reliable brand names came through in the National League, where Mike Schmidt won his sixth home-run title, with forty downtowners, and Bill Madlock, the Pirates' short-stroke Zen master, captured his fourth batting title, at .323.

Among the moundpersons, LaMarr Hoyt, of the White Sox, won twenty-four games (and the Cy Young Award in his league), mostly by the useful expedient of throwing strikes; he walked just thirty-one batters in two hundred and sixty innings. The National League, for reasons I don't understand, produced not one twenty-game winner, for the first time in fifty-two years, but did wind up with both earned-run leaders: Atlee Hammaker, of the Giants (2.25), and Rick Honeycutt, of the Dodgers (whose 2.42, compiled in the American League before he was traded out of the league by the Texas Rangers, held up in the books). During this season, three famous hurlers—Steve Carlton, Nolan Ryan, and Gaylord Perry—sailed past Walter Johnson's previously inviolate record of 3,508 lifetime strikeouts. Perry, who announced his retirement late in the summer, went home with 3,534 whiffs (and with the secret recipes for his famous jellies still intact), but Ryan, at 3,677, and Carlton, at 3,709, are still motoring. Carlton's two hundred and seventy-five strikeouts were the most in either league in 1983, and this was the fifth time he has topped his league.

All these heroes and Lee MacPhail, too. Mr. MacPhail is the president of the American League and, since late July, the author of the most discussed legal ruling in the land since Marbury v. Madison. This, of course, was his fair and sensible resolution of the monumentally entertaining pine-tar fuss, which came to pass during a July Sunday afternoon at Yankee Stadium when George Brett, of the Royals, rapped a two-run, two-out homer against Goose Gossage, thereby putting his team ahead by 5–4 in the top of the ninth—only to have the runs disallowed and the homer turned into an out on a ruling by the umpires, who accepted an ex-post-facto protest by Yankee manager Billy Martin that the pine-tar stickum on the handle of Brett's bat extended beyond the eighteen inches above the bat knob specified by the regulations. Brett, in demurral, attempted thuggee upon the arbiters and was excused for the rest of the day, but the Royals protested the game, and after a few days they were upheld by

MacPhail, who, citing "the spirit of the rules," ordered the
homer restored and the contest resumed at a later date. The
remainder of the inning was played without incident a few weeks
later (before an audience of 1,245 second-year torts students),
with the Royals holding their 5–4 lead, and the teams swapped
the won (and lost) game on their records. Mr. MacPhail's statement attempted to mollify his umpires by deploring the fuzzi-
ness of the frequently amended baseball rule book but pointed
out that the intent of the rule was simply to remove an offending
bat from the game, and that there was no evidence of any sort
to suggest that Brett's homer had been aided or abetted by goo.
(The rule, in fact, appears to have been written in order to keep
pine tar from discoloring balls in play, and thus is intended to
deprive *pitchers* of an unfair advantage.) For me, the MacPhail
decision is bathed in the clear sunshine of fairness and common
sense, but the immoderate responses to it by the Yankees suggest
the extent of the distemper and the almost frantic distractibility
of so many people now connected with the sport. George Steinbrenner said that if the Yankees lost a pennant because of the
ruling it would not be safe for Mr. MacPhail to continue living
in New York. Billy Martin, who cannot exactly be faulted for
trying the ploy in the first place, said later that in making the
ruling Lee MacPhail had encouraged every kid in the country
to "go ahead . . . and cheat, and they can get away with it,"
and then told his players during a team meeting that they had
been bilked. If this was intended to inflame his troops for the
remainder of the campaign, it did not succeed. At the end of the
summer, Mr. Steinbrenner, looking back at the foolish crisis,
said he thought that the game and its emotional offshoots might
have cost his team a pennant, and there, for once, I agree with
him.

Mr. MacPhail, who is retiring as league president but who
will serve now as head of the owners' Player Relations Committee (a brilliant appointment, given his unflappable good sense
and the approach of another negotiation of baseball's basic contract with the players, in 1984), was twice required to suspend
Billy Martin during the summer because of the manager's intem-
perate disagreements with the umpires. In the Stadium press-
room one evening late in the season, I ran into Dick Butler, who
is the chief of umpires for the American League, and made some
reference to the hard times his minions had experienced in these
and many other public disagreements, but Butler, who is as
gentle and courtly in manner as his boss, dismissed the matter

cheerfully. "It's always the same," he told me. "It's been this way ever since I can remember." He went on to say that only a day or two earlier he had happened upon some correspondence from the early nineteen-thirties in which Clark Griffith, the president of the Washington Senators, had complained angrily to A.L. president Will Harridge about the abilities and intelligence of the league's umps. "It was exactly like this year," Butler said. "Nothing was different—well, except for one thing, I guess. Nowadays, nobody calls my umpires Bolsheviks."

◆ ◆ ◆

DAVE RIGHETTI, THE BIG YANKEE LEFT-HANDER, PITCHED A no-hit game against the Red Sox on July 4th,* and in September Bob Forsch, of the Cardinals, threw a 3–0 no-hitter against the Expos, and then Mike Warren, a twenty-two-year-old Oakland rookie, did the same thing to the White Sox. None of this is entirely surprising, nor should we be struck dumb with wonder by the news that there were no no-hit games at all during the 2,106 major-league encounters played in 1982, and that Bob Forsch's and Mike Warren's no-hitters came along within three days of each other. In baseball, Yogi Berra has told us, you don't know nothing. What we do know, perhaps, is that there is a splash of luck when any pitcher, no matter how imperious or crafty, gets by twenty-seven batters without seeing one harmless grounder bounced through the middle or a half-hit flare drop untouched in short right field. This late little scattering of no-hit games statistically illuminates the same essential attribute of the game. Luck does matter in baseball, as well as brilliant and resolute performance, and the proportions of the mixture—a recipe as subtle as the béarnaise at La Grenouille—are exquisitely pleasing. If the sport were easier—if it rewarded only the Carltons and Ryans (and Rices and Schmidts) of the game and never the Forsches or the Mike Warrens—we would almost know the outcome of every game in advance. If it were much easier— if there were a no-hitter every week and a grand-slam homer every evening—we would gossip or snooze or read in the stands until the ninth, for only the score would matter, and the constant surprises of baseball would seem only eccentric or else would elude us altogether.

*Righetti was moved to the bullpen the following year, where, as expected, he became the Yanks' prime late-innings stopper.

Baseball's placid exterior and smooth, scheduled flow of games conceal so many possibilities for astounding circumstances that we old fans, picking up the morning paper or tuning in to the late-night sports, wait almost smugly for word of the newest first-ever play or utterly unexpected series of events. Early this August, the California Angels, playing a home game against the Minnesota Twins, appeared to have matters comfortably in hand when, already leading by 2–1, they put their first two batters on base in the bottom of the fourth, only to crash headlong into Yogi Berra's dictum. The next California batter, Ron Jackson, hit a low line drive to third baseman Gary Gaetti, who flipped to second to double off the lead base runner, and in plenty of time for the relay over to first, which beat the other retreating Angel base runner to the bag. Triple play. The next pitch of the game—delivered by Tommy John to the Twins' Gaetti, the leadoff batter in the top of the fifth—was smashed over the fence, and the *next* pitch, to Tom Brunansky, also departed the premises, tying the score of the game, which the Twins eventually won by 4–2. Three successive pitches, good for three outs, two runs, one ruined game, and uncounted broken hearts. According to the records, this had never happened before in major-league baseball. And no one could quite remember an inning like the one that the Orioles came up with a couple of weeks later, in a game against the Blue Jays at Baltimore. The Orioles had rallied for two runs in the bottom of the ninth, tying the game at 3–3, but in the process had used up their last catcher, who had given way to a pinch-hitter—a spendthrift maneuver that now required Baltimore manager Joe Altobelli to send a reserve infielder, Lenn Sakata, out to catch in the tenth. The visitors led off the extra inning with a home run and a single, thus bringing on a new Baltimore pitcher, Tippy Martinez. The Torontos, one may assume, had noted the presence of Sakata behind the plate, and were understandably eager—a bit overeager, in fact—to test him with attempted thefts of second, but they never did find the answer. Martinez instantly picked the base runner off first. He walked the next man but also picked him off, then surrendered a single, and notched the third out with his third pickoff of the inning. Ah, baseball. No one, I think, was particularly surprised when Sakata won the game in the bottom of the same inning, with a three-run homer.

Another extra-inning contretemps came along in a bitterly contested game at Pittsburgh's Three Rivers Stadium on September 9th, at a moment in the race when the Expos, the Phillies, the Cardinals, and the Pirates were clumped within a game and a half of each other in the upper stories of the National League East. Tied with the Pirates at 3–3 in the top of the thirteenth, the Phillies had base runners Willie Hernandez at second and Mike Schmidt at first; Pittsburgh hurler Jim Bibby, facing Joe Lefebvre, let go a wild pitch, but while Hernandez scampered to third, Schmidt, who had somehow considered this remote set of possibilities beforehand, oddly held his base. Not so oddly, when you think about it: with first base still occupied, Bibby, a right-hander, was deprived of the option of walking Lefebvre, a lefty swinger, in order to bring up the next man in the Philadelphia order, Garry Maddox, who bats right. Lefebvre singled, thereby winning the game (it turned out), moving the Phillies into first place for the moment, and certifying Schmidt as a genius—all in one stroke.

◆ ◆ ◆

I SAID EARLIER THAT THERE WERE NO LATE, GREAT PENNANT races this summer, but that is not to suggest that there weren't some brisk and telling patches of action along the way. On that same second weekend of September (the focal point of the baseball summer, it turned out), the Phillies and the Pirates split their next pair of games in thrilling fashion, in contest where the lead or tie was repeatedly surrendered, bitterly rewon, then lost again. By taking the rubber game, the Phillies remained a bare half game out of first place, behind Montreal; later in the week they went home and swept the Expos in a doubleheader, knocking them out of the lead for good, and then embarked upon an eleven-game winning streak, which captured the flag.

Matters were less parlous in the American League on that same weekend (the White Sox, in the A.L. West, had already spread-eagled the field and were leading the nearest competition by a full fifteen games), but there was a sudden little stir of speculation when the Yankees won the opening game of a four-game set at the Stadium against the league-leading Orioles, to climb into second place, just four games back. The Saturday doubleheader, a twi-night affair, brought out fifty-five thousand fans and produced a horrific (for the Yankees) dénouement, which started in the top of the ninth inning of the opening game, with the score tied at 2–2. Shortstop Roy Smalley threw wildly to first, putting the Orioles' Lenn Sakata on base; a sacrifice moved him along to second and brought on Goose Gossage, who walked Rick Dempsey and then faced the left-handed pinch-hitter Joe Nolan; Nolan took a breaking ball for a strike, fouled off five consecutive fastballs, and then singled cleanly to center (against a sixth heater), to put the Orioles ahead. A double by Cal Ripken brought in another counter, and a bit later John Lowenstein, a left-side pinch-hitter, whacked Gossage's second pitch over the right-center wall for a grand slam—to an accompanying sudden silence that suggested an electric plug pulled out of the wall. When Gossage and the Yanks came in off the field at last, they were booed. The Orioles also won the second game, and the game on Sunday, wrapping up the Yankee season for good.

Hindsight is easy, but nothing about the Orioles-Yankees weekend surprised me (except for Gossage's throwing six fastballs in a row to a good left-handed hitter). Indeed, the games perfectly confirmed what we have all known for so long but have somehow failed to understand in its entirety. The Orioles, not the Yankees, are the dominant American League team of our time. They had come into the Yankee series on a roll: twenty victories in their past twenty-five games. This was an entirely typical sort of momentum for them in the late going; their September-October record this year (21–12), under manager Joe Altobelli, sustained almost exactly the same killing late-season winning percentage (.638) that they had compiled during the previous fifteen years, under Earl Weaver, who retired last fall. Since their first pennant, in 1966, the Orioles have won three World Series and lost three, while the Yankees are 2–2 in that same span, but the Orioles have taken seven divisional titles since the split-league plan went into effect, fourteen years ago, as against five for the Yanks. The Orioles, in fact, have won more games than any other team in the majors in the past five years and in the past ten years and (someone went to great pains to dig *this* out) in the past twenty-seven years. Why this is so is something we can get to shortly, when talking about the playoffs and the World Series, but the heart of it, clearly, is that the Orioles always cling to and personify the idea of a team, while the Yankees, by declaration and policy, prefer the idea of winning. Stated this way, the rival propositions seem to tilt unfairly toward the selfless, semi-anonymous, all-for-one fellowship of the O's, if only because so many of us were taught to strive for such an ideal back when we were in school. But the celebrated and extremely successful Yankees, with their purchased stars, enormous salaries, and bumptious, self-publicizing ownership

and management, have given such a good account of themselves
in competition that they have taught us—or should have taught
us by now—that sweetness and selflessness are not automatically better. The many strands that go into the fabric of a winning or losing franchise include the club's market area and
audience potential, the financial resources of its owners, its
scouting personnel and minor-league program, its luck (above
all, its luck in avoiding injuries to significant players), and, in
the end, its baseball philosophy. Fans incline toward the current
personality and practices of their chosen team, as long as it
shows sporadic faint signs of life, but I think we in the stands
are capable of a little distance as well, and perhaps even a baseball philosophy of our own. The brusquely capable Baltimore
style perfectly suits my own fancy, for the Orioles, by long
observation, have proved both approachable and thoughtful, patient and combative. Their players instinctively avoid the attitudes of moneyed sullenness that so many teams fall victim to
once they experience good fortune, but they also remember what
matters in the end. They win.

◆ ◆ ◆

IN THE QUICK, FLATTISH NATIONAL LEAGUE PLAYOFFS, THE VIS-
iting East Coast champs presented the first-day Los Angeles
audience with a gemlike miniature sample of Philadelphia-style
basic baseball: a 1–0 shutout by Steve Carlton (with a bit of help
from the bullpen), built upon—cantilevered upon, perhaps—a
solo first-inning home run by Mike Schmidt. The unsatisfaction
of such an opener was probably not entirely dispelled in the next
night's game, which the Dodgers won by 4–1, since three of the
Dodger tallies resulted directly or secondarily from Phillie errors. Fernando Valenzuela, never quite dominant, hung tough
and got the win, as he so often does. Game Three, played on
the chemical lawns of Philadelphia's Veterans Stadium, also
lacked zing, since the Dodger starter, Bob Welch, was forced
to depart the scene in the second inning, when he was laid low
by a recurrence of a hip affliction—a terminal blow to the Dodgers' hopes in the series, I think. The Phillies got a good outing
from their starter, the tall twenty-four-year-old curveballing
rookie Charles Hudson (he had pitched in a postseason playoff
game last year, too: between the Peninsula Pilots and the Durham Bulls, of the Class A Carolina League), and won by 7–2.
Gary Matthews, a veteran Philadelphia left fielder, who had

been frequently benched during the regular season, had himself a day: two runs, a homer, two singles, a base on balls, and four runs batted in. The next evening, he resumed at once, with a first-inning three-run homer bombed into the central sector of the left-field loge seats, which more or less settled the game and the National League pennant right there, since Carlton was back on hand and (with his compeers) cruised to win, again by 7–2. This is not, to be sure, a very extensive summary of these semifinals, but the truth of the matter is that the Dodgers never distinguished themselves or looked even vaguely like champions in this little stretch of games. This was a problem-marred, transitional year for the Dodgers, in which they had to make do with a slow, weak-armed outfield, an error-prone infield (with a converted outfielder, Pedro Guerrero, at third), and a catcher, Jack Fimple, who was hurried up from the minors because of injuries to his predecessors on the job. They will all do better in the coming seasons, and God or their other skipper, Tom Lasorda, deserves awe for bringing them so far in this one.

The American League championships, although concluded in the same short span, were more *like* it, starting as they did with a successive pair of genuine pitching masterpieces—the rain-soaked opening 2–1 win by the White Sox ace, LaMarr Hoyt, and its riposte the next evening, when Baltimore's rookie right-hander Mike Boddicker fanned fourteen Chicago batters in the course of a 4–0 shutout. Hoyt, tough and tubby, showed us his specialty, which is zipping the ball over the plate: he threw first-pitch strikes to twenty-six of the thirty-one batters he faced, never fell behind in the mid-counts, and walked no one. Boddicker, who is slim and dark-haired, dismissed batters by the handful without ever really overpowering anyone. A prime new graduate of the Baltimore School of Sensible Pitching, he relies upon a couple of curves, a modest fastball, a slider, and a changeup-sinker thing, and, above all, upon the perfectly controlled changing speeds with which he offers up his repertoire. The two games, in addition to these heroics, seemed to offer multiple hints and lessons. Right from the start, I felt certain that LaMarr Hoyt would win, as he did, but it was odd that his teammates could never quite break things open in that first game; leading against Scott McGregor by 2–0 at the mid-way point, they somehow contrived to put ten base runners aboard in the last three innings without scoring any of them. Baltimore, for its part, at last scored a run in the bottom of the ninth, on a double by Dan Ford and then a single by Cal Ripken, and thus had the typing run aboard when Eddie Murray grounded into a force for the last out. Insufficient rallies are rarely brought up or dwelt upon in losing clubhouses, and it was more than interesting that several of the Oriole players and coaches pointed out this ending after the game and spoke of it almost with satisfaction. The Orioles' dispassionate group perception of baseball is not something I have previously encountered; it's as if there are twenty-five academicians out there with birdies on their caps. They had lost this game, to be sure, but they had kept things close, even against a LaMarr Hoyt, and had had a chance to win it at the end, with their best man up at bat. A tying double or a winning homer cannot be counted upon in that situation, of course, but the chance for one had been made, which is the way Baltimore likes to do things.

The next evening, just after Boddicker's memorable outing, I talked with his pitching coach, Ray Miller (he was wearing a faded T-shirt that advertised his pitching precepts: "31 SAYS [Miller is No. 31] WORK FAST, THROW STRIKES, CHANGE SPEEDS, HOLD 'EM CLOSE"), who professed himself not quite ravished by Boddicker's fourteen strikeouts, since he so much prefers the more energy-efficient mode of dismissing batters on ground balls and pop-ups. What he did like, however, was Boddicker's beautifully modulated tempos. "He's got a range of from sixty-four to eighty-six miles per hour, from low on his slider to high on his fastball, which is what you're after in this business," he said. "The whole concept is to know what the guy up at bat is looking for but to throw it at a different speed than he expects." Someone said that the Chicago batters, over in their clubhouse, were saying that they had been less than awed by Boddicker's heat, and Miller smiled contentedly and said, "That's just music to my ears. I love it when the other batters complain about our pitchers throwing nothing."

The third game (which I had to watch, to my dismay, from a distance, by television) brought out some mid-game rumbles when Chicago's rookie slugger Ron Kittle was accidentally plunked on the knee by Mike Flanagan and when Rich Dotson, the Chicago hurler, then hit Cal Ripken and brushed back Eddie Murray in response, but the deeper cries of pain came from the overflowing throngs of Chicago fans when the Orioles, profiting from long blows and an inordinate number of bases on balls from the Chicago pitchers, blew away the Pale Hose, 11–1. The next game—the last of the year for the White Sox, it turned out—was distressing to watch and wait through, so edgy and exciting in its multiple crises and endlessly prolonged resolution that I was almost glad I was not on the scene to see and hear and taste such fierce and enveloping anxiety and hope and ultimate heartbreak. (Players have told me, by the way, that it is infinitely easier to be in such a game than to have to sit and watch it, since the concentration and physical movements of playing release one, a little, from the pain of waiting and speculation.) Inning after inning, the two teams put up zeros on the scoreboard, with the accidents and adventures of play seeming to sway first in one direction and then in the other, yet there was so little to choose between the two that after six full innings each team had come to precisely the same point in its batting order, with four hits and five stranded base runners apiece. Britt Burns, the big, heavy-bodied Chicago left-hander, pitched out of a frightful situation in the sixth and another one in the eighth, to baying cries of relief from the Comiskey Park faithful, while his Baltimore counterpart, Storm Davis, gave way to Tippy Martinez on the mound in the bottom of the seventh. This was when the White Sox blew their best chance of the day. I think in retrospect that the key to the game was not just some very bad baserunning by the White Sox—which turned three hits and a successful hit-and-run play and an Oriole balk into no runs at all—but the icily executed Baltimore defensive play in the middle of this crisis: a cutoff peg and a waiting, watching-over-the-shoulder rundown between short and second that was suddenly redirected into a 7-5-4-2 out at the plate. That and the scarcely noticed fact that the Orioles had changed pitchers, while the Sox had not. When Chicago failed to score in the eighth (a fine running catch by John Shelby in deep center field took an extra-base hit away from Carlton Fisk) and again in the ninth (Martinez struck out Rudy Law, with two on), the feel of the game was wholly altered, for it was clear that Britt Burns must be close to exhaustion and that his manager, Tony LaRussa, did not have enough confidence in his bullpen to bring in a successor. In the end, it was one of those special but not wholly rare games that are settled by some players who never get into the lineup at all—in this case the left-handed Baltimore pinch-hitters Jim Dwyer and John Lowenstein, waiting in the dugout, whose presence and reputation persuaded LaRussa to try to stay with Burns for at least one or two batters more. (A light sometimes clicks on, I have found, if I can remind myself to think about the movable pieces, on the bench and in the clubhouse, that remain available to each manager in the latter stretches of a close game.) With one out in the top of the tenth, the Oriole right fielder, Tito Landrum, whacked a home run into the left-field upper deck, and then three successive singles and a sacrifice, all struck against Burns' successors, made it 3–0, and turned out the arcs in Comiskey Park until the spring. In spite of White Sox malfeasances on the bases and near-total collapse of their power hitters Kittle, Paciorek, Luzinski, Fisk, and Baines (who in four games batted a collective .183, with one run batted in), there was a nobility to this last game that should bring pride to the White Sox players in time, and balm to their supporters. It was the game of the year.

Those Comiskey Park fans had more fun than anyone this past summer. Their club, for a wonder, did not adhere to its ancient tradition of a second-half collapse but went quite the other way, surviving a very rocky start and then suddenly finding itself at midseason and thundering home with a 22–9 record in August, followed by a 22–6 September. The turnaround seemed to begin on June 15th, with LaRussa's decision to move Carlton Fisk up to the No. 2 slot in the order. Fisk batted .319 in the second half, and probably helped even more with his handling of the pitchers; three starters—Hoyt, Dotson, and Floyd Bannister—had a combined record of forty-two wins and five losses in the second half. The best things of the year seemed to happen at home, where Greg Luzinski three times bombed a home run up onto the left-field roof (no one had ever done it more than once in a season), and Kittle put two up there, too, and had thirty-three others for the season. And then there was the evening when Fisk and Luzinski and Paciorek hit back-to-back-to-back (well, I guess not, but something like that) home runs in the first inning. The noisy Chicago style became known as "winning ugly"—a numbingly publicized slogan picked up from an oxymoronic slur about the club made by Ranger manager Doug Rader. Anyway, by the time the last home stand was over, 2,132,821 fans had come to the old white pagoda of Comiskey to see the Sox—the most in any summer since they began to play ball there, back in 1910.

I missed the whole scene, and I'm sorry I did. I'm not certain that I've ever appreciated the Chicago White Sox enough, since I did not grow up in that great baseball city and never joined the holy order of Sox believers. Loving the White Sox, it should be understood, means hating the Cubs; there can be no middle ground. I learned this years ago from a friend in college, who lived and (much more often) died for Ted Lyons and Luke Appling, and this year in September I talked with a White Sox fan in exile—a woman now living in New York (she is in television news) who grew up in Chicago in the nineteen-fifties and early sixties—who told me that matters still stood the same back home. "For me, the White Sox have the same image that Chicago does," she said. "That *grittiness*. There's nothing lovely about it. When most people I know think about Chicago, they sort of mean the Cubs and the North Side. I mean, they don't know the city at all. The Cubs are just one safe elevated ride away, but we Sox people were way off on the dangerous South Side. I *hate* it that the Cubs don't have lights. It's typical—they just don't think they have to do anything for their fans. Who can go to games in the daytime, anyway? Just rich people and kids. The Cubs are so damned boring. They don't have that street feeling. Did you know that Harry Caray, the broadcast guy, has gone over to the Cubs from the White Sox? Can you *believe* that? That's like changing sides in the middle of the war. It's like joining the Nazis."

She had begun to glare at me. Then she said, "You know, I *hate* it that the White Sox finally won after I'd left town. It's just like them to do that. I'll bet they're not going to win the playoffs—or if they do they'll lose the World Series. You'll see. I can't stand it when they lose, but I'm ready for it. You have to hold back at times like this. You have to know about the Sox if you're going to care about them."

◆ ◆ ◆

THE WORLD SERIES, SO CLEAR IN FORM AND OUTCOME, WILL be revisited only briefly here. Its neighbor-city participants had inspired a few writers to call it the Amtrak Series, and the first two games—a swift, neat opening 2–1 win by the Phillies, followed by a 4–1 Baltimore victory the next evening—went by so quickly that they suggested two Metroliners swooshing past each other in opposite directions on some marshy Chesapeake-side straightaway. Three unencumbered home runs—by Joe Morgan and Garry Maddox, of the Phils, and Jim Dwyer, of the Orioles—produced all the scoring in Game One, in which the Phils' John Denny, their best pitcher this year, threw his curveball on the corners all evening, setting down the O's in neat little packages of three and getting the home crowd home (and out of a drizzly rain) in less than two and a half hours. The jammed-together, cheerful (under the circs) Baltimore fans were again conducted in their noise-making by their self-appointed leader,

Bill Hagy, a local cabdriver, who has announced his retirement from the tummler post next season. (Unlike some of his counterparts and imitators in other cities, he is not paid by the team, and, indeed, has refused any emolument for his work.) He is the inventor of the unique Orioles letter-cheer, executed in body language, and I noticed that his handwriting has become minimal and blurry over the years, like the signatures of other famous men. Game Two brought back Mike Boddicker, who outpitched the other junior, Hudson, and won by 4–1—another impeccable outing for him, since the only Philadelphia run was unearned. The Baltimore staff at this juncture had surrendered four earned runs in fifty-four postseason innings. Boddicker did not look quite as awesome as he had against the White Sox, but when I thought about it I realized that this was probably only because he had stuck more closely to Ray Miller's ideal—striking out a mere six batters and, of course, walking none. After the game, Jim Palmer was in ecstasies of appreciation of his young teammate's stuff. "That change of speeds reminds you of Stu Miller, the old slowball pitcher years ago," he said. "I remember batting against Stu in a spring-training game when I was nineteen years old, and he suddenly came in with a fastball up *here*, and I almost had a stroke. But it's Mike's curveball and his control of it that gets me. I charted pitches for five of the games he pitched this year, and I was amazed. Steve Stone had that one great year for us when he threw all curveballs, but this was even better. I've never seen anything like it in all my years in baseball."

The Baltimore offense, which had not been getting much lift from its third and fourth batters, Cal Ripkin and Eddie Murray, was given a leg up by John Lowenstein, who had a single, a double, and a home run for his day's work. As everyone knows by now, he plays half of left field for the O's, giving way to Gary Roenicke on days when the other team has a left-hander on the mound. (Lowenstein is an original. When a young reporter asked him one day if anyone knew the origin of the one-handed catch now universally practiced by outfielders, Lowenstein said he was pretty sure it had begun with a player named Pete Gray—yes, the Pete Gray who played a season for the wartime St. Louis Browns in spite of having only one arm. When he is asked from time to time if he might be willing to talk about how it feels to be a Jewish major-league ballplayer, Lowenstein usually obliges with a thoughtful, in-depth probing of his feelings on the matter, with appreciative references to great baseball forebears like Moe

Berg and Hank Greenberg and so forth, without ever quite explaining that he himself, as it happens, is not Jewish.) Here Brother Low, as he is called in the clubhouse, responded to the clamorous press with the low-key eloquence that has become an Orioles' trademark. "There's never any talk around here about a platoon system," he said. "That would be too glamorous. We don't have a Jim Rice on this ball club, so it works very well for us to have two or three men in left field. We just relish the accomplishment that different people can bring to the position." All right, but it should be added that Baltimore *almost* has a Jim Rice out there in left. Between them, Roenicke and Lowenstein accounted for thirty-four homers and a hundred and twenty-four R.B.I.s during the regular season, which is nice work for a committee.

And so we went to Philadelphia and to Game Three—the hard game of the Series for both sides, I think—and when it was over, with Baltimore the winner by 3–2, there was a sudden sense in me and many other onlookers about how the rest of the week might go. The immediate problem for Baltimore in the game was Steve Carlton, who had been resting from his winning appearance in the Phillies' final playoff game. On this day, I noticed, he seemed to be missing one part of his repertoire, which is a three-quarter-speed rainbow slider that suddenly drops out of the strike zone like a mouse behind the sink, and he gave up some uncharacteristic hard-hit blows, pulled to the left side (mostly for outs), in the early innings. Carlton, like most great pitchers, is an indomitable closer—very hard to beat in the late innings no matter what stuff he may have—and it seemed forehanded and lucky that the O's got him out of there in the seventh, with a double by Rick Dempsey and a pulled hard single by pinch-hitter Benny Ayala, which tied the game at 2–2. (Ayala's stated batting philosophy, by the way, is a bit simpler than Yaz's multipart cogitations: "I look for something white moving through.") Ayala then became the winning run, scoring a moment or two later when Dan Ford's hard grounder skidded on a wet patch of the infield carpet and ricocheted off shortstop Ivan DeJesus' glove: a no-fault error. One prime recipient of this gift was Jim Palmer, who was in the game in relief of Mike Flanagan and thus gained the win. He had endured a difficult season, suffering back problems and tendinitis, and at one point had been sent down to the Orioles' Class A Hagerstown team to recover his form. He took this all in good part, becoming a stand-by bullpen operative in the postseason, and his work in this

game, by his own admission, looked more like throwing—
careful throwing—than pitching, but he was delighted with the
win. When he and Carlton were in the game against each other
for a few minutes there, we were looking at five hundred and
sixty-eight lifetime victories.

The particular problem for the Phillies—or a symbol of the
problem, at least—was Pete Rose, who got into the game as a
pinch-hitter in the ninth after spending most of it sombrely
watching the proceedings from the top step of the dugout, with
his white-gloved fists tensely clenching and unclenching. He had
been benched by Philadelphia manager Paul Owens, who put
Tony Perez on first in hopes of getting a little sock into the
lineup—not an inconceivable turn of events, since Pete had had
one single to his credit so far—but Rose was at no great pains
to conceal his distress and irritation over the demotion. The
press hordes made much of the little scandal, of course, and Joe
Morgan uncharacteristically lost his temper in the postgame
clubhouse when the reporters, after Rose's swift departure,
turned their questions toward the gentle Perez. Morgan's sense
of propriety was offended; he felt that professionals (including
Rose, although he did not say so) should have handled all this
more calmly. Rose, in fact, had previously embarrassed the club
by not admitting a fielding lapse in Game Two, when he left first
base uncovered in a bunt situation that specifically called for
him to stay in place: no play was made, the bunt helped win the
game, and the fans mistakenly blamed Morgan for the uncovered base.

These trifling contretemps are set forth here because they tell
us about a much deeper problem that afflicted the Phillies all
year. Paul Owens became the Philadelphia manager in the middle of July, replacing Pat Corrales at a moment when the club
was in first place in the flaccid N.L. East but scraping along just
one game above the .500 level. Owens, the incumbent general
manager, took on the field directorship because the Philadelphia
front office foresaw that only a man with his authority and reputation would be able to enforce some difficult alterations in the
Phillie lineup of famous and very well-paid older stars, who by
now had made it plain that they weren't good enough to win.
Owens installed a platoon system of his own, resting Pete Rose
and veteran outfielders Gary Matthews and Garry Maddox
whenever it seemed advantageous to do so, and reshuffling his
batting order. Everyone in the lineup but catcher Bo Diaz, third
baseman Mike Schmidt, and shortstop Ivan DeJesus became a

replaceable part, in fact, and Owens made frequent use of the lesser-known outfielder Joe Lefebvre and, later on, of a rookie first baseman, Len Matuszek, and outfielder Sixto Lezcano. None of this was easy (Rose's first benching ended a seven-hundred-and-forty-five-consecutive-game streak for him), and no one on the club took it with particular grace. In September, Mike Schmidt indulged himself in a public outburst of criticism of Owens' managing (it came at the moment when the club was embarking on its eleven-game winning streak), and even during the Series, after it had become plain to everyone that the changes had worked and that the team had outdone itself at the end, there were mumbles and grousings from some of the famous principals. Owens himself—he is a tall, stooped, gentle-spoken man, with odd white eyelashes, who carries a packet of Gelusil in his uniform pocket—summed up his club during the playoffs with a musing little aside: "We have an old team and a middle-aged team and a young team." Three teams from which to make one—to make a Baltimore, say.

Pete Rose and Joe Morgan were given their release by the Phillies in the week after the Series ended, and it is expected that Joe Morgan will soon decide whether to retire or to join the Oakland A's for a final season as a designated hitter. It is painful for us to see old players go, and infinitely harder when they prolong the inevitable process. Morgan went into September at the bottom of the National League batting averages, but then took fire, at one point running off thirteen hits in eighteen at-bats, and on his fortieth birthday enjoying a four-for-five game with two homers—a beautiful goodbye, if he can but see it that way. Pete Rose, who has slowed down perceptibly in the field, batted .245 this year—sixty-three points below his lifetime average. He will be forty-three next spring, by which time he will have signed on with some club or other, for he is in obdurate pursuit of Ty Cobb's 4,191 lifetime hits. He needs eleven more hits to pass the four-thousand mark, where only Cobb has gone before him, and two hundred and two more to set the new mark. I hope he can do it in one great last rush—an eleventh two-hundred-hit season, with great festivals at its close—but I suspect it may be a much longer journey for him, and for the rest of us as well.

◆ ◆ ◆

Rose, in any case, was back in the lineup for Game Four, and had two hits and scored a run and batted in another—not quite enough to win it. You could say that the Orioles' pitching (Storm Davis, plus Sammy Stewart and Tippy Martinez) won again, or else that it was Orioles second baseman Rich Dauer who did it, with his three hits and three runs batted in and a neatly turned double play to stop a big Philadelphia inning. It was a taut, hard game, in any case, with the Orioles pulling it out by 5–4, and if I believed that managers ever actually win ballgames I would say that Baltimore manager Joe Altobelli won this one, because of what he and his accomplished bench (the "role-players," as they like to call themselves) pulled off in the sixth inning. Trailing John Denny (a right-hander, remember) by 3–2, with Oriole base runners at second and third, he unexpectedly wheeled in the left-side-swinger Joe Nolan as a pinch-hitter; when Nolan was intentionally walked, Altobelli produced Ken Singleton, who switch-hits and was thus proof against any Philadelphia countermove to a lefty pitcher. Singleton walked, driving in a run and tying the game (Sakata came in to run for him), and when Hernandez, a left-hander, did at last come in to pitch, the batter awaiting him was John Shelby, who also switches, and who now, batting right-handed, hit a sacrifice fly that drove in the lead run. Baltimore's fourth successive pinch-hitter, Dan Ford, fanned for the last out, but the marionette show was not quite done, since Altobelli, by moving one incumbent fielder, Dauer, from second base to third base, found room in his defensive deployment for two of the pinch-hitters and for Sakata, too (but none at the same position as the man he had replaced), in the bottom half of the inning. I apologize for this digression, which perhaps needs an accompanying flow chart, but for those of us who were keeping score Altobelli's moves suddenly looked like the moment onstage when the shining red balls vanish from the cup and reappear—count them!—in the magician's fingers, and there was a further glow of pleasure when we suddenly realized that Altobelli somehow still had his three best right-handed backup hitters—Roenicke, Ayala, and Landrum—available on the bench for later use, if needed. Managers try this sort of stuff all the time, but rarely does it work out as elegantly and inexorably as it did here. To be sure, there is always some luck involved in such maneuvers (think of Altobelli's embarrassment in that August game against the Blue Jays, when he ran out of catchers and had to play Sakata behind the plate), but when things come out right you see behind them a kind of nerve and a games intelligence that freshen our appreciation of the sport. Chess is harder, but anyone who thinks these managerial moves are a snap should think back to 1981—another year when the American League had to make do without a designated hitter in the Series—and how Yankee manager Bob Lemon and his staff, in losing to the Dodgers, repeatedly found themselves flustered and outmaneuvered in these old games of pinch and switch.

Joe Altobelli, who put in fourteen years as a minor-league player, coach, and manager in the Baltimore system (he later managed the Giants for three years and then coached at third base for the Yanks, before taking up his post last winter), has a strong instinct for the Baltimore outlook on baseball. "My moves weren't *that* hard to make," he said mildly. "It wasn't the result of meditation, or anything. I had the players available, and that's the big thing. And how hard is it to send Singleton up to pinch-hit, when he's had five hundred at-bats, or Shelby, who's been in there all year for us?"

Most of the Orioles regulars are long-termers with the club (which in recent years has lost to free-agency only one player it hoped to keep, pitcher Don Stanhouse), and most of them talk about Baltimore style with the same tempered earnestness, but in each case, I felt, their views seemed to represent a private set of convictions or discoveries, with none of the numbing, faked-up "positive values" that the boyish Los Angeles varsity exudes when it expounds upon Dodger Blue. Ken Singleton, now in his ninth year with the club, who was converted from designated hitter to a pinch-hitter for this series, talked to the reporters about how much more difficult it was to get up on short notice and make a single crucial appearance at the plate, and expressed his awe of people like Dwyer and Ayala, who do it all the time. "There's a certain atmosphere here that's conducive to winning," he said. "On other teams, guys get upset with their roles if they're not playing all the time. Not here." Dauer, who batted .235 this summer but maintained that he'd had a good year, said, "If we're here, we must all be playing well. When you come up in an organization that's had a Brooks Robinson and a Mark Belanger, the defensive part is instilled in you. You know that's part of why you win." And Jim Palmer: "We don't have any ups and downs. We come out here and hope we'll win. It's a calm feeling. Earl Weaver had a lot to do with it. He never overreacted early in the season, so by September we'd be in business again. Joe is the same. We had two seven-game losing streaks this year, but, as he said, nobody pointed the finger at anyone else. Stable organizations don't overreact. You do your best, send out good pitchers, and hope you can go on doing what you've done all year.''

Stable organizations run deep, and the calm Baltimore way of winning that Palmer was talking about seems to have grown out of a pattern of sound management that began with its first general manager, Paul Richards, who was steering things when the club came to Baltimore, in 1954. (It had been the hapless St. Louis Browns franchise.) He was succeeded by a near-Plantagenet line of brilliant executives: Lee MacPhail, Harry Dalton, Frank Cashen, and the incumbent (since 1975) G.M., Hank Peters. (Dalton is now the general manager of the Milwaukee Brewers, who won the A.L. pennant last year, and Cashen holds the same post with the up-and-coming Mets.) Above them, in the owner's office, were Jerold C. Hoffberger and then (since 1979) Edward Bennett Williams—each an exception to the twin mold of drearily conservative or flamboyantly egocentric owners—and around them, so to speak, in various farm and coaching and scouting posts, was a passel of sound, much-admired field men: Jim McLaughlin, Lou Gorman, George Bamberger, Ray Poitevint, Ray Scarborough, and the present-day super-scout, Jim Russo. Some of these worthies have retired or moved along to higher posts with other clubs (Ray Scarborough died last year), but each of them, I think, must have felt a proprietary glow over the Orioles' home-grown grand success this autumn.

◆ ◆ ◆

IN THE SERIES, EDDIE MURRAY AND MIKE SCHMIDT EACH RAN into oppressive difficulties in trying to do what he had been doing all year, which was to hit the ball to distant parts and win ballgames. Schmidt talked at length with the writers about his failures (he was batting .063 after four games), and said that the Orioles pitchers were making him chase a lot of pitches that were up and out of the strike zone, and that he was making adjustments in his swing; Murray, for his part, said nothing and made no adjustments (he had had two singles so far, for .125), as is his custom, but it seemed certain that he was unhappily thinking back to the World Series of 1979, when he failed repeatedly at the plate while the O's dropped the last three games in a row and lost to the Pirates. Now he came up in the second inning of the fifth game and whacked a monstrous homer into the upper tiers in right field—"It would have been a homer in Grand Canyon," Pete Rose said later—and followed up in the fourth with an even longer, two-run job that bounced off the center-field scoreboard, where the ball just missed hitting the "M" of his own name up there at a moment when the message screen was listing the American League R.B.I. leaders. Rick Dempsey hit a home run and also a double, and scored the last run, and the O's, behind McGregor's 5–0 shutout, were World Champions. Dempsey was voted the Most Valuable Player—a lovely choice. He is a first-rate catcher, durable and energetic, with a powerful arm and great agility behind the plate, but with few of the offensive abilities that usually go with the job. This summer, he batted .231, with four home runs—about average for him. Dempsey's attitude toward the game has always been summed up for me by the way he wears his cap in the field—turned backward, because of the mask, but with the brim bent up in a cocky little flourish. Like most of his teammates, he seems to have an unquenchably high regard for himself. "I've got a lot of good hits for this club down the years," he remarked early in the Series. "I get pinch-hit for a lot late in the game, so I've gone plenty of weeks when I was oh-for-two and then came out of the game. I figure if I'm hitting .250 here it's the same as .280 someplace else. We just have a different way of doing things here."

◆ ◆ ◆

FOUR

Easy Lessons

THERE'S NOTHING LIKE AN ALL-EXPENSE-PAID LATE-winter vacation under the palms and within sight and sound of batted baseballs to give a sensitive man a deeper appreciation of the nature of guilt. Each year in March, I journey to Arizona and then to Florida, or vice versa, to watch a sampling of the current and future major-league ballplayers do their morning stretching exercises on dew-dappled outfield lawns (lately these workouts are being done to bouncy aerobic-rock sounds and are led by a young woman in shorts and leg-warmers who is clearly in better shape than anyone else on the field) and then test and disport themselves in batting cages and on practice mounds—engaging in B.P. and Infield and Shagging and Flip—and eventually play a few innings of morning B-Squad ball or an afternoon exhibition game, and each year this excursion brings me such freshets of pleasure that I must find new excuses within myself to justify such dulcet bystanding. Duty, for instance. I am there at the camps as a reporter, to be sure, having been dispatched sunward to search out the news and the special sense of the coming season, and there is no sterner or more assiduous newshawk to be found on the demanding Scottsdale-to-Sarasota beat than yours truly. Even the most casual morning invitation to take a dip in my motel pool or to make a fourth at middle-aged doubles finds me puritanically glum. "Not a chance!" I cry. "I'm *working* today." And work I do, carefully noting in my notebook the uniform number and the unremarkable batting mannerisms of some hulking young stranger now taking his hacks in the cage, and checking his thin line of stats (.266 and eight home runs in Danville in 1981) in my team press guide, and then eliciting clubhouse quotes from a grizzled bullpen millionaire about the current state of his damaged wing ("Hurts like a bastard. . . ."), and, later in the day, raising my mid-game gaze from the diamond to observe the gauzy look of departing rain clouds lifting from the jagged rim of some distant desert peak, and then entering *that* in my notebook (with the pen slipping a little in my fingers, because of the dab of Sea & Ski I have just rubbed on my nose, now that the sun is out again and cooking us gently in the steep little grandstand behind third base). I watch and listen and write, filling up almost as much space in my copybooks as I do in October at the World Series, and entering on my scorecard the names of third-string non-roster substitutes who filter into the game so late in the day that even the geezer fans and their geezerettes have begun to gather up their backrests and seat cushions and head off home for beer and naps. Guilt, as I have said, is the spur, for it is my secret Calvinist fear that baseball will run out on me someday and I will find nothing fresh at the morning camps, despite my notes and numberings, or go newsless on some sun-filled afternoon, and so at last lose this sweet franchise. Baseball saves me every time—not the news of it, perhaps, so much as its elegant and arduous complexity, its layered substrata of nuance and lesson and accumulated experience, which are the true substance of these sleepy, overfamiliar practice rituals, and which, if we know how and where to look for them, can later be seen to tip the scales of the closest, most wanted games of the summer. Almost everything in baseball looks easy and evident, but really learning the game, it turns out, can take a lifetime, even if you keep notes.

Let's face it: spring training is a misnomer. Thanks to aerobics, racquetball, high-tech physical-fitness centers, California-chic wives, and a sensible wish to extend their very high salaries through as many years as possible, most major-league ballplayers stay in terrific shape all year round now. Back in the straw-suitcase days, it took a month to six weeks to work off winter beer bellies and firm up poolroom-pale bodies, but contemporary players have told me that a single week of batting practice and rundown drills would make them absolutely ready for Opening Day. What with performance records, autumn visits to the Instructional Leagues, and almost daily reports from the winter-ball leagues in Latin America, most managers have a pretty good notion of the capabilities of the rising minor leaguers in their organizations, and are not likely to be badly startled (or much convinced) by a .485 spring average put together by some anonymous rookie outfielder during the exhibitions. The pitchers, to be sure, do require all of March and a little bit more in order to get their arms in shape, and the process—early stretching and tossing, the first three-innings stints, then harder stuff and longer outings—cannot be hurried or shortened, since there must be days of recuperation after each game or batting-practice workout. Spring training is really for the pitchers, then—and for the writers, who need this slow, sleepy time in which to sweeten their characters and enlarge their perceptions of what truly matters in our old game. I offer as example an apothegm uttered by a friend from the *Chronicle*, a budding Solomon whose views have already been heard in these pages. It was in a week of dazzling weather in Arizona, and this time we were sitting side by side in the narrow press box of Scottsdale Stadium, watching the Giants vs. (I think) the Brewers. Late in the sixth inning, he looked irritably at his watch and said, "Damn. Yesterday's game was already over by this time."

"Right," said I, arising and gathering up my notebook, media guides, pencils, and scorecard. (*My* deadline was weeks away.) "And thanks, Dave. See you at the pool."

◆ ◆ ◆

IN WINTER HAVEN, ON THE VERY FIRST DAY OF THIS SPRING jaunt, I found Ted Williams out in right-field foul ground teaching batting to Von Hayes—a curious business, since the Splendid Splinter, of course, is a spring batting instructor for the Red Sox, and Hayes is the incumbent center fielder of the Phillies. Hayes was accompanied by Deron Johnson, the Philadelphia batting coach, and the visit, I decided, was in the nature of medical referral—a courtesy second opinion extended by a great specialist to a colleague from a different hospital (or league). Von Hayes is a stringbean—six feet five, with elongated arms and legs—and his work at the plate this year will be the focus of anxious attention from the defending National League Champion Phillies, who are in the process of turning themselves from an old club into a young one in the shortest possible time. Since last fall, they have parted with (among others) Pete Rose, Joe Morgan, Tony Perez, and veteran reliever Ron Reed, and later this spring they traded away Gary Matthews, their established left fielder (Matthews, in fact, was intently listening in on Ted Williams' talk to his teammate Hayes), to the Cubs. Two years ago, in his first full year in the majors, Von Hayes hit fourteen homers and batted in eighty-two runs for the Cleveland Indians—sufficient promise to encourage the Phillies to give up five of their own players (including the wonderful old Manny Trillo and the wonderful young Julio Franco) for him. Last year, Hayes, troubled with injuries (and perhaps unsettled by the nickname Five-for-One, bestowed on him by Pete Rose), batted a middling-poor .265, with six homers—reason enough for a call to Dr. Ted.

"Lemme see that," Ted Williams was saying, and he took Hayes' bat and then hefted it lightly, like a man testing a new tennis racquet. "Well, all right, if you're really strong enough," he said, giving it back. "But you don't need a great big bat, you know. Stan Musial always used a little bitty drugstore model. So what *do* you want? You know what Rogers Hornsby told me forty-five years ago? It was the best batting advice I ever got. *'Get a good ball to hit!'* What does that mean? It means a ball that does not fool you, a ball that is not in a tough spot for you. So then when you are in a tough spot, concede a little to that pitcher when he's got two strikes on you. Think of trying to hit it back up the middle. Try not to pull it every time. Harry Heilmann told me that he never became a great hitter until he learned to hit inside out. I used to have a lot of trouble in here"—he showed us an awkward inside dip at the ball with his own bat—"until I moved back in the box and got a little more time for myself. Try to get the bat reasonably inside as you swing, because it's a hell of a lot harder to go from the outside in than it is to go the other way around."

Hayes, who looked pale with concentration, essayed a couple of left-handed swings, and Willams said, "Keep a little movement going. Keep your ass loose. Try to keep in a quick position to swing. When your hands get out like that, you're just making a bigger arc."

Hayes swung again—harder this time—and Williams said, "That looks down to me. You're swingin' down on the ball."

Hayes looked startled. "I thought it was straight up," he said. He swung again, and then again.

"Well, it's still down," Ted said quietly. "And see where

you're looking when you swing. You're looking at the ground about out here." He touched the turf off to Hayes's left with the tip of his bat. "Look out at that pitcher—don't take your eyes off him. That and—" Williams cocked his hips and his right knee and swung at a couple of imaginary pitches, with his long, heavy body uncocking suddenly and thrillingly and then rotating with the smooth release of his hips. His hands, I saw now, were inside, close to his body, while Hayes' hands had started much higher and could not come back for a low, inside pitch with anything like Ted's ease and elegance. Nothing to it. Hayes, who has a long face, looked sepulchral now, and no wonder, for no major leaguer wants to retinker his swing—not in the springtime, not ever—and Williams, sensing something, changed his tone. "Just keep going," he said gently to the young man. "Everybody gets better if they keep at it."

Hayes kept at it, standing in and looking out at an imaginary pitcher, and then cocking and striding, while Williams stood and watched with Deron Johnson, now and then murmuring something to the other coach and touching his own hip or lifting his chin or cocking his fists by way of illustration—a sixty-five-year-old encyclopedia of hitting, in mint condition: the book.

When I left, he was in deep converse with Gary Matthews, who had asked about the best response to a pitcher's backup slider after two fastballs up and in. "Why, *take* that pitch, then!" Ted cried. "Just let it go by. Don't be so critical of yourself. Don't try to be a .600 hitter all the time. Don't you know how hard this all is?"

◆ ◆ ◆

I ACCOMPANIED THE RED SOX DOWN TO SARASOTA TO WATCH Tom Seaver work against them the following afternoon—his first American League innings ever. Seaver, as most of the Northern Hemisphere must know by now, was snatched away from the Mets over the winter when that club carelessly failed to place him on its protected twenty-six-man roster prior to a "compensation draft"—a process that permits a team (in this case, the White Sox) that has lost a so-called Type A player to a free agency to select as recompense a player from a pool of players with other teams that have signed up for the plan. This misshapen schema is a monster child spawned by the owners as a part of the settlement of the player strike of 1981, and there is considerable evidence that its headstrong fathers may now wish to disinherit it. Shortly after the Mets' humiliation, the Yankees experienced a similar shock (the circumstances were a little different) when they lost a freshly signed top pitching prospect, Tim Belcher, to the Oakland A's in another compensation kidnapping. The Mets, in any case, suffered a horrendous double embarrassment: first, for the forfeit of their old hero figure—an Odin brought back to the fold last year, amid many trumpetings, to finish his days in Shea-Valhalla as the steadfast elder leader of a corps of shining young Baldurflingers—and, second, for the clear evidence that it somehow did not occur to them that the pennant-hungry and publicity-hungry White Sox might find some use for a highly motivated and splendidly conditioned veteran star pitcher (Seaver is thirty-nine) with a lifetime earned-run average of 2.73. The Mets people, to their credit, have rent asunder their blazers and strewn dust upon their razor-cut pates in public penance for their gaffe, and no further criticism of them will be put forward here.

The first glimpse of Tom in Chisox motley—neon pants-stripes, the famous No. 41 adorning his left groin—was a shock, though, and so was the sight of him in pre-game conversation with his new batterymate, Carlton Fisk. I took a mental snapshot of the two famous Handsome Harrys and affixed to it the caption "Q: What's wrong with this picture?" (A: Both men are out of uniform.) Then the game started, and Seaver's pitching put an end to all such distractions. It was a prime early-spring outing—three swift, harm-free innings that included a couple of bases on balls and four strikeouts. There was a good pop to his fastballs, and he wheeled in some thoughtfully located sliders and curveballs as well, and once it was clear that he was going to be all right out there I sat back and took pleasure in all the old looks and ways of him—the thick, strong legs and droopy shoulders, the grave gaze catcherward for the sign, the audible *"Hunh!"* that sometimes accompanied the in-driving thrust of his big body in mid-delivery (Ted Williams had said that he doesn't hear enough grunts from the mound nowadays), and then the mitt flipped up vertically to take the catcher's return peg.

In the clubhouse after his stint, Seaver declared himself satisfied with his work—perhaps more than satisfied. There had been some small technical problems—his release point was a little flat at times—but that wasn't surprising, because he'd been nervous about this outing. "I wanted to prove to the guys that I can help this ball club," he said. "They don't care who you are. They want to know if you can still pitch—especially at the age of thirty-nine. This is a team that wants to win. They've had a taste of it, and they want more. What our game is all about is proving things to your own team."

He went over the three innings almost pitch by pitch, making sure that the writers had their stories, and they thanked him and went off. A couple of us stayed on while Tom unwrapped the big icepack from his shoulder and started to take off his uniform. I think we wanted reminiscence or philosophy from him now—something about motivation or the shocks of unexpected trades or the wearing down of an athlete's will with the years—but what we got was much better: mechanics. He talked about tempos of early throwing in the first few days of spring—a murmured *"one, two, three-four . . . one, two, three-four"* beat with the windup as his body relearned rhythm and timing. He went on to the proper breaking point of the hands—where the pitching hand comes out of the glove—which for him is just above and opposite his face. Half undressed, he was on his feet again and pitching for us in slow motion, in front of his locker.

"What you don't want is a lateral movement that will bring your elbow down and make your arm drop out, because what happens then is that your hand either goes underneath the ball or out to the side of the ball," he said. "To throw an effective pitch of any kind, your fingers have to stay on top of the ball. So you go back and make sure that this stays closed and *this* stays closed"—he touched his left shoulder and his left hip—"and this hand comes up *here*." The pitching hand was back and above his head. "It's so easy to get to here, in the middle of the windup, and then slide off horizontally with your left side. What you're trying to do instead—what's right—is to drive this lead shoulder down during the delivery of the ball. That way, the pitching shoulder comes up—it *has* to go up. You've increased the arc, and your fingers are on top of the ball, where they belong."

I said I'd heard pitching coaches urging their pupils to drive the lead shoulder toward the catcher during the delivery.

"Sure, but that's earlier," Tom said. He was all concentration, caught up in his craft. "That's staying closed on your forward motion, before you drive down. No—with almost every pitcher, the fundamentals are the same. Look at Steve Carlton, look at Nolan Ryan, look at me, and you'll see this closed, this closed, *this* closed. You'll see this shoulder drive down and this one come up, and you'll see the hand on top of the ball. You'll see some flexibility in the landing leg. There are some individual variables, but almost every pitcher with any longevity has all that—and we're talking now about pitchers with more than four thousand innings behind them and with virtually no arm troubles along the way.''

Someone mentioned Jerry Koosman, who had gone along from the White Sox to the Phillies over the winter, and Seaver reminded us that he and Koosman and Tug McGraw and Nolan Ryan had been together on the 1969 World Champion Mets and that they were all still pitching in the majors, fifteen years later. ''Nolan Ryan's still pitching *and then some*,'' he said. ''We all had good fundamentals, and our pitching coach, Rube Walker, stressed the right things—don't overthrow, stretch out your work with a five-day rotation, and keep those sound mechanics.''

There are other ways to pitch and pitch well, to be sure, Seaver said, and he mentioned Don Sutton as an example. ''Sutton's exceptionally stiff-legged,'' he said, ''but he compensates because he follows through. He doesn't do this.'' He snapped his right arm upward in a whiplike motion after releasing an imaginary ball. ''The danger with a stiff front leg is recoiling.''

He picked up the remaining pieces of his discarded uniform and underwear and tossed them into a canvas hamper. ''What is the theory of pitching?'' he went on. He sounded like a young college history lecturer reaching his peroration. ''All you're doing is trying to throw a ball from here to here.'' He pointed off toward some plate behind us. ''There's no energy in the ball. It's inert, and you're supplying every ounce of energy you can to it. But the energy can't all go there. You can't do that—that's physics. Where does the rest of it go? *It has to be absorbed back into your body.* So you have to decide if you want it absorbed back into the smaller muscles of the arm or into bigger muscles of the lower half of your body. The answer is simple. With a stiff front leg, everything comes back in *this* way, back up into the arm, unless you follow through and let that hand go on down after the pitch.''

''But isn't that leg kick—'' I began.

''The great misnomer in pitching is the 'leg kick,' '' he interrupted. ''That's totally wrong. Any real leg kick is incorrect. Anytime you kick out your leg you're throwing your shoulders back, and then you're way behind with everything. You've got to stay up on top of this left leg, with your weight right over it. So what is it, really? It isn't a leg kick, it's a *knee lift*! Sure, you should bend your back when you're going forward, but—'' He stopped and half-shrugged, suddenly smiling at himself for so much intensity. ''I give up,'' he said. ''It's too much for any man to do. It's too much even to remember." He laughed—his famous giggle—and went off for his shower.

◆ ◆ ◆

I GOT LUCKY IN ARIZONA THREE DAYS LATER, BECAUSE HERE was Don Sutton working five sharp innings for the Brewers against the Giants in Scottsdale, and I could think about mechanics some more. Sutton gave up two singles and a solo home run (to Jeffrey Leonard), and got a passel of ground-ball outs with his down-breaking curve, which he throws, oddly, with his forefinger crooked up on the ball and the fingernail cutting into a seam. For a while there, I thought he *was* snapping his arm on the recoil—he comes straight over the top, right-handed, bobbing over the front leg and finishing with so little twist or drop to his body that it almost appears to be attached to a vertical wire somewhere—but when I concentrated I thought I could see his pitching arm moving so fast after the release that his hand, a blur, actually did come down past his left knee before it slowed, stopped, and rose again. I wasn't sure, though, and I checked this with him when we met in the dingy wooden visiting-team clubhouse after his outfield sprints. Sutton has fashionably cut gray curly hair and a lean, humorous face; he looks and sounds like his pitching style—slick, spare, smart. Within a couple of weeks, he would turn forty and begin his nineteenth season as a big-league starter.

"Yes, my arm comes way down," he said at once. "I transform the strain. My mechanics are fundamentally sound, because I do what comes naturally to me. We're all unique. To take a guy like me and turn him into a drop-and-drive pitcher like Tom Seaver would have made for about a one-year career, and to make Tom into an over-the-top curveball pitcher would have done the same to him. Seaver has powerful legs and butt muscles and a strong upper body. All my effort in pitching comes from my upper legs and lower back, and I've worked over the years to keep them strong."

Sutton's shirt was off by now, and I could see the lean, tightly drawn shoulder muscles moving beneath his skin. His body looked tailored. He told me that Red Adams, his pitching coach with the Dodgers years ago, had worked with him to establish and refine his pitching form—"He found my slot" was the way he put it—and had given him four checkpoints to watch for during his delivery. Raising his arms, he faced me and went through a slow-motion delivery. "One: Start square," he said. "Two: Quarter-turn. Three: Pause at the top and tap. Four: Go on through and *don't stop*." He did it all again, even slower this time. "Starting square, looking directly at the plate, and making no more than a quarter turn is important, because if I do this"—he bent his body a little farther away from me on the pivot, going from nine o'clock to about ten-thirty—"if I get that far, I can't make up for all that body action by the time I turn the ball loose. The quarter turn keeps me together. The tap at the top"—he wiggled the toes of his right foot, the mound foot, while his hands were still together above his head—"allows the upper part of my body to catch up with the bottom half and then throw and follow through. It's a one-beat pause. If I *don't* tap, then I'll just rush ahead, so I'm twisted way over here, while my arm is still behind. When I do tap, it's—" And he finished his motion beautifully, with the arm going down and through and then rising again. He had looked almost nothing like Seaver during all this—he was more of a machine, less menacing—but then, near the end of it, I saw the lead shoulder drive down and the back shoulder fly up, bringing the pitching arm up high and through, exactly like Seaver's. They were the same, after all.

That was enough mechanics for the moment, and I asked Sutton how he felt about baseball now, in this last, or latter, part of his career.

"I don't care any more or any less about the game than when I started," he said. "I still think it's a fabulous profession to be in. Sometimes we get a little unrealistic about the role we play in things. Being a professional athlete doesn't solve world hunger or stop crime. It's not going to cure cancer or build houses for people. It's not as important as we think it is. What I do for a living isn't that big a deal to me, then, but the fact that I can do it is a real big deal, because it was the goal I set for myself. I love the competition. It's as simple as that."

◆ ◆ ◆

I FOUND REGGIE JACKSON PLAYING IN A B-GAME BETWEEN THE Angels and the A's the next morning. He'd been waiting out a pulled leg muscle, and these were his first at-bats of the spring. He rapped a little single to right, struck out, and stroked a double against Ray Burris which the center fielder, out by the 410-foot mark on the wall, gloved but could not hold: a real Reggie-blow. He was D.H.-ing for the Angels—it's his regular position

now—and between his turns on deck and at bat he came out and
stood in the sun with some of the writers along the low right-
field fence and took care of the day's ink. Reggie loves to talk—
we all love what we're good at—but now, for the first time, he
was talking about the end of his playing days, or the chance of
that. He had an abysmal season in 1983—a .194 average, with
fourteen home runs, the last of which came in July. In the
campaign just previous, he had tied for the league lead with thirty-
nine downtowners. He has four hundred and seventy-eight lifetime home runs, and Angel-watchers last summer had the
impression that he was so eager to reach the five-hundred plateau
(he would be the thirteenth player there, ever) that his big stroke
came apart under the strain. He will be thirty-eight later this
spring, and there can't be many seasons ahead. He looked the
same as ever—large and friendly and anxious to please, and in
great shape—and it was hard to ask him how he felt about closing down his career.

"I often think about coming to the end," he said. "It's fairly
real—it's a possibility—and I can't say it doesn't bother me. It
isn't a big event or anything, but what I'd like now is to leave
on my terms. If I had another year like last year—and that wasn't
a bad year, it was *horrible*—then I'd have to go. I'd feel defeated.
It isn't just slowing down, not being able to do what you've
done—that's understood and accepted. You can deal with that.
But we're talking about maybe not being able to play baseball
at all—the end. In some ways, I won't mind. The position I've
been in is that of an offensive leader who is counted on to produce. If I play in a hundred and fifty games, I'm expected to put
a number on the board in a hundred of those games. That's the
kind of pressure you don't mind doing without, especially if
you've accomplished some goals along the way. So if I can do
what I think I can do this year—hit maybe twenty-five home
runs and eighty-five R.B.I.s, just get back in Reggie's groove—
then I don't think I'd miss the game after that. But if I didn't—
if I was asked to leave—it would be a whole lot different. I'd
miss baseball if it came to that. It's *how* you go."

I asked if he felt that people expected him to fail now, where
once they had expected him to succeed.

"I'm always under pressure," he said. "I always feel that.
Even in this game—a little B-game. I got that base hit and everybody reacted to that. I could feel it. Then I struck out—it
was the first changeup I'd seen all year—and I could feel the
pressure of *Uh-oh, you didn't succeed. What are people think-*

ing? The pressure goes on and off for me now even from one at-bat to the next.''

Someone asked if most older players didn't have to bear this sort of burden, and Reggie agreed.

"If you're over thirty-five and you've done some things in this game, you develop—if I'm using the word right—you develop a certain braggadocio, a bravado about yourself, but you know you're being watched in a special way, because this is a young man's game. If you do have some bad games, people notice it and write about it and talk about it, and you begin to think, Hey, why are you knocking me now? Even when I'd had a good season, like two years ago, I'd be asked how I measured it, how I felt about it, and that brought defensive responses. You can understand that. So listen. If I get one more good year, give me a pat on the back. Give me a feather and I'll wear it in my cap.''*

◆ ◆ ◆

ONE OF THE UMPIRES IN THAT MORNING GAME WAS PAM Postema—a quick, slim, cheerful arbiter from the Pacific Coast League, who is the only woman ump in the business. I'd seen her work some games last year. The word on her is that she is an outstanding ball-and-strike ump and that she doesn't take any guff out there. At one point in the spring, there was a rhubarb on the field, and coach Herm Starrette, of the Giants, told her to go back to her needle and thread, and she threw him out of the game. Here in Phoenix, she was talking to some friends after the game—she said she'd been hit on the toe with a foul the day before and was dying to get off her feet—when a fan leaned out of the stands and handed her a ball to sign. "Just give me your autograph, will ya, honey?" the man said.

Postema took the ball and the pen and said, "You want me to sign it 'Honey' or do you want my name?"

◆ ◆ ◆

LUCKY KIDS GET TO BE BATBOYS IN THE SPRING GAMES—MOSTLY the sons of coaches or club executives or older players, who come and visit their fathers during the spring break at school. For a while in March, the Oakland batpersons were Kacey and Carey Schueler, the daughters of Ron Schueler, who is the pitch-

*See page 139 for the feather.

ing coach for the A's. Another A's sprout on hand was Jim
Essian III, the son of the veteran backup catcher, who was the
smallest batboy on view anywhere. He is four years old, and he
wore a green sunsuit on the job, with manager Steve Boros' No.
14 inked on it, fore and aft. He had all the moves out there.
Dave Kingman, who has caught on with the club as a designated
hitter this year, bombed a moon shot up onto the left-field embankment against the Cubs' Scott Sanderson, and when Kong
came around third James III was waiting about ten feet up the
line from home, with Kingsman's bat under his arm, and he
gave him a high five—high for him, low for Dave—as he came
by.

◆ ◆ ◆

AS IT TURNED OUT, I DID HAVE A SCHEME OF STUDY THIS SPRING,
and that was to listen to older ballplayers talk about their trade.
I didn't plan it that way, but once it began to happen I was ready
to go back for more. Rookie fireball flingers and unknown
nineteen-year-old sluggers who can hit the ball five hundred feet
into the mangrove swamp are the prime drawing cards of spring
baseball—the equivalent of royal palms to Florida or giant cactus
to Arizona—but over the years I have discovered that while it is
exciting to watch the kids and think about their futures, it does
not nearly match the pleasure of listening to the older players
tell you what they have learned over many thousands of major-
league innings. Tom Seaver, Don Sutton, and Reggie Jackson
don't have much in common at first glance except their age and
their long success, but what I picked up from them all was an
absorbed pride in work that accompanies, and sometimes even
exceeds, the self-pride and love of challenge that lie somewhere
near the center of every professional athlete. We envy and admire ballplayers because they get to do brilliant things under
contrived but excruciatingly difficult circumstances; if they like
themselves in the end, we can forgive them, I think, for it is
much clearer to them than to anyone else how truly hard it was,
every day, to play this game well, or at all.

Rusty Staub, the old man of the young Mets, had an amazing
season in 1983. Employed almost exclusively as a pinch-hitter,
he batted .296 over a hundred and four games, and rapped
twenty-four pinch hits—one short of the all-time record. His
eight consecutive pinch hits, in June, tied another record, and
so did his twenty-five pinch runs-batted-in for the season. All

this came to pass in his twenty-first season; he started as an outfielder with Houston in 1963, when he played a full season, with more than five hundred at-bats, at the age of nineteen. Along the way, he became the first people's favorite—*le Grand Orange*—with the newborn Montreal Expos; then held down right field for the Mets in the early seventies (I can still see him catching a drive by the Reds' Dan Driessen and crashing heavily into the wall out there—and holding the ball), batting .423 in their second World Series, in 1973; then played for the Tigers, the Expos again, and the Rangers; and came back to the Mets in 1981. I talked with Staub one bright, breezy morning while we sat on a little green bench outside the clubhouse at Huggins-Stengel Field, where the Mets train. He is a large, thickly built man, with pink eyelashes and oddly pale skin and a self-contained, polite way of speaking. He was a few days short of his fortieth birthday.

"Most of the men who have played into their forties have been pitchers," he said. "The players who have made it that long are a group that's had talent and a tremendous dedication to staying in shape. People like Yastrzemski, Pete Rose, Joe Morgan, and myself took pride in how they played every day. They didn't give. They never said the hell with today, we'll get 'em tomorrow. Every game mattered. As my career went along, I saw a lot of players with great ability who didn't stay in the game as long as they could have, because they seemed to lose their desire. Even way back when I was with Houston, people were saying I only had a couple of years left, but I knew better. I'm pleased and proud I've been able to stay in this game and still play with the young guys."

Staub said that he had found it much easier to accept his role as a pinch-hitter once Keith Hernandez came over to the Mets from the Cardinals last June. Before that, Dave Kingman had been playing first, although Staub was convinced that he himself could have helped the club more at that position. Hernandez deserved the job, in Staub's estimation, and that made a difference in his own mental adjustment to his limited duties. "You've really got to have a positive attitude about yourself to be a pinch-hitter," he said. "As frustrating as hitting is, there's just no comparison between it and pinch-hitting. You're going to come up to bat in a great many situations where the game is on the line, and no matter what sort of streak you're on you're going to make some outs, and they'll be outs that hurt. You're going to let down your teammates. It's wonderful when you do get up there and put your team back in the game, or get the hit that ties it up, or the hit that wins it, but when you make the out, that's *tough*. You have to be mentally strong about it, because you can't redeem yourself until the next opportunity, and that may not be until a week from now. You have to have a great belief in your own abilities and worth to go through that and not get down.''

He talked a little about the more technical side of the work—staying loose in the clubhouse during the game with exercises and a skip rope, so as to be in gear when called upon, and keeping his short stroke (a thing of beauty; how well I can see it!) at the plate. ''If there's anything I've worked at, it's to be intelligent about the pitchers,'' he said. ''I try to give the outstanding pitchers full credit and not do too much with the ball. Take what's there. If there's a really good left-hander with a breaking ball''—Staub is a left-handed batter—''you can't be up there wheeling for the fences. Most of the time when I'm up, I'm only after a base hit. Going after an extra-base hit is a little different, and sometimes you can have that in mind and succeed. Not a *lot*, though.'' He shook his head.

''I don't get to play in the field much now,'' he went on, ''but I used to work on that part of the game as much as I did on my hitting. It's strange, but quite a few people who are known as hitters do the same thing. That's why I spent so many hours thinking about the other aspects of the game. One of the greatest compliments I ever got was when Ron LeFlore called me one of his top ten base stealers in the game, not because of my record''—Staub has forty-seven lifetime stolen bases—''but because I'd studied it so much. I knew the pitchers and their moves, and I think I was able to help him become such an outstanding man on the base paths.''

I told Rusty that I'd always had the impression, watching him, that no part of the game had come naturally to him. Every aspect of it—running, hitting, picking up the ball and throwing it—looked to me as if it had been studied and practiced endlessly and somehow mastered.

''What you saw is right,'' he said. ''I discovered at a very early age that nothing was going to come easy for me, that I'd have to work to have any success. I compliment my dad and my mom and my kid coaches and high-school coaches, who all made me want to do things the right way—and to know myself. *That's* the biggest challenge for any player: to know in what situation you might have a tendency to back off a little and not do very well—from an injury, say, or for any reason—and then

to learn to overcome that. Learning to face the people you have
to face and how to do things then. It's—Well, I don't think I
want to get into that. It's rough.''

What he did want to get into, it turned out, was the part of
the game from which he is now exiled—playing outfield, that
is. "I probably got as much pleasure from playing defense as
anyone who ever played this game," he said. He was smiling a
little now. "I took great pride in being able to throw the ball
hard and with real accuracy. For ten or twelve years there, I
probably threw the ball from the outfield as well as anybody in
my league, and I definitely threw as accurately as anyone. I
know I made myself into an outstanding outfielder, and when I
slowed down a little I found that I loved playing first base well.
When I made an outstanding defensive play, that was as good
as a base hit any day. As good or better.''

◆ ◆ ◆

AFTERWORD: RUSTY RETIRED AFTER THE 1985 SEASON AND SO
missed out on the Mets' glorious pennant season and World
Championship the following year; he has joined the Mets'
broadcasting crew. He rapped out nineteen more pinch hits over
his last two seasons—each under extreme duress, for the Mets
had risen into serious contention in their division by then. To
me, his finest moments came in late September of 1984. I was
at Shea Stadium when he smote an eighth-inning two-run pinch-
hit single that beat the Phillies and clinched second place for the
Mets. He came out of the dugout for a standing O (a practice he
deplores), waved his cap, and disappeared—done for the year,
I assumed. *Almost* done. The next night (I was away, worse
luck), with the Mets again in the soup, manager Davey Johnson
again rang for the specialist, and Staub whacked a game-winning two-run homer in the bottom of the ninth. It was Rusty's
only home run of the year (and his two-hundred-and-ninety-first
lifetime), and the first for him since he turned forty, back in
April. He struck his very first home run back on June 3, 1963—
Don Drysdale was pitching—when he was a nineteen-year-old
first baseman with the Houston Colt .45s. Rusty Staub thus qual-
ifies as the second player ever to hit major-league homers as a
teen-ager and in his forties; his companion in this feat is Ty
Cobb. Stat of the year.

◆ ◆ ◆

FIVE

Being Green

ONE DAY IN JUNE LAST YEAR, I TOOK A RIDE ON THE
BART subway line from the Embarcadero station,
which is near the foot of the Bay Bridge in downtown
San Francisco, all the way out to the Coliseum station, in Oakland. It was about a twenty-five minute trip, which took us under
the bay and then out into the sunshine and along the East Bay
shore, but it seemed a lot shorter than that. The BART (for Bay
Area Rapid Transit) car I was in was clean and shiny and almost
empty—it was early afternoon—and the train zipped along in a
pleasing, slithery way, so quietly that you could converse with
a friend in a living-room tone of voice. I was glad about that
part, because Roy, my companion on the little trip, is a prime
talker. Roy lives in San Francisco and I live in New York, and
anybody sitting across the aisle from us in the BART car could
have sorted us out in about four seconds. Roy was wearing faded
tan corduroys, a pink Izod alligator T-shirt, and beat-up tennis
shoes; the handle of a tennis racquet protruded from a blue
canvas bag between his feet. His thick brown, casually cut hair
covered the tops of his ears, and his long, interesting-looking
nose was peeling a bit. He had a year-round sort of tan, and he
was clearly in terrific shape: a Californian. Roy is forty-four,
but he looks seven or eight years younger—*ten* years younger.

94

He is a nonpracticing lawyer, a former coach of the University of California freshman crew, a former professor of law at Boalt Hall (the University of California law school at Berkeley), and an active Class A tennis player. I had agreed to pick him up at the Golden Gateway Tennis Club, where I turned up just too late to see him in action in a doubles match, but we didn't talk tennis on the ride out to Oakland; we talked baseball.

"The different ways that baseball reaches its audience are extremely important, because of their effect on the fans," Roy said to me at one point in the subway. "The fans in the stands have an entirely different perception of the game than somebody watching it on television. Sometimes I think of baseball almost as something that exists like the notes on a sheet of music, which has to be performed—performed again and again, well or badly, sometimes brilliantly—in order to go from an inchoate to a choate state. It's performed in the stadium with fans there to watch it, *in attendance*, and they are important—a real part of the process, whether you're aware of them or not. It's not a studio game. Did you ever go to a game where nobody seemed to be watching, really watching, or when there were so few people in the stands that they didn't seem to add up to a crowd? It's a totally different experience. It reminds you of that tree falling in the wilderness: if there's nobody to hear it, is there any sound? If there's nobody in the stands who really understands what's going on, you don't really *have* a baseball game. The delivery systems of baseball are a great concern now—or should be. Television is more important than ever, of course, with the new network contract the clubs have signed, and with cable coming on so strong, but televised baseball is almost an auto-immune disease. We're consuming ourselves. We're attacking our own system. Baseball can't really be taken in on television, because of our ingrained habits of TV-watching. Anybody who knows the sport understands that the ninth inning is as valid as the first inning—that's why real fans always stay to the end of a game. But we don't watch TV that way. If the other team scores four runs in the first inning we go *clicko*, or else we flip the dial and watch Burt Reynolds. On TV, the primary emphasis becomes the score and the possibility of the other team's changing it, and so we miss the integrity of the nine innings and those multiples of three—three strikes and three outs. People can't learn to watch baseball that way; they're just learning to watch television."

Roy speaks in almost subdued conversational tones, with very few gestures or emphasized phrases to make a point, but the intensity of his gaze—he has wide-spaced brown eyes—and the elegantly turned and finished shape of his ideas sometimes make me think that I am a juror in the sway of a subtle and riveting barrister. Yet there is no sense of pleading or performance in him; he simply thinks more clearly than most people I know, and compliments his listener by his wish to convey his discoveries with the same gravity and excitement that he has brought to searching them out.

"Baseball is a terrific radio sport, by contrast, because radio feeds our imagination," he went on. "I was a Tiger fan all the time I was growing up, and I have a perfect memory of George Kell and Hoot Evers making certain plays that I heard but never saw. I almost remember them to this day. I'd be lying out on the grass at home listening to the game, but I was really there in the ballpark. I think baseball has survived all this time because of its place in our imagination—because we've chosen to make the players and the games something larger than they really are. But television has just the opposite effect. The players are shown so closely and under such a bright light that we lose all illusion. It's the same reason we're having such trouble with our politics—our one-term presidents and our senators and mayors and representatives who are held in such low esteem. We can't find the old feelings that we had about F.D.R. or about Ted Williams. The best way to get rid of a hero is to put him in front of that camera. Nobody can stand such close scrutiny. Nobody can survive it in the end. Whether we want it or not, our approach to the game becomes iconoclastic and cynical."

He paused and shook his head a little, half smiling at his own concern. We sat in silence, swaying with the motion of the train, and then we talked a bit about some games and players each of us had seen in recent weeks.

"Everyone in baseball is so afraid of losing," Roy said at one point, "But I've begun to think that, for a team, learning to lose is a very important part of the game. It can be the greening of a team. You have to learn to *wait* in baseball, and losing tests that capacity. When you have a good team that's playing badly, everybody has to be patient—the players, the organization, the media, the fans. Every team runs into losing streaks during the season, but when it happens there's a tendency to react as if it's a crisis that requires immediate surgery. The players press and start to change their batting stances, the writers ask shrill questions, and the front office hides out. Everybody goes into a bunker mentality, and that's exactly the wrong thing to do. Winning looks so easy when it's happening, but I think there are some ways of winning that are a whole lot better than others. I'm like any other fan: I love it when my team is winning big, and the hitters and pitchers all seem to be on a tear. That brings high scores and excitement, but it also brings losing streaks when everybody comes down. The clubs that do best in the end are the ones that have one player getting hot and then another and then another, each taking his turn carrying the team. But losing has it uses, if you can remind yourself. You don't make changes when everything is going right. It's only when things seem to be in a state of disaster that you get any progress in this world.''

Our train began to slow for another stop, and Roy reached for his blue tennis bag. "This is us," he announced. He smiled and said, "If you want a homily, I've got one: The easiest thing in sport is to win when you're good. The next easiest is to lose when you're not any good. The hardest—way hardest—is to lose when you're good. That's the test of character.''

We got off the train and walked down the empty platform and up a flight of stairs in the sunshine and onto a footbridge that spanned the tracks below. At the other end of the bridge, a ball-park was waiting for us—The Oakland–Alameda County Coliseum, where the American League's Oakland A's play. The place was empty. There would be a game here that night, but at the moment there wasn't another human being in sight, and the only sound was the click and whir of a couple of sprinklers at work. The triple decks of green and yellow and orange and red seats curved smoothly toward us, right and left, throwing a hard glaze of color back at the sky, but when we walked up to the high wooden fence that ran around the center-field perimeter there was a gleam of rich green visible through the narrow slats of the fence, and a sudden delicious whiff of lawns. Roy put down his bag and pressed one eye up against the fence. "I love this view," he said. "Look at that grass! It gives me goose bumps every time.'' We stood there a minute together, savoring the moment, and I wondered to myself how many other baseball owners would approach their parks this way—like a fan, like a boy. He ran the joint: Roy Eisenhardt, the president of the Oakland A's.

◆ ◆ ◆

THE TWENTY-SIX MAJOR-LEAGUE BASEBALL OWNERS ARE A much more diverse group than is popularly supposed, but it is hard for fans (including this fan) always to keep that in mind.

The obtuseness and arrogance of the owners' majority position during the negotiations over the renewal of baseball's basic agreement between the owners and the players in 1981 was largely responsible for the strike that closed down the game for seven weeks in the middle of that season, inflicting extensive psychic and financial damage on the sport; the image we were left with was that a band of willful millionaires seeking, by main force, to solve the game's financial problems by putting an end to the fundamental structure of free agency, thus miraculously returning the business of baseball to its antiquated nineteenth-century pattern of owner-patroons and captive players. The bitterness and wreckage of the strike probably did away with that dream for good, but the bumptious public posturings of a handful of the owners continue to obscure the relative modesty and anonymity of their peers; maybe that will always happen. So far this year, we have been blessedly spared George Steinbrenner's customary tantrums and tirades—the firing of still another Yankee manager, the public haranguing and harassment of some of his well-paid stars if they fail always to perform at the level he demands—but other owners have hurried forward to play his Mister Bluster number, at the expense of the fans. In Seattle, a publicity-hungry novice owner, George Argyros, enraged the fans and inflamed the local media by firing the talented young Mariner skipper, Rene Lachemann, in a singularly vapid re-enactment of baseball's ritual sacrifice of good managers of hopeless teams. In June, a band of limited partners in the Boston Red Sox, under the leadership of a general partner, Buddy LeRoux, attempted to seize control of that ancient flagship by means of a sudden, flimsy-looking legal coup—an embarrassing adventure that will embroil the club in the courts for many months to come. This selfish little war broke out on the day that the Bosox were preparing to stage a sentimental reunion of the famous pennant-winning 1967 Red Sox at Fenway Park, and, of course, it ruined the party. Roy Eisenhardt, who still thinks of himself as a novice in the business, is at sensible pains not to stand aloof from his fellow-owners or criticize their deportment, but since his arrival on the scene, late in 1980, when the club was purchased by his father-in-law, Walter A. Haas, Jr., then the chairman of Levi Strauss & Company, it has been plain to me and to a great many other people that Eisenhardt's new involvement in the old game is founded on an intellectual and spiritual appreciation of the sport that has hardly been articulated since the time of Branch Rickey. I care about baseball, too, and worry about its future and its ultimate fortunes at the hands of its current keepers, so I have made a point of calling on Eisenhardt whenever I'm in California or Arizona (where the A's train), and sharing his company during some of the trials and disappointments and surprises of his team's extremely adventurous journey across the past few seasons.

The business side of baseball is a high-risk, low-return enterprise, as difficult to learn and predict and bring under control as the game out on the field. The franchise that Walter Haas purchased from Charles O. Finley on November 6, 1980, for twelve million seven hundred thousand dollars was a much better ball team and an even shakier corporate structure than anyone in the incoming group had quite expected, in spite of extended advance scouting. Andy Dolich, the A's' vice-president for business operations, told me that the A's offices inside the Coliseum had an abandoned-warehouse look when he first arrived that December. "It was like a quonset hut here," he said. "There was one dusty telephone in the reception room, and nobody in sight, and when you picked it up nothing happened. Inside, we found some old trophies jammed together to hold a lot of loose files, and when we took them down we found that they were the club's World Championship trophies from 1972, '73, and '74. There were six employees in the whole office, including a receptionist, and we discovered that only nineteen percent of the incoming phone calls were ever answered. So we had a job to do."

The turnaround that the Haas-Eisenhardt group has achieved in the past two and a half years can only be suggested here: the development of a six-team minor-league farm system (all six finished at the top their respective leagues in 1982, and two won league championships), at a cost of three and a half million dollars a year; the establishment of a thirty-seven-man scouting and player-development staff (the A's had no independent scouts in 1980); a club-record attendance of 1,735,489 last year, in spite of the team's fifth-place finish (the A's drew just over three hundred thousand in 1979); the setting up of an intensive and inventive marketing and publicity program, which includes classy, lighthearted television commercials (Sample: a slow-motion closeup of the great A's base stealer, Rickey Henderson, churning into high gear on the base path, to an accompanying Mission Control voice-over countdown and down-range weather forecast); and the computerization of almost everything, including pitchers' and batters' and fielders' records (via a small computer available to manager Steve Boros) and ticket sales and general revenues (via a Hewlett-Packard 3000 computer, with flanks on the order of a Greyhound bus, set up in a back-room vault). Further effort and money (more or less as expected, the club ran up a five-and-a-half-million-dollar deficit in the first two full seasons of the new regime) have gone into a community-affairs plan that now includes more than thirty separate programs involving schools and hospitals and libraries and other local charitable and educational ventures. (More than forty thousand youngsters signed reading "contracts" with the A's this summer; when each one has read a specified number of books before the resumption of school, he or she will receive a Certificate of Education Achievement, signed by Roy Eisenhardt and Wally Haas, and two free tickets to an A's game.) A more noticeable change is the abolition of the quonset-hut look of the offices, by means of bright carpets and paintings and murals (there are many blown-up photos of the team's famous ancestor club, Connie Mack's Philadelphia Athletics, and of baggy-uniformed Hall of Famers like Lefty Grove, Chief Bender, and Jimmie Foxx—a reflection of Eisenhardt's conviction that ancient games and bygone heroics mean almost as much to baseball fans as yesterday's box score), and by the perpetually crowded look of the front-office rooms and corridors (there is now a full-time, full-press staff that numbers more than fifty). The telling ingredient in the club's management-side effort may be beyond précis, for it lies, one senses, in the looks of that staff and in its demeanor, which is youthful, laid back, and fully engaged. There are a great many women and blacks on the roster—hardly a commonplace in big-league offices—and very few of the people you pass in the hall ("Hi, there!") appear to be immediately threatened by the arrival of a serious birthday. Some of these post-collegians are, in fact, club executives: the bearded, bespectacled, shyly smiling executive vice president, Wally Haas (the son of the principal owner and Roy's brother-in-law), whose main engagement is with community affairs; Andy Dolich, who some days actually wears a necktie; general counsel Sandy Alderson, who has curly hair, rimless eyeglasses, and an athlete's shoulders (an associate of Roy Eisenhardt's San Francisco law firm, he went to Dartmouth, as did Eisenhardt, and later served in the Marine Corps, ditto, and now runs five miles over the San Francisco hills six mornings a week, often side by side with Roy). Sometimes on a busy afternoon, the next young man to pass you in the hall—he is wearing a striped yellow sweater, rumpled white jeans, and Adidas, and is nibbling on a Toll House cookie—goes by almost unnoticed until he speaks ("Hey, how're you doing?"), and, flustered, you wave and smile back. Roy. Mickey Morabito, the team's press-relations director, who previously held the same post with the Yankees, once said to me, "Because of the way baseball is structured, only the people at the very top tend to be important, and everyone else feels underpaid and undervalued. But not here. This is a casual office—no one is too uptight or too shy to go in and talk to Roy, and we all have a lot of leeway in how we do our jobs. You have to have good people to make that work, and that's just what we do have."

Charlie Finley, who brought the A's to Oakland in 1968, ran a different sort of show: a one-man band. A self-made million-aire insurance man, he ruled the club in absentia—by telephone from Chicago, for the most part. (Sometimes he listened to broadcasts of entire games over the long-distance phone.) He got rid of sixteen managers in twenty years, wrangled with play-ers and commissioners, inflicted buttercup uniforms and "Hot Pants Day"'s and team mustaches and a mascot mule named Charlie O on the fans, but he also built up the wonderfully exciting and combative Reggie Jackson-Catfish Hunter-Sal Bando-Joe Rudi ball club that dominated both leagues in the early nineteen-seventies. When free agency arrived, Finley turned off the switch and divested himself of his stars and his scouts—and, in time, his fans. The stripped-bare look of the Coliseum offices was a paradigm of the A's status in the Bay sports scene when the Haas family took over the club. Walter Haas, who is now sixty-seven and has moved on from the routine management of Levi Strauss (he is chairman of the executive committee, and the company is now headed by his brother, Peter E. Haas), is almost the precise opposite of his predecessor. The great-grandnephew of the original Levi Strauss, who sold his first blue-jeans to prospectors in the gold rush, Haas inherited a major family fortune and a family tradition of modest hard work and dedi-cated, nearly anonymous community service; he may be the only trustee of the Ford Foundation whose name does not appear in *Who's Who*. His decision to purchase the A's—made in con-cert with his son and son-in-law, since it was his intention from the beginning to turn the whole shebang over to them—was motivated by his conviction that an imaginatively operated, community-oriented sports franchise would be the best and quickest means of doing something useful for the racially and economically distressed city of Oakland. Haas is an informal and extremely courteous gent, with pink cheeks and ruddy good looks. He is a serious trout fisherman and tennis player, and perhaps the world's No. 1 rooter for and benefactor of his alma mater's football team, the University of California Golden Bears. I first met him about a year after he had purchased the club, and he told me that he was not very well informed about baseball and that he expected not to have any serious day-to-day involvement with the fortunes of the club. Last March, in Scottsdale, during a dinner with Roy and several of the team's baseball counsellors, he listened intently all through a multicourse conversation about the problems and expectations of thirty or forty different Oakland pitchers and catchers and fielders and hitters, and then leaned across the table and murmured to me, "I take back what I said last year about not getting hooked. This is a whole lot harder than the pants business."

Charlie Finley's neglect of the shop was a considerable boon to the early Haas-Eisenhardt plans for upgrading the franchise. ("That contrast in reputations was a public-relations *dream*," Andy Dolich said to me.) Another asset was a spirited young ball team, piloted by Billy Martin. The very first Eisenhardt decision was to keep Billy in place—and, in fact, to increase the scope of his authority by making him director of player personnel as well, thus putting him in charge of training all the club's ballplayers at every level. The young Oaklands included outfielders Rickey Henderson, Dwayne Murphy, and Tony Armas, whom many baseball writers were calling the best picket line in either league, and a staff of durable, strong-armed pitchers, led by Mike Norris, Rick Langford, and Steve McCatty.* The remainder of the roster was of lesser quality, with notable shortfalls in infield defense and relief pitching, but in 1981 the club jumped away to a terrific start by winning its first eleven games in succession, and although it declined a bit after the lull of the midseason strike, it captured the American League West half-pennant by dispatching the Kansas City Royals in three straight games, in the strike-imposed, appendixlike miniseries that year. To no one's real surprise, the A's then lost the championship playoffs, being swept by the Yankees in three straight, but several events in that series stuck in my mind. For one thing, the team president did not accompany the Oakland players to New York, where they were to open with two games at Yankee Sta-

---

*Durable for about two seasons, that is. By the end of the 1983 season, four of the five starters were gone, laid low by arm miseries.

dium—a curious, almost unique turn of affairs. No one could
explain it to me at the time, but later on, when I knew the team
and its people better, I understood. Eisenhardt had decided to
stay home and watch the games on television because he sensed
that his persona and presence, which were at such a remove
from the public attitudes of George Steinbrenner, might make
for headlines and distraction, and so diminish from the accomp-
lishments of his young ballplayers. And then, when the action
swung out to Oakland, where the Yankees' Dave Righetti ended
the A's season with a 4-0 shutout, it became clear to me that the
fans out there, although badly disappointed, were not disheart-
ened or angry about this unhappy finale. They remained to the
end of the game, all forty-seven thousand of them, cheering and
yelling in the sunshine, and when the game was over they stayed
on and cheered some more, at last summoning their heroes back
out onto the field for a final roaring thank you and farewell.

The next year—last year—was different, of course. Like a lot
of other fans, I was paying much closer attention to the A's this
time around, but nothing really went right all year. It rained
ceaselessly in spring training, and the pitchers' arms never quite
got in shape, and then a long and debilitating series of injuries
meant that the club's thin line of regulars rarely played together
on any given day. McCatty and Norris both went on the disabled
list with shoulder problems, and the club pitching sank from its
3.30 earned-run average, which was second-best in the league
in 1981, to 4.54 in 1982, which was next to worst. Rickey Henderson did set an all-time, both-leagues record with his one
hundred and thirty stolen bases, but that wonder seemed to boost
the team's home-attendance figures more than its place in the
standings. The club finished fifth, twenty-five games behind the
division-leading Angels. A further casualty was the manager,
Billy Martin, who, in psychological terms at least, was also
disabled during the summer's hard going. Losing has always
been a special hazard for this intense, bitterly driven man, and
his team's misfortunes visibly wore down his confidence, his
ability to lead his troops, and, in the end, his self-control. This
had happened to him in other years, of course, and with different
clubs, but the shock of it and the sadness of it were not less
because of that. One day in late August, Martin indulged himself
in obscene telephone harangues directed at two officials of the
club (he had asked to have his contract extended by five years,
and the wish had not been granted), and then, in a rage, demolished the furniture and fixtures in his clubhouse office. He

was released in October, after the end of the season, and since then, of course, he has resumed his post at the helm of the Yankees. For the A's, it turned out, almost the only resemblance to the 1981 campaign was the final home game, when the fans again stayed to the very end—it was a meaningless game against the Royals—and then once again summoned their players back to the field with their sustained and even more surprising cheers.

ANYONE WHO MOURNS THE DECLINE OF BASEBALL AS A FAMILY game should try to arrange a visit to the owners' boxes in the first-base, upper-deck sector of the Oakland Coliseum, from which vantage point I took in a swatch of A's home games in late May this year. A stream of visitors—A's brass, A's scouts, an occasional reporter, friends and relations, friends of friends— kept changing the dimensions of the party, but the regulars there included Roy Eisenhardt and Wally Haas; Walter Haas and his wife, Evie; Roy's wife, Betsy, and their daughter, Sarah; and a large, cheerful retired Oakland cop, Sarge Ivey, who directed traffic at the door, dispensed beer and soft drinks, and rooted louder than anyone else. Everyone was really in the games, except perhaps for Sarah, who was four months old; once or twice in the middle innings Betsy took Sarah over to the back of an adjoining box for a quiet meal. For the Saturday-afternoon tilt, we were joined by Sarah's brother, Jesse, who is four years old, and by Wally's daughters Simone, who is nine, and Charlotte, four and a half (Wally's wife, Julie, who is a textile designer, was away in New York on a business trip), and by three or four small cousins, whose names and ages and connections I didn't quite catch, and by a couple of babysitter fans as well. Jesse wore a full A's uniform (the all-white home-game getup), with "JESSE" across the back. Charlotte wore a pretty flowered Liberty-print dress and a player-size pair of official A's wrist-bands. Toys and clothes and sandwiches and modelling clay and raisins scattered themselves around the box carpets, and Jesse and Charlotte climbed back and forth over the knees and feet of their parents and grandparents and the other baseball people there, who absently caressed them or gave them a hand up while they stared past them and down at the riveting business on the field.

   The A's were playing the Yankees, so the games had the sense of omen and anxiety that the famous Gothamites bring to every park they play in around the league, and there was a further edge of significance to it all this time, for this was Billy Martin's first trip back to Oakland, and hordes of fans had showed up to welcome him with loud and cheerfully mixed messages. They were good games, it turned out, and the special quirks and flavors of Oakland rooting added to our pleasures—a gap-toothed cheerleader known as Krazy George (he is a former school-teacher who is paid by the A's for his appearances), who whanged on a tambourine and conducted the multitudes with Wagnerian passion, and the popular "A's Waves" way of cheering, during which the customers suddenly rise and yell, section by section, quickly and in unison, round and round the park, madly waving their arms and screeching together in a rolling, accelerating vortex of fervor and foolishness.*

Eisenhardt watches games with an abstracted, almost silent intensity, sometimes chewing on his thumb. Wally is more vocal, and tends to groan when things are going poorly; occasionally he rises from his seat, groaning, and turns his back on the field. The senior Haases, who usually sat behind me, commented to each other on almost every pitch, and clapped for every particle of Oakland good fortune. The Friday-night opener, which pitted the Yankees' Bob Shirley against the A's veteran Tom Underwood, went the right way from the outset, when the Oaklands scored three runs in the first inning and added another on Rickey Henderson's homer in the second, to move off to a 4-1 lead. "Good!" said Evie Haas. "Wonderful! Now let's get more!"

"I know you," Walter said. "You always want the score nine to one."

"There's such a *logic* to nine to one," she said.

Earlier, I had stood with Eisenhardt down on the field in a little fenced runway that connects the A's' dugout to the club-house, where he remains during the first few pitches and outs of almost every game. Just before the game, he talked briefly with his chief groundskeeper and with one of his security people, and during the anthem (a cappella, by Mickey Thomas, of the Jefferson Starship band, to faint accompanying Eisenhardt winces) his gaze roamed around every corner and level of the field and park. He was housekeeping, but once the game began he gave it his absolute attention. He seemed even more preoccupied than usual, and for a moment I wondered if it wasn't because of the presence of Billy Martin over there in the wrong

---

*The innocent optimism of this early report on the accursed Wave phenomenon suggests the happiness of that anonymous bygone southern gardener who first spied the pretty green tints of the kudzu vine along the back borders of his rose-beds.

dugout. Before this game, reporters had searched out Roy for his comments, and to one of them he said, "This weekend is nothing like the press has made out. It's nothing to be 'handled' by me. Billy came to find me when he got here, and I went to find him. We're friends. There's nothing to be 'patched up' or discussed. A decision was made last year. Neither one of us wanted it, but we both accepted it. No substantive issues were created. I don't want to quantify a friendship. O.K. ?"

O.K. The reporter didn't exactly love this reply, but its content was clear, all right. A day or two later, in a quieter moment, Eisenhardt said to me, "These games were a coda for Billy and me. It's like when you meet your ex-wife at a party somewhere for the first time after your divorce. It happens, and then it's over." And he went on to say something about how pleased Billy had seemed to meet the new baby, Sarah, for the first time, and how affectionate Billy had always been with Jesse and with Wally's daughters. "Billy is wonderful with kids," he said. "He has that touch. It's a great gift."

Roy's preoccupation, I realized, was with his team. Uncertainty surrounds every ball club from April to October, but there were more than the usual number of doubts and hovering question marks about this particular club, starting with its new manager, Steve Boros—a scholarly, low-key baseball man in his mid-forties who had coached for the Expos and the Royals and had managed for six years in the low minors, but who was taking the helm of a major-league team for the first time. Injuries and disappointments had brought down the 1982 A's, and this year the club was already in the same sort of trouble. Third baseman Carney Lansford, who had come over from the Red Sox in a trade for Tony Armas and was expected to solidify the left side of the infield, had missed a lot of early-season games because of the death of his infant son, and was now laid up with a sprained wrist. Catcher Mike Heath and pitchers Dave Beard and Rick Langford were also sidelined (Langford had just gone on the twenty-one-day disabled list), and another starter, Steve McCatty, was coming back from severe shoulder problems and so far had made only a few brief appearances in relief. For all this, the club stood at nineteen and seventeen in the young season, one game behind the division-leading Texas Rangers.

Many chief executives of big-league teams could match this list of apprehensions and misfortunes, for most of the twenty-six clubs stumble along in a condition of semi-shock and disrepair during the better part of each season, but the burdens of baseball reality are even heavier for an owner who has chosen a particular path out of conviction rather than economic necessity, and not only wants to win but wants to succeed. Eisenhardt, I knew, had strong feelings in this regard. "Anybody who just sets out to win, who promises his fans that their club will be a winner, is in trouble from the start," he once said, 'because it's built in that even the best club will win six games and lose four, and this means that almost half the time your fans will be in a state of outrage. We want fans to come to the park for the baseball—for the pleasures of the game and of being at the game—and if we also happen to win, then fine. We want to be respectable and competitive, and we want to win our share of everything, including championships. But the way to do that is by being patient and foresighted. You can't just buy it or grab for it—we've already seen too much of that in the game, and its results."

Although the Oakland club is paying its players net salaries of more than eight million dollars in 1983, out of its major-league operating budget of twenty-two million dollars, I knew that the Haas fortune would certainly permit the club to bid in the blue-chip free-agent market for an occasional high-priced slugger or pitcher—a Dave Winfield, a Floyd Bannister, a Don Baylor—if Eisenhardt and the Haases so desired, but no moves have been made in that direction. Back in spring training this year, I had tried to probe Eisenhardt's resolution about such matters by asking him if he would ever consider making an expensive late-season trade for one star pitcher or hitter if he felt that such an acquisition would probably nail down a pennant. This stratagem has become a commonplace in the latter stages of every season; the Milwaukee Brewers did it in August last year, when they acquired Don Sutton from the Houston Astros, taking over his salary of three-quarters of a million dollars and dispatching three of their highly regarded minor-league prospects to the Houston club.

"I'd think a long time before I tried it," Eisenhardt said. "If the deal includes the transfer of good young players, it means you're just mortgaging your future for the present. Qualitatively, what's the worth of winning the whole thing versus the worth of being competitive each year? No one wants to accept second place, but unless you actually win the World Series you'll see yourself as having lost in the end. I enjoyed watching Bud Selig's team in the World Series last year"—the Brewers, that is, who lost to the Cardinals in seven games—"but I don't think Bud enjoyed it much. I hope I'd resist the Golden Apple. But then, of course, coming along year after year with a team that never has a chance of being there is much, much worse.''

THE YANKEES NEVER DID QUITE CATCH UP IN THAT FRIDAY-night game, although there were some troubling moments along the way: Tony Phillips made two frightful errors at short, and the visitors put the tying runs aboard in the eighth before Oakland reliever Steve McCatty got Ken Griffey to pop up for the third out, with the bases loaded. But the situation was never really critical, as it often seems to be when the A's are playing—the team has a chronic difficulty in scoring runs, especially in late innings—and there was time and ease enough in the game for me to enjoy the look and feel of Oakland baseball: the eight World Championship banners (five won in Philadelphia, three in Oakland) arrayed across the outfield perimeter; the new home-game uniforms that have replaced Charlie Finley's garish old tavern-league greens and yellows; and the youthful beat and bounce of the brilliant ballpark music. The A's sound apparatus is a state-of-the-art system, and Roy and Wally have enjoyed themselves in the selection of its repertoire. When Steve Baker came in to relieve Tom Underwood during the Yankee seventh, we heard Carole King's ''You've Got a Friend,'' and when Tom Burgmeier very soon arrived to relieve Baker, the Beatles' ''Help!'' piped him aboard. The Yankee relievers, of course, heard Johnny Paycheck's ''Take This Job and Shove It.'' The Oakland victory song is ''Celebration,'' by Kool and the Gang, and fans slouching out to the parking lots after a tough loss are sometimes reminded that ''It's Not Easy Being Green.'' Ballpark organists also play mood music, of course, but for me the mighty Wurlitzer can suggest only hockey or prayer.

The A's won by 8–4, with the last two Oakland runs scoring in ravishing fashion in the bottom of the eighth, when Tony Phillips laid down a dandy suicide-squeeze bunt, to score Kelvin Moore from third—and Davey Lopes from second, too, when the flustered Yankee pitcher threw the ball away. Showing Billy Martin the squeeze play is like hawking lavalieres on the sidewalk in front of Tiffany's, and when it happened Roy said, ''Getting the right count to set up the squeeze bunt is as good as the next-to-last move in Scrabble. Once it got to three and one, we had them.''

He was smiling and youthful when the game ended and we

all trooped out of the box, and I was happy, too. Last summer, I had visited the A's during a particularly dreary string of home-game losses to the White Sox and the Blue Jays. One of those beatings had come in a game in which the A's had led Chicago by 5–0 in the middle innings, but then the White Sox sluggers hit a couple of monstrous home runs, and the A's died at the plate once again—and on the base paths and the mound, too—and the visitors finally took it, 7–6, in the tenth. After that game, I got a lift into San Francisco with Roy and Wally—a trip of long silences and desultory broken-off sounds of mourning. "I wouldn't want to be in that clubhouse tonight," Wally murmured at one point, and Roy said, "That game is a perfect example of why you can't do anything about a season like this. There's just no place to *start*." There was another longish stretch of uninterrupted highway hum, and then Roy, in a faraway, musing sort of voice, said, "You know, this sport might be a whole lot more interesting if there were no such thing as a home run. You could put up this enormous wall . . ."

◆ ◆ ◆

EMIL ROY EISENHARDT (THE FIRST NAME IS VESTIGIAL) GREW up in South Orange, New Jersey—a suburb just west of Newark that is so self-consciously tidy and green that it looks like a World's Fair replica of a turn-of-the-century village—in what he describes as "the middle of the middle class." His father, who died in 1980, was the director of purchasing for New York University, and his mother, who is seventy-two, taught college English and then linguistics in the New Jersey state-university system. Each of his parents had been the first family member to attend college. Roy's paternal grandfather, an immigrant from Germany, was a baker. (The Eisenhardts are Catholic, but the combination of Roy's name and his marriage into the Haas family has caused many people to assume that he is Jewish.) Roy, who has a younger brother and sister, was a versatile, extremely energetic member of his class at Columbia High School, in nearby Maplewood, where he belonged to the dramatic club, played bass drum in the band, and held down right field on the baseball team, in spite of inordinate and incurable shortcomings at the plate. He was also a Boy Scout, a home carpenter, and a woodworker, and he took piano lessons—as he still does: he tries to play a half hour to an hour every day, partly because Chopin and Schubert allow him to put baseball entirely out of his mind for the moment. Roy was a year ahead of his age in school, and what he remembers most about himself then is his immaturity. "One of the important things back then was to have everybody like you," he once said to me. "When I went to Dartmouth"—he was in the class of 1960—"I fully expected to be elected president of my fraternity, but I wasn't—a wonderful thing, because the shock of it began to shift me away from that external system of validation. I began to care more about my own ideas and values, and a little less about what people thought of me." Another shift was away from baseball to rowing; he made the Dartmouth first boat, but thinks he wouldn't have at a larger university. He was a naval R.O.T.C. cadet at Dartmouth, but switched into the Marine Corps upon graduation, serving two years on active duty in Okinawa (this was just before the American involvement in Vietnam), and rising to the rank of captain in the reserves. Law school ensued. He graduated thirteenth in his class at Boalt Hall, in 1965, and spent a further year studying tax law in Germany. "I loved the law, it turned out," he says. "Not the practice of it so much as its ideas—the idea of our trying to define the rules we're going to live by—and its examination of the history of ideas."

By the late sixties, Eisenhardt was a young married lawyer in San Francisco, with a passionate fan's interest in the San Francisco Giants. His first wife, Auban Slay, whom he married in 1965, told me that as she joined him at the altar during their wedding Roy whispered, "The Giants are leading, 3-1, in the fifth." (They were divorced in 1976, but remain on amicable terms; Auban Eisenhardt is also a lawyer in San Francisco.) Roy Eisenhardt's work at his firm, Farella, Braun & Martel, was mostly in business law—conglomerations, real-estate acquisition, and the like—and in 1974, when that palled, he began teaching law at Boalt Hall. A little later, he took over as coach of the U. Cal heavyweight freshman crew. "Maybe that's what I really am—a teacher," he once said. "I'd love to teach anything—how to grab an oar, how to paint a wall." By 1979, he was a full-time professor at Boalt Hall, teaching courses in commercial law, bankruptcy, and real property. He tried to continue there on a part-time basis after taking over the A's late in 1980, but the double load was too much. "I still miss it," he says. "Sometimes I feel like Kermit in 'The Muppet Movie,' when he says, 'Why did I ever leave the swamp?'" A close friend of Roy's, Dr. Hirsch Handmaker (he is a nuclear radiologist, and now has come aboard as director of medical services with the

A's), does not quite agree. "The job with the A's was *exactly* the right chance for Roy at that moment in his life," he said to me. "The person and the place and the work came together in a miraculous sort of way. If you're a fan of destiny, you really appreciate it."

Destiny had also brought Roy and Betsy Haas together at a Chinese-cooking class. They were married in 1978. After I had come to be sufficiently at ease with Roy to raise the question, I asked him how he had felt about marrying into such a wealthy and distinguished family.

"It was the best thing that ever happened to me," he said. "There hasn't been a moment of discomfort about it, and that's because the Haases are all so unintimidating and open and modest. They all have a basic and proper sense of values, and a great sense of humor. Everything about Walter reflects his sensitivity and feeling of concern. We talk almost every day—not so much for business as for the fun of it. The whole family is the same. I am in awe of the subtlety and passion of Wally's involvement in our community efforts. He has a genius for sensing the proper areas and people for us to see, and for figuring out how we can be of use to them. The same sort of thing was true of Walter Haas, senior—Walter's father—who ran the company before Walter did. He was still going to work on the bus every day when he was ninety. I remember a conversation he had with Betsy and me a few weeks before he died. He asked us if we were concerned about the future—how things were going in the country. We both said yes, we were, and he said, "So am I, so am I." There he was, an old, old man, and he wasn't thinking back and being sore about the New Deal or anything like that. He was worrying about what our country would be like for young people in the next twenty or thirty years. You can't beat people like that."

Bill Rigney, the white-haired, angular savant who serves with the A's as Assistant to the President in Baseball Matters (he is a former manager of the Giants, the Twins, and the Angels, and he also does color commentary on the A's' telecasts), told me that Walter Haas had once asked him for whatever special advice he thought would be most useful to a newcomer to the game. "I told him, 'Don't fall in love with the players,' " Rig said. " 'They'll do beautiful things for you out there. They'll pitch a great game or drive in the winning run, but they're also young and they can't know and they don't care, and they'll break your heart, a lot of them, before you're through.' " I asked if he thought Roy needed the same warning, and Rig said, "No, I think he's got it figured out. But I hope he'll never lose the kind of concern he has for his players. I've never seen the like of it in baseball."

I had this conversation with Rig in the living room of the Eisenhardts' narrow, comfortable house in the Cow Hollow section of San Francisco (a pink palazzo at the end of the same block belongs to Bob Lurie, who owns the San Francisco Giants), where we were having cocktails with Roy and Betsy and Rig's wife, Paula, before going out to dinner together. Roy joined us, and we stood together at a big window looking out at the hillside, crowded with rooftops and tilted backyard gardens, which fell away steeply toward the bay, and, beyond that, at the sunlit banks of evening fog that were beginning to swirl in from the sea. Roy pointed down to his own garden and said, "I was doing a lot of digging up and replanting down there last summer, just when the team was beginning to go bad." He laughed and shook his head. "That's the best-dug dirt in northern California."

As we left, Roy pointed out (at my request) several large and elegantly finished pieces of furniture in the house that he had made in his basement workshop, including a new nine-foot white-pine toy cabinet for Jesse, with lathed split-turnings on the corners, four doors, and eight interior-latch drawers on oak runners. "It's an antidote," Roy said of his woodworking. "You can complicate an easy job and try to make things come out perfectly—and I can listen to our road games on the radio while I'm doing it."

We said goodby to Betsy (the babysitter had crumped out, and Betsy was staying home with the kids), and she turned to Roy at the door and said, "Got your keys?" He shook his head and went off in search of them, and Betsy said, "He just can't pay attention to some things. Last year, our car broke down, and it sat out there in front of the house for days and days before they came to fix it, and when they opened the door there was Roy's wallet under the front seat."

Roy returned and happily jingled the keys for us to see.

"Good," said Betsy, kissing him. "No midnight pebbles against the windows tonight."

◆ ◆ ◆

THE SECOND GAME OF THE YANKEE SERIES, ON SATURDAY afternoon, was almost better than the first. The sun shone, and the soft winds blew, and thirty-eight thousand baseball-entranced fans roared and cheered and made waves, while the pitchers—Mike Norris for the A's and Shane Rawley for the Yanks—and fielders on the greensward together wove a lengthening skein of brilliant, scoreless innings. Norris, in a lather of intensity and mannerism on the mound, fanned nine batters with his screwball and darting heater, and Tony Phillips turned Dave Winfield's rocketed grounder into a double play, and Dwayne Murphy cut down a Yankee base runner at third base with a mighty peg from center, and the A's truly seemed to be having all the the best of it until, in the bottom of the eighth, Mike Davis made a trifling, young-ballplayer's sort of mistake on the base paths that amputated an Oakland rally, and the Yanks, suddenly reprieved, put Willie Randolph on second with a walk and a sac (Norris, kicking the dirt on the mound, was positive that the ball-four count had been strike three), and scored him when Winfield muscled a single into center against a tough, tough Norris pitch, up and in, and that was the ballgame, of course: 1-0 Yankees. Walter Haas, getting up from his seat in the box after the last out, said, "Boy, that was a game to remember. That's the way baseball should be played. Nuts."

The postgame gathering in Steve Boros's office was a reflective one, with Eisenhardt and Rigney and Sandy Alderson and Bill King—the A's' bearded, soft-spoken veteran radio-and-TV announcer—and Karl Kuehl, who is a "motivation coach" of the A's' minor-league players, filling up the circle of chairs, and the local writers and TV and radio people quietly coming to get Boros's comments and going out again. "We gave the fans their money's worth, I think," Boros said finally. "I'll sleep all right tonight, because those guys played an outstanding game. I could heat my house all winter with the energy Mike Norris had in the dugout between innings. He really wanted this one."

Roy was nursing a can of Tab, and he nodded to the writers who came and went. "It was an aesthetic game," he ventured at last.

"The worst thing about this kind of game is having to read about it again in the papers tomorrow," Sandy said.

"We've scored one run in the ninth all year, against seventeen for the other guys," Bill King said.

Roy made a down-curving gesture with one hand and said, "Our effort has been sort of Sisyphean—I have to admit it," and Boros nodded in agreement.

I wondered briefly about how many other manager's-office

dialogues might have included the word "Sisyphean" in a post-game exchange, but the question didn't seem to matter, because I'd never attended postgame meetings elsewhere that regularly included the owner. But Roy was always there, listening. I had discussed this matter on several occasions with a friend of mine named Glenn Schwarz, of the San Francisco *Examiner*, who has been on the A's beat for many years.

"Right from the start, he's sat there and paid attention," Schwarz said. "He did it with Billy, and now he's doing it with Steve. He's ceaselessly curious. No other owner in baseball could get away with it without making the writers and the manager incredibly nervous, but Roy is so informal and so open that you really don't notice that he's there at all."

One clear glimpse of Eisenhardt's relations with his players had been offered to me last year, when a little group of Bay-area baseball writers—the regular beat people, including Glenn Schwarz—came to call on Roy to ask him about one member of the club who was known to have, or was strongly suspected of having, major difficulties with cocaine.

"Well, it's a fair question," Eisenhardt said. "You guys will have to decide whether to write it or not. The whole question of drugs and athletes is extremely complicated. Players used to go out and get drunk, and everybody thought that was manly and funny. I think the great sums of money we throw at the young players probably have something to do with it. I understand how ballplayers are under a lot of pressure, and I don't want to toss any easy societal values around here as a solution. I don't know what the answer is. We're going to have to learn a lot about this in the next few years—and I don't mean just in sports."

One of the writers asked if the player knew that Roy knew he used cocaine.

"I really can't say for sure," Roy answered. "Maybe the best thing for him would be for him to know that we know but to notice we're not doing anything about it, because it's up to him to solve it. It's his choice in the end. I know I kept on taking piano lessons for so long when I was a kid because my parents told me I could quit anytime." He shrugged. "You'll have to decide what to do about this story," he went on. "What this means to the success of the team and what its value is as a news story seem worth about two cents compared with the damage the story might do to him as a man."

The writers did not write the story.

◆

THE SUNDAY YANKEE GAME WAS ANOTHER PIPPIN, MATCHING up the Yanks' Ron Guidry against the slim Oakland rookie right-hander Chris Codiroli. The Yankees led by 1–0 in the early going, and then by 2–0 after six, but the quality of play was even better than what we had seen the day before, and the crowd was enthralled. But the game was a killer, it turned out. Rickey Henderson tied things up with a two-run homer in the bottom of the eighth, but the A's instantly gave back the runs in the ninth with some shabby infield play and a throw to the wrong base by Mike Davis. A promising rally against Goose Gossage in the home half was cut short when base runner Wayne Gross took off in a pointless extempore attempt to steal third and was thrown out easily. It was like a door slamming shut. "Oh, what a way for a game to end!" Boros said in his office. "It looks bad and it feels bad, but you have to live with it somehow."

"It's a seventh chord," Roy said. "It's like the end of 'A Day in the Life.' " He did not smile.

Roy's intensity at home games and his pain over each loss by his team is matched by almost every owner I have observed at close quarters, but not many of them seem to have an accompanying composure, as he does, which arises from a habitually, almost compulsively, reflective attitude toward the sport.

I heard some of these longer views on the final day of my Oakland sojourn, when I called on Roy at lunchtime in his small, windowless office in the Coliseum. This was a bare eighteen hours after that sudden, odious end to the Yankee series, but I found that Eisenhardt could smile about it by now, albeit a bit stiffly. "One of the reasons I hate that kind of loss—that particular turn of events—is that I'm the kind of person who likes to do things myself," he said. "When I first went into law practice, I insisted on typing all my own letters, to make sure they were done right, but then one of the partners pointed out that I wasn't entitled to that sort of luxury anymore. And you certainly can't do that in baseball. You have to turn things over to the players in the end. That's the way the game *is*. It's really much harder on the manager, who gets the blame when something goes wrong out there. I can always hide, or point out that I have no discrete function around here. But I'm connected, all right. I know I've never had so many people working for me—and I never dreamed of such a thing—and I can't conceive of another job, unless it's in high elective office, where you have the chance to affect the way so many thousands of people feel at the end of the day. The fans, I mean. Sometimes I wish I could control that, but I don't really want the power to go down and place the ball on the field so that the game always comes out the way I want it to. Well, maybe I'd enjoy that once—for one game—but after that it would be boring, and it would mean the end of it all, of course. I think we all know how much George Steinbrenner wants that. Sometimes I see George as Lennie in 'Of Mice and Men,' when they gave him that puppy. You squeeze so hard that you stifle the thing you love.''

Roy ordinarily lunches at his desk, but at his suggestion we took our sandwiches (turkey on whole wheat, the invariable Eisenhardt plat du jour) and drinks (a Tab for him, a beer for me) and went down a flight of stairs, through a small door, and out into the vast, sun-struck picnic ground of the Coliseum. We had our choice of fifty thousand two hundred and nineteen available seats, and settled on a nice pair down in the Section 123 boxes, just to the left of the home dugout, where we put our feet up on the seats in front of us (Roy was wearing a pair of distressed wingtips that looked like survivors of his days as a downtown lawyer) and gazed out at the unpeopled greensward and ballroom-smooth base paths, and let the baseball talk flow.

◆ ◆ ◆

BASEBALL TALK AT THE EXECUTIVE LEVEL OFTEN BECOMES money talk, and for a while Roy addressed himself to the chronic fiscal anxieties of his trade. He said that the A's expected to lose from five to six million dollars in 1983, in a budget of twenty-two million dollars, and that a major decline in attendance could make for further inroads. He said he wasn't certain exactly which of the other clubs posted deficits in 1982 but thought it was as many as eighteen or twenty of them. (At the All-Star Game lunch in Chicago last month, the president of the Chicago White Sox stated that the major-league teams had lost a hundred million dollars in the past year.) Help is on the way, however, in the form of a new six-year, one-billion-two-hundred-million-dollar network-television contract, which, starting next year, is expected to produce about six million dollars per year for each major-league club—more than three times the current fixed network revenue. Most clubs, including the A's, have also negotiated, or are negotiating, lucrative new local or regional cable-television contracts, with a wide range of returns, depending on the size of the area market; the Yankees' current fifteen-year contract with the Sports-Channel network is believed to be in the neighborhood of a hundred million dollars, while similar cable rights in Oakland produce less than twenty million for the A's. Not surprisingly, Eisenhardt doubts that the television bonanza will do away with the game's inherent fiscal imbalance, which is perhaps the most implacable of the sports' continuing difficulties, because clubs with limited regional markets (the Mariners, the Twins, the Royals, the A's, to name a few) must somehow compete, on the field and also in player salaries and free-agent bidding, with teams like the Yankees, the Dodgers, the Expos, the Phillies, and the Angels, whose markets are enormously more lucrative. (The A's, of course, must vie with the San Francisco Giants for their audience—the region is counted as encompassing five million people—and all sports franchises in the Bay area are perennially handicapped by the popularity of active outdoor sports and recreation among the indigenes.)

Eisenhardt said that he is also wary of the long-range effect of baseball's reliance on television as its prime source of revenue and its prime delivery system. A sizable number of clubs—the Braves, the Cubs, the Phillies, the Pirates, the White Sox—are owned by organizations with major television interests, and the game, he believes, will inexorably be twisted in order to serve those interests. The Braves, for instance, are owned by Ted Turner, the proprietor of the independent cable-TV network WTBS, who has dubbed them "America's Team" and often schedules the Braves' home games to start at 5:35 P.M., so that they may be safely concluded by eight-thirty-five, when the WTBS evening movie begins.

"Under the new national TV contract, we are obliged to play 'Monday Night Baseball' games here when our turn comes along," Eisenhardt said to me. "That means starting play at five-thirty—and anyone who's driven on Route 17 out here to the park knows what *that* means. And of course, none of the batters can see what the pitchers are throwing in that late-afternoon light. We've altered the game on the field to pay back our debt to the networks and suit the convenience of TV consumers on the East Coast, and the long-range damage may be deeper than we can imagine."

As often happens when Eisenhardt talks, I heard an echo here, for we had circled back to those basic apprehensions about television that he had mentioned to me on our BART ride almost a year earlier. His ideas are consistent and extensively worked, so that they often find their terminus or connection at some other level or corridor of the great multicolumned temple of the game. He appears to see baseball as a whole, in short, instead of in flinders or as mounded rubble, which is the way it often looks to me.

I asked how important it was to him to have the A's in the black within the next few years.

"Internally, it's very difficult to run an organization that isn't approaching the break-even point," he said. "That's ingrained in me and in most people, I think. But in one way this is a matter of psychological accounting. An executive or a millionaire can give x hundred thousand dollars a year to a charity, and nobody questions it or says, 'That's losing money.' But if you put it into an organization that's proprietary and capitalist in form but has as its main goal a charitable purpose, which is to provide the game of baseball to as many people as possible, in as many forms as possible, then you have to put an intangible down in your income statement, which is the psychological value of baseball to the community. That doesn't appear as cash flow, and the bank won't lend you money on it, but it's a very important and positive element in what we're trying to do. Actually, I have some basic doubts whether baseball as a self-contained economic unit *can* operate in the black. One thing I know is that the last thing we'd ever do here would be to cut back on our community projects. The only place I might want to cut down would be on player salaries, but that isn't entirely in my control. Still, it raises the question for us of the ultimate value of a million-dollar-a-year player. What is our return on that? But to go back to your question about how long one would be willing to take a loss, the answer is: I don't know."

He paused, thinking about it. "Of course, revenues can vary appreciably, depending on how well your team is doing," he went on. "Each year's attendance is hostage to your previous year's record. We played very poorly last year, and we're already off by thirty percent at the gate this year. I've begun to see this problem almost as a capitalist-socialist argument: nobody should be *wholly* captive to success or failure, and so forth. It's not exactly a new idea. But it's not the consequence of losing that hurts baseball nearly so much as it is the reactive behavior that tries to insure against loss—the sudden hiring of that additional expensive star player who might mean a pennant, or the signing of a free agent at whatever cost for fear that if you don't get him some rival team will and the odds between you will have shifted.

We all have such a fear of losing that we do things that actually increase the chances of our losing. It's almost certain that your team will lose in the end, because only one team is the World Champion at the close of the season, and you've exacerbated the consequences. To some degree or other, all twenty-six clubs operate this way now, and the truth is that player costs are astronomically high not because we want the gratification and profit of winning but because we have such a fear of losing. We all work under that spectre.''

We sat in silence for a while, watching a lone groundskeeper who was silently moving back and forth on a power roller on the dirt warning track at the foot of the distant outfield fences. Roy tipped back his drink and then put the empty can down between his feet.

"If you asked most owners," he said, "they would say, without giving it a thought, 'Yes, I want my revenues to meet my expenses.' But I don't think that's really the expectation of the public. The fans don't articulate it, yet I don't believe they expect the owner to make a profit from their baseball team. I don't think the players feel that the owners should, or the writers, either, although a lot of journalists seem to validate a team on the basis of how much money you spend. Baseball is perceived almost as a public utility that has been granted a monopoly and is obligated to deliver quality services, so a team isn't looked on with favor when it makes a lot of money. I don't see anything wrong with that notion. We *have* been given a monopoly—that's what each franchise is—and with monopoly comes responsibility. We really are the curators of this game. It's a public asset, and we are the guardians of that asset.

"As I was saying, I don't know that it isn't an anachronism to try to keep baseball going as a form of fee-simple private ownership. If we assume that it has to be affordable and available to all, and if we're not wholly determined to destroy it with television, and if we want every geographical area to have access to it, then I question whether private ownership or major corporate ownership can make it work. That brings us around to the quality of ownership. Can we find people who will care for the game if we tell them that they have to lose money in the process? I'm afraid of the answer to that one. So the only long-range solution I can see is some form of redistribution of profits that will reduce the risks of losing. We have to begin to ask ourselves if we really want baseball in Seattle and Oakland and Dallas–Fort Worth, or if it should be played only in surefire major market centers like New York and Chicago and Philadelphia and Los Angeles. Under the present system, some markets are inherently less valuable simply because of where they are, and not because the local owners are doing a bad job, and we don't really know if the clubs there can survive. It seems to me that the next question we have to ask ourselves is whether the value of each franchise—the value of being permitted to play ball in Chicago or St. Louis or Oakland—belongs to those clubs, or whether it belongs to *baseball*. Is the great tradition and history of the Boston Red Sox owned by that club, or is it owned by the people of Boston or the people of New England or by you and me—by anyone who cares about the game of baseball?"

He laughed suddenly, and said, "I can say the Red Sox, because I know that Sully"—Haywood Sullivan, the chief executive eminence of the Bosox—"won't get mad at me, the way some of the other owners do when I begin to run on this way."

He looked as cheerful and buoyant as ever, and I had difficulty in reconciling such good spirits with the endless and perhaps insoluble difficulties of the problems he had been exploring. "How come you don't get upset about all this?" I asked.

"You're just making Thomas Hobbes' old assumption that the natural state of man is to be bad-tempered," he replied. "But getting mean or low-down really serves no purpose at all. Sure, I get frustrated sometimes, but I try not to show it. The games—the different contests and their outcome—don't really bother me, even when they end the way that one did yesterday. I hope I can be like Betsy that way, who is more and more a real fan. She enjoys the baseball process—the day-to-day, the ongoing soap opera—and she doesn't get too far down about losses or slumps. If you can't do that, baseball will drive you crazy, because of its very high percentage of defeat. Robin Yount succeeds at the plate only one-third of the time. Just think what it would have been like if Beethoven had had to write symphonies that way!"

◆ ◆ ◆

AFTERWORD: NOT MUCH GOOD FORTUNE HAS BEFALLEN THE A's—now officially the Athletics—since these visits to Oakland. The team finished fourth in its division in 1983, 1984, and 1985, and third (in a tie) in 1986 and 1987.* Manager Steve Boros was

*An extended account of the team's tribulations in the 1986 campaign may be found in Chapter 12.

dismissed in mid-season in 1985, and his successor, Jackie Moore, gave way to the incumbent Tony LaRussa two years later. Attendance in 1987 rose to 1,678,921—less than a half million shy of a financial break-even level for the club; that rivalry between the Athletics and the Giants (who won the National League West division in 1987) for the Bay-area audience remains one of big-league baseball's intractable infirmities, but both clubs are clearly on the rise. The Athletics have fared well in the trading market, and the club's flourishing farm and scouting systems have produced home-grown, successive Rookie of the Year slugging stars in 1986 and '87, in the imposing persons of Jose Canseco and Mark McGwire. The team now presents a strong and confident offensive lineup, and some firming up of the infield defense and the chronically laggard pitching corps could take Oakland to a pennant one of these days. These current baseball affairs have been conducted by Sandy Alderson, who is considered one of the outstanding general managers in baseball, while Roy Eisenhardt, more or less by design, has kept himself more in the background.

By design and perhaps in self-defense. I'm not quite objective about the Athletics, but by most measurements they are almost the prototypical contemporary team. They haven't won lately, but their hopes are up, and rightly so. Like most other clubs, Oakland is losing money, but for reasons—a divided market area; limited local television income—that are not within its powers to correct. A pennant would help: wait till next year. Most of the other twenty-five big-league clubs face similar or even less cheerful prospects, but it is my belief that the so-so Athletics are subjected to much sharper criticism than other teams from their fans, from the local media, and from other owners and front-office people—because of their articulate and iconoclastic style of management. Because of Roy. I put this suggestion to him not long ago, and he shook his head but did not absolutely disagree.

"It's true that I've withdrawn a little," he said. "I think I've got a new description for myself: I'm trying to be *well-tempered*. Sometimes I ask myself if it's better to be in the middle of a pennant race, the way we are right now, or to be out of it in September, so you feel free to relax and think about next year. You have to opt for the first choice, but sometimes you wonder, particularly after you lose a game in the ninth, the way we did last night. It takes it out of you. People keep asking why we don't win more, but everybody in baseball demands explanations when you don't win. That's understandable but it's inappropriate. Baseball is ruled by the mathematical laws of chaos. There are too many variables to conclude anything else, and there's some sort of comfort in that, I suppose. It's never easy, but you go on wanting to win. If you didn't, it wouldn't be fun anymore.''

Listening to Roy, I thought back to the last game I attended with him on one of my trips to Oakland in 1983—a night encounter against the Milwaukee Brewers on a Monday evening, which the A's won by 5–4, after a few adventures and surprises along the way. Bill Krueger, the A's' tall rookie left-hander, had matters safely in hand in the ninth, it seemed, with the A's ahead by 3–1, and no one on base. With two outs, he walked two batters in succession, and Steve McCatty, summoned in to shut the door, instantly surrendered a three-run homer to pinch-hitter Roy Howell. Davey Lopes then tied up the game at 4–4, with a homer on the first pitch of the bottom half of the ninth, and we went into extra innings.

◆ ◆ ◆

ROY, BESIDE ME IN THE BOX, HAD NOT MADE THE SMALLEST sound or gesture in response to the Howell stunner, but he whacked me on the shoulder as we watched Lopes's blow sail over the left-field palings. Then he resumed his silent, thumb-biting vigil over the events—or non-events, more correctly—below. The game, it turned out, had a few more moments to go. The Brewers and then the A's each moved runners into scoring position in the tenth, to no avail. The A's got a base runner to third base in the eleventh—and stranded him there. They loaded the bases in the thirteenth, and did not score. The stream of the game became a brook, then a trickle. Pitchers and pinch-hitters came and went; fans promised themselves one more inning and then *one* more, and then gave up, a lot of them, and went home. Manager Harvey Kuenn, running out of substitutes, inserted a pitcher named Jamie Easterly to pinch-hit for his designated hitter, who had been lifted in an earlier inning for a pinch-runner, and then batted him again three innings later. Up in my seat, I drew in fresh columns and boxes on the right-hand side of my box score, writing over the totals columns there and then extending my chart on top of the printed team rosters on the outer margin of the page. The squidgy, messed-up scorecard looked like a child's birthday card, and then I began to notice that all of us there in the owner's box—Roy, Bill Rigney, Wally,

Sandy Alderson, Sarge Ivey, two or three other front-office A's people, and myself (the senior Haases had not come to the game)—were responding peculiarly to this slow and ceaseless crawl of hours and innings. "Come *up!*" Rig yelled whenever a Brewer grounder was rapped in the direction of an Oakland infielder. "Go *through!*" he ordered when the teams had changed places and the hopper had come off Oakland wood. "We have to win, because we're the only ones still watching," Wally pronounced. "Everyone in Milwaukee is home in bed and asleep." Sandy Alderson, observing two lesser A's on the bases and Rickey Henderson coming up to bat, said, "*Now* we've got them. We've got seventy thousand dollars on the bases and eight hundred thousand dollars up at bat. This is it!" But the eight hundred thousand dollars grounded into a force. "Now!" cried Sarge again and again. "Now! You *got* to!" But no one heard or heeded the command. "It's going to be Tony Phillips who drives in the winning run," I announced. "You'll see—it's *always* that kind of player who wins this kind of game. Unless it's . . . uh, Dan Meyer." We sounded like children, boys in a tree house. At last, we fell into silence—a prolonged daze of sleepiness and exhausted speculation—and into a sense of wonder, too, I think, at the endless variety and stubbornness and perfect unpredictability of this sport. The A's won the game in the bottom of the seventeenth, when Henderson scored Meyer from second on a line single to left center and sent us home at last, five hours and seventeen minutes after the first pitch. All of us there in the park—the sixty-odd players and coaches on the field; the weary grounds crew and security people and ushers and venders; the burned-out, crazily remaining handful of fans and their sleepy-eyed children; the writers, whose unfinished stories had been rewarmed for several successive deadlines; and the waiting owner and attendant executives and strategists of the A's—all of us had wanted the ridiculous party over and done with long before then, but our skills and wishes and plans and hopes meant nothing, of course. The difficulty of baseball is imperious, and prevails ever.

SIX

◆

Tiger, Tiger

FALL 1984

B ASEBALL IS WELL INTO ITS WINGLESS, OR BLACK-TIE,
dormant phase, and the only sound from within the co-
coon is the customary late-autumn murmuration of rumors and awards, plus a steady low whine of complaint about
the season just past. Not a good year, I keep hearing. Not much
of a World Series, was it? And what in God's name happened
to those Padre starting pitchers? Oh, if only the Cubs had won
their playoffs—what a Series *that* would have been! And, listen,
why couldn't we have a decent pennant race somewhere, for a
change, with maybe the Dodgers and somebody fighting it out
on the last weekend, the way they always used to, and could you
believe that American League West, with the Twins and all those
losers still in it there at the end? I mean, it was great, in a way,
but what the hell happened to the White Sox, and what happened
to the Orioles and the Phillies—and what *did* happen to the
Dodgers, do you think? And, sure, it was great the way the
Tigers ran away from everybody back in the spring—nothing
like it, out of sight—but even when the Red Sox and the Yankees, with those nobodies in uniform, got so good there in the
second half it was never really close, you know, and, sure, there
were the Mets, but even when they were so hot there in July I
never exactly believed they'd do it—not with those kids pitching

124

and that lineup—but that Gooden's *unreal*, you know, and, sure, if you look at the Tigers you have to say they're great, they can kill you on the bases and the other way, too, with that batting order, and I'm happy for Sparky, because he's an old name, like I was even happy for Reggie when he finally did it, you know what I mean, and—oh, yes, Dave Kingman! I mean, *Dave Kingman*! But why couldn't the Cubs've won that last game out there in San Diego, for God's sake, with Sutcliffe going, and all, and that way we'd've had Wrigley Field again, and some terrific games in the wind there, and something to talk about when it was over, you know?

Only full-bore fans will recognize every note of these stridulations—it is mostly their voice we are hearing—and a brief refresher gloss may be helpful. The Detroit Tigers won the recent World Series, of course, knocking off the San Diego Padres in five games, one over par for the distance; several Tiger luminaries distinguished themselves during the classic, which we will return to in due course, while the Padres, in departing, left some bloody footprints across the record books. Their four starting pitchers in the five games survived for a total of ten and one-third innings, during which span they gave up sixteen runs, twenty-five hits, and eight walks, good for an earned-run average of 13.94; in the unmemorable third game, the Padre pitchers walked the ballpark, handing out eleven bases on balls. The Tigers, by the way, scored almost instantly in each of the games, bringing the initial runs home in either the first or the second inning, thereby providing a dazzling paradigmatic reminder of their regular season, in which they won thirty-five of their first forty games (they were 9–0, 16–1, and 26–4 along the way), for the fastest start in baseball history. Only six other teams have ever led their leagues or divisions wire-to-wire, the most recent of which was the lordly Yankee club of 1927. Jack Morris, the Tigers' right-handed ace, set the tone for their year when he threw a no-hitter against the White Sox in his second start, but Detroit's bolt from the blocks was a true team effort; nine different Tiger pitchers came up winners in the first fifteen games. The team, moreover, did not simply cruise home after its opening burst, as other clubs (the 1977 Dodgers and the 1981 Oakland A's, for instance) had been known to do, but actually increased its lead over the second-place Toronto Blue Jays from seven games at the midseason All-Star Game break to fifteen games at the close (the champions wound up at 104–58), which is a much better indication of their pride and deep talent, given the quality of the opposition in that extremely difficult division.

Three of the four divisions, in fact, sorted out their eventual winners by the first week in August, a full two months too soon, while the fourth, the American League West (the "Mild West," it was sometimes called, or the "American League Worst"), produced a pennant winner of sorts in the final week, when the Kansas City Royals fell fainting across the finish line, with the only above-.500 record in their sector. The Padres, in the National League West, profited from a similar fatuousness in their opponents, since their nearest pursuers, the Braves and the Astros, wound up in a tie, twelve games back and two below the waterline. The Cubs, who overtook the surprising Mets at the beginning of August and whomped them regularly thereafter (they won eight of the nine games against New York at Wrigley Field), were easily the most popular winners of the year, thanks to their antiquity (Tinker to Evers to Ernie Banks et al.); their charming vine-covered and sunlit (there are no lights, no night games) neighborhood ballpark; their long and frightful predisposition to defeat (they led and lost a World Series in 1945 and horribly blew a sure pennant in 1969); and their mighty electronic audience, which tunes in the Cubbies by television in forty-nine states and five foreign countries, via cable station WGN. Suddenly, even the most casual, late-summer sports bystanders perked up at the possibility of a sonorous and perhaps epochal World Series between two famous clubs—the Cubs and the Tigers—played on grass diamonds in venerable city enclosures where teams and heroes were playing baseball when each of us, no matter what our age, first became aware of the game. The Tigers took care of their part of the date by brushing aside the Royals in three quick meetings in the American League championship series, but the Cubs, after administering a pair of quick, wonderfully appreciated drubbings to the Padres at Wrigley Field, went west to finish the job and there fell into a well, or a hot tub, losing by 7–1, 7–5 (an extraordinary game, an all-timer), and 6–3, after leading in each game. *Eheu*, as Mike Royko did not write, *fugaces.*

The sense of unsatisfaction, of diminished expectation and lowered reward, that attached itself to the latter stages of the 1984 season may not be wholly attributable to the one-sided World Series or to the sad and shocking expunging of the Cubs. I think we should remind ourselves that not one of the four teams involved in the league playoffs this year was a finalist in the 1983 playoffs, in which the Phillies defeated the Dodgers, and the Orioles (who went on to win the World Series) eliminated the White Sox, and that not one of *those* four teams had won its division the previous year, 1982, when we saw the Cardinals and the Braves in one playoff and the Brewers and the Angels in the other, with the Cardinals overcoming the Brewers in a seven-game Series. Team inconsistency, a lack of continuity and pattern, has become a pattern all its own in recent years. In the past six full seasons—1979 through 1984—eight different American League clubs have filled the twelve playoff slots, with the Royals, the Orioles, the Angels, and the Yankees making two appearances each; while ten different National League clubs have qualified for post-season play, with only the Phillies and the Dodgers repeating. In all, eighteen of the twenty-six clubs that make up the major leagues have appeared in postseason play in the past six Octobers, and ten different teams have played in the World Series; none has repeated as World Champions.

Some of the reasons for this instability are broadly understood, since they arise, in one form or another, from the central alterations to the game brought about by free agency and salary arbitration: enormous payrolls (averaging in the neighborhood of eight million dollars per club) and the consequent shifting, by trades or by loss to the free-agent market, of older, more expensive players from one club to another, with a resultant smudging of team identity from one season to the next. I don't propose to examine this phenomenon in depth here, since the responses to high salaries and limited-year contracts would require us to explore a very wide range of club philosophies, resources, needs, and plans. To illustrate just a bit, though, a team with a limited audience and small immediate prospects (the Indians, let's say) will often try to trade off a star player near the end of his contract, since it may be unwilling to offer him big enough fresh sums to keep him out of the free-agent market; in return, it will look for some first-class rookie prospects from the other club involved in the trade, thus saving itself the long-range cost of maintaining a full-scale scouting and farm system. Another team (try the Padres or the Angels) will habitually seek to pick up established older players, at whatever price, to fill precise needs in a roster that seems close to becoming a genuine pennant contender. Elsewhere, a change of ownership can inspire a depressed, fiscally cautious club (yes, the Cubs) to plunge headlong into the trading place with fistfuls of dollars and players, while, for its part, a wealthy, conservative franchise with a high record of success may begin to unload some famous but aging regulars in order to make room for shining rookies whom its field personnel now consider to be ready for daily play: the Phillies and the Dodgers both recently embarked on such a course, with unhappy results so far.

A glance through the lineups of some of this year's divisional winners offers useful lessons and variations on these themes. First baseman Steve Garvey, who is thirty-five, joined the Padres two years ago as a free agent at $1.3 million per year, and third baseman Graig Nettles and the famous short reliever Goose Gossage (they are forty and thirty-three years old, respectively) came over in a trade with the Yankees last spring, adding some $2.7 million per year to the San Diego payroll. The 1984 Cubs are virtually a short-order team, grabbed up over the past two years, mostly via the trade route, by their vigorous general manager, Dallas Green, who has put twenty-two new players in place on the club since his arrival in 1981, the year that the team was bought by the Chicago *Tribune*'s parent corporation. Six of Green's regulars, including the entire starting outfield, played for him on his former club, the Phillies. Three fixtures in his 1984 lineup—third baseman Ron Cey, shortstop Larry Bowa, and left fielder Gary Matthews—are in their mid-thirties, and achieved their high reputations and high salaries (they all earn a base pay in excess of six hundred thousand dollars per year, with considerable increments in the form of bonuses and deferred payments) while playing for other clubs that have appeared in the fall championships within the last four years—Cey with the Dodgers, Bowa and Matthews on the Phillies. Dallas Green's most brilliant acquisition for the Cubs has been their youthful second baseman, Ryne Sandberg, this year's Most Valuable Player in the National League, who was virtually a throw-in in a trade of shortstops that brought Bowa from Philadelphia in 1982, but the deal that won the division was the Cubs' acquisition of Rick Sutcliffe, who came over from the Indians on June 13th in a multi-player swap; he won sixteen of seventeen decisions for Chicago over the remainder of the summer, and captured the Cy Young Award as the league's best pitcher. An established, dominant right-handed starter, Sutcliffe was playing out the final months of a contract that released him as a free agent a couple of weeks ago, and at this writing it is not at all certain that the Cubs will decide to bid against the eight clubs that have obtained negotiating rights to him and are expected to drive his salary up to or over the one-and-a-half-million-dollar level. He may even sign with the Padres. The Cubs' No. 2 starter, Steve Trout, is also a free agent, and so are Dennis Eckersley and reliever Tim Stoddard—which suggests that the Chicago pitching staff may have a very different look and capability come Opening Day next spring. And so it goes. The newly crowned Tigers are a stable, mostly homegrown team, as such matters are measured nowadays, but *their* key addition in 1984 was the left-handed short reliever Willie Hernandez, who was successful in thirty-two out of the thirty-three late-inning game-saving situations in which he worked for Detroit, and thereby emerged at the top of the balloting for both the Cy Young and the M.V.P. awards in the American League.

I should add that there are some front-office people and managers and coaches (and baseball writers, too) who see a different cause for the pattern of vapid play by comtemporary pennant-winning clubs in the years just subsequent to their championships. Last year's World Series contestants—the Orioles and the Phillies—finished nineteen games and fifteen and a half games, respectively, behind their divisional leaders this year; the 1982 pennant winners—the Cardinals and the Brewers—wound up twelve and a half and thirty-six and a half games to the bad this year. The baseball thinkers I have mentioned find all this attributable much less to the shifting of personnel from one club to another than to a smugness and a waning of desire among players who have been very highly rewarded at the pay windows as a result of their October triumphs. The notion has a certain logic, and if I resist it to some degree it is because it is so often put forward by some of the arch-conservatives of the game, including the Tigers' manager, Sparky Anderson. I will follow Sparky all the way, however, when he says (as he did in the Tiger dugout before the third Series game this year) that what the sport now badly wants is a consistent winner—a dynasty, if you will. "It's fine for the fans in all those different cities to have a different team in the playoffs each year," he said, "but you also need one *particular* team in there that half the people in the country love and half of them hate: the Yankees, the great Oakland club back in the seventies, the Cincinnati team we had"—Anderson managed the Big Red Machine that appeared in five playoffs and four World Series between 1970 and 1976— "which used to break all those attendance records wherever we played. There should be a club like that in the World Series about half the time. What baseball needs right now is a Muhammad Ali."

Anderson delivered all this in cheerfully matter-of-fact tones (he also insisted he did not blame the players for taking the loot that has been coming their way), and I wish I could persuade some of my friends who are part-time baseball followers to adopt a similarly calm and unpetulant view of money and trades and baseball as a business. It's my impression that it is the late-summer soldiers—the fans who don't pay much attention until the campaigns slip into mid-September, and "magic numbers" and M.V.P. talk begin to turn up in the sports pages—who are most upset by the ironies and realities of contemporary baseball. They are probably the ones who most want an imperial and dynastic old club in the series every October, for that will add a morality-play savor to their tube-watching for a couple of weeks, and will also seem to confirm that nothing much has changed in the old game, which is a lie. For my part, I will happily welcome a defending champion in the October games when one turns up, but I don't think that a brusque, rather slovenly World Series or three flattish pennant races are much cause for gloom. One should not go thirsty at dinner for want of a Château Margaux, and the happier fans, I think, are the ones who find time actually to go to games every so often throughout the season. This summer, I kept leaving baseball and then coming back to it—dropping in on the game, so to speak—and I had as much fun, from first to last, as I ever did. The sport didn't seem particularly Homeric this year—no clanging swordplay in the dust under ancient walls—but more resembled a collage, a ragbag, or perhaps a meadow: bits and swatches jumbled together for our pleasure, and color everywhere.

◆ ◆ ◆

THE CLOSEST MEADOW FOR ME WAS SHEA STADIUM, OF COURSE, and I dropped in on the Mets again and again—not just for those enormous games with the Cubs in midseason but earlier, when the team's repeated successes were still so new and refreshing that a sudden Mets rally to retake the lead or a dandy double play that began with still another elegant move or unlikely stop by Keith Hernandez from deep behind first base would be greeted not only by roars and cheers and applause but by great bursts of delighted laughter all around the stands. Following the Mets back then was like watching a child of yours suddenly being good in a school play or a junior tennis tournament; you didn't know he had it in him. I was at Shea in the middle of June when the Mets beat the Phillies and slipped past them into first place in the National League East—a ridiculous, obstreperous game in which the Mets led by 6–1, then trailed by 7–6 (the clubs took turns batting around, and there were thirty hits for the afternoon), and finally prevailed by 10–7. I was back again the next night, when the downy Dwight Gooden struck out eleven Montreal batters but lost by 2–1 to the dewy Bill Gullickson; and I was there (along with fifty-one thousand and nine others) to celebrate the Glorious Fourth with fireworks and maybe first place again, huzzah!—except that the visiting Astros put a damper on the party by bonking out seven hits (bloops and nubbers, for the most part), good for five runs, in the very first inning, and took it by 10–5. A couple of nights later, the Mets swept a double-header from the Reds, with Ron Darling knocking off his seventh straight win with a 1–0 shutout in the opener (he had a most disappointing second half of the season, partly because the club scored so few runs behind him, and wound up at 12–9 for the year), and the next night it was Gooden again and first place regained, in a great gala, as the Mets hitters dealt most severely with the formidable Mario Soto, battering him for eight runs in four innings, with homers by Mookie Wilson and Darryl Strawberry, and with the firecrackers going off in the upper deck again, and the non-stop cheering, and the banner wavers and sign carriers at work, just like the grand old days of 1969 and 1973. In the stands, the new Gooden strikeout tabulators kept busy, hanging up their big red-on-white "K" placards, one after another, on the front-row railing of the top left-field deck, and I noticed that the custom had spread around the park, with folks waving "K"'s scrawled on newspapers and paper napkins and scorecards. I spotted a kid, down a couple of rows from me in the stands, who would write a "K" in ballpoint on one of his fingertips whenever Dwight struck out another batter, and then waggle his hands in the air for us to see. Then, out on the right-field side, two men put up a huge black "K" done on cardboard—as big as a garage door by the look of it— and held it swayingly aloft. As it happened, this wasn't a particularly brilliant outing for Dwight, and he was allowed to sit down after the sixth, by which point he was ahead by 12–2 in the game, with eight "K"'s up on the rails. It turned out to be Mookie Wilson's night—four hits and four R.B.I.s, with that homer and a stolen base thrown in—and he got the best sign, too: a couple of kids strolling the lower-deck main aisle and holding up "PARTY AT MOOKIE'S!"

The Mets' season, as we know, did not end quite so happily, but Dwight Gooden never stopped. He wound up the year at 17–9 (third best in the league), with an earned-run average of 2.60 (second best), and two hundred and seventy-six strikeouts—the most in baseball this year and the most by a rookie pitcher ever. He pitched two innings in the All-Star Game (he struck out the side in the first one), and finished his season in awesome fashion, winning eight of his last nine decisions and posting a 1.07 earned-run average for that span, with a one-hitter and two sixteen-strikeout games along the way. The most frequent baseball question I hear is "Is he *really* that good?" Yes, he is. Most major-league scouts and managers I have consulted state without hesitation that Gooden is the best young pitcher they have ever seen at a comparable stage—better than Tom Seaver, better than Bob Gibson, better than Herb Score, better than Bob Feller. He is the most vivid first-year hurler *I* can bring to mind since Vida Blue set the American League afire with his twenty-four victories and 1.82 earned-run mark for the Oakland A's, back in 1971, but Blue was twenty-two years old (and technically past his rookie status) and, as I recall, did not quite have the command of his pitches that Gooden has. The Gooden fastball is the genuine article, regularly up in the 92-to-96-m.p.h. range, and delivered with a tight spin that makes the ball look smaller and quicker as it bites through the strike zone; his curve breaks late and sharply downward; and at times he has a first-class change-up, which he can also deliver for strikes, to the deep discouragement of the hitters. I remember a 2–1 shutout he pitched against the Dodgers in Los Angeles early in May (I was watching on television), which he concluded by fanning the side in the ninth, with a changeup in there that Pedro Guerrero swung at and missed by—Well, he would have missed it with a canoe paddle. Gooden is six feet three and about two hundred pounds, with amazingly long legs, arms, hands, and fingers. His motion begins with an exaggerated leg-lift, which brings his knee up higher than his front-side elbow, but everything about the launching is nonetheless balanced, smooth, unforced, and pleasing. It requires some concentration before you begin to pick up his gargantuan opening strike on the mound and the abrupt downward tilt of the left shoulder which inaugurates the mostly over-the-top (about NNW, I make it) delivery, and also pulls his whole body swoopingly to his left just as the ball is released.

For all these elegant kinesthetics, I think I most admire Gooden's thoughtful and untroubled attitude while he is working—the absence of gesture or mannerism on the mound (now and then he flicks the sweat from his face with a downward swipe of his right palm), and his ability to adjust and improve his performance on a given day as the game progresses. Often this past summer, I saw him struggle and sometimes begin to overthrow in the middle innings of a tough game, and I would nod wisely to myself and think, Well, not much longer for you this time, kid—only to watch him recapture his poise and rhythm within a batter or two and resume the little string of "K"'s on my scorecard. His notable weakness so far is his inability to hold runners on first (forty-seven out of forty-nine would-be base stealers were successful against him), but the Met coaches are convinced that a slight tinkering with his delivery in the Instructional League during the off-season will clear up the problem. Davey Johnson, the Mets manager, spoke often and warmly about the youngster's maturity and his continuing eagerness to learn as the season went along. Gooden is reserved and quiet in the clubhouse, and a bit shy with reporters and TV crews, and there is no suggestion that further fame and a great deal more money down the line will much alter him. He is in the habit of calling his father, down home in Tampa, after each game he has pitched. He is nineteen years old, and this was his second full season in professional ball. He will be better next year.

Another manager—Jim Frey, of the Cubs—was being asked about Gooden one July afternoon in the dugout at Shea, after Gooden had shut down his club by 2–1, on four hits, the previous evening. Frey, who was a coach with the Mets last season, was complimentary about the phenom, but when most of the reporters had gone away he sighed and spat and murmured, "If there's one thing I get tired of, it's all these questions about Dwight Gooden's poise. Anybody who can throw the ball across the plate at ninety-five miles an hour up *here* and then comes back with a breaking ball that drops a foot and still comes over down *there* for a strike—why, damn, that man doesn't need poise! But ask me about a pitcher who's just been taken to the back of the bullpen twice in the same inning, then I'll show you a man who needs *poise!*"

◆ ◆ ◆

AS IT HAPPENED, I DIDN'T SEE A MAJOR FIGHT ON THE FIELD this year, or many brushbacks or knockdown pitches of the kind that eventually empty the benches, but it was a testy, bad-tempered sort of season nevertheless—by mid-September, the National League counted twenty-six official warnings to pitchers and/or brawls, which was up by one-third from the total of the previous summer. News shows and editorials have gravely taken up the "beanball epedemic," which they seem to view as a true threat to the pastime, but I am less alarmed. For one thing, "beanball" is a misnomer: no, or very few, big-league pitchers aim for a batter's head (it is too dangerous to a fellow-professional, or, conversely, the head is too small a target if malice is actually intended). For another, the war between the pitcher and the batter for control of the plate (more precisely, for the outside three or four inches of the plate) is the center of the game, of course, and the pitcher's best weapon in that unending contest is a whistling fastball up and in, close to the body or under the chin, that will make the batsman give ground—in his mind or in the batter's box—when the next pitch arrives. "Show me a pitcher who can't pitch inside and I'll show you a loser," the sweet-mannered Sandy Koufax once said. Sometimes, given a certain pitcher and batter at a certain moment in the long, nerve-abrading season, the pitch is to the ribs or the knees, and the batter goes down. Retaliation is then in order, although the rules forbid it and umpires now have the power, as they did not up until seven years ago, to issue warnings to one side or both and to eject a pitcher or a manager for an ensuing provocation. Even this form of peace-keeping is not wholly endorsed by some classicists of the sport, who also dislike the American League's designated-hitter rule, because it exempts the pitcher from ever coming to bat, and thus makes him unavailable for direct retribution if he has plunked somebody. Don Drysdale, the dominating, Hall of Fame Dodger right-hander, believes that the D.H. and the umpires' new pitcher-banishment power have actually increased the chances of some batter's being seriously injured. He points out that more batters are digging in at the plate and that they are much more aggressive in attacking the outer sector of the plate. Because they have forgotten about bailing out, he says, they are forever at risk against an inside fastball that gets away from the pitcher. Someone's going to get hurt.

The matter is usually less grave on the field, as the great Atlanta brawl of August 12th seems to illustrate. This Thermopylae began briskly when the Braves' Pascual Perez drilled the visiting Padres' leadoff hitter, Alan Wiggins, with the very first pitch of the game, and it extended itself lengthily, with many skirmishings and rasslings along the way—mostly because it took three San Diego pitchers four Perez at-bats to nail him in return, in the eighth. Then there was a counter-*counter* essay of honor in the ninth, when a Braves reliever, Donnie Moore, nicked the Padre third baseman, Graig Nettles, which again emptied the dugouts. By the time the firefight was over, sixteen members, including both managers, had been officially excused for the day, and league president Chub Feeney eventually parcelled out eighteen fines and suspensions, including a ten-thousand-dollar fine and a ten-day suspension for Padre manager Dick Williams.

Stern stuff, but once again I sense a decline in the quality of hostilities in comparison with some earlier eras of the game—at the very least, a decline in the language of hard feelings. After the Atlanta fracas, Atlanta manager Joe Torre said that Dick Williams was "Hitler-like," and Williams, in riposte, referred to Torre as "Benito." A couple of weeks later, during an A's-White Sox game at Oakland, Dave Kingman was nailed by a pitch, with a brief ensuing flareup, apparently because somebody in the home dugout had called the White Sox pitcher a "jerk," and Chicago manager Tony LaRussa, swinging from the heels, retaliated by describing the A's as "pimps." Or consider the horrid outbreak of rudeness between the Minnesota Twins and the California Angels, in which there were taunting references made to Angel catcher Bob Boone's celebrated wine collection, and Twins manager Billy Gardner stated flatly that there was enough cork in the bat of Angel third baseman Doug DeCinces to make a fishing bob. It's enough to make one long for the bad old days. The late Ray Scarborough, a redoubtable right-handed pitcher with the Senators and several other A.L. clubs in the nineteen-forties and fifties, once told me that when he was toiling for the Tigers against the Red Sox one afternoon his manager, Fred Hutchinson, was baited from the field by the flamboyant and somewhat unreliable Jimmy Piersall, then a Bosox outfielder. As it happened, Piersall was due to lead off the next half inning at bat, and when the sides changed and Scarborough started out of the dugout to take the field, he muttered, "I know, I know," to his skipper. Hutchinson, a famously dour and direct competitor, beckoned him back. "What you don't know," he said, "is that it will cost you a hundred if you don't hit him." This was a first, as far as Scarborough knew, but he went manfully at the job, only to find himself quickly behind in the count, by 3–0, when Piersall proved wonderfully lithe and rabbitlike under fire. "I sure couldn't afford to walk him," Ray said to me, "so I bore down on the next two pitches, which were called strikes. Then I threw the next pitch behind his back, and Jimmy guessed wrong." He held up two fingers. "Two broken ribs," he announced.

Some surprising names made their way onto the dean's list at the end of the term this year, including Tony Gwynn, of the Padres, and Don Mattingly, of the Yankees, who won the league batting titles with averages of .351 and .343, respectively. Mattingly, it will be recalled, pulled it off by rapping out four hits in the Yankees' very last game of the season, thereby nudging his way past his teammate Dave Winfield, who had begun the day two points ahead. There is no right way to hit, of course, and the two Yankees' month-long day-by-day pursuit of the title offered a wonderful contrast in styles—Mattingly always taking a level, thoughtful cut at the ball, with his arms beautifully extended at the point of contact (he bats from the left side, with his head tilted back oddly as he stares out at the pitcher), while Winfield, as always, looked lunging and prodigal up there, with the various parts of his gigantic six-foot-six frame seeming to depart the launching pad separately, starting with the shoulders, but then all somehow coming together again in the midst of his scary swing (sometimes when he misses a pitch he has to take a twisting leap in the air to keep his balance and comes down yards in front of the plate, like a broad jumper landing). To put it another way, I am always as surprised when Winfield bangs out a base hit as I am when Mattingly doesn't.

Tony Armas, of the Red Sox, led the American League with forty-three home runs, while Mike Schmidt, of the Phillies, and Dale Murphy, of the Braves, wound up together at the top of the N.L., with thirty-six homers apiece. (Murphy is in a rut; this was his third straight thirty-six-homer season.) The American League appears to be working up a monopoly in power hitters, with ten of its sluggers driving in a hundred runs or more during the summer, as against three in the National League; eight A.L. hitters weighed in with more than thirty homers, while only Schmidt and Murphy made the grade in the other league. Boston outfielders Armas, Jim Rice, and Dwight Evans each finished with more than a hundred runs batted in—the first time any outfield picket line had turned that trick since the Cubs' Hack Wilson, Kiki Cuyler, and Riggs Stephenson did it in 1929.

A new American League bopper was Dave Kingman, who joined the Oakland A's this spring after the Mets had given up on him because of his sulks and strikeouts (he batted .198 last year, with thirteen homers) and released him. Freed from New York and the New York writers, which he claimed to despise equally, Kingman came through with a ravishing year as a designated hitter: thirty-five home runs and a hundred and eighteen runs batted in. (He was also quite a bargain for the A's, who paid him only the major-league minimum salary of forty thousand dollars, while the Mets continued to mail him the installments due on the rest of his six-hundred-and-seventy-five-thousand-dollar unexpired annual contract.) Sky King has always been a famously (or infamously) streaky hitter, but his performance during a nine-game road trip in April must have been his best—a three-homer night in Seattle, two subsequent two-homer games, and eight home runs and nineteen runs batted in, over all. Some of the travelling A's on that trip—second baseman Joe Morgan and coaches Clete Boyer and Billy Williams—have watched a fair assortment of the game's best in action over the past twenty or thirty years, and all three said they'd never seen a hot spell to match it. Most of us probably remember Kingman for some enormous downtowner we once saw, but I think we don't yet realize how many of these there have been over the years and how fast they have come. He has hit three hundred and seventy-seven homers in fourteen seasons—one for each 14.65 times at bat. This is the fourth-best ratio in the history of the game, putting him behind only Babe Ruth, Ralph Kiner, and Harmon Killebrew. He has some firsts as well. In May, he hit a stratospheric, straight-up fly ball that disappeared through a ventilating aperture in the tentlike roof of the Metrodome, in Minneapolis, and never came down: a sky-rule double.

Joaquin Andujar, of the Cardinals, and Mike Boddicker, of the Orioles, were the only official twenty-game winners among all the pitchers (Boddicker was 20–11, and Andujar went 20–14, after a 6–16 season a year ago), but Rick Sutcliffe, it should be noted, did even better in his split season (which doesn't count in the record books): 4–5 with the Indians and 16–1 with the Cubs. One might even claim that Bert Blyleven had the best totals of all—a 19–7 and 2.87 year, compiled while pitching, from start to finish, for the lowly Indians. Mike Witt, of the Angels, belongs on this honor roll as well, for the perfect game—no hits, nobody on base at all—that he threw against the Rangers on the very last day of the season. Dan Quisenberry had forty-four saves for the Royals, and Bruce Sutter forty-five (a new

National League record) for the Cards: no surprise *there*, at least. The Pirates led the National League in team pitching and somehow also finished last in their division, while the Manager's Averted Eyes Award (given here for the very first time) went to Juan Samuel, the rookie second baseman with the Phillies, who had fifteen homers, nineteen triples, and seventy-two stolen bases (a major-league rookie record), but also struck out a hundred and sixty-eight times and committed thirty-three errors.

There has rarely been a better vintage of rookies and baseball Yuppies, with a minimal rundown requiring mention of the Mariners' Alan Davis (twenty-seven homers, a hundred and sixteen R.B.I.s); center fielder Kirby Puckett, of the Twins; second baseman Marty Barrett (also of the Bosox); and outfielders Dan Gladden (Giants) and Jeff Stone (Phillies), who batted .351 and .362, respectively, in less than full seasons. The new pitchers were almost better: the aforementioned Messrs. Gooden and Darling, of the Mets; Mark Langston, of the Mariners (17–10, with two hundred and four strikeouts); Roger Clemens, of the Red Sox; Orel Hershiser, of the Dodgers; and Bret Saberhagen and Mark Gubicza, of the Royals. (The funny-name team title went to the Cincinnati Reds, by the way, in a landslide: a roster that included the possible law firm of Knicely, Krenchicki, Bilardello, Esasky & Redus. A trade might even land them Doug Gwosdz—pronounced "Goosh"—of the Padres, who is known to his teammates as Eye-Chart.) And let us conclude our rosters by not naming the eleven managers who were released, or allowed to depart, during the season or just after it—a casualty (or scapegoat) list that inspired the ineffable George Steinbrenner (who has canned ten managers—but not ten *different* managers—in his twelve years with the Yankees) to remark, "It's getting so you can't make news anymore when you make a change. The lack of stability is alarming." Steinbrenner then gave his incumbent, Yogi Berra, a vote of confidence that reminded me of the three-finger handshake that W. C. Fields received from his boss in "The Bank Dick": "Yogi did a very creditable job."

Reggie Jackson, now almost exclusively employed as a designated hitter by the Angels, struck his five hundredth lifetime home run—a vast relief to everyone who knows what pride he takes in such matters. I am not very fond of these Landmarks Commission records, which so often seem to burn out or put down an aging player as he struggles toward some arbitrary plateau. I well remember the repeated mound embarrassments that Lefty Grove experienced when he was straining to notch his three-hundredth victory, and, twenty years later, the sadness and disconcertion we felt as we watched Early Wynn go through the same process; each of them made the grade at last, and instantly retired, diminished by his triumph. Reggie has persisted, however, and has surprised us once again. He knocked No. 500 (his twenty-second of the year, on September 17, against the Royals, out of an eventual twenty-five), thereby joining a most exclusive gents' club; eleven of its twelve previous members are in the Hall of Fame. Reggie, now thirty-eight and with no more real challenges in sight, will be back for at least one more season—clear sailing at last, with a few splendid targets (Mel Ott, with 511 lifetime homers; Ernie Banks and Eddie Mathews, each with 512; and Ted Williams and Willie McCovey, with 521 apiece) in plain view.

A few sweepings remain here on the floor of the Archive Room. Here is the box-score pitching line left by George Frazier, a Cubs long reliever, after a painful outing against the Mets in September:

IP	H	R	ER	BB	SO
0	3	4	4	0	1

Box scores never lie, and the apparent typo in Frazier's little row of embarrassments—a strikeout but no outs (the out would show as "⅓" under the innings-pitched symbol)—is absolutely correct: Darryl Strawberry struck out on a Frazier wild pitch that bounced away from the catcher, and made it easily to first. Another genuine curio is not in the record books but deserves enshrinement somewhere—the umpire's ruling that enjoined Indians outfielder Mel Hall from coming up to the plate with three batting gloves dangling from each hip pocket; an errant pitch might flick one of the gloves, the arbiter decided, and unfairly allow Hall a free pass to first base. This was a sad loss to the game, for Mel Hall does not actually *wear* a batting glove when at the plate. The six white mitts, dangling prettily on his haunches and all aflutter whenever he ran the bases, were purely decorative: the beautiful badge of a hotdog. And, finally, we should probably not forget the midsummer news that three members of the Padres' pitching staff—Eric Show, Mark Thurmond, and Dave Dravecky—were found to be full-fledged, signed-up members of the John Birch Society. Much was made of this in the press, and the hurlers defended their politics stoutly, but I couldn't fit it in anywhere. Everything in baseball means something, but this one eluded me. Two of the pitchers were starters, one was a reliever. . . . Two were left-handed but one of these, Dravecky, was *a left-hander who bats right-handed*. . . . Something is afoot here, clearly, but what? I leave the matter to Bill James, the demon Sabermetrician, who must now devise the first Birchfactor formula and thereby return our game to the pure world of numbers, where it belongs.

EARLY ON THE DAY OF THE FIRST CUBS-PADRES PLAYOFF GAME, Jim Frey went to his bedroom window to check the wind—*too* early, it turned out, for it was four-thirty in the morning and still pitch-black out there. He went back to bed. He got what he wanted, though, for there was a lovely Cubs wind at Wrigley Field by game time that afternoon—blowing straight out, that is, at a good twenty miles an hour—and throughout the day you could hear the shuffle and pop of the flags snapping in the breeze. The scoops of bunting set around the gray-blue facing of the steep upper deck were also astir, and, farther out, the tall center-field flagpole above the great gray-green scoreboard and the rising pyramid of bleachers flew a double row of pennants (team flags, in the order of finish, top to bottom of the National League divisions), which kept up a gala, regattalike flutter all through the shining afternoon. The famous ivy, thickly overgrowing the outfield walls from pole to pole, showed October tints, and the graceful old brickwork of the inner-field façade suggested foot-ball weather as well. There were treetops swaying out along Waveland Avenue, beyond left field, and Sheffield Avenue, be-yond right, and other flags were aloft on the rooftops of the low neighborhood houses there, with a fine range of colors and loy-alties to choose among: Old Glory, Israel, Ireland, Puerto Rico, and, of course, the Cubs. In among the flags, a couple of big tethered balloons shifted and shouldered in the moving air, and the parapets and extemporaneous stands on the roofs were jammed with unticketed, opportunistic fans, who counted them-selves lucky to be close enough to pick up glimpses of the game along with the sounds and sense of it. The angling, early-autumn sunlight illuminated white-and-blue Cubs pennants in the stands around the park and silhouetted a long, sweeping line of heads and shoulders of the spectators in the topmost row of the lower deck, and when the Cubs' center fielder, Bob Dernier, sprinted to his left and abruptly bent low to pull in a line drive, early on, there was a sudden gleam, a dart of light, from his dark glasses as he made the grab. Even the noises of the day—the deep, happy roaring of the fans; the ancient, carny-show strains of the Wrigley Field organ (sometimes playing upbeat old airs like Cole Porter's "From This Moment On")—seemed to reach us with washed and wonderful clarity, and in my seat in the airy, down-sloping lower left-field stands (an overflow press sector), I kept tight hold on my rustling scorecard and stat sheets, and felt at one with the weather and the world. It was as if the entire baseball season—all those hundreds of games and thousands of innings—had happened, just this one time, in order to bring this afternoon to pass; a championship game and the Cubs, for once, in it. Only one possibility could spoil things on a day like this— and I could almost see the same thought on the faces of the holiday throngs pushing along under the stands before game time: the unexpected, awful shadow of a doubt—and even that was taken care of in the quickest possible way. Dernier, leading off against the Padres' Eric Show in the bottom of the first, rocketed the second pitch to him into the screen above the left-field bleachers, and a bare moment or two later Gary Matthews got another shot up into the wind, which landed above and beyond the ivy in left center, a good four hundred feet away. Rick Sutcliffe came up to bat in the third, and *his* homer—a low, hurrying, near line drive over the right-side bleachers: a *shot*— didn't need the wind at all, and it told us, if any doubt remained, what kind of day this was meant to be. Chicago won, 13–0.

Before we say goodbye to the Cubs, who are about to make their sudden departure from this season and this account (they won again the next afternoon, this time playing shortball—speed and defense and the extra base—for a neat 4–2 decision), another lingering look at the Friendly Confines and its team may be forgiven. The Cubs' great success in 1984 and their abrupt termination in the championships can best be appreciated if we remind outselves about the team's unique place in the sport. The Cubs are the Smithsonian of baseball, a caucus of institutions, many of which were on view during the playoff festivities. "Mr. Cub," Ernie Banks, who put in nineteen years' distinguished service at shortstop and first base, reappeared in uniform as an honorary member of the 1984 team and threw out the first ball (a trick flip from behind his back on the mound) before the first game. The next day, the ritual was performed by Jack Brickhouse, who had broadcast thirty-four years of Cub games before his retirement, in 1982; his successor in the booth, the incumbent Harry Caray, is a *transferred* institution, who had previously put in eleven years' work with the White Sox. Bill Veeck, who sat in the center-field bleachers through the season and the playoffs (I spotted him there through my binoculars, with a Vincent van Gogh straw hat on his bean, a beer in his hand, and his pegleg comfortably out in the aisle, while a stream of friends and writers and well-wishers came by to shake his hand and spoil his view),* was most recently in baseball as the owner and chief executive of the White Sox, but his father, William Veeck, Sr., was president of the Cubs from 1919 to 1933, and Veeck the Younger grew up in Wrigley Field and had his first job in the business with the team thereafter. It was Bill Veeck, in fact, who persuaded the Wrigleys to plant ivy out along the outfield walls, in 1938. Steve Trout, the southpaw who pitched and won the second playoff game against the Padres, is a son of Dizzy Trout, who pitched and won a game against the Cubs in their last previous postseason adventure, the 1945 World Series, against Detroit. And so on. The best-known Cub fixture, of course—almost an honored institution—is defeat. No other club has had a manager who described his team's home fans as unemployables, as did a recent incumbent named Lee Elia, and no other franchise has taken so mild a view of its own fortunes as to allow its team to amble along with no manager at all, as the Cubs did from 1961 to 1965, when the day-to-day direction was handled by a rotating board of coaches. Leo Durocher took over after that and whipped the team up into second place a couple of times, but the last pennant, in '45, is still so vivid in the memory of the fans that this year in Chicago I kept hearing references to Hank Borowy, the pitcher who won the first and sixth games of that World Series, and lost the fifth and seventh.

We won't know for some time where the 1984 Cubs will fit into this sweet, dismal history, but I think we can already do honor to the principals—Dallas Green and Jim Frey, and the newborn or new-bought stars on the field—for reversing this deep-running tide so precipitately. There was no preparation for this at the beginning of the year, when the Cubs, fifth-place finishers the year before, lost eleven straight games in spring

---

*I almost walked out there to pay my respects to Veeck, a favorite old friend of mine, but then I decided that I didn't want to add to the distracting crush of admirers around him. So many reporters wanted to interview him during the playoffs that he was forced to set up a schedule of incoming telephone interviews at his house; one writer told me he had got his story at seven-twenty in the morning. Bill Veeck died fifteen months later, but I treasure this distant last glimpse of him at home in his favorite old ballpark and relishing a game. Baseball, he always said, should be *savored*.

training, but some late trades suddenly filled the team's needs—
a leadoff man, a center fielder, more speed (Bob Dernier, who
came from the Phillies on March 27th, took care of all three),
more and then still more pitching—and they began to win and
began to be noticed. On June 23rd, before a national television
audience, the Cubs beat the Cardinals, 12–11, in eleven innings,
in a game in which Ryne Sandberg, their remarkable young star,
hit two home runs against Bruce Sutter—one in the ninth and
another in the tenth (with two out and a man aboard), each time
retying the score. "Sandberg is the best player I have ever seen,"
Cardinal manager Whitey Herzog said afterward.

It is the cub fans who will have to sort out this season—most
of all, the unshirted, violently partisan multitudes in the Wrigley
Field bleachers, who sustain the closest fan-to-player attachment
anywhere in baseball—and I will not patronize them by claiming
a share of their happiness during the summer or pretending to
understand their pain and shock at its end. Baseball, as I have
sometimes suggested, is above all a matter of belonging, and
belonging to the Cubs takes a lifetime. But to Chicago the Cubs
are something more than just a team. Wrigley Field is almost
the last of the old neighborhood ballparks, and the antiquity of
the place (it was built in 1914, two years after Fenway Park
opened for business in Boston) and the absence of night ball
there (the Wrigley family believed that the crowds and the noise
would be an affront to the nearby residents) remind us what the
game once felt like and how it fitted into the patterns of city life.
I took a little stroll around the blocks off to the north and east
of Wrigley Field one morning before game time and fell into
conversation with a short, cheerful young woman named Debra
Price, who was out jogging. She was wearing a sweatshirt with
huge Cubs emblazoning, and was accompanied by her black
cat, Dufus, who runs with her. She told me she had lived just
around the corner, on Kenmore Avenue, until August, when she
took a job in Denver (she is in labor relations), but had come
back for the games because her old roommate, Karen Miller,
had been lucky enough to get hold of a pair of tickets. "I was
going through a bad Cubs withdrawal out there," she said. "It
used to be incredibly convenient living so close to the park here.
You could walk over at nine in the morning and pick up your
seats for that afternoon. It was always easy to get seats, because
the team wasn't going anywhere. I can't quite believe this whole
year, or understand it. I'm a little young to be a real Cubs fan,
but I think I qualify. I was there two years ago the day Bill

Buckner got his two-hundredth hit of the season, and Jody Davis has been sort of a constant for me. There's a lot of character and sentimentality in what the Cubs are. They've always seemed older than the White Sox in this town—I don't know why. They have this kind of *humor* about them. The Cubs are outside the realm.''

On Grace Street, I paid an impromptu visit to the House of the Good Shepherd, a convent whose sizable, unmarked backyard parking lot has been a public secret shared by suburban Cubs fans for forty years or more. The parking revenue now accounts for more than a third of the annual budget for the convent, which does its main work in family care. I was told by a pleasant, impressive nun named Sister Patricia, who said she respected and admired the Cubs for sticking to daytime ball. She wouldn't quite declare her own feelings about this year's team, but I thought I could tell that she was—well, *pleased*. I asked about a vender I had seen out on Grace Street who was selling wonderful T-shirts with the message "THE CUBS—A TICKET TO HEAVEN," but Sister Patricia shook her head. "Not ours," she said. "That's outside the walls." When I took my leave, I noticed that the sister who let me out was wearing a little paper Cubs logo—the red letter "C" inside a circle of blue—over her heart on her white habit.

The side blocks off Grace Street were made up of elderly detached three-story houses, with scraps of lawn and flower beds out in front; the grass had a worn, late-summer look to it, and the low-hanging tree branches were heavy with dusty leaves. Here and there, the narrow concrete sidewalk had a half-circle cut out, making room for a fat tree trunk. I could have been in Keokuk or Kirksville, but whenever I crossed a street I could look off to my left a couple of blocks and see the great back wall of Wrigley Field. Down another street, Clifton Avenue, I came upon a man named Barry Flanagan, who was carefully brushing a fresh coat of green paint on his front stoop. When I stopped to talk, we were joined by his father, James Flanagan, a retired gent with a ruddy face and gold-rimmed glasses. The senior Mr. Flanagan was born in England—there was still a trace of that when he talked—and used to root for the West Ham football team, but he took up the other game when he came to the new country and the Cubs' neighborhood. The Flanagans had been in the same house for twenty-seven years, and before that they had lived just next door. They were great Ernie Banks fans, of course. They could *hear* the games, Barry told me, but couldn't quite see them—not even from the roof. I had the feeling that they didn't get around to going very often. "I can tell by the people walking home after a game whether they've won or lost," the elder Flanagan said. "When the Cubs lose, they're saying, 'Oh, we should have done this, we should have done that.' Some days, if there's been a bad game, they trample the flowers a bit. But it's nice having the Cubs. You know there's always going to be parking space right after the games, when you're coming home from work."

I said goodbye and headed off for the park, and all along the street I noticed yellow signs put up in the lower windows of the little houses: "NO NIGHT BASEBALL"—a response to the rumor, back in midsummer, that the postseason games in Chicago might be played under some temporarily installed floodlights in order to placate the demands of the networks for night ball and its vast audiences and numbers. Now (it's only to be expected, I suppose) Dallas Green is talking about building a new ballpark somewhere for the Cubs, with more seats, improved parking, and, of course, night baseball.

◆ ◆ ◆

I WATCHED THE REST OF THE N.L. PLAYOFFS, OUT IN SAN DIego, by television: some fine pitching by Ed Whitson in the 7–1 Padre victory in Game Three; the riveting attacks and ripostes of the next game, in which Steve Garvey again and again surpassed himself—surpassed possibility, almost—in the 7–5 Padre victory that tied things up; and some useful work by the top two hitters in the San Diego lineup, Alan Wiggins and Tony Gwynn, in the team's 6–3 comeback victory over Rick Sutcliffe in the Sunday finale. Garvey, it will be recalled, batted in the second San Diego run in Game Four with a double; tied it with a single in his next at-bat; drove in the go-ahead run in the seventh; and, with matters again tied, whacked the game-winning two-run line-drive homer in the ninth, against Lee Smith; five runs batted in for the day. Garvey has his detractors, who are put off at times by his smiling, TV-host persona, but I am not among them; I was startled by his great day at the plate, but not surprised. What I can't decide, even at this distance, is whether Jim Frey should have taken out Rick Sutcliffe, his star and stopper, much sooner in the final game, when he proved unable to hold a three-run lead. To be sure, Sutcliffe had often found himself in similarly horrid places during the summer, as all pitchers do, and had pitched out of them, but even in the middle innings of this game, before the Padres had been able to put anything together at the plate, he had looked uncharacteristically uncertain and unhappy out there—an amazing and disconcerting sight. The pressure of such a too short series is killing, of course, and a deepening and palpable weight and doubt about the outcome of this last game had begun to swing against the Cubs well before it began. It's second-guessing, but I would have pitched Sutcliffe on Saturday.

The Padre fans, it will be recalled, kept up an unending, unquenchably ferocious din through all those games at San Diego's Jack Murphy Stadium. They actually seemed to make a difference, and thus had some part in the great comeback—all the Padre players said so at the end—but I must confess that I resented them a little, once their team had triumphed. The Padres had not come close in their fifteen previous years of campaigning, never finishing above fourth place, and I did not think that their supporters quite understood the kind of waiting and the hope and pain that Cubs fans know by heart. Now, to be sure—since the playoffs, I mean—the Padres have been in a World Series and lost it, which changes everything. Their fans have won and *then* lost, and they are in the game at last.

These games—and the American League championship series as well—were contested without the supervision of major-league umpires, who were striking for a larger share of the playoff and World Series (and All-Star Game) profits, and for a distribution of that share among all their members instead of among the few who actually worked the games. The impasse was resolved before the Series by the intervention of the brand-new commissioner, Peter Ueberroth, who came down very strongly on the side of the umps—a most surprising and (to me, at least) pleasing turn of events. The playoff games were supervised by locally recruited amateurs—college and high-school umpires, for the most part—who looked a bit tense and ragged on the field but who, very fortunately, never had to make a crucial call. Some people in baseball can't accept even the smallest disruption of their sport—among them a crabby scribe friend of mine, now with the Chicago *Tribune*, who watched the first Cubs-Padres game from his regular perch in the press box and, in his column next morning, stated without hesitation that the home plate ump-for-a-day had missed twenty-three ball-and-strike calls through the first seven innings.

◆ ◆ ◆

THE TIGERS, OVER IN THEIR HALF OF THE PLAYOFF DRAW, TOOK care of the Royals in the minimum distance—not an astonishing outcome, given their records; Detroit's 104–58 was the best season put together by an American League divisional champion since 1970, and Kansas City's 84–78 was the worst ever. Dick Howser's young troops gave it their best, of course, but I think the heart went out of them when they came back from a three-run deficit in the second game only to see their stopper, Quisenberry, beaten in the eleventh on a double by John Grubb. I caught up with the teams in Detroit at Game Three—an austere, tense little pitching battle between the Tigers' Milt Wilcox and K.C.'s Charlie Leibrandt. The only run of the game came home in the bottom of the second, when, with one out and men on first and third, Royals shortstop Onix Concepcion and second baseman Frank White were a fraction late in turning a double play (they are more accustomed to the fast infield carpet on their home field), and the Tiger batter, Marty Castillo, ran out the play hard and beat the relay by a whisker. You never know. The other critical moment went the other way. With two outs and a Kansas City base runner aboard in the top of the eighth, Willie Wilson smashed a grounder well to the right of first baseman Darrell Evans—past him, it seemed. Evans made an airborne dive to his right, barely gloved the ball as it came off the bounce, and somehow held on to it as his body slammed into the dirt. The force of the fall made his hat fly off, but he was up in an instant and came scrambling back in the other direction, staggering in his haste, as his pitcher, Wilcox, sprinted over to cover the bag, and Wilson, perhaps the fastest man in the league, barrelled up the line. There was no chance for a play to Wilcox, even if he could have held on to a flipped toss somehow, and the pitcher danced away at the last instant as the two others— runner and fielder—flew together in an amazing double slide for the bag, with Evans winning the event by an inch or so. The inning was done and, a few minutes later, so were the Royals.

I loved the play—I can still see it—but I was even more taken with Darrell Evans' reaction to it, which, for once, gave us a glimpse of the players' responses in these moments of tension and courage that the rest of us pay to watch. Evans is thirty-seven—an old-pro third and first baseman who came over to the Tigers as a free agent last winter, after hitting thirty homers for the Giants. He was expected to add some sock to the Detroit batting order, but he had a disappointing sort of season at the plate—.232 and sixteen home runs. But Evans brings other qualities to any team he plays for. He was team captain on his two previous clubs, the Braves and the Giants, in the first case succeeding Hank Aaron and in the second Willie Mays. This was his sixteenth major-league season but his very first taste of postseason play.

After the game, Evans was a center of attention in the Tigers' shouting, jubilant clubhouse. He has a pale, somewhat pouchy face and a thoughtful way of talking, but now he was voluble. He was holding a bottle of champagne in one hand, but I never saw him take a sip. "A game like that, a time like that—it takes you over," he said. "It consumes you. You're thinking so far in advance, you're making mental pictures of plays two or three pitches ahead. You have to experience it to understand it. It's another level—other guys told me that, but I had to get into it to know what they meant. You feel that there's no one else around but you. You have to take all the responsibility for the game, and it takes it out of you. You know, the other day, after we'd won that game in the eleventh, I had to go and lay down in the training room—I was spent emotionally. You want it to be a little easier than it is, but it can't be that way."

He went on like this, going over the play again and again for different groups of reporters and camera crews that surrounded him in succession, but, if anything, he grew more excited and exalted by his memory of the play and the moment each time he described it. "Everyone *enjoyed* it—everyone in the park!" he exclaimed at one point. "In that situation, you don't have time to think, you just react. You get in sort of a panic—you have to think of *something*. This is what you want from the game. It's what you play for. This is the whole thing."

◆ ◆ ◆

ALL SORTS OF PRAISE SHOWERED DOWN ON THE TIGERS DURING and after the World Series, but the most telling compliment I heard came during the late summer, when several players on three other clubs—the Blue Jays, the Twins, and the Red Sox—separately offered the opinion that the best group of games, the best single series, that their club had played during the year had been against Detroit. The Tigers had won most of those games, but the quality of their play, the combined pressure of their pitching and power and speed, and their day-to-day élan on the field had brought out the finest efforts of their rivals and raised the level of the games to the highest calibre. This is the same sort of spontaneously offered professional endorsement that used to be reserved for the imperial Yankees back in the nineteen-fifties, when A.L. managers would sort out their pitching rotation weeks in advance in order to have their top performers ready for some forthcoming home set with the Bronx Bombers—and, when the games came, they would sell out the park and, most of the time, end up losers. Nowadays, the only evaluation of supremacy in the sport that goes entirely unchallenged is the No. 1 rating given to the Tigers' up-the-middle core: catcher Lance Parrish, second baseman Lou Whitaker, shortstop Alan Trammell, and center fielder Chet Lemon. The quartet is currently without a peer or a close rival, and is now being seriously compared with the Dodgers' early-fifties middle line of Campanella, Robinson, Reese, and Snider. The star qualities of the Detroit four—Parrish's power (he holds the all-time A.L. record at the position with thirty-two homers in 1982) and deadly, quick-release arm; Whitaker's ball-bearing smoothness afield and remarkable hand-speed at bat; Trammell's all-around skill and his consummate calm (coming after Cal Ripken and Robin Yount, he is the third marvellous shortstop in a row to play for the American League in the World Series); and Lemon's range and speed and passion for the game (he is the only outfielder I can recall who actually works on his defense during batting practice)—suggest that their club may not be easily susceptible to the kind of falling off that has afflicted other recent champions after they've won. I also find it significant that the Tigers did so well in a season when many of their regulars (Parrish, Whitaker, Trammell, Evans, Larry Herndon) had poorer records at the plate than they had in 1983. The prime pickup for the team this year, aside from Kirk Gibson's coming of age out in right field, was in pitching, and most of that, of course, followed upon the acquisition of Willie Hernandez. This year's Tigers led their league both in runs scored and in fewest runs allowed: a killing balance. Their fifteen-game winning margin was achieved in the only powerful division in either league, and, as Sparky Anderson kept saying even before the Series began, that was the true championship test.

The Tigers had an *impatience* to win, as we saw all through this Series. Their first two batters, Whitaker and Trammell, got on base in the very first inning nine times in their ten leadoff at-bats over the five games, and scored six runs. The Tigers, as I have said, scored first in every game, and they outscored the

Padres 13–4 over the first and second innings. The corps of San Diego starting pitchers, to be sure, did not distinguish itself in any way, and even in Game Two, which the Padres eventually won, the first three Tiger hitters (Gibson was up third) ripped singles off Ed Whitson on his first three pitches of the day; after the game, the Padre catcher, Terry Kennedy, said that he'd contemplated calling a pitchout on the next delivery, just so he could handle the ball. Once aboard, the Tiger base runners yearned to be farther along. The most significant play of the first game, in the opinion of Tom Lasorda (on hand as a columnist for *USA Today*), was Kirk Gibson's unsuccessful steal of second in the fifth inning—a plain message about the Tigers' battle plan, which was to run, rather than to play it safe and wait for their power to bring people home. Many clubs seem to think that they lack the personnel to make this option available, but hit-and-run and taking an extra base is mostly a state of mind, implanted (or cautiously suppressed) by the manager. The Tiger skipper, Sparky Anderson, is a man of zeal, and his teams at their best give their opponents the impression that they are about to be *buried* in a game—as, indeed, they often are. And this year— let's face it—Sparky had the horses. Kirk Gibson, to name one horse, is a slugger by any measurement, but he is also the fastest man on the Tiger roster. The other prime indicator in Game One (in the opinion of *this* bystander) was an ugly little two-base error by the young Padre left fielder, Carmelo Martinez, in the fourth inning—a misjudgment that seemed to paralyze him, afield and at bat, for the rest of the week, thus adding to the burdens of the Padres, who had already lost another starting outfielder, Kevin McReynolds, because of an injury.

The Padres' comeback win in Game Two was made possible by some startling relief pitching by a young right-hander, Andy Hawkins, and a young left-hander (and terrific screwballer), Craig Lefferts, who between them muffled the Tiger offense over the last eight and one-third innings. The winning runs came in on a three-run homer by their raffish and exuberant veteran designated hitter, Kurt Bevacqua, who did pirouettes and threw kisses to the crowd as he rounded the bases. All this was vastly appreciated by the cacophonous, Wave-running local multitudes—far and away the loudest baseball audience I have ever encountered. Some aspects of the San Diego persona elude me— I am thinking of the persistent, semi-weepy references to the team's late owner, Ray Kroc, the millionaire McDonald's-hamburger man, in the local journals and news shows, where he

was depicted as being almost visibly in attendance at the revels—
but I took pleasure in the game and its result. Most of all, I
admired the top two men in the Padre order, second baseman
Alan Wiggins and right fielder Tony Gwynn, who for a time
almost rivalled the Whitaker-Trammell wizardry at the plate.
Wiggins, who is a switch hitter, is skinny and quick, and a
master of the push bunt—the exquisite little offensive tap that
must be rolled just to the pitcher's left and *past him*, so that the
play (no play at all, usually) can be made only by the inrushing
first baseman. He is a useful foil for Gwynn, who sees an inordinate number of fastballs from pitchers who don't want Wiggins to steal second, and thrives on them; his .351 led the
National League this year, but it was .413 when Wiggins was
on base. Gwynn is chunky and aggressive, and mobile in the
batting box: a left-handed Bill Madlock up there—a pistol.

We repaired to Tiger Stadium for Game Three, the unen-
thralling contest in which the Padres' pitchers almost walked the
ball boys along with everyone else; no explanation for it, nothing to be said. It was 5–2, in the end, with twenty-four base
runners left aboard by the two clubs. Game Four, on Saturday,
was pretty well over by the third inning, by which time Alan
Trammell had hit two home runs into the left-field stands against
Eric Show—one downstairs, one upstairs—each of them with
Whitaker aboard. The Detroit starter was Morris (back from his
victory in the opener), who threw first-class fastballs and down-
breaking split-fingered semi-fastballs, almost all of them strikes;
somebody keeping count declared in the eighth that he had delivered one ball in his previous twenty-one pitches. He won
4–2, cruising.

Morris, who has won a hundred and three games for the Tigers over the past six summers (only the Phillies' Steve Carlton,
with a hundred and six, has more), is an exceptional athlete and
a violent competitor who would succeed, no doubt, with any
club, but Roger Craig has had a part in his making. Craig, the
Detroit pitching coach, is the Leonardo da Vinci of the split-
fingered fastball, which he claims to have invented at his own
California baseball school a few years back, when he was in-
structing teen-agers and was looking for a variant pitch that
would not damage their arms. The pitch is not the old forkball,
which is held more deeply between forefinger and middle finger,
and which, being spinless, behaves a good deal like the knuckler; this delivery arrives more quickly, looking very much like
a fastball until its late little pause and duck, which result in

handfuls of lovely four-hop ground balls. Craig has taught the pitch to anyone on the Tiger club who was interested, including the catcher–third baseman Marty Castillo, who had such success with it on the sidelines that he had sudden wild hopes of becoming a pitcher as well. Craig's prime pupil is probably Milt Wilcox, a veteran righty starter with fourteen years in the bigs; on Craig's advice, he substituted the s.-f.fb. for his rather shopworn slider this year and, despite some chronic long-term aches and frays in his arm and shoulder, came up with a 17–8 summer—by far the best of his career. Craig, by the way, calls the Tiger pitchers' pitchouts and pickoff moves from the bench—not always on pure hunch. Late in the final game, when the Padres had a pinch-runner, Luis Salazar, on first, Craig, who had been eying the Padre dugout from across the field, suddenly announced, "Salazar is going and we've got his ass." So he was and so they did: he was picked off on the next pitch.

Like most coaches, Roger Craig has been around. He coached for the Padres, and moved up to be their manager in 1978 and '79; before that, he had managed and coached in the minors. Early Mets masochists will remember him as a tall, extremely patient mound stalwart who lost twenty-two games for the good guys in 1963—an improvement over 1962, when he lost twenty-four. Before *that*, to be sure, he was a successful starter with the Brooklyn Dodgers. He is an engaging, lanky North Carolinian, with a sizable nose and a pleasing resemblance to the late Slim Summerville. Before one of the games, he was telling some of us about his first look at the major leagues, back in July 1955, when he and another rookie pitcher, Don Bessent, were suddenly called up to join the Dodgers. "I was with our Montreal club on a road trip down in Havana, where I was supposed to pitch on a Sunday against the Havana Sugar Kings," he said, "but my manager, Greg Mulleavy, called me in and said no, I was pitching against the Reds on Sunday, in Ebbets Field. I called my wife collect, and she asked what the hell was I doing calling long-distance all that way, and I said, 'I'm goin' to the big leagues.' Well, Bessent won his game and I won mine—I pitched a three-hitter, and it was the first major-league game I'd ever seen—and when it was over Walter Alston told me I'd better fly back to Montreal and get my wife, since I was a major-league pitcher now. I didn't have but a dollar on me, and I had to borrow the money. Jackie Robinson, he drove me to the airport. I'll never forget that."

TIGER STADIUM, AS THE END DREW NEAR, WAS ROILING AND
pleasure-mad. It didn't quite come up to San Diego for pure
noise, but Detroit fans certainly know how to express themselves. Over the summer, the turned-on Tiger-made throngs
evolved simultaneous clockwise and counter-clockwise Waves
in the upper and lower decks, which then somehow reversed
themselves. Sometimes there came a funny, slow-motion Wave
in the center-field bleachers (always a place of humor and invention this summer), which would be succeeded by a right-to-
left sprint Wave that could circle the stadium (I clocked it) in
twenty-seven seconds flat. There was also the foolish, comical
business of the two bleacher sectors' yelling a beer commercial
back and forth ("TASTES GREAT!" from one side, and then "LESS
FILLING!" from the other) while brandishing fingers and programs at each other. Other worked-up routines involved rotating
hands and jingling car keys—God knows how they started, or
why—and, of course, banner variations on this summer's inescapable "BLESS YOU BOYS" campaign slogan, which, I believe,
was born on WDIV, the local TV channel, no comma and all.
Tiger Stadium is a steep-sided, squared-off city enclosure, whose
boxy dimensions, like those of many ballparks back then, were
dictated by the cross streets and avenues that hem it in. Downtown stadiums like this (Comiskey Park, in Chicago, is the other
surviving relic) seem to hold and intensify the sounds and hopes
and intimate oneness of their crowds, and when you're inside,
watching your team (in its old brilliant home whites, with the
same famous, old-timey gothic initial) violently at play, it's possible to wonder for a moment which decade you are in and
which wonderful, hero-strewn lineup is on view down there, in
the instant of its passing from action to history. Just above my
vertiginous press-row perch, high in the park, I could see the
"ꟽUIGAT≀ ЯƎϼIT" sign on the roof, with each of its tall letters
illuminated in blue neon, and for another odd instant I felt as if
I were in one of those rooftop "ⱢƎTOH" chase scenes in a black-
and-white gangster movie, with the watching crowds breathless
below.
    All through the playoffs and all through the Series so far,
Sparky Anderson had kept telling us that we hadn't really seen
the Tigers yet—the Tigers doing it all: the hitting and the power
and speed all together in one game, the Tigers at their best—but

in Game Five that happened at last. The obligatory first-inning
explosion (against Mark Thurmond this time) was for three runs,
with the first two sailing home, on surges of noise, on Kirk
Gibson's first-pitch homer into the second deck. The third was
scored because Parrish, up next, singled *and then stole second*,
and came in on a single. A bit later, there was a double steal.
The Padres, it will be recalled, obdurately tied things up again
in the fourth, but Gibson, back on first base after a single in the
fifth, tagged up and thundered down to second after a deep fly
to left field—a play one sees very rarely indeed—and when he
scored, a moment or two later, on a very short sacrifice fly, the
Tigers went ahead for the winter.

The rest of it probably didn't matter, but it was nearly pure
pleasure. Aurelio Lopez, the other famous and stubborn Detroit
reliever, worked some quick innings, sometimes seeming to dismiss a San Diego batter with a blur of slicing strokes, like a
Japanese sushi chef (when he and the Padres' Craig Lefferts
were in the game over the same stretch, we had a marvellous
assortment of tough, hard pitching stuff on display); and Garvey
and Templeton pulled off a dazzling three-six double play for
the other guys, with Tempy making the tag on Marty Castillo's
fingertips down at second. Lance Parrish came up in the seventh, and in came Goose Gossage for the Padres (the loud-
speakers played the "Ghostbusters" theme full blast, with the
fifty-one-thousand-voice home-town choir roaring out "GOOSE-
BUSTERS!" in the right places), and Lance busted the Goose,
smacking a line drive into the lower left-field pavilion on the
second pitch, for a two-run lead, and I think it was about then
that I spotted a little parade of stadium venders, in their red-
striped jackets, snake-dancing down an upper-deck aisle with
their boxes held up over their heads.

The party still wasn't over, though, for the Tigers put runners
on second and third in the eighth, with the discouraged Padres'
mistakes helping a bit now, and there was a mound conference
about the open base, at which Gossage somehow persuaded
Dick Williams to let him pitch to the waiting and wildly hopeful
Gibson. I couldn't *believe* it, and neither could Sparky Anderson, in the dugout, who flashed a little one-hand-up five-dollar
bet to Gibson, in the on-deck circle, that Gossage would never
pitch to him—to which Gibson responded with all ten fingers:
Ten bucks he will, and I'm going to hit it out. And so he did,
on the second pitch—a heater down the middle and then, very
quickly, up into the middle rows of Topside Section 436. Gibson

circled the bases, rejoicing as he went, and came home with some very nice totals for the day: two homers, three runs, five runs batted in, ten bucks, and one World Championship. The score at the end was 8–4.

Kirk Gibson was an All-American flanker back at Michigan State, and he chose a career in baseball, as against one with the National Football League, almost at the last moment. Baseball hasn't been easy for him. He played in the minors for two years and then put in the better part of three seasons with the Tigers before he became a regular; a year ago, he went through a tortured .227 season, in which he raged at his coaches and his manager and the local writers and (most of all, of course) at himself. This year, he got it together, and then some; there are many baseball people who think he could be the next Mickey Mantle. He is twenty-seven years old, with a thick neck and enormous shoulders, but when you see him up close—in the middle of a boisterous clubhouse party, say, with his blond hair soaked with champagne, and his pale, darting eyes alight with triumph—your first, startled thought is: Look how young he is! Why, he's just a kid—it's all just beginning for him. Quite a few of the Detroit players look like Gibson; tall and aggressively athletic, with little gunslinger mustaches and an air of great, insouciant confidence. The Tigers are of different ages and temperaments and degrees of experience, but there is a sense about them—I felt it all summer—that they are just beginning. Next year will be different—it always is—and, as Sparky Anderson has said, it will be much, much harder, but still . . . If baseball wants a dynasty, why not start here?*

---

*Why not, indeed? But the Tigers finished third in the American League East in 1985 and again in 1986, fifteen and eight and a half games out; in 1987, they won their division on the very last day of the regular season but then suffered an unexpected elimination in the championship playoffs at the hands of the Minnesota Twins, who went on to beat the Cardinals in the World Series as well. Sparky's Muhammad Ali, an imperial baseball power for our times, has yet to step forward, and each autumn we writers and experts fall victim to the wishful delusion that the skills and vivid demeanor of this year's World Series winner will prevail in the coming season, when in truth the fixed factor in our game just now is that champions do not repeat.

◆ ◈ ◆

SEVEN

Taking Infield

BILL RIGNEY (FORMER INFIELDER, NEW YORK GIANTS; former manager, Giants, Angels, Twins): "Sometimes you should remind yourself that of all the things we have in this game—hits and runs and stolen bases and home runs—the thing we have the most of is outs. So it's important to be able to catch the ball out there and then to know what to do with it. You can't give a major-league team four outs in an inning and expect to win."

Frank White (second baseman, Kansas City Royals): "I don't notice that anybody thinks about defense a lot—not the fans, not all the managers, not even the front office. If they find some infielder who can hit, they're more likely to go with that kind of player than stay with one who can field and not hit much. The theory is that you can always shake another defensive infielder out of the trees when you want one. I don't believe it. Baseball is offense-minded because the fans like that. Defense isn't discussed unless your club is going good and it's close to World Series time."

Clete Boyer (coach, Oakland A's; former third baseman, Athletics, Yankees, Braves): "First basemen have a lot more to think about than third basemen. The shortstop—I don't know what's the hardest play for him. They're *all* hard, I guess. There's not much of a problem for him on the double play, because the whole situation's right in front of him, but the second baseman— he knows he's got to turn that thing, and the guy's breathing down his neck. You can get your legs torn up. More often than not, you see the second baseman turn it when he didn't have a chance, really. The judgment of infielders is something.''

Keith Hernandez (first baseman, New York Mets): ''There's a small percentage of left-handed batters today who are real pull hitters. There's an even smaller number of right-handed hitters who can hit the ball away and up the line. I play away from the bag, and that lets our second baseman play more up the middle than what's done on most clubs. I've got enough range so that I can be very aggressive about going for anything in the hole.''

Dave Concepcion (shortstop, Cincinnati Reds): ''I think being able to play the infield, especially playing shortstop, is something you're born with. You can't learn it—you have to have that ability from the beginning.''

No, we fans will never quite learn this game, but there are rewards in trying. We can't step up to bat or take infield or get to play, ever, but we can look and listen and, most of all, try to make ourselves notice what we've been watching all along. Spring is the best time for this, before we get involved in scores and standings, or are distracted by hope. Players and coaches and managers are more willing to reflect on their profession when you approach them in the preseason: bring a notebook and a good No. 10 sunscreen—mornings and afternoons were a white blaze in Florida and Arizona this year—and, with luck, you can improve yourself in the happiest fashion, which is to learn something you thought you already knew. This March, as the names of the deponents above suggest, I tried to sharpen up my infielding, and within days I felt more alert to all the different ways the ball is picked up and got rid of in the quicker instants of the pastime. Once again, I discovered how much more difficult baseball is than I had imagined. Although these seminars seemed less exacting than those I encountered in a recent survey course in catching, I soon understood that this was because infielding is a fine art, not a science—an aesthetic to be thrillingly glimpsed but, as Dave Concepcion suggested, never quite understood. The conventional wisdom about spring training is that it doesn't mean anything (it is never mentioned in the sporting press after the bell rings), but its languid, noncombative pace suits me very well, I find, not only for the pursuit of some special baseball discipline but because it provides me and the other early fans with a procession of trifling moments and glimpses and connections that feed our intuition about players and teams and skills, and so keep us in the game.

◆ ◆ ◆

I BEGAN MY INFIELD TUTORIALS ON THE VERY FIRST DAY OF MY trip, and I tried to keep at them every day, waylaying practitioners or infield coaches or managers who came my way, and asking them what was hard or easy or unappreciated about their work in the field. I happily took whoever came along—some veterans, some journeymen, a few famous performers, some newcomers. All of them were established professionals. They didn't always agree with one another, of course, and I quickly realized that I lacked the expertise to weigh or evaluate their responses, even if I had wanted to. There is no right way to pick up a one-bounce rocket at third base, or to charge a soft hopper at second and make a whirling flip to the shortstop as he crosses the bag off to your right, and many of the men I talked to said that they themselves weren't always quite clear how they made the hard plays. The personalities of the different infielders—thoughtful, impatient, ironic, exuberant—seemed a very important part of their style of play, as they described it, and the number and variety of the answers I gathered left me with a flickering, videolike impression of the ways infielders do their work, rather than with any freeze-frame rules or certitudes. "How do you do what you do out there?" I kept asking, and the answer was mostly, "Any way I can."

Jerry Remy, who has put in ten years at second base with the Angels and the Red Sox, told me that positioning himself in the field before every pitch required him to pick up the catcher's signal to the pitcher about the forthcoming delivery, to which he added his accumulated knowledge and hunches about the abilities and habits of the batter, and of the base runner (if any). Most of all, though, he had to know his pitcher. "With Bob Stanley pitching, I wouldn't play a dead-pull left-handed hitter the way I would if it was Roger Clemens pitching, let's say, because nobody pulls Stanley. Stanley is easy. He doesn't walk anybody, and you get almost all ground balls, because of that sinker. I played behind Nolan Ryan a couple of years, and you could throw all that stuff out the window, because the batters were just trying to make contact. There were high counts and fouls and walks and—well, it wore you out. Then, if you've got a real quick base runner on first—a Rickey Henderson, say—it makes a tremendous difference in the way the whole infield plays. On bunt situations then, I've got to be cheating toward second base all the time. If the runner fakes a steal and you make one little move toward second to cover, you can be dead: the ball's hit by you. If he's on second, you got to be keeping him close, and that means you might miss anything hit off on the first-base side. A runner doesn't even need a whole lot of speed to make that work. A team like the Tigers doesn't have all that much speed, but they think aggressively on the bases, and that changes the way you have to play them.''

Remy, who is thirty-two, has a narrow face, a small mustache, and a contained, street-smart way of talking. I was surprised and then touched by his willingness to talk about his work at all, for it had been announced only the day before that he was probably finished as a second baseman. Once a wonderfully quick and spirited infielder, he has played with increasing difficulty over the past six seasons, as a result of an accident in July 1979, when he caught his spikes while sliding into home plate at Yankee Stadium. Five operations on his left knee have failed to relieve the intense pain he feels whenever he attempts the twisting pivot at second base in the middle of a double play, and now he was trying to hang on with the club as a pinch-hitter. I suggested to Jerry that he might not want to talk to me just then, in view of the news, but he smiled and made a dismissing gesture. "It doesn't hurt to talk," he said. (Just before the season opened, the Red Sox, trimming their roster to the obligatory twenty-five players, placed him on the twenty-one-day disabled list—a message that the club had decided that it couldn't afford to keep him on only as a pinch-hitter. He took the news in good part—there were no hard feelings, he told me by telephone— and he and Dr. Arthur Pappas, the Red Sox physician, have just decided that one more arthroscopic procedure, the sixth and final surgical tinkering, might possibly relieve his pain. No major surgery would be attempted. "I want this because it will settle things once and for all," Remy said. "I didn't like the idea of just being a pinch-hitter—not playing the infield at all. This way, I can get better and be a real player again, or else that's it—it's over and I'll know it, and I'll go on to the next thing. So it's all right.")

Remy said that the most difficult play for him at second base had always been the one on a ball hit off to his left, with a base runner on first, which meant that he had to turn completely around, spinning three hundred degrees or so and making the throw back to second with the same motion. We were sitting side by side on a railroad-tie embankment next to the Red Sox batting cages, and as Remy described this he made a little half-turn in illustration, with his arms reaching to his left for the invisible ball; the gesture of his upper body was like a snapshot, and I had a sudden flash of Remy in the field again, making the play.

"If that ball's hit at all soft, you're probably not going to make the play," he went on. "But even if you think you've got a chance, you'll tend to rush your throw, and the ball can fly all over the place. You want to try to take the extra second to make that throw. Turning the double play can be real tough, of course. I always try to hit the bag with my left foot when I'm taking the throw. Then I can either back off or go across or go behind the bag, depending on the situation. The hardest D.P. is probably going to come on the throw over to you from third base, because the runner's going to be a little closer. You end up making all different kinds of pivots and throws, depending on who's giving you the ball. When Carney Lansford played here, his ball from third was always the same, and you could count on getting off your own same throw across to first. A guy like Wade Boggs, now, his throw tends to sink. If the man at third doesn't have such good control, or if it's a tough play of some kind for him, I'll try to straddle the bag, if I can get there in time, so's to be more ready. Then when I do go to first—well, I guess I've made every kind of throw there is."

I asked where such things could be learned and perfected, and Remy said that most of his habits afield had been instilled years ago, when he was a young infielder coming up in the Angels system and had worked with a coach named Bob Clear. "I've used the same moves ever since, I guess," he said. "Things like going over to the bag a little bit bent, so you can handle the ball better and get it off quicker. And if you're there a little early, even staying *behind* the base, so if there's a wild throw you're not stretched out by being up on top of the bag. Adjust to the ball, adjust to the base runner. If you ask me after the game how I made the play, I probably can't tell you. If I've got Don Baylor comin' in on me, I'm sure not thinking about how it's done. But at least in certain situations — say, first and third, with less than two outs—you know they'll be coming after you. A select few will take a crack at you every time. Baylor's probably the best at it—or he was when he could run better. Hal

McRae, of course. George Brett. Hrbek does it well. Winfield, because he's so damn big—he can slide five feet out of the base-line and still take you down. Big guys with speed are what you watch for. With all that going on, I don't think there's anybody playing second base who can say he's real technical about it. There's no time for that—you just get it done. You do it in infield practice and then in games, but you don't work on it, if you see what I mean. You take extra batting practice all the time, but in my whole career I never practiced taking extra double plays.''

Marty Barrett, who replaced Remy at second for the Red Sox last year (and batted .303 in the process), mentioned most of the same runaway-truck base runners that Remy had listed for me, and threw in Reggie Jackson and Chet Lemon for good measure. ''You have to have an idea about these guys and how they come at you,'' he told me. ''But knowing the batters—knowing where to play them all, and being with the pitcher—is the main thing. You pick that up quicker than you'd think. I won't have to make as many tough plays this year, because I'll be positioning myself better. Of course, I was up with the Sox for most of '83, even though I didn't get in a lot of games, and I really paid attention to where Jerry played everybody. Position, and all that—the pitchers, the batters—means everything for me, because I don't have that much range. You look at a Frank White or a Lou Whitaker''—the Gold Glove second baseman with the World Champion Tigers—''and they basically stay within a three- or four-foot spot on the field. I really believe they can play a whole game just from there—they're that quick—while I'll be starting from over in the hole to way up the middle. I'm twenty to thirty feet different, depending on the batter.''

Frank White, it turned out, had just about the same ideas as Barrett about positioning. ''I think as you learn the players more, over the years, the great plays are going to come easier, because you're in the right place and ready for the ball,'' he said to me. ''When I first came up, I was making these super plays all over the place—*wow! hey!*—because I didn't know where I was sup-posed to be. When I knew the hitters and knew the pitchers, that kind of slowed down. I'd learned where to play, I'm saying. Maybe I'm playing better now but getting noticed less.'' He laughed.

White is an engaging fellow—an intelligent, invariably cheer-ful star player, with a dazzling smile. He is thirty-four and has played second base for the Royals for more than eleven seasons, winning six consecutive Gold Gloves through the 1982 campaign; the honor (it is voted by each team's players, coaches, and manager) went to Whitaker the last two years, but you can still get an argument in clubhouses around the league about which of the two is the better second baseman. White told me that there was less sudden body contact around his base now than when he came up. "The runners aren't so bad now that they make them slide a little sooner," he said. "Before they changed the ruling, everything was a cross-body block. When we played the Yankees in the 1977 playoffs, Hal McRae took out Willie Randolph with a shot way over beyond the bag at second—you remember that [I did indeed]—and it was legal, because at that time base runners didn't have to slide at all. They could just run right over you. The rules were changed after that, so at least they have to slide first now. Most of the times now when a guy gets taken out it's on the first-and-second situation or a bases-loaded situation, where the man on first isn't being held close, so he gets down at you in a hurry on an average-hit ball. I've only been hit bad twice, and it was in a bases-loaded situation both times. Once was by Doug DeCinces, back in '78, and I twisted my knee. And then I got hit by Dwight Evans once and landed on my shoulder and missed a couple of weeks."

Two damaging collisions in fifteen hundred-odd games: I expressed amazement.

"I'm *awake* out there," White said. "By the time I get to the base, I know if I'm going to get one or try for two. I never bail out. You only have to bail out if you haven't made up your mind." He told me that a second baseman's throw to first under these circumstances is often less than picture-perfect. Like all fielders, he tries to take the ball with his fingers across the seams when getting off a throw, because the ensuing spin makes the peg much more accurate. "You try to grab seams, but you don't always have time for it," he said. "In most cases, your hand sort of goes there automatically. But on the D.P. sometimes I'm throwing over with three fingers, or even with the ball in the palm of my hand. The general idea is any way you can, and as quick as you can. That's why you appreciate having a real big first baseman over there to throw to—a guy like Steve Balboni, here. It's a comfort to your mind."

◆ ◆ ◆

DAVE CONCEPCION HAS BEEN THE CINCINNATI REDS' SHORT-stop ever since 1970. He played in four World Series and five league-championship playoffs in the nineteen-seventies—the glory days of the Big Red Machine—and he has won five Gold Gloves and has been tapped for nine All-Star Games. Nowadays, other shortstops—Ozzie Smith, Alan Trammell, Cal Ripken, Robin Yount (who has moved to left field this year for the Brewers, because of a shoulder problem), Tony Fernandez—are mentioned before he is in most press-box comparative-lit seminars, but none of them has played as well for as long as he has. (It is the opinion of a lot of front-office people, by the way, that there has rarely been an era in the game when there were as many remarkable athletes on view in the middle-infield positions as there are right now.) Concepcion, in any case, is approaching the end of his career. He had bone chips removed from the elbow of his throwing arm in 1980 and an operation on his left shoulder in 1983. He is thirty-six years old, and looks it—a rangy, narrow infielder (he is six-one), with bony shoulders and a careworn expression. He is a Venezuelan, and speaks with a slight accent. He seemed a bit reticent in talking about his position, but then so was I; perhaps we both felt that playing short is almost too difficult to be put into words.

"For me," he said at one point, "the hard play is always the ball that's hit easy and right at you. You don't know if you should charge it or stay back. You're on your heels, and sometimes you have to stop, so the ball can come to you. The hard ground ball, it comes with the bounces right there, and you can always play the right one—the one you have to. You see what I mean?"

I asked about the play in the hole—the difficult chance that sends the shortstop far to his right to grab the ball and simultaneously plant his right foot for the long, quick throw.

"It's tough, because you got to stretch yourself to get to the ball and right away try to make that good throw. You got no time to get yourself set. Making the throw—that's the main thing. Be quick *and make a good throw.*"

Riverfront Stadium has AstroTurf, and for some years now Concepcion has been making his longer pegs over to first base— especially on plays from the hole—by bouncing the ball on the infield carpet. He does this only on artificial grass, where the bounce is true. The innovation seemed controversial at first, perhaps because it looked so much less pleasing and powerful than the full, airborne throw, but now a few other shortstops have taken it up; some players believe that a bounced throw actually picks up speed as it skips off the carpet. "I use it a lot of the time on AstroTurf now," Concepcion said. "I first saw that when Brooks Robinson did it at Riverfront in the World Series of 1970. He got a ball hit down the line way behind third and got rid ot it, *bang!*''—he slapped his hands together—''like only he could do. It bounced, but Boog Powell dug it out, and they got the runner. I couldn't hardly believe it. It was in the second game of that Series, I think. I don't think Brooksie meant it—he had no chance, you know—but I thought about it that winter. I could still see the play. Then I had elbow trouble the next spring, so I began trying it—but on purpose, you know, to protect my arm. Our first baseman—it was Lee May; Perez was later—didn't complain, and I kept on with it. On turf, it's a good play. Brooks Robinson started it, but I registered the patent.''

We discussed some other matters—grabbing seams, relaying the catcher's signals to the third baseman, what it was like to play with Joe Morgan at second base all those years (it was great), why you should always get to the bag early if you're making the throw from second on a double play (because you may throw low but you'll never throw wide that way)—and then there was a pause. ''Defense, it always meant a lot to me,'' he said unexpectedly, glancing at me to be sure I understood. ''Batting gives you some great moments, but defense, it's—Defense is a joy to me every day. I think fans like defense next best to the home runs. I really think that. A lot of guys can catch the ball and make the great play, but not a lot can throw the ball with control. Decent hands and a steady arm is what you want. You got that, you got it made.''

Keith Hernandez is more outspoken and more intense than Concepcion—he exudes confidence and precision in conversation, just as he does on the field—but you hear the same pride in his work when he talks defense. ''I can win a game with my glove just as easy as I can with my bat,'' he said to me. ''The most difficult thing when you're a young player and you're trying to establish yourself is to learn to separate that part of it from the rest of your game. You get in a slump and you tend to take it with you out onto the field. Now when I'm going bad up at bat I make it a point to be good at what I'm doing on defense.''

Hernandez, of course, is *very* good at what he's doing at all levels of the game. He batted .311 for the Mets last year, and finished second to the Cubs' second baseman, Ryne Sandberg, in the postseason balloting for the league's Most Valuable Player. I have hesitated to mention defensive statistics here, since there are so many variables (team pitching, grass and artificial playing surfaces, and so on), but the easiest way to convey Hernandez' exceptional range and mobility is to point out that he had one hundred and forty-two assists in 1984, while the nearest National League first baseman had fewer than a hundred. Hernandez committed eight errors last year; Steve Garvey, who plays first for the Padres, did not make an error all year, but he accounted for only eighty-seven assists.

Not quite believing such evidence, I once asked Hernandez' manager, Davey Johnson, how he appraised the man's work. "That's easy," Johnson said. "He's the best I ever saw."

"I'll make more plays than some, because I'm willing to go so far in the hole" is the way Hernandez explained it. "The hard play for me is when I have to throw overhand from the hole back to a pitcher who's breaking for the bag. It's like being a quarterback throwing to an end on a look-in pattern in football. I want to try to get the ball to him before he gets to the bag—about two steps before, if I can—so he can catch it and then look for the bag. The 3-6-3''—this is the pleasing play when the first baseman takes a grounder, wheels to the shortstop to retire a base runner going down to second, and gets back to his base in time to take the return throw to beat the batter—"used to be tough for me, but it's not so bad now. About six years into my career, I suddenly realized—it just came to me—that there was no point in my waiting around to see if I'd made a good throw in that situation. If I've thrown it away, I've thrown it away. Now I throw the ball and then turn my back and run straight to the bag. You want to be there to take that throw back, because it's the hardest thing in the world for the *pitcher* to get all the way over and make that catch."

I asked if any other first basemen made the 3-6-3 that way.

"Not that I've noticed," he said.

What I understood in time—it just came to me—is that there is nothing defensive about Keith Hernandez' thinking about defense. "How many right-handed hitters can hit the ball up the line to right?" he asked me at one point, and then answered his question at once. "A few. Sandberg does it very well. Moreland does it. Maybe a couple of others. It's funny, but almost nobody who bats left-handed in my league can really pull the ball down the line. If that's true, there's just no point in playing the line so close. In the late innings, you're supposed to stay up next to the line if you're defending a one-run lead, so you won't let a ball get by you for extra bases. Everybody knows that—it's almost a rule—so you see them all playing three feet from the line. But I'll be six feet or more away from it, depending on the batter and the pitch, and that's fine with Davey Johnson—we agree. If you ask most players and managers about it, they'll say yes, of course, you get beat more on balls hit into the hole—it's nine times out of ten, I think—but they don't play it that way. It's ridiculous.''

PLAYING THE INFIELD REQUIRES A PERPETUALLY HONED ANTI-cipation, and if you make yourself watch for them you can almost always notice the little quirks and twitches that each player at an infield position uses to bring himself onto his toes at the instant the pitch is delivered, with his body poised in preparation for a ball suddenly smashed in his direction. (Frank White believes that this constantly repeated preliminary little hop, made thousands of times over a season, wears down infielders' knees and quadriceps muscles over the years, and may be even more damaging in the long run than playing on AstroTurf.) What you can't pick up, for the most part, is the accompanying small dialogue of signals that constantly flies about this four-man perimeter a moment or two before that—the language of defense. As I have indicated, both the shortstop and the second baseman peer in at the catcher to pick up his sign to the pitcher about the next pitch—a sign that cannot be seen by the first or third baseman, of course. They—the middle pair, I mean—will lead or edge a bit to one side or the other in response, and if the pitch is to be a breaking ball, one or the other will also relay the message to the infielder at his corner—to the first baseman if there's a left-handed hitter up, or to the third sacker if it's a right-handed hitter. A word will do it: if Leon Durham, a left-handed swinger with the Cubs, is to see a breaking ball from Ron Darling on the next pitch, let's say, Keith Hernandez will hear his second baseman, Wally Backman, say "Keith!" at the instant that Darling is at the top of his windup. It's a trifle—perhaps only a mental knock-on-wood—and probably doesn't help much, but it's there if the first baseman or third baseman wants it. Some *don't* want to know. Jerry Remy said that one of his Boston first sackers, George Scott, never wanted the signal; another, Carl Yastrzemski (he often played first in the latter stages of his career), did want it. There are other messages as well—notably the hand signal or glove flick or special glance between the shortstop and the second baseman with a base runner on first, which determines who is to cover second on the coming play. This, too, is a response to the catcher's sign to the pitcher, for the man who covers will be the one less likely to have the next pitch hit to his side. A common semaphore here is a quick grimace flashed by one man or the other to his partner behind his raised glove—a closed-mouth mime for "Me" or an open mouth for "You." It's nothing much—kids might make up a code like this—but it can be needed thirty or forty times in a game, and it's always done. The keystone pair must also understand which of them is to make the first try at a ball that is chopped over the pitcher's head and short of second—a very hard chance that is usually taken by the shortstop, since his momentum is toward first base. But they must *know*. Frank White said that all this comes as second nature to him by now, but that sometimes the burden of so many repeated and altered fragments of intelligence—letting the shortstop know, letting the first baseman know, and sometimes relaying signals from the bench to the Royals outfielders about which direction to shade in a tough situation—can suddenly be too much. "I get a mental blowout now and then," he said. "I can't handle it, and then I tell my coaches I'm going to beg off from that for a couple of days and let the shortstop be the main man. The mental strain is unbelievable sometimes."

Buddy Bell, the Texas Rangers' third baseman, doesn't want to know the next pitch to the batter. "I gave up looking for signs on breaking balls, because I found I was cheating too much," he told me. "I was counting on it, and I'd begun putting myself out of position. I'd rather just go on the situation and what I know about the batter." Then he added, "Besides, we've had a big turnover of pitchers on this club in the past few years." This took me a minute: Bell was saying that there weren't many Ranger pitchers just now whom he trusted to put the ball where it was meant to go on the next pitch—to throw what the catcher had asked for.

Bill Rigney had already mentioned the same thing. Rig (he is sixty-six years old, but still has the eager gaze and lanky quickness of gesture of the born infielder) said that he had noticed a recent decline in strategic conversations between infielders and pitchers in hard situations—the moment when a shortstop or third baseman might step over to the mound in a jam and murmur, "Where do you want me? How are we going to come at this guy?" Rigney said, "I can remember times on the Giants when there were men on base and all, and I'd go in and ask Sal Maglie or Larry Jansen, and they'd say, 'With this guy, play him in the hole, because the way I pitch him, that's where he's going to hit it.' But I noticed with some other pitchers we had, they'd always say, 'Play him straight away.' That was because they didn't know *what* the batter was going to do, or where the pitch would be. They had no idea.''

Buddy Bell is the nonpareil third baseman in his league—perhaps in both leagues. He looks all wrong for an infielder—he's six feet two, with powerful shoulders and a long upper body; with his blond hair and mild blue eyes, he reminds you of a Southern Cal football player. Actually, he grew up in Cincinnati, and is the son of the Reds' (and dawn-Mets') outfielder-slugger Gus Bell. Buddy Bell played third for seven years with the Indians and is now starting his seventh season with the Rangers at the same position. He's thirty-three years old, and last year batted .315 and picked up his sixth consecutive Gold Glove. He has an outstanding arm, he is durable (he plays about a hundred and fifty games, year after year), and his manner is efficient, pleasantly brusque, and (you learn in conversation with him) ironic—essential attributes for a third baseman, it seems, if you stop and think about the position a little: they must deal with those bazooka shots that are lined past them or *at* them, and must also cope with the sneaky, skulking bunt down the line, baseball's shiv in the ribs. When they fail, as they often must, they look terrible—flat on their bellies in the dirt behind the bag, or foolishly grabbing at the bunted ball in the grass . . . and missing it altogether.

''I play a deeper third than most,'' Bell said to me, ''and that kind of takes the do-or-die away from the play on that hard-hit ball down the line. You can cover more ground if you're back a little deeper and can still make the throw. Third basemen need a rock-hard body—I hope we're getting away from the rock-hard hands a little. No, you really need some kind of hands to play the position now. The infields aren't as good as they used to be, and with the artificial turf now . . .'' He winced and shook his head. ''Defense is the most important part of the game. If you don't believe that when you start out, you learn it pretty soon playing third. You let a ball go through, and it's probably the ballgame. I'd say that ninety-five percent of the pitchers have serious trouble in a game if there's been an error at third and a ball's gone through that shouldn't have. Most of 'em sort of blow up after that. So you're out there not only protecting yourself and your team but knowing that the pitcher is relying on you to do well. Dimensional ballplayers''—he meant the ones who can play all aspects of the game—''are easy to find, because there aren't all that many of them.''

I asked how he tried to defend against the obligatory-bunt situation—the strategic late-inning tangle that begins with base runners on first and second, no outs, and an unthreatening, bottom-of-the-order batter up at the plate.

"On that play—well, first, it depends on who the runner is coming down to third, and who the pitcher is," he said. "Then, if the ball's bunted down toward me I try to draw an imaginary line up the infield between the pitcher's mound and the third-base line, and anything that's hit to the right of it should be mine. Either way, I've got to call it—yell to the pitcher which one of us is going to make the play, or try to. But that's a tough, tough chance. You have to make the decision, and if you don't make it right you may not get the runner you want—you may not get *anybody*. I don't mind the swinging bunt"—the sudden surprise tap, for a base hit—"so much, because it's just a yes-or-no thing: you make the play or you don't. There's no think in it."

Rigney had said that there was more of an effort being made these days to defend against that late-inning must-bunt situation than there had been in his time, and he cited the Chinese-fire-drill set plays that send the first and third basemen charging in on the squared-around bunter, with the second baseman dashing to cover first and the shortstop whirling over to race the front base runner down to third base.

Clete Boyer agreed. "Baseball is a lot of little things," he said. "You keep learning them and trying them out. There's always something new."

Clete is forty-eight now and looks a little heavier than he was when he was playing third base for the Yankees and the Braves, back in the sixties—he put in sixteen years at the hot corner, in all—but it's hard to think of him in anything but a baseball uniform. He and his brothers, Ken and Cloyd, make up one of baseball's first families. (Ken, who died a couple of years ago, also played third base, of course, mostly for the Cardinals, and later managed the Cards, too; Cloyd, a pitcher, is now a coach with the Syracuse Chiefs.) Clete talks baseball almost stolidly, with a little Ozark legato in his husky voice—the family comes from western Missouri—but his face lights up wonderfully once he gets into it a little.

"There are those bunt situations you plan about, and all," he said to me one morning in Phoenix, "but I still think the hardest play at third is when you've got a man on second who can steal a base and a left-handed batter up at the plate who can bunt.

You've got to play up front on the grass and you know what they're thinkin'. My great example for that kind of trouble is Aparicio and Nellie Fox''—Luis Aparicio, the Hall of Fame shortstop with the White Sox and the Orioles in the nineteen-fifties and sixties, and his stellar Chicago second-base teammate, Nelson Fox. "They could work that just perfect. If there's none out or one out, I've got to guess on each pitch if Luis is going to steal or if Nellie's up there to bunt. If I think Luis is stealing and he breaks, I got to get back and cover third, and then if Fox bunts the ball it's a base hit. If I break in two steps instead of one toward the plate, I can't get back—it's all over. Fans look at you playing back on the grass and grabbing that big line drive, but that play's routine, really. The other part is where the game is played.''

We went back to the must-bunt a bit, and after a while I suddenly realized that Clete had changed sides in the midst of the conversation. He was like a chess Grand Master expounding upon the Nimzowitsch Defense who had shifted over to the white pieces. "You can't always protect against that bunt in the same way, you know,'' he said. "You can't always charge, or stuff like that, because I can kill you once I see that. I think you might have your third baseman charge that bunt two or three times in a season, but not more, and that would depend on who you had running at second base. We''—he meant the Oakland A's—"beat Cleveland three times in the last two years because they always charged their third baseman and first baseman. When that happens, I tell the batter either to take the pitch or else hit away. Forget the bunt, and if you swing don't give me a little half-assed effort up there. Don't fall into their trap. Mike Heath hit a ball that went three inches past Toby Harrah's head one day, and we win the game. Last year, Tony Phillips hit a little plinker up the middle for us, but their second baseman was goin' over to first to cover, and the shortstop is way down here by third, and nobody can get near the ball. We got five runs in the inning.''

◆ ◆ ◆

THE SCHOOL TERM IS OVER, BUT I THINK WE SHOULD CALL BACK our distinguished infield faculty for a few more pointers. I did not talk to these players and coaches in a group, of course, but the same subjects kept coming up. There was a great deal of talk about infield surfaces, for instance—grass versus artificial turf. (Six parks in the National League now have the chemical carpet, while six have grass; in the American League, there are four synthetic-turf diamonds and ten natural.) "If you got a turf field, you have to have middle infielders who can *move*—people who can cover a degree of ground very quickly," Frank White said. "I've played on turf all my career. It's a cleaner game— no bad hops, no dust blowin' in your face, or stuff like that. Turf shows all your natural ability—your quickness, your leg strength, your range. Most of all, it tests your durability, because it does wear you down. You also find out that when you're planting your foot to make the throw over to first you almost have to take an extra little jab-step on turf. It grabs your leg so quick you'll lose your balance without that, and *that's* hard on your legs, too. My biggest complaint about turf is the pounding you take."

Jerry Remy likes the better bounce on the carpet, too, but almost nothing else. Ground balls hit right at him are less of a strain on turf, he said (*everyone* said this), but the ball seems to pick up speed after the bounce. "I hold my glove a little looser playing on turf, because the ball can spin right out," he said. "I play back, of course—sometimes I'm so deep I wonder if I can ever get the ball over to first in time. But even then somebody will hit a little bouncer up the middle that goes right by you, and you think, My God, how did *that* go through? I like to hit on artificial grass, but I don't like to field on it."

Bill Rigney told me that, as a group, the athletes playing the middle infield now were undoubtedly better than the ones who had played in his time, and that this was due in great part to the demands of artificial turf. "A few years back, a lot of clubs were just making do at short and second, but that's impossible nowadays," he said. "If you think about it, you begin to notice that the teams who get to play in the Rose Bowl every year" —this is Rigneyese for playing in the World Series—"are the ones who can put an Ozzie Smith or a Cal Ripken out there. Yount and Frank White and Trammell and Sandberg and that little Whitaker—there's a whole gang of them. I admire them— even though Mr. Ozzie has made so many kids coming up try to play one-handed, the way he does. But, you know, there's been a price. That pretty play by a shortstop or a second base- man on a ball hit over second is just about gone. That was one of the nicest things in the game—you enjoyed it—but now almost anything that's through the box is gone. It's a base hit."

Steve Garvey, whom I saw for a few minutes before a Padres- Giants game in Arizona, told me that it was the shifting back and forth from one surface to another that took it out of your legs in time. "I'm fortunate that I've always played on grass at home, but you go out on the road and onto AstroTurf, and your legs suddenly get that pounding," he said. "Then you come back to grass again and your legs stretch out more, and on the second day you'll have a lot of soreness, no matter how good condition you're in. It's like running on pavement and then on the beach." Wet AstroTurf is more slippery than grass, he added—or, rather, is slippery in a special way. Relays from the outfield that strike wet turf become hockey pucks that can shoot right past the cutoff man.

White said that it seemed to take him three or four days of playing on a different surface, either grass or fake grass, before he was quite comfortable again. "What I hate," he said, "is being at home for a couple of weeks and then arriving at a grass-field park on the road, and there's been rain there, or else there's a ceremony before the game or something, so you don't get any infield practice. I just wonder what I'm going to be able to do out there. It shakes you up."

Infields have a barbered look, and infielders compare notes about the "cut" of the various parks—the dimensions of the circular pattern of infield dirt, that is. Municipal Stadium, in Cleveland, recently enlarged its cut; before that, Remy said, it was ridiculously small—almost like a Little League field. "Nobody wants to be back on the grass, so that cut really limited your play," he said. "Anaheim has a big cut, which gives you much better range. I like that, but it's kind of strange there, because everybody looks farther apart. It's like you're playing a different game."

Artificial infields used to be all the same—hard and quick—but now there are variations. The surface at the Metrodome, in Minneapolis, is called SuperTurf, which is softer and spongier than AstroTurf, and thus more forgiving to the infielders' legs, but the bounce is ridiculously high; an infield chop can sail ten feet over the first baseman's head on the first ricochet. For all that, Remy said, he found the bounce there a trifle more consistent than it is on the AstroTurf at Toronto, for instance. Frank White told me he was looking forward to the brand-new turf at Royals Stadium, which has just been refinished with a softer, quick-drying carpet—AstroTurf-8 Drainthru—which is said to offer the closest resemblance to real grass that has yet emerged from the laboratories.

Yankee Stadium has real grass, of course, but Remy dislikes

the hump-backed infield there. "The whole thing slopes away toward the outfield," he said. "It's worst of all from the pitcher's mound on down to the second baseman. Sometimes I get the feeling there that the batter is standing *above* me. You've got to stay real low on a ground ball, or else it can shoot under your glove. You even see that happen to Willie Randolph sometimes." Remy paused and then smiled a little. "Look," he went on, "don't get me wrong about Yankee Stadium. I'd rather play there than anywhere, because of all it means. I *love* to play there."

Infields, whether grass or turf, are as interestingly various as the men who play on them. The grass infield at Jack Murphy Stadium, in San Diego, for instance, is famously unreliable, possibly because its groundskeepers are employees of the city's Parks Department. Garvey told me that it played differently during each Padre home stand last year. "They never could seem to find the right composition," he said. "One time, you'd come home and find that the dirt was so firm that your cleats could hardly dig into it. The next time it would be low tide at the shore. They say it will be better this year, but we've heard that before."

Jerry Remy likes the Fenway Park infield, where the grass is thick and well watered; the bounce there is low but consistent. The dirt at Tiger Stadium is a little quicker than at his home field, he told me, but the grass is slow and kept high—an advantage from a defensive point of view but not much fun to hit on. American League players have complained for years about the infield at Arlington Stadium, the Rangers' home park, where the midsummer Texas sun bakes the dirt to a brick-hard finish, but Remy said it didn't bother him much. "You just expect it to be fast, and it is," he said. "It's like spring training—*all* spring training infields are hard. I think Oakland gives me more trouble than any of the other parks. The dark infield dirt there is O.K. for the first couple of innings, but for some reason it gets chopped up during the game—by the base runners and all—and by the sixth or seventh inning it's like a plowed field. I always figured I was lucky if I finished a series there with nothing against me."

Interdependence was another persistent topic on my "Meet the Infield" show—a recognition that a brilliant pitching staff or an outstanding defensive infielder would in time add to the reputation of adjoining players on the team. "I've always thought it was that super Baltimore pitching staff that's made Dauer such a good defensive second baseman over the years," Clete Boyer

said. "He knows where to play, and with those pitchers—
Flanagan and Palmer and McGregor and the rest—he's playing
right, because of their location. It's always the same. Whitey
Ford made me a great third baseman. Mel Stottlemyre made me
a great third baseman."

Rig mentioned the Baltimore pitchers, too, but added that
Dauer's partners at shortstop for Baltimore—the extraordinary
Mark Belanger and his successor, Ripken—hadn't exactly handicapped the man. All my consultants brought up Belanger sooner
or later, and almost everyone added, as an afterthought, that
Belanger would probably have had a much harder time making
it in the major leagues today, because of his inferior batting.
Belanger, who won gasps and laurels for his range and sureness
at shortstop over an eighteen-year career that ended in 1982,
was a lifetime .228 hitter. Infielders nowadays are expected to
contribute more offense, and Ripken and Ryne Sandberg are
shining role models for the eighties: two years ago, Ripken batted .318 for the Orioles, with twenty-seven home runs and a
hundred and two runs batted in; last summer, Sandberg hit .314
with the Cubs, with nineteen homers and nineteen triples. Each
won a Most Valuable Player award for his efforts. "In my eleven
years, I never saw anybody play shortstop better than Mark Belanger, but he'll never make the Hall of Fame," White said.
"At least, I don't *think* he will. Nobody is called a great ballplayer now unless he can hit. But home-run hitters who can't
really play in the field at all are called great all the time—you
notice that."

Ripken and Ozzie Smith, Whitaker and Trammell and Sandberg—the same names and Gold Gloves popped up again and
again in my interviews, while the older men often went back to
Belanger and Aparicio, and also to Brooks Robinson, and to Bill
Mazeroski, the splendid Pirates second baseman of the nineteen-
fifties and sixties, and to Marty Marion, the tall, elegant Cardinal shortstop of the era just previous. There was no surprise
in this, of course, but what I noticed was that my consultants,
almost as a group, would then quickly make mention of less
celebrated practitioners in their trade and go out of their way to
say warm things about them. They almost *preferred* them, it
seemed, because their skills were on a more mortal level. (I had
observed this same phenomenon a couple of years ago when
I was talking to catchers; many of them made an initial respect-
ful reference to Johnny Bench but then spoke much more warmly
and happily about other, and perhaps lesser, men in that hard

trade.) Rigney, for his part, brought up Manny Trillo ("Such an *easy* player, with those great hands and that good instinct for the game—one look and he always knew where the play was"), and Clete Boyer mentioned Larry Bowa and Bucky Dent. "Bowa can catch the ball hit to him and throw the man out," he said, in his plain, positive fashion. "Bucky could make all the plays. Doesn't have a great arm, doesn't have great speed, but he gets the ball hit to him, and he knows the hitters. That's what you need to get those twenty-seven outs. The fan appreciates the great play, but the coaches and managers sitting in the dugout appreciate the everyday play."

Fair enough. Baseball skills at the major-league level are astronomically beyond the abilities of us in the stands, as I have said, and it is somehow good news that we can never really or wholly understand how the great plays are done, either, no matter how hard we try. If we knew it all, the game would seem less, rather than more. But steadiness, day-to-day accomplishment at the skill positions, is something we can grasp, and now, perhaps, look upon with deeper respect. I should add, too, that I haven't taken up anything like the full range of infield skills and maneuvers in this brief field trip. Rundowns, relays and cutoffs, pickoffs, and the pure mechanics of gloving the ball and then getting rid of it must await some later lessons. If I learned anything from my talks this spring, it was to try to pay closer attention to the game, even to its quickest and yet most familiar moments. Frank White took some time in the Royals clubhouse one day to show me how he makes the tag play at second against a stealing base runner. He wants the base between his feet, he said, and the catcher's throw should be taken in the center line of his own body, and the glove and ball should then be swept straight down—you don't reach out for the incoming ball and pull it back and down, because that takes longer. If the man stealing is a slovenly, spikes-up slider, White may try the play with the base just outside his left foot as he faces the base runner, and then, taking the ball down from a bit more to his left now, make the tag higher up, on the man's thigh, to stay out of trouble. Yes, of course, I understood. A day or two later, I saw Dave Concepcion make that play against Tony Fernandez in a Reds–Blue Jays game in Dunedin. Concepcion took the peg from his catcher, Brad Gulden, a foot or so above the bag and let his mitt droop down toward Fernandez' incoming foot, but at the same instant he leaned his right leg and the entire right side of his body away from the play, toward left field, as he began to depart the scene even while arriving there. Fernandez, sliding, tagged himself out and never made contact with the shortstop at all. He simply wasn't there. It's magic.

◆ ◆ ◆

NEAR THE END, I FOUND COMFORT IN FLORIDA, TOO—AT TERRY Park, in Fort Myers, where the Royals get their spring work done. Fort Myers is seventy-five miles down U.S. 41 from the next-nearest Gulf Coast diamond (at Sarasota), and this distance seems to have preserved the sweetness that I had lately missed in some other spring parks. Dowager nineteen-twenties palms line the narrow downtown avenues of Fort Myers, and some of the old folks coming into the stadium at game time tote little plastic bags of seashells that they have plucked from the beach that morning.* In the park, there is AstroTurf within the bases and green grass beyond—possibly a metaphor representing the 1985 Royals, who have very young pitching and a comfortably mature defense. One afternoon in the press box (an upright, boxy shack that perches on top of the grandstand roof like a diner on a siding), I was startled by a stentorian squawking—"Whooh!" . . . "Whooh!" . . . "Whoo-ooh!"—that progressed by slow degrees around the stands below me, from right field to left. I made inquiry, and was told that this was the Screecher, an ancient local species of fan, who had not missed a Terry Park game for many years. He was Mr. Bruce McAllister, who brought his unique avian rooting here more than twenty years earlier, back when the Pirates were the spring incumbents; before that, I learned, he had screeched at old Forbes Field, in Pittsburgh.

Earlier that day, I had a rewarding conversation with Joe Cunniff, a Chicago teacher who takes the winter semester off every year in order to be near baseball. He is a spring assistant to the Royals' P.R. people, watching over things in the press box, keeping statistics, and the like. The rest of the year, he teaches music and art at De Paul University and the City Colleges of Chicago—adult-education courses, for the most part. He told me that his baseball vacation at Fort Myers was a cultural counterpart of his fellow pedagogues' summer trips to Greece and

_____
*These happy grounds are now lost to big-league baseball. The Royals gave up their Fort Myers camp in 1987 and moved to Orlando, where their spring workouts form part of a "Boardwalk and Baseball" theme park.

Italy. Cunniff is in his upper thirties—an engaging, thick-set baseball zealot with a black mustache and a shy, polite way of talking.

"I love that sound of bats cracking in the morning air," he said at one point. (We were sitting in the cool, shady Royals dugout during batting practice.) "Every year, you see a new player in the games here who sticks out in your mind. Last year, Jack Morris came down here with the Tigers and struck out six of our batters in three or four innings, and I called my brother in Chicago that night and told him that Morris would be unbeatable during the season. Sure enough, Morris came to Comiskey Park in the first week of the season and threw a no-hitter against the White Sox. My brother was *impressed*."

Cunniff said that he'd started out as a White Sox fan as a boy in Chicago, but that in recent years he had become entranced by the pleasures of the bleachers at Wrigley Field and had just about made the great moral switchover to the Cubs. "I suspect that if most people in Chicago really told the truth they'd admit that they're perfectly happy when either team does well, and that they secretly shift over and begin to root for that team and claim it as their own," he said. "Baseball's really about fun, you know, and I don't think we have to have these deep antagonisms. But now the suburbs have discovered the Cubs, and I think it's going to be different from here on. I almost preferred it when they were in last place, and we regulars would be out there in center field, cheering them on. It's the best life you can imagine. Down here, I care about the Royals—they're a great team and a great organization. I go see them and root for them when they come to Chicago, and that way I get to see the writers I know and my other friends in the press box."

One of those friends, Tracy Ringolsby, of the Kansas City *Star-Times*, told me about his favorite moment of spring training at Terry Park last year. An hour or more after the final game of the 1984 spring season, he and a *Star-Times* colleague, Mike Fish, were alone in the press box, clicking out their final preseason wrapups, when they noticed a lone figure out on the diamond. The stands were empty, the players and the groundskeepers had long since left the field, the bases were up, and an angling sun illuminated the field below. The man out there was not in uniform, and he had no glove, but he had stationed himself at shortstop and was taking infield practice—the last workout of the year. It was Joe Cunniff. Unnoticed in their perch, Ringolsby and Fish watched, mesmerized ("It was beautiful,"

Ringolsby told me. "It took your breath away."), as Cunniff charged an invisible slow hopper and flipped sidearm over to second. Then he grabbed a bullet line drive down by his heels and whipped the ball over to first quickly, trying to double off a runner. Then he flew into the hole, far to his right, pulled down the hard grounder, planted his foot, and made the long peg over to first, waiting an instant for the ump's call over there, and then slapping his fist into his phantom glove in triumph: *out!* He had made the hardest play at the hardest position in the game.

EIGHT

◆ ◆ ◆

Summery

MIDSEASON BASEBALL IS A PICNIC AT THE BEACH. WHAT the experienced visitor cares about just now is not so much the water sports or who is ahead in the young people's relay races but the great family chowder cooking here just above the tideline: a warm upbubbling of innumerable tasty ingredients—some hearty and reassuring, others tantalizing and sharp-flavored—which requires many anticipatory sniffings and discussions, and perhaps an icy beer or two to deepen the long afternoon. The metaphor will not be extended by references to the ominous thunderheads gathering off to the west (Will they strike and spoil things?) or to the unpleasant behavior of the picnickers on the next dune. No half season in recent memory has presented so few clear conclusions or has rewarded us more generously. The standings at this writing show three muscular teams in fierce contention in the American League East (in descending order, the Blue Jays, Yankees, and—back a bit now—the Tigers), with the Orioles and the Red Sox only lately beginning to slip from reasonable hope; the California Angels ahead of a plodding pack in the A.L. West; the Padres and Dodgers shoving and shouldering past each other by turns at the top of the National League West; and four attractive competitors (the Cardinals, Mets, Expos, and Cubs) having at each other, often

179

in astounding fashion, in the excellent N.L. East, with the Cubs now falling a bit to the rear. But nothing seems fixed or certain in this summer of 1985 except the certainty of surprise; winning streaks and losing streaks have turned up like summer lightning, exciting or scaring the citizenry and leaving the nearby landscape with an abruptly altered look and feeling. The Minnesota Twins lost nine games in a row and then won ten in a row in the early going; then they *lost* ten in a row. The Toronto Blue Jays, six and a half games in front of their bunch by the first week in June, helpfully dropped six straight games, while the Red Sox, more or less at the same time, suddenly turned savage and won six straight; neither performance proved characteristic. (Bobby Cox, the Toronto manager, ended his team's downturn by managing a Blue Jays game from a seat in the visiting-team bullpen in Milwaukee—"A terrible view," he said later, "but I'd tried everything else.") The Cubs, who won so often and so vividly last summer, got in the spirit of things by losing thirteen straight in the middle of June—and tying an all-time club record. I have consulted a good many front-office and dugout and press-box experts in recent weeks, but no one has seemed to know quite what to make of all these zigs and zags; I lean toward the Gnostic explanation put forward by Fra Wade Boggs, of the Red Sox: "It's the moon."

The Mets, with a six-game and two four-game losing streaks and then a league-high winning spurt of nine straight to their credit so far, have looked as loony as anyone. Loonier. On June 11th, in Philadelphia, they lost to the Phillies by 26–7. The winners' total was the largest number of runs scored by a National League club in forty-one years. Von Hayes, the Philadelphia leadoff man, hit two homers in the first inning, the second one a grand slam, as the Phillies, who had scored twenty-five runs in their previous nine games, put sixteen on the board in their first two turns at bat. And so on—on, perhaps, to the rain-interrupted Mets-Braves game in Atlanta on July Fourth, which was settled at 3:55 A.M. with the Mets on top by 16–13, after nineteen innings; almost everybody (including fourteen pitchers) got to play—which is what one likes to see in these holiday pick-up affairs—and the postgame fireworks began right on the dot of 4:01 A.M. I partook of this encounter at home, and turned off my set well after midnight, after watching the Mets bullpen blow a three-run lead in the bottom of the eighth inning: a decision rivalling Brown v. Board of Education in its wisdom and foresight.

A season of this jumbly sort does not yield to summary or invite extended speculations about the multiple off-the-field issues and crises that continue to afflict the pastime, and neither will be offered here. Like many other fans this summer, I have been going out to the park more often than has been my early custom (attendance is up by seven percent over 1983's banner total and, if we are given an uninterrupted season, seems certain to exceed a total of fifty million for the first time ever), and I can hardly wait to get back there again. What follows, in any case, is a seining of the notes and scorecards and clips and moments that I kept during a couple of busy weeks at the old ball game.

◆ ◆ ◆

I WAS THERE AT SHEA STADIUM WHEN RON DARLING, THE BEST right-handed part-Chinese Yale history major among the Mets starters, shut out the Cubs, 2–0, in the opener of a spirited four-game set in the middle of June. It was the first meeting of the year between the two clubs, and forty-two thousand of us turned out for the fun and angst. Darling's opposite was Rick Sutcliffe, the bearded, six-foot-seven Chicago right-hander, who beat the Mets three times last year in the course of his dazzling 16–1 Cy Young summer and seemed to personify his team's absolute dominance over the young Gotham nine after midseason in 1984. Both squads on hand this time looked a bit frayed, thanks to many recent injuries and losses, and the series, which had lately seemed certain to be fought around the parapets of first place, turned out to be for second and fourth. No matter. There was enough intransigency and mutual dislike on view to hold our attention, with Darling spilling the red-hot Leon Durham with an inside pitch in the second, and Sutcliffe, in a responsive reading, nailing Clint Hurdle in the neck (after two outs: Cy Young pitchers are no dummies) in the bottom half. It seemed to me that Sutcliffe, who had just returned to action after a hamstring pull, was a mite below his best out there, but there was nothing easy or offhand about the Mets' win, with their runs coming on a fourth-inning solo homer by Gary Carter and a fifth-inning double by Danny Heep, which scored the hastening Wally Backman all the way from first. An inning or two later, with matters still at 2–0, Frank Cashen, the Mets general manager, paused by my chair in the press box and murmured, "Typical game for us—right? Another laugher." He wasn't laughing. The Mets, who were then batting a team .230, have been starving for runs all year, and pulling for them has sometimes seemed like rooting for low-cost housing or a higher literacy rate: a good cause but not much fun.

Darling, who went the full nine, repeatedly ran up high counts (or "deep" counts, in the current cant) on the batters, but I noticed that he was often able to deliver his breaking pitches for strikes in such straits, and that he threw first-pitch strikes when defending a lead in the late innings—certifying marks of the arrived, professional moundsman. Now in his second full season as a starter, Darling has put aside some of the reflective self-doubt that he sometimes displayed on the mound when things weren't quite going his way (the rap against him, which I used to hear even in his own clubhouse, was always that he might be "too smart" to be an effective big-league pitcher), and his post-game interviews are less winsome as well. "In the past, I've let walks bother me, but I'm a better pitcher now," he said. "It's a natural evolution—I'd worry about myself if I wasn't."

In the next game, Ed Lynch, a bean-pole right-hander, gave up a run to the Cubs in the very first stanza and then shut them down with six lonely singles for the rest of the evening, as the Mets took it by 5–1. It was Gooden-time the next night—a 1–0, nine-strikeout gem, which ran his record to 10–3—and no lessons to be learned, for once, except the unanswerable logic of overpowering stuff. I missed the game, being caught up in the social ramble (in Satchel Paige's phrase), but found time now and then to tiptoe away to a television set in the next room and there await the next Gooden high heater or glimpse another leaning, distraught batter punched out with the unfair curveball. In some ways, I have decided, it's almost better to catch Gooden on the tube, where the slow-motion replay can show us the real dimensions of these chronic mismatches. Something was clearly wrong with the Cubbies (the Gooden whitewashing was their eighth loss in a row), and I even felt a few unfamiliar pangs of compassion the next afternoon as I sat in the sunshine, in company with my teen-age son, and we joined thirty-seven thousand Mets-roarers in their noncompassionate bayings ("Sweep! Sweeeep!") as the good guys won again, 5–3, and the series concluded with the Mets suddenly a bare half game behind the Expos at the upper end of the standings. The Mets pitcher this time was Sid Fernandez, a thick-bodied left-hander who hides the ball behind his shoulder and then delivers it with an awkward-looking sudden lurch and arm-snap. He reminds you of somebody jumping out of a closet. The mannerism is effective but tiring, and I was in perfect agreement with Davey Johnson when he brought on Roger McDowell in relief after six innings, by which time Fernandez had already set down ten batters on strikes. The crowd was almost as much of a story as the game— the attendance total of 172,292, achieved without benefit of a promotion or weekend date, was the largest four-game turnout in club history—and we in the stands comported ourselves with exuberant and proprietary disbelief. With the Mets behind by 1–0 in the third inning, George Foster came up to bat with two out and the bases loaded, and was greeted with considerable unoptimism by the experienced fans in my sector of the mezzanine. "You're a thief, George!" a man just off to my left announced. "You're stealing the money! Sit down, George— you're gonna strike out again!" I disapprove of financial references in these public debates (Foster is paid about two million dollars per year by the Mets), but I have so often seen Foster wave harmlessly at strike three or rap a mighty four-bounce grounder to the shortstop under these circumstances that I recognized these sounds as the cries of a true Metsevik. This time, Foster took a strike and hit a low, hard line drive that ate its way hurriedly through the mild summer air and disappeared behind the right-center-field fence, for a grand slam. The ensuing noise and emotion were predictable, but loudest, I think, there in the forward rows of Section 501, where we had all turned to scream happily at Foster's recent tormentor—who was on his feet like the rest of us, with an enormous, unrepentant grin on his face. He'd got what he wanted.

• ◆ •

I HAVEN'T SEEN PETE ROSE IN A GAME YET THIS YEAR, BUT I will, I will. As most residents of our nebula must know by now, Pete is very near to Ty Cobb's once unapproachable lifetime mark of 4,191 base hits. At this writing, he is thirty hits short of that famous goal and closing fast, but, strangely enough, the daily "Rose Watch" box, which has been a sports-page stuffer for more than a year now, has almost obscured the sort of season Pete has been having. Playing first base for the Cincinnati Reds and benching himself every fourth or fifth game, usually when there is a left-handed pitcher going for the other side (he is the Reds manager, too, of course), he has kept his average close to .280 for most of the year; in spite of a recent and perhaps predictable slump, he is tied for third in the National League in on-base percentage. He is officially forty-four (but possibly forty-six) years old, and plans to go right on playing and batting once the Cobb plateau is reached—perhaps for another two years, perhaps more. His interviews are all line drives; they take your breath away. Explaining to one reporter (Mike Sheridan, of *Baseball Bulletin*) why the new record would not tempt him to ease up, he said, "Say you get to interview the one person you've always wanted to interview. Does that mean you stop writing?" He concluded a talk with Peter Gammons in the Boston *Globe* (one of the most entertaining lectures on hitting I've come across) this way: "Sure [Cobb's record] is great. It won't make me the greatest hitter who ever lived: it will make me the man who had the most hits. But the statistic I'm most proud of is that I've played in more winning games than any man on earth."

There will be an enormous dissection of the Cobb-Rose numbers when Pete Day arrives—perhaps early in September—but the only way I can make such figures come alive in my imagination is by comparing them with the lifetime statistic put together by some other distinguished and durable batsmen. Thinking about this the other day, I went to the record books and looked up the first two famous hitters who came to mind—Charlie Gehringer and Rod Carew. Gehringer, a Hall of Famer, played second base for the Tigers from 1924 to 1942, for sixteen of those nineteen years as a full-season regular, and batted a lifetime .320. He had seven two-hundred-hit seasons, and finished up with 2,839 hits, which still leaves him 1,352 short of the Cobb total. If we employ in the equation his average number of at-bats per year over those sixteen best seasons and assume that he continued to hit at that same robust .320 clip, we find that he would have had to continue to play for just a bit less than *eight* additional years in order to catch up. Rod Carew, who will be forty this year, is in his nineteenth season and holds a lifetime .330 batting mark—the best of our time. If we overlook his 1985 work to date (he is batting a sub-par .262 for the Angels) and permit him to begin the year over again, he would do so with 1,262 fewer hits than Cobb, which means that he would have to sustain that same splendid .330 average into September of 1992 in order to draw even. There is just no comparison—except with Pete.

Cobb compiled his total over a span of twenty-four years, from 1905 to 1928 (he played for the Athletics in his final two seasons, and for the Tigers, of course, before that), but in fewer games; for one thing, seasons were a bit shorter then. For another, Cobb's lifetime batting average of .367 stands at the top of all the lists—he was the best batter the game has ever seen— while Rose came into this season, his twenty-third, with a lifetime .305. He has had to work a lot harder to get where he is today, then—he has twenty-two hundred more at-bats so far than Cobb—but hard work has been what he is all about. One can only begin to guess how many parents and music teachers and camp counselors must be using his name these days, in repellent, exhortatory fashion, to languid feeders, reluctant scalesplayers, or wimpy canoeists: "C'mon! Let's see some Pete Rose, there, fella!" He is in the language now.

Players and managers think about Rose just as much as the fans and the writers do. One day in June, Cub manager Jim Frey told a few of us about the awe with which Pete's teammates look upon his energy and furious dedication. Frey, who was once a coach with the Orioles, recalled a story that Terry Crowley told about Rose when Crowley (an outfielder, and prime left-handed pinch-hitter and designated hitter) returned to Baltimore in the mid-seventies, after a brief stint with the Reds, where Rose was already an established star. The Reds, in Crowley's account, were flying home to Cincinnati one night after an extended and exhausting road trip; it was after one o'clock in the morning, and the players who weren't asleep in their seats were dozily thinking about their coming day off—the first break in the Cincinnati schedule in weeks. Just before the plane landed, Rose came up the aisle and woke up Terry Crowley and his seatmate, Merve Rettenmund (likewise a good-hitting ex-Oriole outfielder, albeit a righty.) "Listen," Rose said urgently. "How would you each like to earn an extra hundred bucks? I need a couple of guys to throw about a half hour each of batting practice to me tomorrow morning. Can you be at the park by ten o'clock?"

Frey pointed out that Rose, who is a switch hitter, wanted to bat against both a left- and a right-hander. "Probably it was *more* than half an hour for them, the way Petey goes," he said, shaking his head. "Crowley couldn't get over it. The man is slightly amazing."

◆ ◆ ◆

I HAD PLANNED TO TAKE IN CUBS-METS PART II, SCHEDULED
to open at Wrigley Field the following week, but a sudden,
Bambi-sweet inner wish not to observe the further sufferings of
the Cubs prompted me to cancel—a mistake, of course. The
Cubs, after experiencing another painful house call from Doctor
K in the opener (Gooden's eleventh win of the year, and the
Cubs' thirteenth straight loss), turned on their oppressors and
won the two remaining games in more characteristic fashion,
rapping five home runs along the way. I went instead to Toronto,
where the first-place Blue Jays and the visiting third-place Red
Sox staged a running three-day burleycue that alternately be-
mused, dismayed, piqued, bored, drenched, inflamed, enter-
tained, and (now and then, a *little*) rewarded the frazzled
onlookers. The night before my arrival, the Bosox had blown a
four-run lead in the process of losing to the Jays by 6–5, to drop
four and a half games back (the Tigers were in second), and
after observing but a few innings' worth of my old favorites'
current style of play I knew for a certainty that this would be
another dry summer in New England. The Bosox starter, the
left-hander Bruce Hurst, and his mates gave us a thoughtfully
illustrated progressive demonstration of the many ways in which
a ballgame may be lost; here a misplayed outfield fly, there a hit
batsman, now a gift stolen base for the opposing team, now
(heigh-ho!) another, *now* a baserunning botchup for us, then a
delightfully amateurish sandlot peg from the outfield, and—oh,
yes—here's a *wild pitch*! and soon thereafter (note the difference, please) a passed ball, and so on, ad infinitum, or, rather
ad 7–2 Toronto, which seemed very much the same. During the
evening, I came to know and perfectly understand some previously challenging and difficult-looking baseball data; how Mr.
Hurst could have won but four of his last twenty-six outings (a
bare month later, however, he had amazingly reversed his form
and fortunes, running off five consecutive victories as a Bosox
starter); how Hurst's successor on the mound, Mr. Mark Clear,
could have recently permitted fifty-three consecutive stolen bases
by enemy base runners (including two by the now retired tank
car Greg Luzinski); and who will lead the league once Bill James,
the Pythagoras of baseball theoreticians, devises a best-hitter/
worst-base-runner formula: Bill Buckner, by a mile. All this, of
course, is most unfair to the home-team Blue Jays, who took
these many gifts with modest good grace and sometimes show
us the brighter aspect of the pastime as well. Jimmy Key—a
brisk, poised young left-hander—threw a tidy five-hitter; first

baseman Willie Upshaw hit a homer; and centre (in the local style-book) fielder Lloyd Moseby whacked three singles and stole second and third on successive pitches (*cf.* Clear, *supra*).

The Blue Jays, runners-up to the World Champion Tigers in their division last year, have the second-best won-lost record in all baseball over the past two and a half seasons (behind the Tigers and a hair better than the Yankees), but have somehow remained invisible in the process. "Nobody knows us," the veteran third baseman Garth Iorg told me cheerfully. "We go on the road, and you hear the fans saying 'Who's that shortstop?' and 'Who's their first baseman?' NBC passed up a chance to put us on their 'Game of the Week' the other day, against the Tigers, and the guys in the clubhouse were saying, 'What's the *matter* with those people? We're the best two teams in the league!' I told them maybe it was to our advantage—it takes the pressure off a little—but it does seem funny, doesn't it?" Catcher Ernie Whitt said, "We were on one 'Monday Night Baseball' network thing this year, and I hear the ratings went down. It's been that way around here since Day One. I figure people will wake up and discover us in the playoffs in October."

A *Globe & Mail* sportswriter characterized the Jays for me as "decent but unexciting," and a Toronto friend of mine named Alison Gordon, who used to cover the Blue Jays for the *Star*, seemed to be lumping the players and the fans together when she said, "We're not a very colorful lot."

Some firmer causes for this epidemic anonymity also suggest themselves. The Blue Jays came into being as an expansion team in 1977 and stayed wholly out of harm's way for their first five years, hidden away in Canada and seventh place. Manager Bobby Cox came aboard in 1982, and the club climbed to fourth the next year and into contention thereafter, but the talented present roster was built up patiently and economically, without recourse to the kind of blockbuster trade or multimillion-dollar free-agent signing that wins sudden attention and expectation in the sports media. Whitt and Iorg (along with pitcher Jim Clancy) are surviving members of the club's original expansion draft, and starting outfielders Jesse Barfield and Lloyd Moseby and pitchers Jimmy Key and Dave Stieb—the latter now perhaps the most formidable starter in the American League—were selected in the annual rookie drafts, while outfielder George Bell, pitcher Jim Acker, first baseman Willie Upshaw—locally the best-known, best-loved Blue Jay since the retirement of John Mayberry—were found at bargain rates in the little-used minor-league draft; Damaso Garcia, a fixture at second base since his arrival, in 1980, was picked up in a six-player trade with the Yankees; and the veteran hurler Doyle Alexander, who went 17–6 for the Jays last year, was signed after the Yankees gave up on him and handed him his outright release in 1983. The quick mind and cool eye most responsible for this un-Steinbrennerish merchantry belong to Pat Gillick, the club's executive vice-president for baseball operations, who is much admired (and perhaps unpleasantly denigrated) in the inner circles of baseball for his discovery and signing of so many brilliant young Latin-American players, most of whom were first spotted as school-boys by a legendary regional scouting director, Epy Guerrero. Three of the present Blue Jays—George Bell, infielder Manny Lee, and the ravishingly talented young shortstop Tony Fernandez—hail from Guerrero's home town, San Pedro de Macorís, in the Dominican Republic, as did Alfredo Griffin, Fernandez' predecessor at short, who went over to the Oakland A's last winter as part of a trade for a much-needed bullpen stopper, Bill Caudill. There is no draft system for young ballplayers who live outside the United States, and the Blue Jays' diligent, old-fashioned scouting in the islands and elsewhere to the south makes them, to my way of thinking, the modern equivalent of Branch Rickey's old Cardinals. It also further explains the semi-anonymity of the 1985 Blue Jays, if one believes, as I do, that all Latin-American stars, from Roberto Clemento to Joaquin Andujar, have been habitually overlooked or slighted in our baseball consideration. A Latino playing in Canada is doubly ignored, although in some sense he has become the most American player of all.

Dave Stieb, Toronto's king of the hill, was scheduled to start the next Red Sox game, a Saturday-afternoon affair, but manager Cox, having got word from the weatherman of the imminent arrival of heavy rainstorms, held back his ace at the last moment and sent out a young right-hander, Ron Musselman, to essay his very first major-league start. Cox, of course, did not want to waste an outing by Stieb—a hard-luck pitcher (and legendary moaner), whose record at the moment stood a bare 6–5, despite an earned-run average of 2.16—in a possible rainout, and he very nearly got away with his gamble. Musselman confined the scary Boston sluggers to a couple of runs during his stint; Tony Fernandez delivered the catch-up and go-ahead runs for the home side with a two-run round-tripper, to make for a 3–2 Blue Jay lead in the bottom of the fourth; and the spattering rains held off just long enough to force the dawdling, languishing, heavenward-hoping Bostons to make their third out in the top of the fifth before the players were forced to take shelter—a legal victory, of course, if play were to stop there for the day. Then it *rained*—downward and side-blown sheets and skeins of water that streamed down the glass fronting of the press box, puddled and then ponded on the lumpy, too green AstroTurf playing field before us, and emptied the roofless grandstand around the diamond. Glum descendant clouds swept in, accompanied by a panoply of Lake Ontario ring-billed gulls (a celebrated and accursed local phenomenon), who took up late-comer places upon the long rows of backless aluminum benches in outer right field and then settled themselves thickly across the outfield swamplands as well, where they all stood facing to windward, ready for a fly ball, or perhaps for a visiting impressionist French film director ("Quai des Jays," "Toronto Mon Amour") to start shooting. Rain delays are hard on writers, who cannot just go home—as most of the intelligent Toronto fans were now deciding to do—and are enjoined from visiting the clubhouses or asking the umpire in charge (it was Joe Brinkman) why he won't reconsult his bunions and call the damned thing once and for all. I had plenty of time (three hours and sixteen minutes, as it turned out) to work up my notes; to share in the tepid, onrunning press-box jokes (there had been a guest party of Ojibway Indians at the game, it was discovered, and we worked over the rain-dance variations at excruciating length); to catch up on local baseball history (Babe Ruth hit his very first home run as a professional into the waters of Lake Ontario in 1914, while playing for the visiting minor-league Providence Grays against the Toronto Maple Leafs in the long-defunct park at Hanlan's Point); and to memorize the unlikely configurations of the Blue Jays' Exhibition Stadium. The place is the home field of the Toronto Argonauts, of the Canadian Football League, and the baseball diamond has been tucked off into one corner of the rectangle, with an added-on, boomerang-shaped grandstand section adjacent to the diamond and a temporary curving outfield wall that cuts oddly across the long gridiron, forestalling rolling eight-hundred-foot home runs but imparting an unhappy, overnight-tent-show look to the place. General-admission seats are in the roofed football grandstand, which begins out by the left-field foul pole but then, since it adjoins the football sidelines, departs from the baseball premises at an ever-widening-and-disimproving angle. Fans do sit there, however, even in its farthest reaches—there were some there now, patiently waiting out the deluge under cover. I asked a resident writer how far it was from home plate to the top row of the outmost grandstand sector, and he said, "That's Section 51. I don't think anybody's ever paced it off, but I tried using a little trigonometry once and I made it out to be around a thousand feet. The folks in the lower rows out there are even worse off, because they can't see over the outfield fence, but you see them down there, too, some-times. I think they bring radios."

The Toronto fans, I need hardly add, are *fans*. Even in the closer sectors of Exhibition Stadium, the seats are uncomfort-able and sight lines abominable, but the rooters turn out in very large numbers (2,110,009 of them last year) to cram themselves into the intimately serried, knee-creasing grandstand rows and to cheer with more discriminating loyalty and sensible hope than they used to back in the early days of the franchise. Ontario fans—particularly those off to the west of Toronto, in sectors like Wingham and London—used to be Tiger rooters, but most of them have switched over in the last couple of seasons, and the Blue Jays have supplanted the hapless hockey Maple Leafs as the No. 1 team in town. The seventh-inning stretch (to return to the stadium) is a wholesome little session of sing-along cal-isthenics, directed by numerous Ken and Barbie look-alikes in sweatsuits, to a fight song called "O.K., Blue Jays!," and al-most everyone joins in happily. Happily and for the most part soberly, if only because each row in the stands is forty-one seats wide, aisle to aisle, making beer vending an impossibility. A new stadium—a dome, perhaps with a retractable roof—has been promised by the province, but it sounds years away. A World Series played at Exhibition Stadium would hurry the project wonderfully.

Around suppertime, the rain lessened and then turned itself off, the fog banks began to show pinkish gleams (greeted by "Here Comes the Sun" on the loudspeaker), the Zamboni—after a brief, embarrassing breakdown—thrummed back and forth across the green carpet, sucking up water and spouting it off-field, the gulls flapped off to other engagements, and a hand-ful of fans (kids, mostly) reappeared and filled up the good seats around home: not enough of them to make a Wave, for once. The game resumed, with new pitchers, and the Blue Jays lost, 5–3—almost a foregone conclusion, it seemed, although I wasn't quite sure why. Bobby Cox, who can't *stand* to lose, missed the second part of the odd little double header, having become embroiled during the delay in argument with Brinkman the Rain King, who gave him the heave-ho. None of it could have happened on grass.

The next afternoon, in the Sunday sunshine, Stieb had at the Red Sox at last, and whipped them, 8–1, impatiently setting down their hitters with his tough fastball, a biting slider, and some unsettling off-speed stuff as well; he didn't give up a hit until the sixth inning. Tony Fernandez hit a triple and a double— to date, he was sixteen for twenty-seven against the Boston pitchers for the year—and Rance Mulliniks, who switches with Iorg at third base (they were both well over .300 so far), socked a home run. Fernandez, who is twenty-two years old, gets rid of the ball at short with an oiled swiftness that makes you catch your breath; he switch-hits, starting with his hands held high but then dipping at the last moment to a smooth, late, flat-bat stroke that meets the ball in classic inside-out style and drives it, often to the opposite field, with power and elegance. There are others in the Blue Jays lineup whom I admire and enjoy, including the crisp Damo Garcia, at second, and the quick, strong young outfielders Bell and Moseby (they and the regular right fielder, Jesse Barfield, who didn't start on this day, will all turn twenty-six within two weeks of each other this fall), but, watching them here, I still could not envision them and their teammates holding on through the summer against the likes of the Tigers and the tough oncoming Yankees, and then playing in and perhaps winning a championship elimination or a World Series. I had discussed this feeling just before the game with Tony Kubek, who handles the Jays' color commentary over the CTV television network (he also works the backup "Game of the Week" shows on NBC), and then with Buck Martinez, the veteran Blue Jays catcher, who replaces Ernie Whitt against the lefties. In different ways, both of them echoed the same doubts.

"There's nobody on the club who scares you, which is what you see on so many other teams in this division," Kubek said. "Or, rather, *two* guys scare you—Parrish and Gibson with the Tigers, Murray and Ripken on the Orioles, Winfield and Baylor on the Yanks. Maybe it'll happen here, maybe somebody will come along, but I don't quite see it. You know, a lot of people picked us to win this year, and that changes how a club thinks about itself. Some of the guys have become a little defensive in their thinking. You can see that Gillick built this team to fit this ballpark. It's a hitter's park, with the carpet and the short fences, but I always feel we're a little light when we get into those bigger parks on the road.''

Martinez said, "I cut that photograph out of the paper yesterday that showed Bill Buckner putting a flying block on Garcia in the Thursday game and showed it to some guys in the clubhouse. I said, 'This is the difference between winning and being a bunch of good guys, which is what we are so far.' I played five years on the Royals, with people like George Brett and Hal McRae, and I saw how they play this game. McRae always said, 'If you can't be good, you got to be rough.' You remember that slide he put on Willie Randolph in the playoffs, don't you? Now the game has changed a little, and the people take that sort of thing more personally, almost. But that's the kind of play that can get into an infielder's mind and maybe make for a moment of hesitation later on and win a game for you. Stieb is like that for us, but he's a pitcher and too often it's directed against himself. There were times on our last road trip when we could have used a little more of that McRae stuff, that Thurman Munson personality—somebody who'll get a leadoff double when you want it most, or knock somebody down at second. Maybe it'll come—you never know.''

Ah, yes. Yogi Berra has enunciated this same great principle ("In baseball, you don't know nothin' "), and so, too, in his own field, did the late Fats Waller ("One never knows, do one?"). With one out in the bottom of the fourth, I lifted my gaze from my scorecard to see, on the instant, a fastball delivered by the Boston hurler, Bruce Kison, ricochet off the shoulder—*high* on the shoulder—of the Toronto batter, George Bell. A certain testiness had been evident all along in this series—going back to Doyle Alexander's very first pitch on Thursday evening, which had nailed leadoff man Steve Lyons right on the chest (or, more precisely, on the "S" of his "BOSTON" road-uniform logo)—but Bell's response, even under such duress, was surprising. Batless, he reached the mound in full sprint and aimed a sudden high, right-legged karate kick at Kison, which mostly missed its mark. Bell then spun quickly and landed a fairish one-two combination (fists, this time) to the chops of Rich Gedman, the pursuing Boston catcher. Now batting .666 for this one turn at bat (if we may agree that he had fouled out against Kison), Bell retreated toward third base in a wary backward-boogie style, apparently inviting other participants, just emerging from their dugouts, to share the action, which they did, in typically earnest but inefficient fashion. When it was over, Bell was banished from the proceedings and Kison permitted to continue, though under admonishment. A tall, bony right-hander, now in his fifteenth season in the bigs, Kison knows the outs and ins of his profession, and earlier in the game he had somehow allowed a little off-speed pitch to sail behind the head of Ernie Whitt, who here stepped up to bag again—and walked, muttering. An end to the affair, one might have imagined, but writers of these summer operettas do like that last, excessive twist to the plot. Whitt, coming up to bat again, with one out in the sixth, found Kison still on hand, although tottering, for he had just walked the bases full. Whitt poled the first pitch over the right-field fence—it was the first grand slam of his entire baseball career—and circled the bases talkatively, taking time to direct the appropriate phrasings and rhetorical flourishes toward the mound as he went. The tableau looked like an eccentric windup toy from Bavaria, with the circling outer figure, in the white uniform, twitching his arms and waggling his jaw as he went from base to base, and the central inner player—the little man in gray—rotating more slowly but in perfect concentric rhythm, so as to keep his back turned to the other chap all the way around. I much preferred this baseball keepsake to the George Bell model, but of course it will take the rest of the summer to learn what it meant, if anything, to the Blue Jays.

As it turned out, an even more vivid exemplification of that McRae stuff, that Thurman Munson personality, was presented to the Blue Jays by the man who had enunciated the need for it in the first place, Buck Martinez. While behind the plate for the Jays in a game out in Seattle (I saw the moment on a television replay that night, a couple of weeks after my visit to Toronto), Martinez took a peg from the outfield and attempted to tag an onflying Mariner base runner, Phil Bradley, who collided violently with the catcher. Martinez, knocked onto his back, suffered a broken right fibula and dislocated ankle. Somehow, he held on to the ball and made the out, and then, half rising, threw toward third base, where another Seattle base runner, Gorman Thomas, was now swiftly approaching. The throw went wild, and Thomas turned third and headed for the plate. George Bell picked up the ball in left field and fired it home, where the dazed and badly injured Martinez, still down and writhing, caught it on the bounce and tagged the runner, thus accounting for both putouts in the double play—possibly the last but certainly the most extraordinary moment of his baseball career.

HITTING IS THE HOVERING CENTRAL MYSTERY OF THIS SPORT, and continues to invite wonder. Tommy Herr, a decent singles- and doubles-hitting second baseman with the Cardinals, batted .276 last year and drove in forty-nine runs—almost exactly matching his career averages, compiled in the previous five summers. This year, batting third in a much altered lineup, he has led the league in hitting over most of the first half (he is at .330 at this writing) and has sent teammates already on base scurrying home in great numbers; his three home runs and seventy runs batted in to date have turned the writers to the *Baseball Encyclopedia*, where they have divined that he may well become the first National League to bat in a hundred runs or more while hitting fewer than ten home runs in the process since Dixie Walker did it (116, with nine) for the Dodgers in 1946. Some contributing reasons for Herr's sudden prosperity will be presented a little farther along, when we take a closer look at the Cardinals, but I love to think about the absolute unpredictability of this almost typical turnabout; every year, it seems to me, something of this sort comes along and is then made to look logical and almost inevitable by us scholars and explainers of the game—none of whom, of course, had any idea beforehand where and to whom it would happen. Baseball, to its credit, confirms continuity and revolution in equal parts, thus keeping its followers contented but attentive. Pedro Guerrero, unhappy all spring at third base with the Dodgers, was returned to his old position in the outfield on June 1st, and responded by whacking fifteen home runs in the month of June, a new National League record—a new record, *of course*. Carlton Fisk has hit twenty-six homers for the White Sox so far this year, thereby tying his full-season best in a career stretching back over sixteen major-league summers; he leads both leagues in downtowners to date and seems a good bet to erase Lance Parrish's one-season total of thirty-two homers, the most by any American League catcher.* Sudden extraordinary performance at the plate is never truly explicable, then, and even the batters themselves aren't much help. "I'm in a good groove," "I'm in that realm," or

---

*Fisk set the new record with thirty-seven homers, four of which came while he was in the lineup as a designated hitter—a record, that is, but just barely.

"I'm seeing the ball real good" is what you hear, and the words are accompanied with an almost apologetic little shrug.

It's all right, then, for the rest of us to feel the same way. The two hottest hitters of 1985 are Rickey Henderson and George Brett, and while I thought that I was seeing them real good during several turns at bat this year, I still don't know how they do it. Henderson, facing the Orioles' Mike Boddicker and Sammy Stewart one night up at the Stadium, rapped three singles and drove in three runs (he also stole a base) in the course of the Yankees' 7–4 victory, and somehow looked a bit off his form in the process. A week earlier, while the Yankees were administering a frightful three-game pasting to these same Orioles down in Baltimore (they had forty-four hits along the way), Henderson went eight for nine in the first two games, and ten for thirteen over the three, at one stretch getting to first base safely ten straight times. Like a perfectly cooked roast, his June statistics look wonderful no matter where you slice them: a three-for-four night against the Tigers, with two home runs; a one-for-three effort against the Orioles again, with four stolen bases again; and so forth. It is this almost unique combination of batting eye, power, and speed that makes him so dangerous, and when you see him approach the plate (with that preliminary little baton-twirler mannerism, during which he alternately taps the head and the heel of the bat with his gloved hand) and then fold himself down into his odd, knock-kneed, doubled-over posture as he awaits the pitch you suddenly perceive what a mean little knot of problems he presents to the pitcher. His scrunched-down strike zone means that he is almost always ahead on the count (Earl Weaver has said that Henderson draws walks as well as anyone he has ever seen in the majors), but the pitcher, uncomfortably aware of his devastating quickness on the base paths, is unwilling to settle for ball four and thus very often gives up a line drive instead. Again, these explanations look easy—except for the last part: the hitting. His stroke is at once so quick—almost an upward and outward jump at the ball—and yet so full and flashing . . . Well, I give up. The Stadium throngs love him, of course, and he has been very much at the center of the Yankees' vivid drive to the fore (*almost* to the fore) in the past two months.

I saw Brett in a stretch of three games against the Angels in Kansas City, at a time when he had just returned to the Royals lineup after a spell on the bench with a hamstring pull. He has always been prone to injury, and almost always seems to return to action at full bore—this time with ten hits in his first twenty at-bats. Brett, who is thirty-two, took off twenty pounds over the winter, and looked younger and more cheerful than I had seen him in years. He was meeting the ball well (here we go again) when I saw him, showing that full, exuberant cut every time, and was hitting a lot of long fouls, but he didn't do much, except for a three-for-three performance in one fourteen-inning game, finally captured by the Royals—almost an amazing day, at that, since he walked on his four other appearances, thus ending up on base seven times. A couple of days later, after I'd left town, Brett went three for three against the A's with two three-run homers; starting there, he ran off a .538 week, with three doubles, two homers, a triple, and eleven runs batted in.

I have written so often about Brett's batting style—going back to his great .390 summer in 1980, and before—that I will not attempt another likeness here of that uniquely pausing, balanced, and then suddenly free and whirling grace. Observing him repeatedly at work there on his home field, though, it did seem to me that one part of his swing—the cocked, attentive tilt of his head as he awaits the ball, and the the abrupt downward tuck of his chin as he watches his bat drive through at the pitch— is especially satisfying to an onlooker. In some strange fashion, Brett always appears to be watching himself being a hitter. There is a considering, almost intellectual presence there, even during the most violent and difficult unleashing of forces, and it suggests—it almost *looks like*—that waiting and expectant inner self, the critical watcher, who remains at rest within each of us and is spectator to all our movements and doings, however grand or trifling. Even crossing a street, we can find ourselves in that good groove sometimes, and take note of it with secret surprise.

◆ ◆ ◆

BY THE TIME JULY CAME AROUND, EVERYONE WAS TALKING about the Cardinals—about their wonderful combination of fine pitching and good hitting (they have been leading the league both ways); about the rookie flier, Vince Coleman, who plays left field and has been stealing bases at such an amazing clip; about Tommy Herr and about the big cleanup hitter, Jack Clark, who came over from the Giants in a trade during the winter; and—oh, yes—about Willie McGee, in center, who bats second and has thus done a few things that help account for Coleman's success on the bases, just behind. This is the way ball teams should *work*, it suddenly seems.

I kept missing the Cardinals—their baseball schedule always had them going off in the opposite direction from mine. But then I saw my chance and jumped on a plane and went up to see them play the Expos in Montreal in an afternoon game—went up and came home again the same day, just for the game—and caught up on my studies. Vince Coleman, who is muscled like a cheetah, hit a single and stole a base; he is less flashy than Rickey Henderson on the bases, but the man can scamper. Tommy Herr hit a single and got a base three times; Ozzie Smith made a couple of lazily beautiful plays at short, easy as pie; and Willie McGee had a single and a double and a home run and a stolen base—the same silent, scrawny-necked, semi-apologetic Willie McGee who so pleased and surprised us all back in the World Series of 1982, just before we forgot him again. (The last time I looked—as this was written—McGee had passed his teammate Tommy Herr, and was leading the National League in batting, at .339) The day in Montreal went as promised, I mean, and I even found time to congratulate Whitey Herzog, an old favorite of mine, for the kind of team he had this time, and for the way he had put it together—even trading away an excellent, established left fielder, Lonnie Smith, the moment he was sure about Coleman. "This team is all right, for my park," Herzog admitted—his park, Busch Stadium, has the artificial carpet—"but if I was playing at Wrigley Field or Fenway I wouldn't want to go this way. Geography makes all the difference in baseball these days."

It was a holiday in Montreal (Dominion Day—or Canada Day, as they now call it), and there was a nice medium-small crowd (everyone else was at the shore, I decided) cheering vociferously down below me in the deep, echoey circular strip mine of Olympic Stadium. A great blazing-white horseshoe of sunlight slid slowly across the billiard-table-green mat below, and I again recalled a remark once made by the long-gone, unforgotten Dick Allen: "If a horse can't eat it, I don't want to play on it."

There was the game, too, and in time—very quickly, in fact—that took over, and though I was glad to have Herr and Coleman and McGee and others in plain view at last (I almost felt like a scout, because of my trip), I also began to pay attention to the Montreal pitcher, a fledgling righty (he had just turned twenty-one) named Floyd Youmans, who was making his major-league début. He, too, was there just for the day, having been called up from the club's Class AA Jacksonville team to make an emergency appearance on the mound when the Expos had found themselves with an inordinate number of pitchers invalided to their *liste des blessés*, but he had been told before the game that his next stop would be back down at the Indianapolis AAA farm, no matter how well he did here today. Perhaps freed by this news, he resolutely worked his way once and then twice through the tough Cardinal batting order, giving up an occasional base on balls or a longish fly-ball out, and here and there a base hit, but also fanning a Cardinal or two, including Jack Clark, whenever he most needed the out. He had the Cardinals shut out after six innings, by which time the Expos were ahead by 2–0. Then Coleman touched him up in the seventh with a single through the middle—his first time on first base. Vince took an enormous lead, paused, and then flew away on the hit-and-run—an awesome jump, as promised—and Willie McGee socked a high, sailing home run into the Montreal bullpen to tie it. Youmans departed, and the disappointed Expos fans saw him off with a grateful, stand-up round of applause and then sat down quietly and tried to regather hope. I was happy when their team hung in and won the game at last, 3–2, on a single off the third baseman's glove by the grand old Montreal favorite André Dawson, in the bottom of the tenth. It was only the Expos' fourth hit of the game—four hits amassed against *six* Cardinal pitchers: I'd never heard of such a thing. Whitey's bullpen is a Sargasso for National League hitters this summer—no end to it and not much fun.

On my way home, I kept thinking about the Cards and their new look, and I recalled how Jim Frey, whose Cubs had lately dropped three games to the Cardinals at home, kept returning to the Redbirds in conversation one day. "This Coleman reminds you of a lot of fast young guys in their first year up," he said. "He plays like Tim Raines did, or like Willie Wilson did in his first two years. You look around and he's up at bat and the other team has got the third baseman playing in, the second baseman is in by two full strides, and the first baseman's up on the grass. You got no choice. The way the man's going, he's going to steal a hundred and twenty bases in his very first year up. When the season started, everybody was sayin' they got seven leadoff men and Jack Clark, but you can throw that out the window now, because of Coleman and the way they're hitting. The whole club is always going from first to third. The one who's overlooked is McGee. He can run as good as anybody. He can bunt the ball, he can top the ball and get on base, he can hit the ball for distance, and he can run and catch the ball in the outfield. He's like No. 2 in everything on that club. You look over at Coleman, with McGee at bat, and he's got that big lead, and you can't make him back off an *inch*. He always gets that amazing jump. In a couple of years, they'll be calling him a great left fielder—you wait and see.''

Only self-assured veteran managers talk about rival teams and players in this fashion, and when you listen to a Jim Frey or a Whitey Herzog in midseason, you begin to sense that they are perpetually involved in two levels of baseball—the game at hand or just ahead, which they are trying to win, and the deeper difficulties and returns and surprises of the other game; baseball as a discourse or discipline, baseball as a way of thinking. Earl Weaver talks this side of baseball more gracefully than anyone I know; in his postgame chats he compliments the writers by including them in his inner excursions and musings, and by the time he's done you're convinced, at least for a glimmering instant or two, that you've seen how this game works. The little man was in splendid form up at Yankee Stadium during the Orioles-Yankees game I have mentioned, in spite of his team's failings. He had only just come back from his two-year self-retirement—brought back, it has been hinted, by a half-million-dollar salary and the offer of another chance to work in the Baltimore organization, where he has passed the better part of his working life. (He said he had turned down several previous bids from other clubs.) His postgame seminars were a treat, as usual. Any day now, I expect to walk into Weaver's office after a game and find waiting ushers, with programs and flashlights. One night there at the Stadium, he was simultaneously stripping a chicken leg and himself as he fielded our questions, usually cutting them off before they were quite finished—he is quick—and then fitting his answers into the main discourse of the evening. Weaver is the only mid-size, middle-aged executive I know who can sit behind a desk with no clothes on, as naked as a trout, and never lose the thread of his thinking.

Here he reconsidered a brilliant peg by Dave Winfield that had cut down an Orioles base runner, Ripken, at the plate—the big play of the game, it turned out—and wondered along with his questioner, whether it had been right to send him home. ''Yes, it was an outstanding throw,'' he said, ''but still . . .'' He paused, considering, and then put the matter to rest: ''What the hell—if he scores, it's a great play.'' In the eighth inning of the game, with his club well behind, Weaver had unexpectedly employed an Oriole outfielder, John Shelby, at second base, where he filled in for the weak-hitting Dauer, who had departed for a pinch-hitter. (This was a few days before the Orioles signed Alan Wiggins, the talented former Padre second baseman, who had been permitted to leave that club after revealing his continuing difficulties with cocaine addiction.) Shelby had looked adequate on one chance out there, and more than a bit awkward on another, which went by him, or *off* him, for a base hit. "On the second ball, he tried to get in front of it, though it's way off to his right." Weaver said. "That's what you're taught to do in high school, and maybe he's never had that play since he was in high school. I know about this because I used to manage in Class C ball and D ball, where you have kids who come to you right out of high school. But up here if that ball's hit over to your right"—he was suddenly on his feet, wearing only his shower clogs—"you just get over this far and backhand the ball, like this. You don't try to make a great play, or anything, but if you time it right you look real good. If you don't time it right you look silly. Oh, I *love* this stuff. . . ." He resumed his seat, for the tactics. "If we're losing, Shelby at second gives us an extra move, and I'll go with it. That way, I got his bat in there, and if we tie or go ahead then Lennie Sakata goes out to hold things down. But if I bat for Dauer the old way, then Lennie goes in right away. This is an extra move for me. If you're losing, go for offense. Look for that move." His eyes were shining.

NINE

Quis

TROUBLE IN THE NINTH. THE VISITING TEAM HAS JUST scored, to draw within a run of the home side, and there are base runners at first and third, with one out and the heavy part of the batting order just coming up. Even before the runner crossed the plate, the manager was on his way to the mound, and now he turns toward his bullpen and touched his right arm. The murmurous noises of anxiety in the park give way to applause and the fans' relishing cries of an outcome now almost foreseen as the bullpen car arrives and yields up its famous passenger, the great reliever. He is whiskered and hulking, and his impatient right-handed warmup pitches—seven seeds and a final down-busting curveball—bring gasps and little bursts of laughter in the stands. The No. 3 batter stands in and takes an instantaneous called strike—a fastball under his fists. He lays off the next pitch—a breaking ball, away—then swings hard at the next fastball and ticks it foul to the screen. Another fastball arrives, and he swings late and raised a feeble little pop foul, which is devoured by the first baseman. Two out now. The cleanup hitter, a large left-handed slugger, digs in and takes a ball, takes a strike. He cuts violently at the next delivery, a letter-high fastball, and misses, swinging cleanly through the pitch and then half-stumbling in the box to keep his balance. The first-

201

base and third-base coaches clap their hands reassuringly—hang in there, big guy—but thirty thousand fans are on their feet now, screaming for the K. A slider here would break this batter in half, but the man on the mound has no such idea. Glowering, he leans in for the sign, stretches and stares, and delivers the inexorable heater—up and out of the strike zone, actually, but the bat has flashed and come around just the same, and the game is over. Ovations and euphoria. Handshakes and high fives in the infield, hugs in the stands. Aw *right*, we did it again!

Another ninth, in another city. The Kansas City Royals are leading the visiting Yankees, 5–2, and Royals manager Dick Howser has brought in his prime short reliever, Dan Quisenberry, to finish up. Quisenberry is a slim, angular right-hander, with sharp shoulders and a peaceable, almost apologetic mien. He has pinkish-red hair, a brushy ochre mustache, and round pale-blue eyes. Nothing about his looks is as surprising as his pitching delivery, however. He is a true submariner—a man "from down under," in baseball parlance—and every pitch of his is performed with a lurching downward thrust of his arm and body, which he must follow with a little bobbing hop off toward third base in order to recover his balance. At perigee, ball and hand descend to within five or six inches of the mound dirt, but then they rise abruptly; the hand—its fingers now spread apart—finished up by his left shoulder, while the ball, plateward-bound at a sensible, safe-driving-award clip, reverses its earlier pattern, rising for about three-quarters of its brief trip and then drooping downward and (much of the time) sidewise as it passes the batter at knee level or below. One way or another, the pitch almost always finds part of the strike zone, but most people in the stands—even the home-town regulars in Royals Stadium—are so caught up in the pitcher's eccentricities that they don't always notice this. The oversight is forgivable, since Quisenberry is not a strikeout pitcher. But he doesn't walk batters, either; in his six hundred and thirty-five major-league innings (going into this season), he had surrendered a total of eighty-four bases on balls—one for each seven and a half innings' work, which for him comes out at about one walk every fourth game—and had plunked only two batters with pitched balls. Yet Quisenberry when pitching invites more similes than stats. His ball in flight suggests the kiddie-ride concession at a county fairgrounds—all swoops and swerves but nothing there to make a mother nervous; if you're standing close to it, your first response is a smile. At other times, the trajectory of the pitch looks like an expert trout fisherman's sidearm cast that is meant to slip the fly just under an overhanging clump of alders. The man himself—Quis in mid-delivery—brings visions of a Sunday-picnic hurler who has somehow stepped on his own shoelace while coming out of his windup, or perhaps an eager news photograper who has suddenly dropped to one knee to snap a celebrity debarking from a limousine.

In the Yankee game, Quisenberry dismisses his first batter, the towering Dave Winfield, on a harmless bouncer to short. The next hitter, Dan Pasqua, who bats left-handed, numbs a Quisenberry sinker down toward third base, where the spinning ball worms its way out of George Brett's glove for an infield single. Ron Hassey, another lefty swinger, takes a ball and then jumps on a high delivery—an up pitch: a mistake—and smashes the ball to deep center field, where Willie Wilson pulls it in with his back almost against the fence. Willie Randolph steps up to bat, swings and misses on a sinker, takes two balls, and then whacks a sharp single to center, sending Pasqua scooting around to third. The tying run, in the person of Mike Pagliarulo, comes up to the plate, to the accompaniment of some nervous stirrings in the Kansas City stands. Batting left-handed, he fouls off the first pitch, swings at a sinkerball that slips away from him and off the outer edge of the plate, takes a ball, and then stands immobile while another sinker, again backing at the last instant, catches the inside corner, low, for a called third strike. End of game. The crowd, although happy about the win, does not exactly split the sky in honor of this pitching performance, but in most ways it has been a typical outing for Dan Quisenberry: a couple of hits—one of them a half-hit bouncer to the wrong side of the infield—two solid pokes, one of which went for an out; no walks; no runs (one run would have been almost more like it); and another game safely put away. Quisenberry experienced some uncharacteristic pitching difficulties in the first half of this season—the game just set forth was played on July 23rd—but the official save that went into the record books that evening was his twentieth of the year, which put him ahead of all other American League relief pitchers in that department. It was his third save in four days, in a little string that eventually added up to six saves in six consecutive appearances. Last year, Quisenberry had forty-four saves in all, the most in his league, and figured in sixty percent of the Royals' winning games; the year before that, he set an all-time record with forty-five saves, although a

National League pitcher, Bruce Sutter—then with the Cardinals, now with the Braves—tied that figure in 1984.

Baseball's save rule (to get this out of the way, once and for all) has grown in significance in recent seasons, along with the rise of the short-relief specialist—that is, the man who comes in late in the game, sometimes only to nail down the last out or two (or *not* nail them down, as the case may be)—yet there are very few fans who can say for a certainty what constitutes an official save. The ruling states that the pitcher who is granted an official save when the game is over—it appears as an "(S)" next to his name in the box score—must be the finishing pitcher but not the official winning pitcher. He must furthermore pass one of three additional qualifications:

(a) he enters the game with a lead of no more than three runs and pitches at least one inning, or

(b) he enters the game, regardless of the count on an incumbent batter, with the potential tying run on base or at bat or on deck, or

(c) he pitches effectively for at least three innings.

That "effectively" is a judgment call, made by the official scorer, and there is sometimes hot disagreement about it up in the press box. There is also general disagreement about the value of saves as the ultimate yardstick of a relief man's work. Certain pitchers—Quisenberry is among them—almost never come into a game when their club is trailing, and therefore tend to accumulate more saves by the end of the year than some of their rivals. Some variously weighted combination of saves, earned-run average, and games won probably constitutes the fairest means of measurement, but here, as in other parlous areas of the pastime, the final word must be left to the writers and the fans, and to the thousand late-night logomachies.

Since Quisenberry adopted his submarine style, at the beginning of the 1980 season, his second in the majors, he has notched a hundred and seventy-five saves—twenty more than Sutter's total for those five years and forty-five more saves than those accumulated by Goose Gossage, the ex-Yankee and present Padre star, who may be recognized as the model for our classic fireballing bullpen ace in the imaginary inning above. The elegant and obdurate Rollie Fingers, who still performs for the Milwaukee Brewers at the age of thirty-nine, after experiencing some recent serious arm and back difficulties (he sat out the entire season of 1983), he compiled three hundred and twenty-four lifetime saves, the most among all relievers, past or present, but his best five seasons, even when counted non-consecutively, do not bring him within twenty saves of Quisenberry's work in the nineteen-eighties. No one else comes close. By a different measurement—saves plus wins—Quisenberry, with a total of two hundred and eight in this decade, is also well ahead of the pack. Quisenberry himself, a habitually modest man, would argue with some of these figures—with their significance, above all—but we must embarrass him by suggesting that he may just be on his way to being the most successful practitioner of his odd calling that the game has ever seen.

Prototypes have a burrlike hold on our baseball memories, and most of us, thinking back to great relief pitchers of the past, will first come up with some Gossage-like dominator like Dick Radatz, the monster-tall Red Sox flinger who struck out more than one batter per inning in a short career back in the sixties; or, a decade earlier, the dangerously nearsighted Ryne Duren (his first warmup pitch, preserving an image, was often a ten-foot-high bullet to the backstop), who enjoyed two splendid seasons with the yankees before flaming out; or perhaps even Al Hrabosky, the bearded, angry-looking performer of the Cardinals, Royals, and Braves over the past decade, who habitually turned his back on the batter between pitches while he muttered imprecations and inspirational messages to himself, and then strode balefully toward the rubber like a Bolshevik entering the Union League Club. There is no shortage of thrilling fastballers among today's short-relief specialists—the Cubs' Lee Smith and the Yankees' Dave Righetti come to mind at once—but over the years the lonely specialty has in fact attracted a whole character actors' guild of different styles, quirks, looks, and dimensions. In my boyhood, relief pitchers seemed fatherly and calming; they were called "wily" in the papers. Johnny Murphy (*Fordham* Johnny Murphy) sometimes strolled in from the Yankees bullpen (then a shadowed alley between the grand-stand and the bleachers in right field) to set things right in the late afternoons, especially if Lefty Gomez had started the game. Hugh Casey, toiling for the Dodgers in the nineteen-forties, ran up a lifetime winning percentage of .718 (fifty-one wins and twenty losses), which has yet to be topped by anybody out of the bullpen. Pitching against the Yankees in the fourth game of the 1941 World Series (I was there, sitting in the Ebbets Field upper deck in deep left field), Casey threw a spitball to Tommy Henrich that struck him out, swinging, to end the game—except that the ball, diving into the dirt, eluded catcher Mickey Owen, allowing Henrich to gain first base. Down a run, the Yankees rallied instantly for a 7–4 victory. A few years later, the ebullient Joe Page had become the celebrated Yankees stopper—the first young, or young-*looking* (he was almost thirty when he found his proper niche in the pastime), relief man in my experience. Jim Konstanty—a stolid, blue-collar sort of pitcher—won sixteen games and saved twenty-two, all in relief, for the Whiz Kid Phillies of 1950, and was the surprise starter in the first game of the World Series that fall; he lasted eight innings, giving up one lone run, but lost to the Yankees' Vic Raschi's two-hitter. Elroy Face, a forkballer, who looked almost dwarflike on the mound at five feet eight and a hundred and fifty pounds, pitched in eight hundred and forty-eight games (mostly for the Pirates) in the fifties and sixties, and accounted for a hundred and ninety-three saves; he was 18–1 in 1959—to this day, it scarcely seems possible—with all the decisions coming in relief. Once you start thinking about them, the relievers, the great extras, begin to come back in a flood: Ron Perranoski, the shining Dodger Stadium favorite, who went 16–3, with twenty-one saves and a 1.67 earned-run average, in 1963; Tug McGraw ("You Gotta *Believe!*"), who pitched so stoutly and stood for so much in two unexpected Mets pennants and one glorious Phillies World Championship; Mike Marshall, the chunky, hard-burning right-hander (he had a graduate degree in motion studies, or "kinesiology"), who worked for nine clubs during a fourteen-year career and twice somehow led his league in relief wins, losses, and saves, all in the same year; and Dick Hall, a lesser nova, perhaps, but a stalwart in innumerable significant games for the rising young Orioles of the sixties (he was a Swarthmore graduate who had started as an outfielder with the Pirates, and his cramped, twitchy pitching delivery, somebody once wrote, reminded you of a man feeling under a bed for a lost collar button). Kent Tekulve, the Pittsburgh praying mantis (he went over to the Phillies this spring), saved thirty-one games for the Pirates in 1978 and again in 1979; his skulking, up-from-under mound style much resembled the Quisenberry mode—for reasons we shall get to in a moment. All these, then, and Hoyt Wilhelm, too. A silent, withdrawn man with an odd, twisted tilt to his neck and head, Wilhelm did not win a job in the majors until he was twenty-nine, but then stayed on, with the Giants and eight other clubs, for twenty years. A knuckleballer first, last, and always, he threw the pitch with so little strain to his arm and psyche that he was able to establish lifetime records in five different pitching categories, including most wins in relief (one hundred and twenty-four) and most games pitched (one thousand and seventy—eighty-three more than his nearest rival, Lindy McDaniel, and a hundred and sixty-four more than Cy Young). He went into the Hall of Fame this summer—sailed in, with all seams showing.

It shouldn't be surprising that so many vivid and stout-hearted bullpen performers come flooding forth in this fashion once we pull the cork, but I still think that relief pitchers are slighted or faintly patronized in most fans' and writers' consideration. Ask somebody to pick an all-time or all-decade lineup for his favorite team or for one of the leagues and the chances are that the list will not include a late-inning fireman. Even with the best of the short men, the brevity of their patchwork, Band-Aid labors; their habitual confinement in faraway (and often invisible) compounds during the long early stretches and eventful midpassages of the game; their languorous, cap-over-eyes postures of ennui or lassitude—are they *asleep* out there?—for the first two or three hours of the event; their off-putting predilection of disorder and incipient disaster; the rude instrusiveness of their extroverted pitching mannerisms into the staid game-party; their reckless way of seizing glory, or else horridly throwing away a game nearly in hand, all in the space of a few pitches—all these confirm some permanent lesser status for them: scrubs, invisible weavers, paramedics, handymen. The slur persists, I think, in spite of clear evidence that relief men—the best of them, at least—are among the most highly rewarded and most sought-after stars of contemporary baseball. Five short-relief specialists—the Dodgers' Mike Marshall in 1974, the Yankees' Sparky Lyle in 1977, Bruce Sutter in 1979, Rollie Fingers in 1981, and the Tigers' Willie Hernandez last year (he appeared in eighty games for the World Champions, with thirty-two saves and an earned-run average of 1.92)—have won the Cy Young award in their leagues, and Fingers and Hernandez also walked off with Most Valuable Player honors in those same years.

Scouts and players, managers and writers whom I consulted on the matter this summer were nearly unanimous in their selections of the best relief pitchers ever. They placed Fingers at the top of the list and then, in differing order, named Sutter, Gossage, and Sparky Lyle (who retired in 1982 with two hundred and thirty-eight lifetime saves). Almost none of them mentioned Quisenberry, and it seemed peculiar that when I brought up his name nearly everyone said something like "Oh, yes—I guess you'd have to put him in there somewhere, wouldn't you? He's a strange one, but he sure gets the job done." I couldn't tell from this whether it was Quisenberry's gently weird pitching style or his refreshing off-the-field manner (he is quick and comical, and much given to startlingly free-form images and put-ons during interviews) that has caused this persistent oversight, but I knew by now that it would come as no surprise to Quis himself, who has yet to win a Cy Young Award, even though he outpolled Hernandez last year by winning both the Rolaids and the *Sporting News* "Fireman of the Year" awards in the American League, each for the third straight year. If there is anything to my theory that relief pitchers are still a bit patronized in baseball because of their oddity, then here, too, Quisenberry belongs up near the head of the line.

◆ ◆ ◆

"RELIEF PITCHERS LIKE TO PITCH—THAT'S WHAT WE ALL HAVE in common. We're banded together in that small environment, and then the call comes and we're catapulted out into the screaming masses. It feels good to start thinking and getting ready to pitch. Then you run in—past the umpires and the infielders. That's when I feel absolutely the best—the moment when I'm back in there, into things, in a close game. Until that happens, you're not really part of the game. You're not part of anything."

Dan Quisenberry and I were sitting in the March sunshine at Terry Park, the Royals' spring-training camp, in Fort Myers, Florida. It was early in the day, before the morning calistenics and the first batting-practice pitches, and there was an easy, beginnning-of-things taste to the place and the time of day and the part of the year we were in. This was the first of several meetings I had with him during this baseball year—one-inning or two-inning talks, so to speak, almost like his own forays into the game—during which I hoped to get a clearer idea of his difficult profession. It was pleasant work, it turned out. Quisenberry's face is open and untroubled, and he speaks in a cheerful, self-deprecating fashion that seems to preclude silences or hesitancies on either side of a conversation. On this day, he was wearing his white, home-uniform pants, royal-blue spikes, and a pale-blue T-shirt. Up close, he seemed bigger than I had expected (he is six feet two and weighs a hundred and eighty pounds). He was thin but not frail, and although he is thirty-two his upper body somehow looked as if it might have grown an inch or two overnight, like a teen-ager's. It was late in the spring preseason, but his naturally pale skin didn't show much of a tan; it was more like a glow, and the hairs on his forearms were an odd, yellow-gold color. There was a dab of chewing tobacco tucked in the middle of his lower lip.

"Most relief pitchers are pretty aggressive," Quis said a bit later. "They want to get a lot of attention, and you can see some of them getting psyched up out there on the mound. Gossage gets psyched. Al Holland gets psyched. There are guys who—you know, jump around and raise their fists and all. But there's such a thing as a casual aggressiveness, too. Sutter and Rollie Fingers are more calm. They're cool under pressure, and you can see them figuring things out out there."

I asked him if he thought Sutter and Fingers were better at their profession than he was, and he said, "Yes, they're the best. They've done it longer. It's nice to have a couple of good years and good stats and all, but the great ones are the ones who get it up year after year after year. But sometimes I see them getting roughed up, too, and suddenly giving up three or four runs in a game, and I think, Boy, *they* can do that, too—it can happen to them, just like it happens to me! Being a relief pitcher is such a roller-coaster sort of thing. You're either a hero or the exact opposite, depending on what just happened. Everybody's coming down on your head, or else you're almost a religious icon if you've won. Neither reaction is totally accurate. If things go wrong, I think you always feel bad. You've failed the starting pitcher and let down your teammates, who have played two hours to get that lead, not to speak of your family and the fans who live and die with you every day. But somehow we can deal with that—which isn't to say there isn't a kind of a stab about taking a loss. I think short-relief people are always anxious for the next thing. We know we're always about to get another chance. We'll be back out there the very next day, most times, while the starting pitcher has to wait four or five days before he gets back in there, and the long reliever or fifth starter might have to wait *ten* days. There are different kinds of strain. The starting pitcher has to get the same guys out there or four times in a night, which I don't, but then he doesn't need any mental toughness for the next four days. I think I'd hate that."

I asked him if he ever felt overmatched in a game, or oppressed by the fact that he always had to work in difficulties, a perpetual underdog.

"Well, I was a fan of the Braves and the Orioles when I was growing up, in the early sixties, and after that, of course, I was for the early Mets, like everyone else," he said. "I always liked Tony Cloninger, who wasn't all that good a pitcher. So I guess I identified with underdogs. I still prefer the underdog position, but with my numbers it's harder and harder for me to feel that way. Sometimes I think I *should* be the underdog, because I'm a major-league pitcher with very few resources. I just don't match up physically with the real athletes in the league. I can know these things, but when I'm on the mound I forget all that, and there are some days when I know I'm being effective. Now it's more like playing King of the Hill. I'm not supposed to lose in a save situation, *ever*, and there's a weight that comes with that, with trying to be the best. But there gets to be a kind of an appetite about getting saves. It almost can't be fulfilled—you want that 'S' after your name, you want to maintain that level."

Some short-relief specialists prefer to come into a game at the beginning of the eighth or ninth inning, instead of a bit later, when there are men on base and more trouble at hand; Goose Gossage, for instance, always liked the full-inning option when he was with the Yankees, and fretted because his last Yankee manager, Billy Martin, did not often oblige him. I asked Quisenberry how he felt about this, and he told me that he had no preference at all. He said it in such an uncharacteristically vehement way that I thought at first I had misunderstood him. There was a gang mower working up and down the outfield lawn near us at that moment, and I repeated the question in a louder voice; just then the machine cut off suddenly and my words came out in a shout, and we laughed together.

"I have no preference," Quis went on, more peaceably. "I think I'm going to pitch every night, and I like the uncertainty of that. It doesn't matter to me if I come in to start an inning or with the bases loaded, and it doesn't matter to me who's up at bat. I don't have any choice, so it doesn't matter. If I had a choice, I'd say bring up your Class A team and I'll pitch to *them*. I also don't like it if my manager or my pitching coach asks me if I want an inning tonight, just to get my work in, or asks me if I'm tired after a lot of appearances in a row and might want the night off. My answer is that I want to be told what to do. I want to pitch when you need me."

It took me a while before I quite saw the elegance and use-

fulness of this attitude. Relief pitchers, of course, deal almost
exclusively with dire straits: it comes with the country. If they
start to worry about this, if they think about worst-case or best-
case situations or which hitters they'd rather not pitch to in a
jam, they have made matters infinitely harder for themselves.
Quis had simply turned off that kind of anxiety; it had ceased to
exist for him. He is good at this—it is almost as much a part of
his repertoire as his sinkerball. "When I'm away from the park
or at home, I try not to think about my work at all," he told me
on another occasion. "This job would be a killer if you couldn't
do that. There's plenty of time for me to worry from the sixth
inning on."

◆ ◆ ◆

ONE FINGER DOWN, BY ANCIENT TRADITION, IS THE CATCHER'S
signal for a fastball, but whoever is catching Dan Quisenberry
knows that one finger means the sinker. Quis doesn't *have* a
fastball. For the sinker, he holds the ball with the seams and
tries to throw without undue stress or snap; it arrives at about
seventy-eight or eighty m.p.h. and, ideally, executes a small hip
swerve as it crosses the plate. Quisenberry likes to give the
impression that he has nothing much to do with the action of the
pitch or its results. "I've always felt that when I throw it something wonderful is going to happen—something good for us,"
he said to me once. On another day, he suddenly asked, "Have
I ever told you about my agreement with the ball?" I said no,
and he said, "Well, our deal is that I'm not going to throw you
very hard as long as you promise to move around when you get
near the plate, because *I want you back*. So if you do your part
we'll get to play some more." He watched my reaction to this
with considerable relish, and then elaborated in less Oz-like
fashion. "I've got good control and some movement, but there
are guys around with better sinkers than mine. Greg Minton is
one. Jim Acker, who's with Toronto. Bob Stanley. Mine is generally around the plate and low. You can't start it out at the
batter's knees, because if you do it's a ball. If you want it inside
on a right-hander, you kind of throw it over the middle a little
and let it run in—hopefully *down* and in. If it's going to be
outside to a left-hander, you're throwing it to the outer half—the
outer half of the plate to him, that is—and it's supposed to go
down and away. If you want it inside to him, you throw it off
the plate, and it's meant to run back over. But of course if the

ball doesn't do its job, if it starts dancing all over the place—well, then it's going to get hurt."

Even when it is doing its job, the Quisenberry sinker is apt to have adventures. He gives up something on the order of one hit per inning, and a lot of his outs come on hard-hit balls that seem to be hit right at one of his infielders. "Magical things keep happening behind me," Quis often says, and he points out that the Kansas City second baseman, Frank White, has extraordinary range and hands, and that White's two partners at shortstop in recent years—first U.L. Washington and now Onix Concepcion—are scarcely less talented. The infield at Royals Stadium is AstroTurf, which should be a considerable handicap for a man who throws so many ground balls, but his defense makes up for that, it seems. George Brett, the Royals third baseman, told me that when the team won a pennant in 1980 Quisenberry's infielders ragged him with references to his "30-30-30 Club"—thirty saves, thirty strikeouts, and thirty great plays made behind him. "He's a comfortable guy to bat against," Brett said. "Guys go up there looking to hit the ball. He's like Scott McGregor, of the Orioles. You feel good batting against him, every time, and at the end of the game you realize you've gone oh-for-four—a *comfortable* oh-for-four."

Quisenberry, in any case, has some other pitches, and he has worked incessantly to widen his repertoire. It took him until 1982 to develop an effective breaking ball, and last year he came up with a changeup that he at last felt confident about. He tinkered with a forkball for a time but had to junk it. When the Royals made a barnstorming visit to Japan at the end of the 1981 season, Quisenberry mastered the knuckleball—a nasty shock for American League batters the following summer. But the knuckler doesn't quite work for him anymore, for some reason. "If the knuckleball was my wife, I'd divorce her," Quis said. "She's not consistent, she's not reliable—I just can't depend on her at all. I can throw it great in warmups or playing catch, but in a game now I just use it to show the batters that it's there. If it's done right, it's the most fun pitch to throw in the world. The good knuckleball pitchers throw it just about all the time. With them, it's a stronger relationship. I think I'm just about out of new pitches. I can work on locations and different speeds, but there isn't much more I can think of. I wish I could throw the overhand curveball. Wouldn't *that* be a surprise!"

Back at Terry Park, Quisenberry had told me about his conversion into a submariner, which came about on that very field in the spring of 1980. He had been called up from Omaha in the middle of the previous season, at a time when the Royals were desperate for any kind of a middle-innings relief man who could get people out; he was far from their first choice for the job, but he stuck on, and even accounted for five saves; mostly, he was the setup man for Al Hrabosky, who was then the club's short-relief honcho. Quisenberry was a standup sidearm pitcher then, with virtually no breaking ball. Jim Frey succeeded Whitey Herzog as the Kansas City skipper the next spring, and early in the training schedule Quisenberry had a very bad outing against the Pirates. After the game, Frey asked him to throw for him on the sidelines, to see what he had. After about fifteen pitches, Frey began saying things like "Are you throwing as hard as you can?" and "Is *that* the way you throw your breaking ball?" and Quis concluded that there might be a quick turnaround just ahead in his career. A day or two later, Frey told him that he'd set up a sidelines appointment for him with Kent Tekulve, the great Pittsburgh submariner, when the Pirates next came down from Bradenton to play.

"I thought he was just going to give me a few pointers," Quisenberry said, "but when the day came Jim said to Tekulve, 'We want this guy to be like you. He throws a little like you already, but basically he doesn't have shit.' So it was a total makeover. Tekulve showed me there were three basics to the motion, which were: sit on your back leg, bend at the waist, and, most important, extend the left leg—my front leg—way beyond the normal point out ahead. He told me to open up about six or eight inches beyond what's normal, coming right at the plate with the leg, and not to put that foot out heel-down at first, which is your natural instinct. This opens your body up a whole lot more, and it lets you stay low and keeps your arm low. If I don't get way out there and do that, I land *here*"—Quis was on his feet now—"with this front leg locked, and I start and end standing up, throwing the old sidearm way. I've always got to fight that. It's a battle for me, in spring training and all through the season, because when the ball comes up, the way it wants to, I've got nothing. Staying down like that is a strange feeling when you first try it, because you're totally off balance and you keep thinking you're going to fall over sideways. If I don't make this little hop at the end of the motion, I *do* fall over.

"Well, I didn't like this at all. Frey and a lot of our coaches were watching, and I was throwing all over the place and bouncing the ball before it got to the plate. Teke kept saying, 'Hey, that's a good pitch, that's the way to throw,' and I'm thinkin', I have no *idea* what I'm doing. But Jim liked it, and two days later he put me in another game—it was against the Pirates again, but Tekulve wasn't here—and I did real well. I was on my way.''

Yes. That summer, Quisenberry, who had never run up more than fifteen saves in a season during his five-year stay in the minors, saved thirty-three games for the pennant-bound Royals, and also went 12–7 in the won-lost accounting, while appearing in a league-leading seventy-five games. He won a game and saved another one against the Yankees in the American League playoffs. He had another win and another save in the club's losing six-game World Series against the Phillies, but in fact pitched poorly in the classic, unexpectedly giving up some walks and being charged with two of the team's losses. It was clear that he was very tired at this point, but by most measurements it had been quite a year.

Other submarine-style pitchers have thrived in the majors, to be sure, though never in great numbers. The list is headed by the unfortunate Carl Mays, a starting pitcher who won two hundred and eight games while in the employ of the Red Sox, Yankees, Reds, and Giants, more than sixty years ago, but is remembered now only as the man who threw the pitch that struck and killed Ray Chapman, of the Indians: the majors' only fatality. Eldon Auker, another starter, won a hundred and thirty games while toiling for the dangerous Tigers of the nineteen-thirties, and subsequent underhanders included Dick Hyde and Ted Abernathy, relievers who both worked for the Washington Senators (although Abernathy's most successful years came when he pitched for the Cubs and then the Reds), and the capable Cecil Upshaw, a nine-year bullpen stalwart with the Braves in the sixties and seventies. I asked Quisenberry once why more people hadn't taken up the submariner's way after he had demonstrated how successful it could be. He said that in fact he had tried to pass along the Tekulve Method to several pitchers—Dick Howser, his present manager, had no objection as long as he wasn't tutoring pitchers on contending teams in the American League West. ''He's tried to help,'' Howser said, ''but most guys can't seem to stay with it for long. What you're leaving out of the equation is Quisenberry's maturity and personality. I can't explain it. Everybody can talk about it and analyze it, but nobody can tell you why some people have that winning attitude and others don't. I've been around some great ones in my time—Sparky Lyle and Gossage and now Quisenberry. They were very different people, but they all had that special thing. They're unselfish. They don't want adulation, but they absolutely relish the situation. They don't have the luxury of making mistakes. And you have to remember that it takes real courage to change yourself over like Quisenberry did, and stay with it until you get it right. If it doesn't work for you, it can be the end of a career.''

Quis had a good two innings against the Rangers on my last afternoon at Fort Myers. He retired the side on five pitches in the eighth and gave up a harmless single—a bouncer over the mound—in the ninth to nail down a K.C. win. It was another save, if that mattered. He worked quickly, the way he always does, and the sinker was there, although it wasn't quite on the corners yet. After the game, he seemed boyish and exuberant, exhanging japes and smiles in the clubhouse with Renie Martin, another Kansas City reliever, who is a close friend. (Martin didn't make the final cut, and pitched in Omaha this year.) Quis's blond three-year-old son, David, was in the locker room that afternoon, and several of the tall Royals players stopped by to speak to the little boy. Children are a rarity in some clubhouses, even during spring training, but the Royals seem to be strong on family. On our way into the clubhouse, Quis had introduced me to his wife, Janie, and their five-year-old daughter, Alysia, and to Janie's parents, Fred and Pat Howard, who were visiting from California—a pack of Quis-groupies together on the lawn, waiting to drive the man home for a swim before supper.

Inside, Quis told me that he would probably pitch one more time in Florida before the regular season began. His expression changed a little. "It's about to start," he said. "We're a week away, and to do what the club wants me to do I'm going to have to be great. Rollie's got to be great, Sutter's got to be great, Gossage's got to be great. . . ."

I said that most people didn't work at jobs where greatness was exactly a daily prerequisite, or could be measured.

"Yes, there's a tension that comes with that, and when the season comes that tension will be there all the time. It's starting to happen to me now. I've begun to wonder when that little click will come, when the switch will go on. I don't know where it is—here in the heart or in the brain, or what. I don't know how I turn it on, but somehow it happens every year."

◆ ◆ ◆

THE NEW SEASON BEGAN IN DESULTORY FASHION FOR QUISEN-
berry. Four times in April, he failed to hold a lead or a tie score
in a game he had entered. He steadied for a time, but then was
horribly racked in an inning against the Orioles, very nearly
blowing a 9–4 Kansas City lead. The worst was just ahead: an
exhibition game against the Royals' Omaha farm club, when
Quisenberry, instead of recovering his form, gave up three singles, a stolen base, and a pair of earned runs, all in one inning.
Almost everything he threw was hit, and hit *hard*. Quisenberry,
telling me about it later, said that he had felt as if he were in the
middle of a pinball machine. "I thought, *Uh*-oh," he said. "I
knew it was time to climb down from whatever kind of weird
flight I'd been on and catch the next plane back."

He turned things around for a while, starting with a tidy effort
against the Yankees his next time out (it was an NBC "Game
of the Week" presentation). After that day, Quisenberry put
together a dazzling stretch of work, during which he surrendered
one lone run (it was unearned) in eleven appearances; he picked
up seven saves in eighteen and a third innings pitched, and his
earned-run average shrank from 5.60 to 2.75. He was back on
track, or so it seemed. His next game, however—at Comiskey
Park, on June 1st—was a nightmare. He faced six White Sox
batters in the seventh inning and retired none of them, surrendering five hits and three runs; when Howser took him out of
the game at last, it was only the third time in his major-league
career that he had failed to finish an inning.

I went out to Kansas City at the end of June, to see the Royals
play a weekend series against the division-leading California
Angels. The Royals were in fourth place, four and a half games
behind the visitors, and I was pretty sure that Quisenberry
blamed himself to some degree for their disappointing record to
date. Things had gone better for him since the debacle in Chicago, and his earned-run average had been slowly dropping for
three weeks, but he had been cuffed about here and there as
well. He told me that he felt confused and frustrated by the
season's unexpected turn of events, and that at times pitching
hadn't been fun for him. "It's too big a part of me for it not to
be fun," he said. "There has to be an element of that, or the
game will drive you crazy. I've known times before when I could
throw everything pretty well and still lose, and I'd feel all right,
but if balls are being hit off my forehead or keep bouncing against
the outfield wall it's—Well, it gets chaotic."

A week or two before my visit, Royals pitching coach Gary

Blaylock had noticed on a game videotape that Quisenberry's left foot wasn't landing far enough out in front and to the left as it came down in mid-delivery; he was blocking himself out a bit, and his sinker wasn't sinking much in consequence. Quis made the correction, and it helped. When Quisenberry told me about this, I pointed out that this was exactly the chronic problem that he had described for me during spring training. "Yes," he said at once, "so why is it always so hard?" He threw his hands up in mock despair. Part of the trouble—most of his early trouble, perhaps—was the money. Quis said that back in April and May he had noticed that he was squeezing the ball on the mound in difficult situations and that he'd often found himself trying to throw the perfect pitch: a ten-foot sinker, a nine-foot breaking ball. He said he'd even tried to throw a ninety-mile-an-hour fastball here and there—insanity for him. "Why would I try anything like that at *this* point in my career?" he said. Others on the club noticed, of course. "He had that one streak when he'd just signed the contract and he seemed uptight, like he was trying to prove to himself and to everybody that he deserved all that money," George Brett told me. "I'd go over to see him, and he'd be stuttering on the mound when we talked. It even seemed as if he'd forgotten where he was supposed to be on some plays, so I'd have to tell him. It wasn't like him at all. Now that's all over with, and he's back to his old loose self. You take a look at him after a game and can't tell if he just got the save or took a loss. He's always the same—you count on that."

Last winter, the Royals front office completed a revolutionary reshaping of its salary structure, which included the offer of extraordinary lifetime contracts to three of the team's established stars: George Brett, Willie Wilson, and Dan Quisenberry. The decision was not the result of any pending salary negotiations with the three (Quisenberry was in the third year of a four-year contract, which paid him about eight hundred thousand dollars per year) but seemed intended, rather, to guarantee their presence in the Kansas City lineup for the remainder of their professional careers, and to free them—the players and the Royals management, and perhaps the fans as well—from the trauma of future high-level contract struggles and the possible loss of any or all of the stars to free agency if an impasse should develop. The three contracts are differently constituted, but in effect they make the men co-investors in major real-estate holdings now belonging to Avron Fogelman, of Memphis, who owns forty-nine percent of the Royals franchise. Under Quisenberry's plan, he will be paid about six million dollars for the next six seasons' work (including this season), but tax-sheltered real-estate reinvestments in that same time will return him something on the order of forty-five or fifty million dollars over the next forty years. No other team, it should be added, has made any such generous or wide-sweeping arrangement with a group of players who are still in the middle years of existing contracts.

Quisenberry looked uneasy when I suggested that his new contract might have been the immediate cause of his early troubles on the mound, and only later in the season, when I brought up the question again, did he say—quietly and almost in an offhand way—that, yes, the money might have had something to do with it. Plainly, he didn't want to make excuses for himself—most of all an excuse with such impossible proportions and overtones. Paul Splittorff, a recently retired Royals star pitcher, who is a close friend of Quisenberry's (Quis calls him "one of my life heroes"), has no doubts about the matter. "Early this year, Quis said he felt strange about the new contract," he told me. "He kept saying that this money was crazy—how important was what he did in baseball to the scheme of the world, and things like that. I kept telling him that they had come to him with the money, not the other way around, so he shouldn't feel the pressure. But this kind of thing always happens. You're the same kind of player, no matter what they're paying you. If you're a lifetime .280 hitter, that's what you are, and you can't make yourself into a .300 hitter because of the money. It's even tougher on Quis, because if he tries to throw five miles an hour faster—which is inevitable—he's in trouble. Of course he's happy about the money, and surprised, but, being the kind of man he is, it's hurt him, too."

None of these quandaries and surprises were apparent in Quisenberry's demeanor when we met in the spacious Royals clubhouse on Saturday afternoon. The coming game, a night affair, was still hours away, but Quis, who habitually arrives very early at the park, was already in uniform and ready for the next thing. Like other veteran ballplayers I have encountered, he seemed exceptionally contented in his clubhouse; he looked almost dug in, and, watching him there, with his friends and his mail and his keepsakes (there was a child's red fireman's hat, with a red headlight on it, perched on top of his cubicle), I thought of the Badger at home in his slippers, in "The Wind in the Willows." Quisenberry is a genial and respected figure in the clubhouse (he is the Royals' player representative: their elected union delegate in the Players Association), and so many

overlapping conversations were swirling around his corner of
the den that I was glad when he suggested that we walk out to
visit his other place of business—the bullpen. There were a couple of other players in view outside as we strolled across the
warm ungrass—the home bullpen is in right field at Royals Stadium—but the sunstruck table of the field and the rising tiers of
gleaming empty seats encircled us in a silent bowl of light.

"There's Charlie Leibrandt over there, throwing up on the
sidelines," Quis said, nodding his head toward one of the Royals playing catch. He watched for my reaction—this is a first-
year-Little League baseball joke—and I laughed in spite of
myself. "This year's bullpen is starting to develop," he went on.
"It's a good group. Each year, the makeup of the pen is a little
different, and the feeling changes. Our new man out here is
Mike LaCoss"—LaCoss, an experienced National League right-
handed pitcher, had been signed as a free agent over the winter—"and we're getting to know him a little. We call him Buffy
and Izod, or Izoid, and Buffenstein. I never know where all the
nicknames come from. He likes to mix it up—get on guys and
have them get on him. He's an expert bridge player, or thinks
he is. Then there's Mike Jones, Joe Beckwith, and John Wathan,
the catcher—he always sits a little bit apart—and the rest. Joe
watches All-Star wrestling, and he likes to show us all the new
holds. Renie Martin used to bring pencil and paper, and he'd
draw little cartoons of things that happened in each game. Mike
Armstrong and I used to do some games in Spanish—I just
remembered. Broadcasts, I mean. Of course, neither of us could
speak Spanish, but that didn't stop us. The trouble with bullpens
is that they keep changing. The people in them come and go,
so you can't always keep things going. Last year was a good
crossword bullpen, but we're not so big on that this year for
some reason. But we still do the crossword in the paper first
thing every day, and then Izod looks at the bridge hand and tells
us how Omar Sharif would have played it. The early part of the
game is given to the starting pitcher and the other guys on the
field, and Muggsy—Jimmie Schaffer (he's our bullpen coach)—
sets the tone. We're critical, I mean. If a pitcher in the game
gets behind in the count, he says, 'How can you not throw strikes
with *that* garbage?' and you know he's saying it about you when
you're in the game. There's a total freedom in the bullpen—
freedom of speech, freedom of action. One of the great things
about baseball is that everything gets out in the open."

I asked if he'd heard from the others in the pen when he was having troubles this year, and he said, "Oh, sure. I was called Firecan and Arson and—well, much better stuff than that, if I could remember it. Silence would be terrible under those circumstances. We get on everybody, except there's sort of a compact about the rookies—you go easier with them. And then of course you don't say much to the next man who's going to come into the game—he's off in his little world, getting ready."

Quisenberry, I'd been told, starts to get ready after the sixth inning or so. He becomes withdrawn and abstracted, preparing for what is to come. Players call this "putting on your game face."

We had reached outer right field by now, and Quis pointed to a spot on the AstroTurf about twenty feet short of the right-field foul pole. "This is where the ball landed when Robin Yount hit a shot against me here once. Clint Hurdle dove for it and missed, and it turned into an inside-the-park home run. Sometimes when you're sitting over here in the pen, you can see a line drive disappear into the right-field corner, with the right fielder chasing it. Then the ball comes flying past you on the ground, going in the other direction, and then here comes the fielder again after it, like a dog after a rabbit. It's a great sight."

He stopped, and began pointing out various places in the empty right-field stands above us. "Two girls from Topeka sit up there, most games," he said. "They drive all the way here for the games, and then drive home again. Up there, there's an old gent we call Colonel Sanders—he has that look. Then there's a great fan named Joe Hess, who has a long white beard. He's Santa Claus, of course. There's a guy in Army fatigues who comes a lot—I call him Phnom Penh—and there are three or four grandmas who sit together over here: old sweethearts. You get to know the real fans. Some Sunday games, on days when it's real hot, I get out the ground crew's hose and spray the fans, who line up to hang over that incline over the pen. I only do it in the middle of the sixth inning, and the fans who want to cool off come over and crowd around for it. It's a custom by now, I guess."

We reached the bullpen—a row of orange grandstand seats under an oblong fibre-glass roof and behind a high chain-link fence, with one larger, round, overstuffed black chair in the corner: Muggsy Schaffer's throne. The phone to the dugout was on an adjacent wall. There were a dozen or more little marks scratched on the telephone receiver box, and when I pointed them out Quisenberry said they were left over from the previous season, when the bullpen people had begun keeping track of the outstanding fielding plays made by the new Royals first base-man, Steve Balboni—plays that, in their judgment, his prede-cessor at the position, Willie Aikens, would probably *not* have made. Behind the bullpen chairs were two pitcher's mounds and two home plates set out along a stretch of lush, beautiful grass—the only natural lawn in the park. It is a small irony of contem-porary baseball that the Royals' George Toma is considered the best groundskeeper in the business and now has no grass to cultivate except in the bullpens and down some tilted strips of turf that surround the celebrated Royals Stadium fountains, be-yond the fences. Quisenberry pointed out Toma's office, which is under the stands, to one side of the bullpen, and then took me into a vast concrete equipment shed stuffed with mowers and rakes and rollers, a couple of John Deere tractors, coils of thick hose, and so forth. Just beyond this was a long, upcurving con-crete tunnel, which held more equipment; several cars were parked in the tunnel.

"This is all wonderful," Quis said, "because what you want most in a bullpen is distraciton. During a long game, you can walk over here and visit with George. His office is air-conditioned, and sometimes he'll give you a cup of coffee or some of that iced tea he's made by leaving a pitcher of water and tea bags out in the sun all day. You can watch TV there or read the horticultural news on his bulletin board. You can sit in one of the cars and turn on the radio, and sometimes even bring in another game that's being played somewhere. There are odometers and things. There are the ground-crew guys to talk to. Sometimes you can even sneak a ride on George's Suzuki tricycle."

I asked Quisenberrry about the requisites for a good bullpen, and he mentioned distance from the fans ("You don't want to hear *everything* they're saying to you"), some kind of roof for rain protection, a good bathroom, and a screen to keep balls from getting loose on the field when you're warming up. He much prefers enclosed bullpens to the ones that border the outer stretches of the playing field in foul ground. California's bullpen is beyond the fence, and so are the pens in Chicago, Yankee Stadium, and Baltimore; Oakland and Minnesota and Toronto have sideline pens. And so on. Seattle has a sideline pen and no bathroom; the visiting pen there was moved from right field to left field last year, and a player who needs to use the bathroom has to come in between innings, passing both dugouts along the way. (Quis had begun to sound like a *Guide Michelin*, and I began to envision glyphs illustrating the amenities and points of interest for a young pitcher making his first grand tour of the American League.)

The Royals Stadium bullpen's bathroom is outstanding, Quis said: air-conditioning, heating for cold nights, a door that locks, a sink, and a mirror. The Fenway Park can, by contrast, has no light and no sink, and the door doesn't lock.

I asked about the odd bullpens in Tiger Stadium, which are sunk below ground level in foul territory, with a little screen above them to protect the occupants's heads from foul balls.

"We used to make out that's a submarine," Quis said eagerly. "We'd make those pinging sounds, and if a ball came near us it was a depth charge, and we'd fire our torpedoes. If the ball bounced off the little screen, that was a direct hit, and we'd panic and then ask for damage reports. Then there's always Cleveland, which is interesting in a different way. They've gone and reversed their home-team and visiting-team pens this year, too. The pens there are down the line, but they do have shelter and plenty of grounds equipment and all. That and the biggest spiders in the league. Now that they've put us on the other side of the field, I don't know if the spiders will be as good this year. I don't know their names yet. It's always wet and damp in Cleveland, and there are lots of mosquitoes, but you can catch the mosquitoes and feed them to the spiders—just toss them into the web. There's almost always a rain delay there, so there's plenty of time for all that." He was laughing.

There are bullpen legends, of course—the bullpen pitchers who have put on groundskeepers' uniforms and joined the crew sweeping down the infield in the middle of a game, and so forth. Jim Colborn was the first Kansas City pitcher to think of that one, years ago. Quisenberry joined the Royals too late to see Colborn throw his no-hitter against the Rangers, back in 1977, but he knows the story. Colborn, a free spirit, was so entranced with his work that day that he became convinced that he would pitch *another* no-hitter on his next outing, and insisted that he wouldn't need anybody in the bullpen that day to back him up. All the relief men obliged him and stayed in the dugout when the game began—except for one cynic, Steve Mingori, who trudged on out as usual. Mingori watched Colborn pitch to three or four batters and then got to his feet and began to wave frantically for more help out there. He was right, it turned out: Colborn got bombed.

• ◆ •

DAN AND JANIE QUISENBERRY LIVE IN A HANDSOME STONE CO-
lonial house on a breezy hilltop in the still-rural Leawood section of Kansas City; the house is new and still not much
furnished—the family moved in only last fall—but there is space
and light and airiness everywhere, indoors and out, and a sense
of beginning permanence. The view down the sloping lawns
takes in a couple of other sizable houses in the distance, a stand
of old, dark trees, and, closer at hand, a new, major-league
jungle gym. Before lunch there one day in June, Alysia did
tricycle wheelies on the brick patio for a visiting out-of-town
writer while Quis broiled chicken on a Weber grill; David,
overstimulated by the occasion, went briefly to pieces and was
sent up to his room, but recovered in short order ("I'm better
now," he announced from the head of the stairs) and was wel-
comed back as we sat down to lunch. Dan said a grace while
we all held hands around the table.

The Quisenberry's are more fortunate than most baseball cou-
ples, for he has stayed with one team ever since he made it to
the majors, and now he and Janie know they will be in Kansas
City for good. They have made friends there outside of baseball,
and belong to the Village Presbyterian Church, in nearby Prairie
Village. (Quis has granted himself a dispensation from Sunday
services during the season.) They are considerably involved in
the Harvesters program, a branch of the national organization
that enlists restaurants and groceries and chain stores in the
process of distributing food to the urban poor. An American
League official told me recently that he had run into the Quis-
enberrys in the Royals' offices on opening day this year, and
when Dan went off to talk to someone there, he ventured to say
something to Janie about Quis's new contract. "Yes, we're really blessed," she said at once. "Just think of all the things we
can do for other people now, for the rest of our lives." During
my visit, however, I sensed in both Quis and Janie a strong wish
for privacy in these matters, and we returned to baseball.

Earlier on, at my request, Quis had dug out some thick old
clip books, and, looking through them, we found a short strip
of faded yellow Sports-Ticker tape: a double row of numbers,
followed by the notation "WP QUISENBERRY"—his first major-
league victory, in a road game against the Rangers on July 22,
1979. Janie had joined us—she is shy, and calm, with a sunburst

smile—and she shook her head at the sight of those first box scores and two-inch, bottom-of-the-column mentions of a red-haired sidearming rookie reliever. "We used to die for a little clip like that," she said, "but now he pitches so much I just can't handle all the cutting and pasting. We always tell ourselves we'll catch up after the season is over." The stories grew more frequent, and headlines began to appear (the Kansas City *Star*: "QUISENBERRY: AH, RELIEF!") as we turned the pages, and then there was a 1979 item about Quis being carried off the field in Detroit after being struck on the knee by a line drive off the bat of the Tigers' Ron LeFlore—a ferocious batter who had previously ended the career of the famous knuckleballer Wilbur Wood with a similar shot through the box. "I was listening on the radio," Janie said, "and I remember the announcer saying, 'And Ron LeFlore may have sent another pitcher to an early retirement,' and I turned right around and said, 'But we just *got* here!' " Quis recovered quickly, though, and when 1980 rolled around, the pasted-in headline and feature stories and box scores began to take up more and more space on the pages of the clip books. Looking at these now, Quis shook his head. "At first, I kept thinking that the batters weren't trying," he said. "They were major-leaguers and I was getting them out, but I thought they'd figure me out once they began to pay attention. They kept saying, 'Wait till we see this guy next year,' and I didn't know if they were right or not."

But by 1980 Quisenberry was a submariner, and the batters found themselves in deeper difficulties. "CAN QUIZ MAINTAIN PACE?" reads a headline in the Kansas City *Times* of June 27, 1980, and a *Sporting News* box from August 9, 1980, shows Quis leading everybody in the league in the Rolaids "Fireman of the Year" standings. He had arrived—even in his own mind—at last. "There was a road trip to Boston and Baltimore and New York after the All-Star break that year, and somewhere along in there I began to think that maybe I wasn't going to be too bad after all—that it wasn't just flash, and I wasn't just fooling them somehow."

It had taken a while, starting back in Waterloo, Iowa, in 1975—the Royals' bottom-level, Class A minor-league club; he moved up to the AA Jacksonville club later that summer, then slid back to Waterloo the next year. After two more years at Jacksonville, he and Janie decided to try winter ball in Mexico; he played for Guasave, on the Mexican west coast, and was traded to Mazatlán (Maury Wills was the manager there) on Christmas Eve of

1977. "It was horrible—a disaster," Quis told me. "We were both sick all the time, and I was about 2–4 for the winter, and my E.R.A. was up in the fives and sixes. I had nothing but a breaking ball, and those were the best hitters I'd ever seen. It was about then that I decided to be a sinkerballer. We'd gone to Mexico to see if I couldn't break out of AA ball, but it didn't work—I went right back to Jacksonville and stayed there the whole year." Slowly, things did begin to pick up, though; he had fifteen saves that summer, and in 1979 he made the AAA Omaha club—his last stop before the majors, in July. He had been a sidearmer since college, by the way, and his Waterloo manager, John Sullivan—he is now the bullpen coach for the Toronto Blue Jays—took one look and very quickly moved him into the bullpen. "I thought it was a demotion," Quis told me. "But after a while I noticed I was getting into a lot of games, and I decided it was fun. You never know, you know."

Quis was born in Santa Monica and grew up in Culver City and then Costa Mesa, California. His parents were divorced when he was seven, and his mother remarried and had more children; his older brother, Marty, was a good athlete and a submarine-style pitcher—a better pitcher than he was, Quis insists—who did well in junior-college ball and expected to be picked up in the major-league draft; when it didn't happen, he gave up baseball for good. He became a minister in the Vineyard Christian Fellowship and is now a family counsellor; the two brothers are still very close. Dan grew up thinking mostly about sports, too—he has kept in touch with most of the kids with whom he played street basketball and street football and Little League baseball back in Costa Mesa—and he wanted to become a professional ballplayer but knew almost from the beginning that he didn't have the size and physique for it. "What's happened really *is* a dream," he told me. He followed his brother to Orange Coast College and then moved to La Verne College, where he won thirty-one games over two seasons; he pitched an astounding one hundred and ninety-four innings there in 1975 and, somewhere along the line, shifted over to a sidearm style, to ease the demands on his arm. Then he, too, was skipped over in the draft, in a year when the twenty-four major-league teams selected more than seven hundred young players in that process. "It was a crusher," Quis says. "I'd done some other things in college"—he met Janie at La Verne, where she was an education major—"but I hadn't concentrated on anything except baseball. I didn't care for anything else in the world." His college coach at La Verne, Ben Hines, made some calls, however—to front-office people in Detroit, Baltimore, and Kansas City—and in time the Royals said they just might have a spot. Quis drove up to Santa Ana and was signed by a Royals scout, Rosey Gilhousen. "The contract was for five hundred dollars and a bag of chew to be named later," Quis recalls. "Well, I think they threw in a bat and a Royals banner, and maybe a sticker for my car. I was on my *way*!"

The basic Quisenberry style is humorous and invariably modest—a throwaway mode that is more central to the man than his eccentric pitching. I offered the guess that this sort of response, this habitual presentation of himself as an athlete who had succeeded mostly because of repeated and unexpected strokes of pure good luck, might be a way of concealing something. Was it possible that he did not want to admit his own powerful competitive urges?

"Well, I *used* to be competitive," he said. "I mean, I used to be competitive and show it. When I was a kid, I cried when I lost—I was one of those. In junior college, I lost a game once and when it was over I stuck the nozzle of a shower in my mouth and turned on the water. I was so frustrated I just did that and drank water until I vomited. Another time, I couldn't find the ball I wanted to warm up with, and I threw a whole bag of balls around the locker room looking for it. I couldn't stand things."

I asked what had happened to that Dan Quisenberry, and he said, "He grew up, I guess. I don't do stuff out on the mound—throw my hands up when I strike out a guy, and all. I don't like to show up the other player. I still like to win, but I don't like excuses. I don't like guys who brag on themselves. I have to talk to the press like everybody else, but I really don't like to talk about myself, to say what percentage of winning games I've been in and all that stuff. I try to stay away from that." He paused, perhaps sensing that he still hadn't quite answered my question. "Yes, I'm competitive," he said. "At this level, everybody is intensely competitive. What I want is to keep that extreme level of concentration but still keep the fun in the game. You have to do that if you're going to succeed over a period of time. You have to relax and let the unconscious part of you do the playing. The dinosaur brain has to take over. But I work at things, too. I'm trying to be very good at baseball and to keep it from being too important in my life. I have to live on that border all the time."

◆ ◇ ◆

IN BASEBALL CIRCLES, QUISENBERRY'S HUMOR IS TALKED ABOUT almost as much as his pitching—in fact, the two attributes, or sides of him, often seem to be woven together in the players' and writers' minds: a funny guy who throws funny, too. Here, as well, the man may be slightly and persistently misperceived. He makes occasional appearances on the winter-banquet scene, and the laughter rattles the glassware, but he does not tell jokes or dredge up ancient and improbable baseball anecdotes. He is fresh and playful and surprising, and you are sometimes disarmed by the notion that he is as pleased and startled by what has just come out of him as his listeners are. Asked by one writer for his thoughts about the infamously bumpy diamond in Oakland Coliseum, Quis suggested that the club might try dragging a dead whale across the infield. After he had given up a game-winning pinch-hit single in a 1982 game against the Angels, he was asked if this was not the worst possible way to lose a game. Quis took the reporter's question literally, and came up with a dozen or more worse possibilities: he could have balked a man around the bases; he could have thrown ten wild pitches; a sudden earthquake could have jostled a third-out fly ball out of Amos Otis' glove; and so forth. His line "I have seen the futre and it is much like the present, only longer" lingers happily in the mind (I comfort myself with it often, like an Armenian reaching in his pocket for his worry beads), but most of his stuff is transitory and ironical, and is clearly intended to prick holes in the unending and ponderously serious business of the post-game or pre-game sports interview. Sometimes Quis delivers playful or patently ridiculous responses to glum questions and then is amazed to see his lines repeated literally in the papers the next day; earlier this year, he told a visiting writer (a man who evidently did not lift his gaze from his notebook during the interview) that his bad spell in April and May was attributable to the fact that he had lifted weights all winter and become overmuscled. He is not evasive, however, and reporters around the league admire and respect him for never ducking out of the clubhouse after a game, no matter how painful its outcome. To me, the japes and verbal pranks look like a form of self-preservation—a relief from the dreary dailiness and intensity of the relief man's lot. "I'm not trying to turn anybody off," Quis said once, "but I've been talking with the writers for six years now and I'm getting kind of bored with myself, really." His friend Paul Splittorff said to me, "The writers come to him for one-liners and stuff, and he feels he should always come up with something. He thinks he can be funny every day, like he pitches every day. The man is funny, but he's not a natural comedian. There's more there than that."

◆ ◆ ◆

QUISENBERRY PITCHED IN TWO OF THE THREE GAMES I SAW THE Royals play against the Angels out in Kansas City, and picked up a win and a save in the process. In the Friday-night game, an almost interminable fourteen-inning affair, he came on in the twelfth, with the score tied at 3–3, and retired the side without incident. Doug DeCinces led off the top of the thirteenth for the Angels with a slick bunt—a base hit—and moved along to second on Daryl Sconiers' dunked, wrongfield base hit. Ruppert Jones hit a low liner to Frank White, which was almost turned into a double play, but DeCinces came around to score on Bobby Grich's clean single to right center. Then Gary Pettis was safe at first on another half-nubbed infield hopper—the fourth hit of the inning. The bases were loaded and Quisenberry looked to be in the soup, but Dick Schofield, pinch-hitting, rapped a bouncer to White, who threw home to start a second-to-catcher-to-first double play that retired the side. Even in an overeventful, unsuccessful inning like this, I noticed, Quisenberry's work seemed brusque and businesslike. Barely pausing between pitches, he leaned, sank, bobbled, threw, hopped sidewise, got the ball back, and did it all over again. His work was funny-looking and profoundly undramatic, and he went about it like a man sweeping out a kitchen.

The Royals got the run back in their half in thrilling fashion, when Lonnie Smith tripled over the center fielder's head with two out, scoring Jim Sundberg from second base. Reprieved, Quis returned to his kitchen—and instantly gave up a leadoff single to Bob Boone. A sacrifice moved Boone to second, and Quis walked the next man intentionally, thus setting up a double play on an infield grounder by DeCinces, which ended the inning; Quisenberry's last pitch, a sinker, splintered DeCinces' bat. The Royals won the game in the bottom of the fourteenth (a walk, an infield out, and Greg Pryor's pinch-hit single to left), and Quis, a winner in spite of himself, faced the deadline-hungry writers in the clubhouse in characteristic style: "My first inning was smooth, my second was stinky, my third—well, I wanted to make myself sick and throw up out there, but we got out of it somehow. I can't complain about those dink hits in the thirteenth, because I made a real bad pitch to Grich and he hit it for the run. I was lucky. Morale would have hit bottom on this club if we'd lost.''

Two days later, before a big Sunday crowd, Quis came in in the top of the ninth to defend Mark Gubicza's 3-0 lead and gave up a leadoff home run to the Angels' Ruppert Jones—a long fly ball that just slipped over the fence in left. Then he retired the side—infield out, fly-ball out, strikeout. The Royals, having taken two out of three games in the set, stepped into third place, only three and a half games behind the Angels, and Quisenberry had his fourteenth save.

I didn't know what to make of it. Quisenberry clearly wasn't pitching very well, but the club was succeeding with him in the crucial short-man role, and no one—Quisenberry least of all—looked concerned, at least in public, about the slovenly, non-imperious nature of his recent owrk. The season still had a long way to go, to be sure, but something else was happening here, too—happening to me, I mean. Because I had come to know him better and had been so taken with his disarming and sometimes boyish ways—his jokes and his dogged modesty and youthful deep seriousness—he had become an amateur to me: a human, life-size figure in a business full of demi-gods, inhumanly talented athletes, and egocentric, self-fabricated public personalities. He was clearly at home in this world, yet he also seemed out of place in it, and I had begun to wonder how such a fellow could succeed in a business where failure is so quickly sought out and resolutely punished. How good a pitcher was he, anyway? It was time to go to some others and ask.

Dic Howser (*he is a calm, laid-back manager, with a light voice and reassuring, small-town-bank-president look to him*): Yes, I'm concerned about him this year, but I'm also concerned when Brett doesn't hit or when Willie Wilson doesn't get on base for us. But I'm not concerned in a big way. I look around the leagues and I see a lot of the top relief pitchers have problems from time to time. You can almost expect it. I still think he's outstanding and he's going to have a good year. With his control—well, you'd better go up there hackin'! I think he knows he has to have a good year in order for us to have a good year. His temperament is deceiving. I think he's been more concerned by these off spells than I've been. I know how intense he is, how competitive. But even if he goes through three or four more bad stretches in a row I'm not going to get fancy and move him into the middle and put somebody else out there to finish up. I've got some confidence in the man. People asked me in the spring if I looked forward to forty or forty-five saves from him again, but that's asking too much. A lot of guys would have a great year with twenty-five saves. We expect Quisenberrry to do better than that, but we don't expect forty-five. We're not that crazy.

Bob Boone (*he has been catching in the majors for fourteen years and, at thirty-seven—he will be thirty-eight in November—is among the oldest day-to-day regulars in the game today; he is articulate and intelligent, and still an artist behind the plate*): Watching Quisenberry over the years, I've come to think his greatest attribute is his control. If you're batting against a guy with a super-sinker like that, you think about trying to get ahead in the count, so you can just take that pitch. But all the experienced hitters know by now that you really can't do that—he won't let you—so you say to yourself, "Well, I'm not going to let him get ahead of me," and you start out swinging at something that's his pitch. He's tough. It's a tough pitch to do much with, and the motion is different. It isn't that you try to hit his pitches harder—that happens against a knuckleballer, like Phil Niekro: you're always trying to hit him a mile, which doesn't help. But it's always hard to put the middle of your bat on Quisenberry's sinker, even though you know about where it's going to be. You're likely to hit it foul, so there may be a tendency on the part of some hitters to try to hit it fair, and that takes them out of their normal swing. All this and he's so durable that he can come at you almost every day. You have to have an amazing arm to be able to do that. The only way to handle him is to get ahead in the game, so you never get to see him.

Gary Blaylock (*at fifty-three, he is in his thirty-fifth year of baseball; he pitched for thirteen seasons in the minors and one in the majors—for the Cardinals and the Yankees in 1959; he became the Royals pitching coach last year, after nine years as a minor-league manager and eleven years as a scout*): With that delivery, he has less strain on his arm than most pitchers, because that underneath way is a natural movement for the arm. Anything overhead—what we think of as the natural way to pitch—is unnatural and puts a strain on the arm, so you get injuries. When you get in trouble pitching, the tendency is always to try to throw harder, and that's when you begin to break down mechanically. That happened a little to him, earlier on.

But he has the greatest temperament for this game I've ever seen, bar none. I'd heard about it before I came here, and it's true. A relief man can stay sharper than most, because he's out there so much, but it's hard to stay tuned to that game situation through a whole season. Maybe it's impossible.

John Wathan (*he has been catching for the Royals for ten years; now he sees spot duty—he loves to catch Sunday games—and pinch-hits; he has a strong chin and dark, curly hair, and an air of cheerful aggressiveness, the catcher's look*): He'll never get the Cy Young, because he doesn't throw smoke and because of how he talks to people. He talks about his Peggy Lee fastball—you know that song of hers "Is That All There Is?"—and it sticks in people's minds. What's amazing is that he's done what he's done so often—about ninety percent of the time. Now people come and say, "Hey, What *happened*?"—as if anybody in this business could do it a hundred percent of the time. He's a steady friend. I love his attitude. He's like the kind of infielder in a game who thinks, Come on, hit the ball to me, when the going is tough out there. That's the guy you want on your side. Plus he's quick-witted. He never has a pat answer. I've heard him asked the same question a hundred times by different writers, and he never answers it twice the same way. You've heard all those quotes of his—the best ones are the ones he steals from me in the bullpen.

George Brett (*one of the great hitters of our time; he has been enjoying his best season in many years; he has clear blue eyes, and talks smoothly and without a hitch—just the way he hits*): I don't think anybody in the league thinks he's easy anymore. At first, he looked like a novelty and people were anxious to go up and get to swing at him. But a man like that, for right-handed hitters—well, I'm a left-handed batter and I've never swung against a left-handed pitcher like that in my *life*. So many guys have had problems with him that now they're trying to go to right field against him, or whatever. You see power hitters trying to slash the ball to right. They're going against their own programs. You saw what happened the other night—all those nubbers, and the hardest-hit ball is right at Frank White. That always happens—it's weird. He does have a way of making things interesting out there. We'll have a two-run lead and suddenly they've scored and they're first-and-third, and then he'll strike somebody out or get a lucky line drive to end it, and he'll look at you like he's saying, "Hey, I was just *kidding*."

Earl Weaver (*he came back to manage the Orioles again this summer—his sixteenth year on the job; his winning percentage of .596 is the fifth-best among all managers ever*): He doesn't get the ballots because he ain't overpowering. And I guess a lot of people figure that left-handed hitters are going to get to him sooner or later—only they don't. Like any real good pitcher, he messes with the batters' heads. He's got that knowledge—watching where the bat is on that hitter, taking a little more or a little less off the next pitch. He's always had a good infield to play behind him, but I think he controls those ground balls a little, too. If he throws that sinker to a left-handed hitter, it may be out of the strike zone. Quis [he pronouced it "Queeze"] don't try to go by too many people, up. A good low-ball hitter like Brunansky, say, he still pitches him low—a little below low. That was always the theory—pitch the good low-ball hitter below low and the good high-ball hitter above high, and you'll have success. And he's *had* success. Good attitude and a real good arm.

◆ ◆ ◆

THE ROYALS STRUGGLED THROUGH THE EARLY WEEKS OF JULY, at one point falling to fifth place and at another finding themselves seven and a half games behind the division-leading Angels. Then the combination of George Bretts' hitting (he batted .538 for one July week, with eleven runs batted in), the team's always exemplary defense, and some stout work by the Kansas City starting pitchers (the team's set rotation of Bret Saberhagen, Charlie Leibrandt, Mark Gubicz, Bud Black, and Danny Jackson is the youngest and probably the best in the American League) began to make itself felt, and by early August the team had taken a secure hold on second place. In later weeks, the Angels and the Royals looked like a pair of championship stock cars leading the pack in the final laps of a big race, with the second-place Royals machine drafting comfortably in the lead car, inches behind the Angels, and seemingly in a position to pick the part of the track where it would slingshot its way to the fore; this happened, in fact, on Friday, September 6th, when the Royals won a doubleheader from the Brewers and took over first place at last. At this writing, they lead the Angels by two full games. Quisenberry did better and better as the summer went along, stacking up saves in little bunches and whittling away at his earned-run average. By the end of the second week in September, he had thirty-four saves—more than anyone else in his league—and his E.R.A. of 2.24 was fifth-best (among all pitchers) in the A.L. Only his won-lost record of 7–8 (he had made the Sunday stats) gave some suggestions of his earlier struggles this year. As usual, he had appeared in more games than any other pitcher, in either league: seventy-five. He had righted himself, after all.*

Needless to say, I was delighted by the reversal of Quisenberry's fortunes. I caught up with him by telephone several times in midsummer, and when we last talked, early this month, he sounded euphoric. "It's been kind of fun, the way it should be," he said. "I don't have to be so cerebral out there now." He said that he had briefly resumed his romance with the knuckleball, but when Oddibe McDowell, of the Rangers, took him deep on a knuckler, late in August (a home run that cost the Royals a game), he broke off the shady relationship, at least for the present. Earlier in the campaign, he had experienced some other nasty shocks. Perhaps the most painful of all was on July 1st, when Quis came into a game at Royals Stadium against the A's in the middle of the ninth, at a point when the visitors, down by 3–1, had put a pair of men on base with none out, and gave up an enormous three-run, game-winning homer to Dusty Baker— a cannon shot into the A's bullpen—and heard boos from the home fans as he came off the field. ("They ought to trade me for the seven hostages left in Lebanon," Quis said to the writers afterward. "I deserve to be locked up and they don't.") This occasional total public humiliation of a relief pitcher is an established occupational hazard, like the bends, and cannot be wholly avoided, but all through July it was clear to Quisenberry that he was pitching a mite higher than usual, for some reason, and was suffering in consequence. He determined to eliminate any pitch in his repertoire that crossed the plate above the batter's knees, and worked conscientiously at that task for several games; it was the first time he could remember in his career that he had been forced to curb his sinker in this artificial, premeditated fashion. By September, though, all such strictures seemed far behind. "I'm not even thinking about throwing the ball up or down," Quis told me. "I'm taking it for granted everything will be down. There was no particular game when this began to happen—it just came along. Now I can be an airhead again out there."

*Quisenberry's subsequent work in the 1985 season and his adventures in the championship playoffs and the World Series are described in the next chapter.

He was joking, as usual—and was talking again, in any case, about the "dinosaur brain" condition that he hopes for when he is actually at work in a game, out there once more in the midst of hideous difficulties—but, because I knew him a little by now, I tried to resist his appealing and carefree portrait of himself. I prefer to think back to the last extended visit I had with Quisenberry, which was in Baltimore in mid-July, a few days after the All-Star Game break. The Royals were just beginning a month-long schedule of games, on the road and at home, against the dangerous American League East clubs, which would go a long way toward determining the kind of season 1985 would turn out to be for them. Nobody knew yet whether their young pitching would jell, as expected, and whether the recent wild outburst of hitting by George Brett would be sustained and could be converted into a steadier offense by the whole team, and whether the permanent installation of Hal McRae in the designated-hitter slot would solidify the Kansas City attack, and so forth. Most of all, of course, the Royals wondered about Quisenberry. He had come out of two bad patches, as we have seen, but the midseason stats (the All-Star Game is the traditional halfway point in the long season) showed that he was ten saves short of his 1984 total at the same juncture, with an earned-run average of 2.79—up from his 2.08 of mid-1984. Some other figures, put together by Kansas City *Star* reporter Tracy Ringolsby that week, were more distrubing. These were more subtle indicators, but by each set of measurements Quisenberry was well off his lifetime averages. Over the years, left-handed batters had averaged .275 batting against him, but so far this year they were hitting .335; right-handers were hitting .236 instead of their habitual .226. Since he came up, in 1979, Quisenberry had only twice seen his hits-per-innings-pitched ratio exceed one hit per inning: it was 1.05 in 1979 and 1.01 the following year. His lifetime H/IP ratio was an elegant 0.94, but so far in 1985 it stood at 1.2 hits per inning. In professional terms, he'd been running a fever, and no one was quite certain when, or if, he would ever get well.

In Baltimore, I asked Paul Splittorff how he assessed his friend's season so far. Splittorff is pale and lean and dapper, with rimless spectacles; at thirty-eight, he looks exactly the same as he did throughout his fifteen-year career as the Royals' prime left-handed starting pitcher.

"With Quis, there are so many little pieces that add up to such a big whole that you're surprised something hasn't gone wrong before this," he said. "It's not just his delivery but the whole thing—the complete man. But he's got it all figured out—I really think he does. The pressures on him are so tough—you have no idea, because he doesn't let it show. His job is the toughest on the roster, because this club is going to sink or swim with him. But he never lets that show. I've seen him very down after a game—there's almost a point where you want to go and cry for him—but he doesn't show it and he never hides. He's superb that way. He knows he's got to be in there the next day, and be ready for that, no matter what just happened."

Splittorff went on to say how much he enjoyed Quisenberry, and told me that if I were a golfer Quis would be no threat: he is a sprayer, with an amazing slice. Then we went back to baseball. "He's in his sixth year, and this is the first time he's come under fire from the fans and the media," Splitt said. "It's remarkable that he's gone this far without having a real downslide, and it's going to be interesting to see how he handles it. It's going to be a big point in his career. I don't anticipate any problems for him, no matter how this year turns out. Whatever comes, he's smart enough to handle it and he has the character he needs to survive."

Quisenberry didn't get into the first game of the Orioles series—the Royals lost, 8–3—and the next day I was unexpectedly called back to New York: a turn of events that ended my plans for another weekend with the Royals. I had a couple of hours that morning before I had to catch the Metroliner, however, and Quis and I spent them together. The club was staying at the Cross Keys Inn—an attractive, tree-shaded suburban hostelry on the north side of Baltimore—and Quisenberry and I visited its little shopping center, window-shopping, and then went into a bookstore. Quisenberry's on-the-road reading this year has included Evan Connell's biography of General Custer, "Son of the Morning Star;" the Elmore Leonard thriller "Glitz;" and "Blue Highways," by William Least Heat Moon. But here he stopped before the juvenile shelves and then asked me in some detail what books my children had counted on when they were growing up and how much reading aloud there had been. Out in the sunshine again, he suddenly said, "You know, I really love the road. Or maybe I love-hate it. I miss Janie and the kids, but this kind of day—being quiet, for a change, and all the time you get to put in with the guys: going out to meals, the camaraderie . . . It's a special part of baseball."

In time, we sat down on a low brick terrace wall, in the

dappled shade. Birds were twittering. Quis was wearing freshly pressed jeans and a gray T-shirt (ballplayers on the road are as neat as cadets). He told me which teams and players had given him the most trouble over the years—Ben Oglivie and Cecil Cooper and the Brewers, by a wide margin in all cases—but added that he always looked forward to getting back to Milwaukee to take another crack at them. "There's also the strange thrill of giving up line drives past your ear that you didn't really see at all—and knowing somehow they missed you," he said.

When he went on, it was in a different tone. "It's been strange," he said. "Here we are in July, and I'm still telling myself 'Keep the ball *down*.' I've had to do a lot more work on the side and a lot more thinking. In spring training, Gary Blaylock and I were talking about our young pitchers—we have a lot of them—and about which ones were going to be his main project this year. And then it turns out that *I'm* the project. If I don't like this, it's not because I expect to be great all the time—I know better than that. But I enjoy pitching the ball and getting it right. I don't enjoy getting it wrong, or getting it half wrong or a third wrong. At the very least, I should throw the ball right, night after night."

He sounded deeply puzzled—more troubled than I'd ever heard him.

"Do you remember that Olympics cross-country skier named Koch—Bill Koch, I think it is?" he went on. I said I did, and Quis said, "Well, in the 1984 Winter Olympics he was one of the big favorites—he'd won a medal eight years before, I think—but when his race came he didn't do well. He finished eighteenth, or something like that, but when he got interviewed afterward he didn't seem upset at all. He looked sort of calm and happy, and he said—I don't remember the words exactly—he said he felt good, because he'd been at his best level in that race. He couldn't have done better, he said, and he didn't need a medal, because he was satisfied with his effort on that day. I've heard the pitcher Ray Burris say the same kind of thing, and Phil Niekro, too. Live with what you've got that day, they're saying. Well, that's the kind of athlete I hope to be. I don't believe in fate. I'm not an advocate of good luck. I know that players get hot, just like teams get hot, and then there are times when they can't do better than what you're seeing. They can't. All this year means is that I've got to go out and do a job when baseball life is tougher. I don't think I should complain, because that's what most major-league players go through every season, year in and year out. I don't know what's going to happen. Who's to say what the kids of the future will say about me—will I be Mr. Normal and experience a lot of hard days from now on, or will I be a hero again? Janie said the other day that if it turns out that I'm pitching in the top third of major-league pitchers now instead of the top fifth, the way it's been, those numbers would still be considered a good career by most people. And I know that—I know she's right.''

He paused and then gave a little shrug.

"This summer—we'll find out about this summer. It would be very weak of me if I couldn't accept a whole year like this. I'm really stuck, though. I'm between a rock and a hard place. I want to have balance—I want to accept failure and accept success, and be human. But at the same time I have these unrealistic goals and ideas on the mound. So part of my fight for balance will never be answered, because I'm expecting perfection.''

◆ ◆ ◆

AFTERWORD: The two seasons since this account was written have been the most difficult in Dan Quisenberry's baseball career. Almost nothing went right for him in 1986, when he finished with a 3–7 won-lost record and an earned-run average of 2.77—his highest since his first full season in the majors. He had finished up with thirty-seven saves in 1985, to lead the league in that department for the fourth consecutive year, but in 1986 he accounted for only twelve. His game appearances and innings-pitched were drastically reduced. He pitched well in patches, but the rocky stretches were longer and more noticeable: no saves in the months of May, eleven outings in July that produced no wins and three losses, and a 5.27 earned-run average. Left-handed batters rocked him with a cumulative .310 for the season. Manager Dick Howser (who left the team in July, when it was discovered that he was suffering from a malignant brain tumor) and his replacement at the helm, Mike Ferraro, stopped wheeling in Quisenberry in his accustomed closing role, and Quis, who knows that his peculiar, fine-tuned stuff cannot be counted upon unless he works regularly, felt ill-used as well as ineffectual. The world had turned upside down for him. He tried to accept this without complaint, as one would expect, but Jack Etkin, of the Kansas City *Star*, told me that the summer had been a ''typhoon of emotions'' for Quisenberry. His difficulties, in any case, were only one part of a horrendous season

for the defending World Champion Royals, who fell into a tie
for third place in their division, sixteen games behind the
pennant-winning Angels; nothing, of course, affected the team
as much as the loss of Howser, who died the following July.

Quis pitched a little better in 1987, but neither of the new
Royals managers, Billy Gardner and then John Wathan, used
him much in his accustomed role; he pitched only fifteen innings
after the All-Star Game break in July. Early in the year, a rookie
right-hander, John Davis, was tried in Quis' old spot, and early
in September, when the club was caught up in a four-team pennant scramble in the A.L. West (the Royals finished second in
the A.L. West, two games behind the Minnesota Twins), the
Royals purchased Gene Garber, an accomplished seventeen-year
veteran short reliever, from the Braves—a final signal, if one
was needed, that they had given up on their old submariner.
Quisenberry's final figures for 1987 were a mixed bag. He finished up 4–1, with an earned-run average of 2.76 and eight
saves, but twenty-eight of the forty-seven baserunners he inherited in game situations came around to score. When the season
ended, Quisenberry asked the Royals to trade him to another
team. "I don't really want to do this," he said. "This is the
only uniform I know. This is the only locker room that I know.
These are the only stadium and front office that I know. These
are the only fans that I know. I'm comfortable with everything
here, except not being a participant."

Finding a new team for Quis will present difficulties, starting
with his $1.1 million guaranteed annual salary; the Royals must
also contrive to separate his baseball pay from his lifetime part-
nership with Avrom Fogelman—the multi-million-dollar real estate contract mentioned above. The Royals' affection for
Quisenberry is undiminished and they will try to honor his wish
to be traded, but his future in the game looks uncertain at best.

The puzzle of Quisenberry's sudden loss of mastery will probably never be answered, but he himself looks on these mysterious reversals with composure now. "I still miss not being the
guy—being out there every day," he said to me at lunch one day
in midseason, "but I'm not miserable all day, the way I was,
thinking how I can get the ball again. I've got peace of mind.
Maybe I'm not the same pitcher that I was. I never got my
E.R.A. under two last year, and my hits-per-inning were over
one. They're a little over one right now. Maybe that's because
I'm not working so much, or maybe it's because my sinker isn't
as good. Maybe my sinker is sunk. Left-handed batters have

always hit me pretty hard, on and off, even in my best years, but now I've lost the luxury of weathering the storm. I still covet that, but I may never be in that spot again in my career. I think there's always been some skepticism about me, because I look funny out there, but it's plain enough that people on the club think I don't have what I had. I don't get into conversations about it. I still want to pitch a lot, but I have no trouble sleeping at night.''

Knowing what I did about Quis, I probably shouldn't have worried about his courage and demeanor under these unhappy circumstances, but reactions elsewhere have been less admirable. Often last summer or this summer, I noticed that when his name came up some baseball people—writers or front-office men: never players—would smile knowingly and say something like, ''Well, yeah, but he was always—you know, just trickin' them.'' And the speaker would waggle his arm and wrist side-arm in a comical, disparaging way. I didn't like this, but then I realized that I had begun to disparage Quis a little, too, in my mind. I would find his pitching line at the bottom of another box score and see that he hadn't done very well, hadn't quite closed down the other team, and part of me would think, Maybe he isn't so good, after all. Maybe he's just a nice guy who did pretty well, considering. Not quite a great pitcher, maybe not exactly a big-leaguer . . . This is bitterly unfair, but what are we to do about it? We want our favorites to be great out there, and when that stops we feel betrayed a little. They have not only failed but failed *us*. Maybe this is the real dividing line between pros and bystanders, between the players and the fans. All the players know that at any moment things can go horribly wrong for them in their line of work—they'll stop hitting, or, if they're pitchers, suddenly find that for some reason they can no longer fling the ball through that invisible sliver of air where it will do its best work for them—and they will have to live with that diminishment, that failure, for a time or even for good. It's part of the game. They are prepared to lose out there in plain sight, while the rest of us do it in private and then pretend it hasn't happened.

◆ ◆ ◆

To Missouri

FALL 1985

BASEBALL HAS HAD THE SHUTTERS UP FOR MORE THAN A month now, but its devotees still hang around outside the old saloon in the evenings, out of habit, recalling the lights and the talk and the smoky laughter, and hoping to hold in memory the way so many of us—old regulars and excited newcomers, families and friends and kids—were swept up in what came to feel like a summer-long party. It went on too long, of course, and some parts of it weren't much fun at all, come to think of it, but never mind—it was a fine baseball summer, and I miss it. Good parties come back to us in a blur of names and shouts and too close faces and overlapped talk, and it would be wrong somehow to try to get every part of that in order later on, even if it could be done. This was the summer when Pedro Guerrero hit all those homers (fifteen of them) in the month of June, and Gary Carter hit all those homers (five in two days and eight in a week) in September; it was the summer when nobody caught up with the Blue Jays, and the autumn when the Royals caught up with everybody; it was the beginning of Vince Coleman and Bret Saberhagen, but also the time of Ron Guidry and Dave Parker, once again, and of Wade Boggs and George Brett and Dale Murphy and Don Mattingly and Willie McGee some more. It was the time of John Tudor vs. Dwight Gooden—two rows of zeros up in lights. It was the year of Tom Herr yet again coming up to bat with Coleman or McGee already on base, and the pitcher out there running the count to 3-1 and then going to the rosin bag. . . . Nineteen eighty-five was when three of the four pennant races were settled on the final Saturday of the season, and when the Giants lost one hundred games, for the first time ever—the last of the proud old flagships to suffer that indignity. It was the summer in which catchers Carlton Fisk and Buck Martinez each separately accounted for two outs on one play at the plate, and in which Tom Seaver, Rod Carew, Nolan Ryan, and Pete Rose made us aware of some larger numbers. It was the year of another players' strike, which came on miserably and unstoppably, continued for two days, and then was settled and instantly forgotten. It was the year when the Cubs lost all their starting pitchers to injury, and when a creeping mechanical tarpaulin caught the fastest man in the National League and probably cost the Cardinals a World Championship. Baseball was in court in Pittsburgh, where cocaine was the topic, and in Chicago, where state and city edicts banning night baseball at Wrigley Field were at issue and were upheld, thereby almost assuring the eventual abandonment of that grand old garden by the restless, neo-Yuppie Cubs. There was no Subway Series in 1985, it turned out; instead, the year wound down to the enthralling, suddenly turned-about sixth game of an all-Missouri World Series, followed by a horrific 11-0 laughter the next day, which simultaneously enthroned the Kansas City Royals as World Champions and the St. Louis Cardinals as world-class soreheads. There was more, to be sure, but this is enough, unless anyone cares to remember that this was also the year when a singer named Mary O'Dowd stood up to deliver the Canadian and American national anthems before a sellout Yankees-Blue Jays game at Yankee Stadium and then utterly forgot both the words and the tune of "O Canada." I'll never get over that.

Toward the end, this baseball summer took on a special savor, a tang of particularity, that brought it to the attention of even the most casual fans. "Quite a season, isn't it?" friends of mine kept saying in August and September, and since most of them weren't folks who had demonstrated any prior fealty to the pastime, it usually took me a minute or two to realize that they weren't talking about the weather. I live in New York, where it suddenly *was* quite a baseball season along about back-to-school time, but I can't assume that my own symptoms of attachment—clicking on the bedside radio in the dark at one in the morning to hunt out a late score from the Coast; lifting my gaze from a book or a magazine to see again in my mind Keith Hernandez sprinting in across the infield to short-hop a bunt (*my God, on the third-base side of the pitcher!*) and then firing to third for the force; opening the newspaper before breakfast to the critical "GB" column in the standings (and knowing beforehand what it would show)—also afflicted families in Winnetka and Del Mar, say, where Cubs fans and Padres fans of necessity went to sleep and woke up thinking about *last* year's baseball. For all that, the game did seem to matter more this summer, perhaps because of Pete Rose, perhaps because of the strike that struck out, perhaps even because of the bad news: the drug trials in Pittsburgh, with their celebrity witnesses, pale-faced and in coats and ties for the day, telling us what we wished not to hear about some of their friends and teammates. Baseball had a record year at the gate in 1985, and the over-all attendance of 46,838,819 included best-ever seasons for both leagues and for the Orioles, the Cubs, the Twins, the Cardinals, the Padres, the Blue Jays, and the Mets, whose 2,751,437 was the highest attendance mark in New York baseball history.

The Mets and the Yankees didn't get to the World Series after all, and neither did the Dodgers (in the end) or the Phillies or the defending-champion Tigers or any of the other grand predictables—not even the vivid and appealing Blue Jays, whose demise in the seven-game American League playoffs was almost insupportably painful to their wildly hoping, secretly doubting supporters. After the playoffs, some friends of mine—and some baseball colleagues, too—confessed that they were finding it hard to summon up much enthusiasm for this year's heartland finalists, yet I have the conviction that the Royals-Cardinals World Series excited and warmed great sectors of the game's fan family by the time it was done. It wasn't an epochal Series— the pitchers were too good (four hundred and fifty-two official at-bats produced four home runs), and the last game should have been called after the fifth inning—but the games were somehow life-sized and pleasing, which is a rare result in this era of ceaseless gargantuan spectacle, which we watch, for the most part, with a deepening inner silence.

◆ ◆ ◆

AT 8:01 P.M. E.D.T. ON WEDNESDAY, SEPTEMBER 11, IN THE first inning of a game with the San Diego Padres in Riverfront

Stadium, Pete Rose stroked a soft single off the Padres' right-hander Eric Show. It was Hit No. 4,192 for Rose, at last putting him one ahead of Ty Cobb's life total on the all-time hit parade, and by the time it struck the ground in short left-center field there were some of us in the land who had the impression that we had already witnessed and counted each of Pete's 3,161 other singles, and even his 13,767 previous at-bats in the majors. I was delighted for many reasons, most of all for Rose himself, whose stroke and style and fervor and ebullient good cheer I have written about for more than two decades now, but I think I was almost more pleased by Pete's next hit—a triple to left, in the seventh—which broke the new record (as will every hit of his from now on) and suggested that baseball as we know it would now be permitted to resume, and that games, not monuments, are its purpose and reward. The "Cobb Countdown" had been a daily feature of the sport pages for better than two years, appearing even on the many mornings when it was dutifully noted that Pete hadn't played the previous evening, or that he'd gone oh-for-three in the game. The slowly oncoming Blessed Bingle had given rise to a whole cottage industry of Rosean artifacts, including 4,192 autographed Pete Rose ceramic plates ($25 to $125 apiece), 4,192 numbered Pete Rose color prints ($175 apiece), fifty silk-screened Pete Rose prints by Andy Warhol ($3,000 apiece), and much more, of course—possibly including a four-thousand-one-hundred-and-ninety-two-percent rise in the national riboflavin intake, thanks to those Pete Rose Wheaties commercials. I did not attend the game, however, being of the impression that I would probably not spot anything there that was invisible to the three hundred and seventy-five reporters and cameramen who were on hand that evening. I'm sorry I missed Pete's company and his jokes and one-liners (there were fifteen mass press conferences in the ten days prior to and including Der Tag), and even his tears when he broke the record. I also treasure some of the footnotes and substats that were turned up by the press moles digging back through Rose's 3,475 prior box-scoring appearances—for instance, his twenty-nine hits against future dentists (Jim Lonborg is one of them); his hundred and thirty-one hits against Hall of Famers (Warren Spahn, Sandy Koufax, Robin Roberts, Bob Gibson, Juan Marichal, Don Drysdale, and Hoyt Wilhelm); his hundred and three hits against the Niekro brothers ("I wish they'd been triplets," Pete said); and his six hits to date against Dwight Gooden, who wasn't born until after Rose had already rapped out three hundred and nine major-league blows.

Pete is great, but Cobb was better, having achieved his famous total (in 1928, when he retired) in four hundred and forty-two fewer games and in 2,339 fewer at-bats; Pete is a lifetime .305 batter, but Cobb, at .367, was the best hitter the game has ever seen. I feel like an old crab in pointing out these obvious discrepancies, but they exist, and the obdurate fact of them makes you wonder about our apparent wish for guaranteed present greatness or historic certification, or whatever it is that has driven us to make so much of this particular milestone. Late in the summer, I began to wonder who it was *Cobb* had supplanted in the lifetime lists, and after spending a happy half hour with my nose in the *Baseball Encyclopedia* I decided that it must have been Honus Wagner (3,430), whom Cobb motored past in 1923, six years after the Dutchman's retirement. But what happened on that September day in 1923? How had the local scribes and fans and historians celebrated the end of the "Wagner Watch," I wondered.* Finding no mention of the moment in several histories of the pastime, I called up Seymour Siwoff, the grand sachem of the Elias Sports Bureau, a Fort Knox of stats, which keeps track of every jot and tittle in the books, not quite including Sunday foul tips in the Federal League.

"Nothing happened!" Siwoff said instantly when I put the question to him. "Just the other day, we tried to come up with some mention of the event. We looked and looked, but there was nothing there. The hype wasn't in. This Rose thing was a sitting target all the way. There was much more of a challenge for Pete in 1978, when he was going after Joe DiMaggio's consecutive-game hitting streak, winding up in a tie with Willie Keeler at forty-four, which is still the best in the National League. *Any* single-season record has a finite ending, so it means something."

Four other life landmarks were celebrated this summer: Nolan Ryan's four-thousandth strikeout (he is alone at this level); Tom Seaver's three hundredth winning game and Rod Carew's three-thousandth hit (these two fell on the same afternoon, August 4th, a great day for newspaper layout men across the land); and then Phil Niekro's three-hundredth win, on the very last day of

*Subsequent archaeology shows that Cobb surpassed Wagner's lifetime hits record on September 20, 1923, in the course of a four-for-four afternoon against the Red Sox at Fenway Park.

the regular season. I was tickled about Seaver's arrival in the
Old Moundsmen's Sodality (he had an excellent, 16–11 year with
the White Sox), and when Niekro made the club, too (they were
the seventeenth and eighteenth admittees), I suddenly remembered that he and Seaver had pitched against each other in the
very first National League Championship game, way back on
October 4, 1969—a terrible game, as I recall—when Tom and
the Mets beat Phil and the Braves, 9–5. Nierkro's No. 300 was
a party, for it came in a game at Toronto that meant absolutely
nothing (the Blue Jays had eliminated the Yanks the previous
afternoon), so everyone there and everyone at home by his set
could pull for Phil, who had come up short in four previous
attempts. He is forty-six, and although he will enter the free-
agent market this winter he must be very near the end of the
line. Watching him out on the mound these past few summers,
with his preoccupied air and his white locks, bent shoulders,
protruding elbows, and oddly rumpless pants, I was sometimes
weirdly put in mind of a colonial-planter hurler puttering about
in his garden, his brain alight with Rousseau and Locke and the
knuckler. In the Blue Jays game, Niekro eschewed his specialty
pitch until there were two out in the ninth and his team was
leading by 8–0; then, smiling at last, he fanned Jeff Burroughs,
an old Braves teammate of his, with a sailing beauty.

What is certain about these plateau observances is that there
will be fewer of them in the seasons just ahead. Don Sutton's
fifth victory next year will admit him to the three-hundred-wins
circle, but then, since there are no other viable contenders in
these categories at present, we can put away the speeches and
the cornerstone trowels for a half decade or more, which is O.K.
with me. After Pete Rose's single bounced in short left field at
Riverfront Stadium that day, a Redsperson painted a white circle
on the field at the point where it struck, so that it might be
AstroMarked for the ages. However, some lunkish football players scrubbed out the spot a day or two later, during a Cincinnati
Bengals workout on the field, which means that the place-of-
the-hit may be forever lost to the ages. Like the site of Custer's
Last Stand, it will have to live on only in our imagination, which
was probably the best place for it all along.

I may be overlooking Preënshrinement—a phenomenon I first
encountered in October, when a veteran baseball-writer friend
announced to me that Dwight Gooden is the greatest pitcher
who ever lived. The Doctor, who turned twenty-one just three
weeks ago, had a great year—there is no argument about that.

His twenty-four wins (he was 24–4 in all) led both leagues, and so did his two hundred and sixty-eight strikeouts and his earned-run average of 1.53. He pitched sixteen complete games, including eight shutouts, and ran off a stretch of forty-nine consecutive innings—from August 31st to October 2nd, when it mattered most to his team—in which he did not allow an earned run. He was the youngest pitcher ever to win twenty games in the majors, and the youngest to win the Cy Young Award, which he can put up on his mantel next to last year's Rookie of the Year plaque. Gooden at work is pleasing as well as thrilling. I have come to expect that midgame inning or two when he turns up the meters and becomes even more dominating out there, closing down the other side at the moment when lesser pitchers, even the best of them, so often look vulnerable and anxious. Like other fans, I'm sure, I also appreciate the inner calm and the businesslike unmannered mien with which he gets his work done, game after game—an austerity of style that is so prettily replicated by the clean, ledgerlike columns of one's scoreboard at the end of one of his outings. I look forward to these and further wonders from Dwight next summer and, barring injury or some unforeseen decline in his fortunes, for many summers to come, and the only way to diminish such a prospect, I believe, would be to turn him into a statue, as my friend has proposed. To watch him that way—to enter a mental checkmark beside each strikeout or shutout from now on, simply to confirm our grandiose evaluation of his ultimate place in the history of the sport—is to lose the pleasure and dangers of the day and our joy in his youth: exactly what we came to the game for in the first place.

It is tempting for us fans to assume that baseball is falling to pieces, like so many other parts of our lives, and that therefore we must prop it up with honorifics and superlatives. Perhaps we should just try to keep our eyes open. What is more pleasurable in the game, I wonder, than to watch Willie McGee, whose .353 batting average, quickness on the bases—he had eighteen triples and fifty-six stolen bases—and scintillating work in center field brought him the Most Valuable Player award in his league? I felt the same sort of satisfaction this summer in watching Don Mattingly up at bat and reflecting on what he has done in his own behalf in his first two full seasons in the majors. Once known as a good wrong-field hitter, with no power and no position (he was shuttled back and forth between the outfield and first base throughout his minor-league career), he settled into place last year as the day-to-day Yankee first baseman, and led his league in hits, doubles, and batting average (.343). This year, he batted .324, with thirty-five homers (fourth best in the league), and led all comers in doubles, extra-base hits, total bases, and runs batted in. He was recently voted the American League's Most Valuable Player—an easy choice, to my way of thinking. His total of a hundred and forty-five runs batted in, by the way, has not been topped in the A.L. since 1949. Mattingly is not notably burly or overmuscled (he is five-eleven and weighs a hundred and eighty-five), but, watching him at the plate, you notice that he is a package of triangles—neck, arms, torso, thighs—that together mesh and turn on a pitch like a drill press; his upper body has the thick, down-slanting droop that we once saw in the hockey immortal Gordie Howe—what Howe's teammates called "goat shoulders." Up at bat (he is a lefty swinger), Mattingly positions his front foot with balletlike delicacy, its inturned toe just touching the dirt, and then tilts his upper body back, with his full weight on the back leg and his hands and bat held close to his body. He hits left-handers exceptionally well, often going with the away pitch and cuing the ball off to left, but he also has enough confidence and power to pull the outside fastball to right field on occasion, to the consternation of the man on the mound. He simply kills anything inside, turning beautifully on the pitch and releasing the bat in an upturned, circular arc—the Stadium Swing, which he has retinkered and polished ceaselessly these past two seasons or more, and which so often cracks or bonks or wafts the ball into the middle-upper deck. In the meaningless last Yankee game of the year—Phil Niekro's outing against the Blue Jays—Mattingly rapped a homer and three singles in five at-bats, but when he also grounded out he flung down his bat, shaking his head at such ineptitude.

Mattingly would be an easy pick as the man most likely to win the next triple crown of batting (highest batting average, most home runs, and most runs batted in, all in a single season—a trick last turned by Carl Yastrzemski, of the 1967 Red Sox), except that he would somehow have to garner more hits than Wade Boggs in the process. Boggs, the Red Sox third baseman, this season won his second batting title in the past three years, finishing at .368, with two hundred and forty hits—a total not exceeded in his circuit since Heinie Manush whacked two hundred and forty-one for the 1928 Browns, in an era when the ball was made of rabbit toes and bathtub gin. Only Babe Ruth, Lou Gehrig, and Ted Williams ever racked up single-season on-base

totals (hits plus walks plus hit-by-pitcher) higher than Boggs'
three hundred and forty this year. It might demean Boggs to call
him an automaton of hitting, except that he *tries* to be an automaton. He eats chicken for lunch every day—not always the
same chicken dish but the one that comes around on his precise
fourteen-day, thirteen-recipe rotation. Before night games, he
arrives at Fenway Park at exactly three o'clock; and he runs his
wind sprints—the same number of them, and for exactly the
same distance—starting at exactly 7:17 P.M. He stands up at the
plate always in the same way—his feet comfortably apart, his
bat well back (he, too, bats from the left side)—and cuts
smoothly at the ball, with his head tucked in and his long arms
extended, and raps it on a low, straight line to all fields, but
most often to left or left-center. He does this *all the time*: in six
hundred and fifty-three at-bats, he popped out to the infield
twice this year. Tik-Tok of Fenway plays similarly afield: whenever he happens to make the last out of an inning by catching a
foul fly in front of the visiting-team dugout (on the third-base
side, in Boston), he will still turn and circle back clockwise,
outside the bases, so that he can return to his dugout by his own
special route; if you study the grass between the foul line just
beyond first base and the home dugout at Fenway Park, you will
see four worn places on the turf—the four steps that Wade Boggs
takes on his way back to where he can get ready to start hitting
again.

◆ ◆ ◆

LATE IN THE SUMMER, A COINCIDENCE OF SCHEDULING OF-
fered the riveting possibility that the Mets and the Yankees could
both move into first place in their divisions by whomping their
main rivals—the Cardinals and the Blue Jays, respectively—in
adjacent home-stand series in the second week in September;
the engagements even overlapped, with the third and last game
of the three-game Cardinals-Mets set at Shea Stadium falling on
Thursday afternoon, just before the opener of the four Toronto-
Yankee games that night. Entranced by sudden visions of an
epochal collision between the two New York clubs in the World
Series this year, the Gotham media performed a dogged mouth-
to-mouth resuscitation of the moldering Subway Series feature,
with many a backward look, via TV or tabloid, at fans in fedoras
cheering on Dem Bums or the Jints against Whitey and the Mick,
et al. (I enjoyed a *Sports Illustrated* photograph of the maga-

zine's intrepid correspondent George Plimpton in the act of descending into the I.R.T., apparently for the first time in his life.) None of this quite came to pass, of course, but the two teams certainly did their part in preparing us for the festival—the Yankees by mounting an eleven-game winning streak (their best surge in twenty-one years) that brought them to within two and a half games of the Jays on the eve of their meeting (they had trailed Toronto by nine and a half in early August), and the Mets with a succession of improbable melodramas on a West Coast trip (a ninth-inning game-winning pinch-hit homer by Keith Hernandez against the Giants; a five-for-five game for Keith against the Padres the next evening; Gary Carter's five homers in two days in San Diego; Darryl Strawberry's thirteenth-inning double against the Dodgers, to settle what had begun as a double-shutdown duel between Gooden and Fernando Valenzuela), which brought them even with the first-place Cardinals as the momentous week began. The ensuing games and discoveries— the best fun of my baseball summer, it turned out—can only be suggested here, perhaps in shorthand:

TUES., SEPT. 10: Yucko Shea weather (drizz., tarps, planes roaring, etc.) for Grand Opening, but Metsie fans stay high in fog. Herr homers vs. Ronnie Darling in 1st, but irrit. St. L. twirler Danny Cox loses temper w. dawdling Foster in bottom of stave & plunks Geo., loading hassocks. Mistake? Yep: H. Johnson rockets 2–1 pitch over R-CF fence, for slam. Fans: "HOJO! HOJO!" Whatta team, whatta guy, etc. Metsies lead 5–1, but pesky Redbirds peck at Ronnie, close to 5–4 by 7th. Bad nerves in stands ("*C'mon*, you guys!"), but kid reliever R. McDowell slams door w. sinker. Mets up by one in NL East. Hard work, whew, etc. F'tnotes: R. Darling 1st NY pitcher to hurl key game on same day his Op-Ed piece (bettering our burg, etc.) runs in *Times* . . . Keith, back home from bad-boy drug testimony in Pitts., gets standing O. in 1st frame. Message of some kind: prob. love. Keith wipes tear, bops single.

WED., SEPT. 11: Dwight vs. John Tudor: 9-inn. double-zip standoff before 52,616. Terrif. strain. Doc great, but pickle-puss Tudor no slouch: slider, change, sneaky FB, in-out, up-down. 3-hitter. Best LH in NL. (Typical ex-Red Sock: so-so at Fens, Superman now. Go figure.) Mgr. Davey J. yanks Doc after 9 (young arm, long career ahead, etc.), & Card slugger Cedeno takes Orosco deep in 10th. Winning blow. Cards-Mets tied for No. 1. (Davey after Nobel Peace Prize or *what*?)

THURS., SEPT. 12, AFT.: Visiting scribes scan road maps, subway maps, for unus. postgame exped. to Yankee Stadium, in Bronxian wilds. Game here at Shea starts with Metsies ripping St. L. hotdog starter Andujar. Back-to-back-to-back doubles for Straw., Heep, HoJo. We lead 6–0 after 2. Beaut. afternoon. Pesky Cards batt. back (see Tues. script), close to 6–5 after four. ("*C'mon*, you guys!") In 9th, McGee (skinny neck, mighty stroke) ties it w. 396-ft. blast to left CF, vs. Jesse again. Silencio. No hope. Home ½ of 9th, Mookie hoofs out hopper to SS, beats peg. Hope. Sac. to 2B by good-old Wally B. Keith up ("KEITH! KEITH!"), strokes daisy-cutter thru 3B-SS hole & Mookie hotfoots home. Yay, yippie, etc. Mets No. 1. Nothing to it. Knew it all along.

The visiting writers found their way from Queens to the Bronx through the rush hour that evening ("It was bumper-to-bumper in that subway tunnel under Grand Central," one of them reported), but the visiting Blue Jays fared less well in the game. Steaming along behind a two-hitter by their ace right-hander, Dave Stieb, they suffered an uncharacteristic spell of nerves in the seventh, when second baseman Damaso Garcia and short-stop Tony Fernandez utterly missed connections on a double play, and Stieb lost *his* connection with the strike zone; thus encouraged, the Yankees scored six unearned runs—the last three of which came around on an enormous home run into the top deck by catcher Ron Hassey—and went on to win by 7–5. The crowd, which had begun the evening by booing the Canadian national anthem, concluded it by chanting obscenities about the Blue Jays, but I forbore from any easy sociological comparisons between the two leagues and the two audiences, since it seemed certain that great segments of the crowd had attended both games, contributing to both ends of the 98,436 total for the odd doubleheader.

I stayed home the next night, enjoying the quieter vistas of Sony Stadium, and watched the Jays put away Phil Niekro by 3–2 and resume their two-and-a-half-game margin. The score suggests a brisk, well-kempt pitchers' duel, but my scorecard, which notes a bare two errors for the evening, is in fact a picture of Dorian Gray, repulsive to behold or think about. Early on, after I had observed the Toronto left fielder, George Bell, mis-play a drive by Bobby Meacham, on which the Yankee shortstop impulsively scurried over to third base, only to find it occu-pied—oops!—by a teammate, Willie Randolph, and then re-turned without hindrance to second base, since no Blue Jay had bethought himself to cover the bag, I realized that some new form of game notation might be needed to capture the special flavor of this one, and so sketched two inky Maltese crosses in the margin of my notebook. Another cross was quickly needed when Ken Griffey, in left for the Yanks, played Al Oliver's single into a two-run triple; and two more crosses appeared in no time when the Blue Jay middle infielders messed up two successive clear chances at a double play. And so it went—two crosses for Tony Fernandez when he twice failed to make contact on a sacrifice-bunt attempt, a fat one for Rickey Henderson when he allowed himself to be picked off first base in the seventh, a two-cross effort by Henderson and Griffey on a looped, catchable fly that bounced between them for a double, a black mark for second-base ump Mark Johnson, who blew the call on Barfield's plainly safe steal of second, etc., etc. When the long night was done, I counted fifteen black marks in my notebook, which had taken on the appearance of a First World War aerodrome under attack by Fokkers.

The Blue Jays beat the Yankees the next day, Saturday, and again on Sunday—winning, without strain or undue effort, by 7–4 and 8–5—and left town with their first-place cushion up to four and a half. Although the Yankees did not fall apart on the field, they certainly did in other quarters. During the Saturday game, George Steinbrenner visited the press rows and there delivered himself of critical comments about the abilities of some of his well-paid stars—predictable deportment for him, with predictable results. "The guys are going to get upset," Dave Winfield said when the owner's remarks reached him. "It's like rattling a stick across the bars of a cage with some animals in it." The Yankees left town in disrepair, and the three Toronto losses became part of an eventual eight-game losing streak. Manager Billy Martin seemed to take sulky pleasure in punishing his players in his own ways: permitting his ace pitcher, Ron Guidry, to stay in a game in which he was pummelled for five home runs; allowing the fine young reliever Brian Fisher to absorb a six-run pounding by the Indians; and even ordering one of his players, Mike Pagliarulo, to turn around and bat right-handed, for the first time in his professional career. (He struck out.) The trip ended with Martin's bar fight in Baltimore—and eventually, one may conclude, with his postseason firing, his fourth and possibly last fall from the post. None of this requires comment here, since it speaks for itself and is part of a long and miserable pattern of events for the once-proud Yankees.

If there is an impatient or aggrieved sound to these remarks, it is not directed at the Yankee players, whom I mostly admire and wish well. I would like to root wholeheartedly for the Yankees one of these days, but somebody is always jumping up and spoiling the view—the owner, the manager, some of the fans. The resonance of the game up at the Stadium has gone sour, and often comes across as being ill-tempered, distracted, patronizing, and frantically concerned with winning. That tone is perfectly represented by the Stadium organ music—if that is the right word for the puerile and infuriating assault of noises, nudges, and schlocky musical references with which the management (it must be a management decision, after all) attempts to cajole the players, bait the visitors, and whip up the helpless captive masses in the stands. The mighty electronic wurstmaker is scarcely silent for the duration of a foul tip, it seems, and its mindless and almost ceaseless commentary abrades the fabric of the game and the soul of the watching fan. This year, forcing myself actually to listen to the thing for once, I tried to pick out the main phrasings and modulations of a mid-inning *concerto furioso*:

Organ: "*Buh* da-da-da-da! *Buh* da-da-da-da! *Buh* da-da! *Buh* da-da! BUH da-da-da-da-da-da!" (theme from "Gaîté Parisienne," here repeated in mad up-tempo.) Pause. "Tah-tah-tah TAHHH!" (Beethoven's Fifth, opening theme.) Pause. "Beedle-di-deet, dah-dah-dah-deet! Beedle-di-tweet, dah-dah-dah-tweet!" (Theme from "Dardanella," for seven seconds.) Pause. "Tah-tah-tah-tah- ta-TAHHHHHHH!" (The "Charge!" bugle call, accompanied by a gigantic illuminated "CHARGE!" command out on the scoreboard.) Then, ominously, as Rickey Henderson comes up to bat: "Buh-buh bum-bum, buh-buh bum-bum, BUH-BUH BUM-BUM, BUH-BUH BUM-BUM!" (Shark music from "Jaws.") Pause for the pitch. Single to center field. Organ, joyfully: "Tee-tah tattle-tah tattle-TAH!" ("Three Cheers for the Red, White, and Blue," quickly segueing into the "Colonel Bogey March.") Pause. David Winfield steps in, to a low-register "Grrummmm buddledy-*dummmm*!" (Crypt theme: Bach? Mussorgsky?) There is a base hit, sending Rickey to third base and bringing us the theme from "Over There" ("The Yanks are coming." Get it?) *fortissimo*, and then, very quickly, an irritating repeated upbeat "Blim-blim blah! Blim-blim blah! Teedle-weedle-dee dah-blim-blim-blah!" which drives me bananas for the minute or two before I can recall it as an asinine and once nearly inescapable commercial jingle for Campbell's soup: "Mhmm-hmm *good*! Mhmm-hmm *good*! That's what Campbell's soup is—mhmm-hmm *good*!" Well, enough of this, I think, except that it should perhaps be added that whenever Mike

Pagliarulo came up to bat at the Stadium he was greeted with
"Funiculi-Funicula"—*except for* the times when he heard "Oh!
Ma-Ma" ("It's the butcher boy for me," etc.). He batted .239
for the year.

◆ ◆ ◆

THE METS RELINQUISHED THEIR MINI-LEAD IN THE NATIONAL
League East when they lost two weekend games in Montreal
immediately after the great baseball party at Shea, and they
never got back to first place. But let's say this the other way
around: The Cardinals nailed down their half-pennant this year
with two seven-game winning streaks in mid-Setpember. At
home in Busch Stadium one night, they beat the Expos, 5–3,
after being behind by 3–2 in the seventh; successive triples by
Cesar Cedeno and Terry Pendleton produced the go-ahead run.
The next day, they trailed the Expos by 6–1 but won the game
by 7–6, with a two-run homer by Jack Clark. The next afternoon, they were losing to the Expos by 5–4, with two out in the
ninth, when Tom Herr hit a two-run homer. It was Pendleton's
turn again in the next game—a two-run triple in the eighth pulled
out a 5–4 win over the Pirates. This is top-grade championship
stuff, of course, and reminds us that the Cards were not just the
little speed-and-pitching windup toy that we had somehow come
to believe. The Mets, for their part, could not seem to put together more than two winning efforts in a row, and lost on three
occasions to the abysmal, gallant Pirates. Mildly afflicted, I fell
into pathetic fan postures: finding an office radio on which to
follow a Mets-Cubs game out at Wrigley Field, and sending
couriers down the halls with inning-by-inning bulletins ("Gary
just hit a grand slam!" . . . "There's trouble in the seventh"
. . . "I think we blew it"); overvaluing good news (Sid Fernandez' two-hit, 7–1 win over the Phillies); betraying my own
"Bench Strawberry! The man may not hit again in our lifetime!"); secretly relishing hard luck in the enemy camp (Jack
Clark was out of the Cardinal lineup with a pulled muscle). On
the last weekend of the month, I passed two afternoons on a
splintery lakeside dock, upcountry from Manhattan, where I
simultaneously took in the lovely slanting sunshine, an occasional beer, and the news, via WHN, from Three Rivers Stadium. There the Mets, closing ground at last, were achieving
some heroics of their own: on Saturday, Jesse Orosco came in
with the bases loaded and fanned the last two Pirates of the day;

on Sunday, Howard Johnson delivered the tying homer in the ninth, and Carter won it with a two-run homer in the tenth. We hugged and danced and did high-fives on our dock, startling the swans.

Down by a bare three, the Mets moved along to St. Louis for their last, crucial series—the games we had been thinking about all summer. Misfortune kept me at home at the last moment, and I had to make do with televised glimpses of the Tuesday classic: Tudor once again, Tudor prim-faced and imperturbable, Tudor the perfectionist, but this time opposed by Ron Darling, who pitched the game of his professional life. They were both gone after ten scoreless frames, and then Strawberry won the thing with one stroke—a humongous, crowd-stilling bases-empty home run in the eleventh that bounced off the digital clock at the top of the right-center-field scoreboard. Da-wight (as Ralph Kiner pronounces his name on television) pitched the next game and won on an off day—it was his last effort of the year—in which he permitted Cardinal batters to reach base in every inning and tinkered like a Mercedes mechanic with his suddenly recalcitrant breaking ball. The Cards scored a run in the ninth, to close to within 5–2, and the last out of the game was a bases-loaded screamer by Tom Herr—bang into the glove of Wally Backman. I think we all knew that this was the Mets' high-water mark. They had closed to within a game of the leaders, with four to play, and it was not a shock or really much of a surprise when they lost to the Cards the next night, 4–3, in spite of Hernandez' five-hit outburst at the plate. The Mets had required a sweep of the series—a fantasy, a child's dream—and there was even a dour satisfaction when that did not come to pass. It is the difficulty of sustained winning baseball, the rarity of sweeps and miracles, that keeps us interested, even when we lose. I did feel bad about missing the Tudor-Darling encounter. Friends back from St. Louis told me that it had been the kind of silent, seizing ballgame that is remembered for a lifetime, and now I have begun to hold on to it in invisibility, like that one boulder in a Japanese rock garden that one cannot see from any vantage point, even though one knows it is there.

I had comfort in the knowledge that other fans were suffering, in other places. The Dodgers kept a cushy lead in their unferocious half of the National League and won without effort, so I exempt their fans (if that's what they are) in this assessment, but rooters for the Kansas City Royals and the California Angels and the Toronto Blue Jays never drew an easy breath after midsummer. Through the late weeks, I kept receiving baseball letters and telephone calls from Alison Gordon, a friend of mine in Toronto, who used to cover the Blue Jays as a beat writer for the Toronto *Star* but now does features. Suddenly this summer, she became, for the first time, an absolute fan; it was like a marriage counsellor falling in love. She and her barrister husband had season tickets behind first at Exhibition Stadium this year, and from time to time she would send me news about the games and the players—Dave Stieb's near no-hitter against the White Sox, George Bell's beginning to look like the team leader and then *not* looking that way—and then, as the Jays hung on and October drew near, about the excesses of the local press (a quarter page per day in the *Star* given to poems and prayers by reader fans; a statement in *Maclean's* by the Canadian author Margaret Atwood that the Blue Jays' challenge to American baseball supremacy was "like Richard the Lion-Heart going out to war," etc.), but mostly, I think, she wanted to lean on me a little because she knew that I was a long-term Red Sox and Mets rooter, which meant that I had been here before. "I can't *stand* it anymore," she said on the phone one morning. (It was October, and the Yankees had unexpectedly risen once again, while the Jays had just dropped three in a row to the Tigers.) "We're going to blow this thing, I know it. I was sitting at breakfast this morning and all of a sudden I burst into tears—I couldn't believe it."

I was wise and gentle and insufferable in response. Pain and trouble, I told her, were what it was all about. She was a true fan now—she belonged. The Jays would pull it out—and if they didn't she would survive. At most, she would feel heartbroken if they lost—not angry and vengeful, like Yankee fans. (That helped: she despises the Yankees.) I pointed out that some true rooters—Cubs fans, Indians people, and the like—never get to pull for a winner in their lifetimes. And so forth. Alison recovered, along with her Jays, at least until they lost the seventh game of their league playoff to the Royals, but in retrospect I think I wasn't being quite fair with her. For one thing, she was fresh to the strains of winning; the daily stabs and downers and sudden zinging highs of it all were nearly new to her, while I, an old addict, could barely recall how I had really felt back in 1967, say, when Yaz was marching the Red Sox to the finish line, or in '69, when Tom Seaver and the Mets made all New York feel young again. What I also failed to tell her was something that I fully understood only at the very end of the season, after the Mets didn't catch the Cardinals, and the Kansas City Royals did catch, in turn, the Angels, the Blue Jays, and, at the very end, the Cardinals themselves. Most of the time, I see now, the place to be is a close second. That way—for a challenging team, for its players and manager, for its fans—there is always the taut, delicious possibility that you will nail the other guys at the very end. If you don't—well, it's too bad, we weren't quite the best after all, damn it, and if only, etc., etc. Long-term leaders like the Blue Jays (who stayed in first place from May 20th until the last hours of the A.L. playoffs) have no such release, and neither do their fans. If your team picks up a game on its pursuers, to go ahead by two, your response is: Great! Now we got 'em! . . . Only, I wish it were three. *Why can't it be three?* Lose a game, and it's: Here we go! I knew it all the time. I can't *stand* it anymore. Your summer is like walking down a long, dark alley with the conviction that a jaguar is about to bite you in the seat of the pants.

We *Metsvolk* regathered at Shea on the last Saturday of the season for a farewell afternoon of scoreboard-watching. The magic number was down to one, and there was a small yell when the Cubs, who were playing the Cardinals out in St. Louis, put a "1" on the board in the fourth, to tie up that game for the moment, but the news before us on the field was all too clear from the beginning. The visiting Expos were cuffing Ron Darling—a homer by Dawson, a homer by Hubie Brooks in the early going—and it was plain that there would be nothing much to shout about today. (I was wrong about *that*, it turned out.) On the board, there were other pennant-settling engagements to think about—the Yankees losing at Toronto (beaten there by Doyle Alexander, a Yankee castoff), the Angels beating Texas (but the Royals, who would play that night, won their game, it turned out, and got to open the champagne). Hopes leaked slowly away at Shea, but no one around us in the mezzanine looked desolate or upset. It was a blowy afternoon, and dozens, then hundreds of paper airplanes took to the air, to the accompaniment of cheers. The Mets had handed out orange-and-blue scarves to the ticket holders (it was Fan Appreciation Day), and suddenly—I don't know what set it off—all forty or fifty thousand of us there began waving our scarves in the air, a festival of butterflies, and then we laughed and applauded and cheered for *that*. Through most of this, two women seated just behind me kept up a sociable running commentary about the day and the team and the season. They were side by side: comfortable-looking, Mets-blazoned ladies in their upper thirties—old friends, by the sound of them. Their husbands were over in the adjoining seats.

"They tried, you know," said one of the women, sounding not unlike a Little League mom. "They didn't have it easy, with all those guys out."

"Yes, what was it with Strawberry—seven weeks, with the thumb?"

"Yeah, and Gary's knees, and then Mookie, you know. Imagine if we'd've had Strawberry all the time, it might be different. But that's the way baseball *is*."

The Mets had been giving away prizes and promotional gifts through the afternoon, and when the loudspeaker now announced a trip to St. Pete for two and listed the seat numbers of the winners, one of my Euripidean chorus girls said, "Why don't they give like a trip to the dugout?," and they giggled together.

On the board, the Cards went ahead by 5–1, and then 7–1, and somebody near me said, "Good. I hope they win by five hundred to one." A few folks began to head home. One man looked back up the aisle just as he turned into the exit tunnel and spotted a friend up behind me somewhere, and he tipped his head back and made a little throat-cutting gesture. He was smiling.

At last, the red light went out next to the Cubs-Cards game on the scoreboard—the Cardinals had won their pennant—and then everyone in the ballpark came to his feet to applaud the Mets. Gary Carter was up at bat just them, and when he grounded out, we called him back—"GAR-EE!" "GAR-EE!" "GAR-EE!"—and he came out and waved his helmet and gave us his engaging grin. Strawberry stepped in, to more yells and cheers, and hit a homer over the right-center-field fence—the first home run of next year, so to speak—and then he got more yells and came out again and waved his hat. It went on a longish while— the Expos batted around in the ninth, and won the game by 8–3, it turned out—but we stayed to the end, almost all of us, and cheered some more for our team, and for ourselves. The lights on the scoreboard gleamed in the late-afternoon shadow, and the clock there said "4:52" at the end. I went down to the clubhouse to shake hands with a few friends and wish them a good winter. The Mets looked tired and almost relieved. There was a joke floating around (nobody could remember who in the clubhouse said it first): "If only Doc hadn't lost those four games, we'd have had 'em then!"—but the players kept coming back to the cheers and the ovations on the field at the end there. They couldn't get over the fans.

◆ ◆ ◆

BACK IN JUNE, I RECEIVED A STIMULATING LETTER FROM A ninety-two-year-old baseball fan named Joe Ryan, of Yountville, California, who wrote to tell me about a trip he made to New York in October 1913, to take in the opening game of the World Series between the Giants and the Philadelphia Athletics. He was twenty years old that fall and was working for an insurance company in Hartford, at a salary of fifteen dollars per week, but he and a colleague named Dave were Giants fanatics and impulsively determined to attend the classic. Mr. Ryan's letter is wonderfully precise, conveying not only news of the sport ("It was a good game, but apprehension turned to despair when Home Run Baker put one of Marquard's best into the right-field stands . . .") but a careful accounting of every penny disbursed during the long-ago two-day outing. *Viz*: Railroad fares for two, round trip: $4.40. Room at Mills Hotel: 80¢ (two nights at 40¢ per night). Resturants: $2.50 (Childs Restaurant breakfast, 25¢ per person; Childs Restaurant fried-oyster dinner, $1 per person). Hotdog lunches: 40¢. Transportation: 20¢ (nickel rides uptown and back via Ninth Ave. elevated). Tickets: $2. Lagniappe: 50¢ (tip to a wino who directed the out-of-towners to a gate at the park where same-day tickets were still available). Theatre tickets: $2 (balcony seats, at $1 each, to see Jane Cowl in "Within the Law"). This last was consolation for the Giants' 6–4 loss to the A's in the opener. "Just to look at Jane helped a lot," Mr. Ryan wrote. "We thought she was the most beautiful creature who had been allowed to live." The total budget came to $12.80, plus a possible 25¢ (Mr. Ryan isn't sure about this) for three Blackstone cigars.

I cite this vivid communication to make a point not about inflationary economics but about inflationary baseball. This year, the league championship series were expanded to a best-of-seven-games format (they had been operating on a best-of-five system since their inception, in 1969), in the interests of augmented television revenues. The Cardinals, as we know, eliminated the Dodgers in the National League playoffs in six games, while the Royals went the full seven in knocking off the Blue Jays. Seven World Series games were then required to establish the Royals as champions: in sum, twenty postseason games. More people watched more October baseball than ever before, which may or may not be a good thing, but I think we can take it as a certainty that in the year 2057 there will not be a single surviving fan who remembers even one of these games with anything like the clarity and pleasure that Mr. Ryan so well conveys. Already, mere weeks after the games, I sense an inner blur and an accompanying incapacity to bring back more than a handful of postseason plays and innings.

Each of the playoffs opened in perfect misdirection, with the eventual losers winning the first and second games. The Dodgers, starting at home, put down Tudor at last, with the help of some slovenly Cardinal work afield, and then administered a gruesome 8–2 whacking to Joaquin Andujar, the combustible Dominican right-hander, who, when in difficulties, persistently damaged himself with angry down-the-middle fastballs; he also bunted into a double play which he proudly did not deign to run out. I joined the action at Busch Stadium, where the Redbirds, playing before the home folks (53,708 loyalists, in 53,708 Cardinal-red ensembles), gave a marvellously quick and instructive lesson in their special style of speedball. The front three Cardinal batters—Coleman, McGee, and Herr—got to bat against Dodger starter Bob Welch in both the first and the second inning and reached base all six times, fashioning four runs out of four hits (one of them a homer), two walks, two stolen bases, and two jittery pickoff-play throwing errors. The Cards won by 4–2, and drew even in the series the following night, when they sent fourteen batters to the plate in the second inning, in a 12–2 walkover—"one of those games," in Ballspeak. The more significant news of the day was the grotesque workplace accident suffered before the game by young Vince Coleman, the Cardinal baserunning flash, who was knocked down and nearly devoured by an oncreeping automatic infield tarpaulin; he suffered a chipped bone in his left leg and did not reappear in further postseason action—a most damaging turn of events for the Cardinals, it turned out.

Game Five was the one that mattered: a fairish pitching duel between Fernando Valenzuela (who somehow gave up eight bases on balls) and the St. Louis bullpen committee (Dayley, Worrell, Lahti), which took over in the fourth and shut down the visitors until Ozzie Smith delivered a sudden little ninth-inning homer, for a 3–2 victory—an amazement, inasmuch as it was his first left-handed home run (he switch-hits and had turned around to face the right-handed Dodger reliever, Tom

Niedenfuer) in 4,277 professional at-bats. Dodger manager Tom Lasorda was understandably testy in the postgame interview ("What do I think about *what*?" he barked at a reporter. "I'm not too happy—all *right*?"), but this Q. and A. was a mere plate-warming compared to the rotisserie broiling that Lasorda endured immediately after Game Six, in Los Angeles. The matter at issue here may be remembered for a while, at least around the Casa Lasorda: the decision of the ever-popular Dodger manager—ahead by 5–4 in the ninth inning—to allow his hurler (the selfsame Niedenfuer) to pitch to Jack Clark, the muscular Cardinal cleanup batter, with first base open and Cardinal base runners at second and third, instead of giving him a prudent base on balls. Clark hit the first pitch four hundred and fifty feet in to the bleachers, for the pennant. Manager Tom, in his defense, had several left-hand-vs.-right-hand, pinch-hitter-vs.-new-pitcher scripts in mind before he made his difficult decision, but I think he must be viewed as a victim of overthink. Back in St. Louis, talking to some reporters in the home clubhouse after the third game, Jack Clark had said, "Both of these teams have decided that there are certain guys they're not going to let beat them, which is why batting in that fourth spot is so hard." Lasorda forgot.

◆

I HAD LUNCH WITH ALISON GORDON IN TORONTO BEFORE THE first American League playoff game. "I'm feeling better," she told me. "I'm all right, *for now*." I didn't see her after that, and I was secretly relieved, for her Blue Jays won the first two playoff games there—a fine 6–1 outing by Dave Stieb and then a surprise tenth-inning comeback victory over the Royals' stellar submariner, Dan Quisenberry—and I was certain that she had begun to think, Well, *maybe*! . . . Out at Kansas City, the Jays put together an early five-run inning, but Doyle Alexander couldn't hold it—George Brett went four-for-four (single, double, two home runs) on the day—and the Royals prevailed. Toronto next pulled out an unexpected 3–1 win with a startling three-run rally against Charlie Leibrandt in the ninth inning of Game Four, topped off by Al Oliver's pinch-hit double against Quisenberry, but signs of fatal turnaround were becoming evident, for the Jays had stopped hitting. They were shut out the next day by the young K.C. left-hander Danny Jackson, and then Mark Gubicza, Bud Black, and the Quis together worked out a 5–3 Kansas

City win that brought the teams even at last. Bret Saberhagen
had to leave the deciding game (we were back in Toronto by
now) when he took a sharp bouncer on the palm of his pitching
hand, but Leibrandt (and Quisenberry again, at the end) held
off the Blue Jays without difficulty, and took the gonfalon with
a 6–2 victory. The Royals' pitching was both wide and deep, it
turned out, and the resultant strain on the other side brought out
some weaknesses—a classic turn of events. The mid-game Kansas City left-handers in the last two games (Black and Leibrandt)
forced the Toronto skipper, Bobby Cox, to wheel in his right-
handed platoons, who then proved helpless against Quisenberry.
The Jays had far less pitching, especially out of their bullpen,
and as the vise tightened, the lightly experienced Blue Jay lineup
became cautious on the bases and began to overswing fiercely
when up at bat; twenty-six Toronto batters were stranded in the
last three games. In the end, everything seemed to turn against
the Blue Jays—some terrible umpiring (it was just as bad for the
other side, but the Toronto players brooded about it), the luck
of the games, the weather, and even the dimensions of their
park. Doyle Alexander, furious over a ball-four call, gave up a
game-clinching double to the next and bottommost Royals hitter, Buddy Biancalana, in Game Six. Dave Stieb, left out there
far too long in Game Seven, watched a windblown pop fly by
Jim Sundberg barely reach the top of the fence out in the too-
short right-field corner of Exhibition Stadium, where it caromed
away for a three-run triple, putting Toronto behind for the winter. I had pulled for both of these teams throughout the season,
so I felt mixed emotions at the end. I should have looked up
Alison Gordon, but I didn't, and after a couple of days she called
me in New York. "I'm all right, but let's not talk about it," she
said. "I just thought I'd tell you a subhead in the *Globe & Mail*
here on the day after the Cardinals and Royals won, damn it. It
says, 'MISSOURI LOVES COMPANY.' "

◆ ◆ ◆

THE MISSOURI BALLPARKS, EAST AND WEST, PRESENTED THE
usual festival buntings, identical grassless lawns, and some
slummocky game accompaniments by the organists. The musical commentary at Royals Stadium, though less oppressive
than the Yankee Stadium stuff, is of a repellent cuteness, while
the resident Schweitzer at Busch Stadium spurs on the crowds
with little more than ceaseless repetitions of a Budweiser jingle.

The Cardinals fans appear to enjoy this custom, I must admit, happily patting their paws together in time to the commercial *Braulied*, but this response is as nothing compared with their enravishments during the pre-game show at Busch, when a gate in the outfield swings open to admit the famous Clydesdales, who perform several galumphing circuits of the field, pulling behind them an ancient, shining beer wagon stacked high with cartons of Bud, with a waggy Dalmation perched on top. The swaying wagon seat, aloft and forward, is occupied by a busy teamster, his fists full of reins, and by August A. Busch, Jr., the diminutive eighty-six-year-old millionaire owner-brewer, bravely waving his plumed, Cardinal-red chapeau as he hangs on for dear life. I had some initial critical doubts about this spectacle, wondering whether the precedent might not encourage Mr. Steinbrenner to cruise the Yankee Stadium outfield in a replica tanker some day, but in time I began to look on the ceremonial more tolerantly, comparing it, rather, to a colorful but puzzling indigenous religious rite, like fire-walking or rajah-weighing or a blockful of beefy, sweating Sicilians groaning under their tottering ninety-foot saint's tower on some downtown feast day—a spectacle, that is, better entrusted to a *National Geographic* photo crew than to an out-of-town baseball writer.

The Series games, seen in brief retrospect, invite further attention to the commanding nature of stout pitching and the diffident pleasures of come-from-behind baseball. Tudor, it will be recalled, won the opener of the classic, out at Royals Stadium, though in less than imperious fashion, barely outpitching Jackson for a 3–1 decision. Charlie Leibrandt, the strong, thoughtful Royals left-hander, threw a near-masterpiece the next evening (his patterns are much like Tudor's, in fact, although his off-speed pitch moves the other way: in on a left-handed batter), surrendering a bare two singles through the first eight innings, but suffered an appalling progressive accident in the ninth, when the Cardinals put together a single and three doubles (none of them exactly smoked) and pulled off a sudden 4–2 win. Manager Dick Howser's decision not to bring in Quisenberry in the midst of these adventures—Quis had been knocked about in uncharacteristic fashion in his last few outings—will not be taken up here, lest the sound of New Year's revels intrude on the consequent lengthy argumentation.

Game Three belonged to Bret Saberhagen, who absolutely awed the Cards with his 6–1 economy cruise at Busch Stadium, as the Royals briskly did away with Andujar (his season had come apart, for he finished and won only one game after August 23rd, when he stood at 20–7 in the campaign), and George Brett reached base in all five turns at bat. It was in this game, I imagine, that the millions watching at home began to *notice* Saberhagen—his perky little half smile on the mound, his beginner's mustache, the wonderful rush of mid-game strikes and outs that he can impose on the batters, and the odd darting of his tongue at the outset of his windup—a mannerism that has given him his clubhouse nickname, the Lizard. The *other* pitcher held our attention the next evening: John Tudor back in more characteristic style—a five-hit, 3–0 shutout, in which only two Kansas City base runners set foot on third. Tudor twice fanned Brett with off-speed, slicing sliders, embarrassing him in the process. The Cards were ahead by three games to one, in what some press-box watchers were calling a dull, one-sided Series.

Tudor had struggled unhappily through the early going this season, and his record stood at 1–7 in late May, when he received a telephone call from Dave Bettencourt, his erstwhile batterymate on the Peabody (Mass.) high-school baseball team, who, while watching the Cards on television, had spotted a minor flaw in his old friend's delivery. Tudor made an adjustment and went 20–1 for the rest of the summer—an astounding turn of events for a pitcher who in almost five full years' work, for the Pirates and Red Sox, had never won more than thirteen games in a season. I went to Bill Campbell for enlightenment— the tall, knob-shouldered Cardinals reliever, who had also worked out of the Boston bullpen when Tudor was there.

"There's no secret to it," Campbell said in the St. Louis clubhouse. "He's learned how to pitch. He didn't do all that bad with the Red Sox or the Pirates, but you're not going to come out looking very good with teams like that, because you can only do so much. Here we've got these rabbits in the outfield, a great big ballpark, and some guys who are going to turn the D.P. It's amazing what that double play will do for a pitcher. When he doesn't get it, he knows he should be out of the inning but he's not, and when that happens over and over again it adds up—it's another sort of year. The big difference might be that John changes speeds more than he used to—that's maturity in a pitcher. He's got a good enough fastball, with a tail on it, and he doesn't mind coming inside—any left-hander who's pitched at Fenway has to be willing to throw inside—but when you can move the ball around the way John does, the changeup becomes a *big* pitch for you. His change looks like a fastball, but it moves away, and you can see what that does to the hitters. They're leaning, they're a mile out in front. You saw what happened to Brett today, and Brett is a great, great hitter. You have to remember that big-league batters hate to have the fastball thrown past them. Here's John, who's already shown them that change-up and then the fastball, so what are they going to do? They *know* the change is coming—it's in the back of their minds—but what they're ready for, every time, is the fastball. And then . . .'' He shrugged. ''Then they get the change and they're out of there.''

Dick Howser, the midsize, sociable Royals manager, loves to talk about his young pitchers—Bret Saberhagen most of all. ''Here's a guy who looks like Mel Stottlemyre and throws like Catfish Hunter,'' he told me out in Kansas City. ''I've been saying he doesn't throw the ball past anybody, but after that game he pitched against the Angels''—a 3–1 complete-game victory that brought the Royals even with California at the beginning of their critical late-season series—''I'm not so sure. His last pitch, to Reggie Jackson, was a ninety-five-mile-an-hour strike, and Reggie didn't *move*. The best pitch in the game was that last one. But it's his control that amazes you. Last year, when he was just starting, he beat the Angels a game and only threw ninety-one pitches. Like Guidry and Stottlemyre and those others, he fields his position and he holds the runners close. He doesn't get beat in those little ways. He's got a great pickoff move, and *that's* something you don't see much with young pitchers, because the good ones have been striking everybody out when they're down in the minors. I kept watching this kid's figures as he came up through our system. There'd be nine innings, with six strikeouts and no bases on balls—that kind of thing. And they held up all the way for him, at every level. You *notice* him.'' He shook his head a little. ''Even his pitchouts are good,'' he went on. ''The ball is up *here* to the catcher—not down there somewhere.''

Pitching coach Gary Blaylock told me that Saberhagen could throw the running fastball, could ride it up and in, and could swing it down and away from the batter. ''And that's all you can *do* with a fastball, you know,'' he said. But in the end he, too, came back to Saberhagen's control. ''I was the Royals' minor-league pitching coach up to last year, so I saw this kid when he first came to work for us, in the Instructional League,'' he said. ''He walked one man in his first twenty-three professional innings. He didn't have a breaking ball when we signed him, but he did have that control right from the beginning, which is hard to believe. He's a quick kid, and he can do it all now, and the hitters know it. He gets on a roll in the middle innings, and the batter is up there looking to hit that first pitch, because he knows he's never going to find himself in that good two-oh, three-one spot. Before you know it, the kid is getting ten or twelve or fourteen outs in a row. I've never seen a pitcher to compare him with.''

Saberhagen did not emerge as the best of the young K.C. flingers until the middle of this past summer, and Howser told me that he was still not sure which of them would be the top man in the long run. A year ago, he reminded me, Bud Black's 17–12 record had been the best among the young starters. The beginning of the Royals' championship, in his view, was the spring-training season of 1984, at a very low ebb in the club's history. Four of its best-known players—Willie Wilson, Vida Blue, Willie Aikens, and Jerry Martin—had been convicted on cocaine charges at the end of 1983, and had served terms in jail; only Wilson came back to the Royals afterward. Three established Kansas City starters—Dennis Leonard, Paul Splittorff, and Larry Gura—were approaching the end of illustrious careers (although Leonard has undergone extensive rehabilitation for a serious knee injury and is still hoping for a return to full form), and no one in the dugout or in the front office expected much good news in the seasons just ahead. Howser, with no other course really open to him, determined to see how far he could go with Saberhagen, Mark Gubicza, and Danny Jackson, who between them had nineteen innings of major-league experience. (Bud Black, a year ahead of this freshman class, was already in the rotation.) Saberhagen and Gubicza began the season as rookie starters, and Jackson moved in from the bullpen late in the summer. Leibrandt, who is in his upper twenties (he had four earlier, fair-to-poor years with the Cincinnati Reds), began that 1984 season in the minors. "We plain didn't have room for him," Howser said. "He only got in three innings' work all spring. But then he pitched his way onto our club from Omaha. He just kind of happened on us. You know the rest."

The rest he meant is that the Royals, in sixth place in mid-July of '84, went 44–27 for the rest of the year—the best record over that distance in their league—on the strength of their pitching, and won their division before being eliminated in the Championship Series by the Tigers. The same pattern showed itself this year, when the Royals, seven and a half games back after the All-Star break, put the Angels away in the last week, but this time they seemed to know all along that they would win. As a team, they finished next to the top in pitching (second to the Blue Jays), next to the bottom in batting (the Angels were lower), and somewhere up out of sight in confidence. The Royals' absolute zest for come-from-behind baseball was not made out of mere cheerfulness or some mad belief in baseball luck but came from a perfect knowledge of their own capabilities. A splendid old adage tells us that great pitching will always beat great hitting and vice versa, but I suspect, in fact, that great pitching builds character. The 1985 Cardinals were a better offensive and defensive ball team than the Royals by almost every measurement, but a persistent edge in pitching can give a young, mild club the carefree look of champions; what their players envisage at the beginning of every game is another string of scoreless or low-scoring innings for the other side—a guarantee that they themselves, the good guys, can always play on even terms with any team in the land. What the Royals showed us repeatedly this fall, on the field and in their clubhouse, was class. You could see it in sudden headline performances like Brett's outbursts at the plate or in successive marvellous outings by Leibrandt, Jackson, Saberhagen, and the rest, but you expect that sort of thing from one source or another during championship play. In these games, though, one also began to notice and appreciate lesser inferences, like Steve Balboni's dogged persistence at the plate, in spite of his repeated strikeouts and pop-ups (he hit thirty-six homers this year, but none at all in postseason play), which ultimately brought him eight Series singles and a .320 Series average; Jim Sundberg's baserunning (of all things) and those two identical super-duper slides into home; Buddy Biancalana's exuberance and pleasure in the game, which showed itself in his errorless and sometimes breathtaking play at shortstop (he was considered something of a joke at the outset of the autumn games, having accounted for more errors than runs batted in during his brief tenure this season); Dan Quisenberry's elegant refusal to complain about his bad luck and unaccustomed embarrassments in several games ("I try never to be the manager," he said after being passed over by Howser in that second-game crisis. "I want to be a tool for him, and not guess whether he should use me now, or not now, or not until the fifteenth inning. He's better at that than I am"); and Dick Howser's open and unpatronizing admiration for the play of his professionals, and his joy at their joy at the end. Sooner or later, he seemed to know, young talent will catch up.

The question that remains, before we get back to the last few plays and innings of the year, is why or how it happened that so many extraordinary young pitchers came to the fore so suddenly in 1985—a season in which the ages of the two brand-new Cy Young Award winners, Dwight Gooden and Bret Saberhagen, together, fall four years short of Phil Niekro's forty-six—a symbol, if I ever saw one. Better training methods, better nutrition, and a generally upward genetic curve come quickly to mind (think of all those young pre-Olympic swimmers breaking world records in every meet, or so it seems), and so does the much more intelligent and intensive present-day coaching of ballplayers at the school and college and minor-league levels. But why has there been no similar flowering of young hitters in the game? We will all be pondering this enigma over the next five years or so—a period in which I believe that pitching will more and more come to dominate the sport—but in the meantime I will relay the words I received from Seymour Siwoff, the Wizard of Elias, when I recently put this question to him.

"It's television," he said at once. "It's gotta be the tube. All these kids have grown up watching baseball on television. They've watched all summer long, ever since they were boys, and they've learned how this game is played. That doesn't help much if you're a batter, because the truth is you're either born with the ability to hit the ball or else you can't do it. You can't *learn* that—it's not like a book or a theory. But pitching—well, anybody can see how that's done. Move the ball around, change speeds, get ahead of the batter, throw strikes. There's no mystery there, and if you're a great young high-school athlete pretty soon you can just start doing it. The batters are in trouble right now, and it's going to get worse. Just wait and see."

◆ ◆ ◆

THE CARDINAL FANS WERE READY TO CELEBRATE A WORLD Championship when they poured into Busch Stadium for the fifth game ("IT'S ICED!" said one fan's placard), but some of the Cardinal players seemed less certain. Although the Redbirds were leading by three games to one, it had not quite escaped notice that the absence of Coleman and the parsimony of the Royals' pitching had shut off the Cardinals' free and easy way on the base paths. (By the end, the team had managed only two stolen bases.) "This is by far the best starting rotation we've seen all year," Tom Herr said to me after Game Four. "They've taken us out of our game, and that's the mark of a good club. We're very tired. I'd sure like to win here tomorrow."

Tomorrow's Kansas City starter was Danny Jackson, who further validated Herr's appraisal by going the full nine, in a 6–1 Kansas City win. Five Cardinal pitchers together struck out fifteen Royals batters—a Ry-Krisp sort of stat under these circumstances. The most discussed (or *only* discussed) play of the game was Sundberg's dramatic slither past catcher Nieto in the second inning, when he touched the bag with his fingertips and was either: (a) safe, as umpire John Shulock called it, or (b) out, as the more distant, fifty-thousand-voice minority opinion had it. Watching closely from my privileged press perch in the right-field third deck, I abstained.

Game Six had it all: an excruciatingly cumulative tension as the two pitchers—Leibrandt for the Royals, Danny Cox for the Cardinals—had at each other over seven scoreless innings at Royals Stadium; dashing and sometimes exceptional infield play (Biancalana far to his right in the seventh; Biancalana far to his left on the very next play); and then the inevitable rip in the fabric, a knife-slit in its suddenness, when Pendleton singled in the Cardinal eighth, went to second on a walk, and scored on a little looped pinch single by Brian Harper. Leibrandt—again the hard-luck loser, it seemed, this time in a game he would remember always—was taken out, and we could see him slumped on the Kansas City bench, with his head twisted back in shock and disbelief. What followed, of course, turned the year around—the very close play at first base in the bottom of the ninth, when the Royals' pinch-hitter Jorge Orta galloped out a nubbed bouncer and was called safe by umpire Don Denkinger as Clark flipped to pitcher Todd Worrell. I was in no doubt about *that* play, since I was watching the game, perforce, by television in eastern Maine, and many cameras and replays quickly showed us that Denkinger was wrong. It was not an outrageously bad call, as such matters are measured—it had been previously topped, or bottomed, by several decisions in the playoffs—and one could even tell how it happened. Umpires call these bang-bang affairs by sound as well as sight—they stare at the bag and listen for the sound of the ball hitting the mitt—and the cresting mass screech of the home crowd at Royals Stadium drowned out Denkinger's chance to pick up the little tap of Worrell grabbing the toss. I can sympathize with the indignation of Cardinal fans and players who may still believe that at this precise instant they were jobbed out of a World Championship, even though I don't agree. Baseball luck in an inescapable part of the game, and how a team responds to a sudden, unfair shock very often turns out to be what matters in the end. The Cardinals, wrongly placed in jeopardy, now lost the game when Clark allowed Balboni's foul pop near the dugout to fall untouched behind him (Balboni then singled), and when—next, with one out—catcher Darrell Porter lost track of a Worrell pitch, for a passed ball: two runners moved up and then scored on Dane Iorg's broken-bat pinch-hit single to right, which won the great game.

The last night's doings—the disastrous 11–0 humiliation of the National League champions—should be passed over quickly. I grieved for John Tudor, who could not throw his off-speed pitch over the plate on this particular day, and quickly let us see how cruelly unprotected a fine-tune control pitcher becomes when so handicapped. He left in the middle of the third, after walking two successive batters, to force in a run—his earliest departure from a game all year. Saberhagen, for his part, was in top form—scudding down-wind, so to speak, and sticking to business out there in spite of the wonderful accumulation of good news and good fortune that came flooding his way at this early moment in his life: a new baby son, born the day before; his M.V.P. selection in the Series; a Cy Young Award just ahead; and his overnight arrival as a wonderfully pleasing and talented new sports hero. He would have won the game, I sensed, if the final score had been 1–0. The Cardinals, by contrast, looked petulant and self-pitying in defeat. Whitey Herzog got himself ejected from the proceedings (not the worst of fates on this particular night) while defending the childish and uncontrollable Andujar, who shortly thereafter got the heave-ho himself for rushing and bumping the umpire in his insistence that two successive wide pitches had to be strikes, because he wanted it that way. The other Cardinals were silent in their suffering, but I think it must be said that this was a popular defeat. From the beginning of this World Series, several Cardinal players had made it plain that they thought of their team as being by far the better club—one that would quickly demonstrate that it had been unfairly slighted by the East Coast and West Coast media—and that it belonged somewhere up there in the panoply of great ball teams. What the "Show Me" World Series may have shown them in the end is that easy assumptions are probably a serious mistake in this pastime. They may have a longish time to think about

their miscalculation, as the ABC game announcer Tim Mc-
Carver pointed out in the latter stretches of that seventh game.
He had been a catcher on the 1968 Cardinals—a better Cardinals
team than this one, in my estimation—who had led their American League opponents, the Tigers, by a three-games-to-one
margin in that Series but then somehow let the thing slip away.
"I haven't been able to forget that for one day since it happened," he said, "and that was *seventeen* years ago."

◆ ◆ ◆

LET US END ON A HAPPIER NOTE. EARLIER IN THE WEEK, I RAN
into Frank Cashen at one of the postgame press parties in St.
Louis. Cashen, the general manager of the Mets, is a bluff,
pleasant gent, with a pinkish Fenian phiz and an invariable bow
tie. He was looking more cheerful than he had at our last encounter, which had been in the Mets' clubhouse following the
team's elimination, and after we chatted a bit about the game
we had just seen he said, "Listen, I was sitting at an owners'
meeting this afternoon—they go on forever, sometimes—and I
suddenly began thinking about all the great two-word phrases
we have in this game. I'd never noticed before. I even started to
write them down. I mean 'Base hit,' 'Strike three,' 'Ball four,'
'Double play.' " He was counting on his fingers now. " 'Line
drive,' 'Stolen base,' 'Home run.' ".
   " 'Rain delay,' " I put in. " 'Rain check,' 'Contract dispute,' 'Free agent.' "
   "No, no—don't do that," Cashen said. "Keep listening:
'Squeeze play,' 'Spring training,' 'Batter up,' 'Dwight
Gooden!' "

ELEVEN

◆ ◆ ◆

The Cheers for Keith

A FEW WEEKS AGO, I MADE A LEISURELY SWING SOUTH and then west to watch the major-league ballplayers going through their familiar rituals in preparation for the long 1986 season, which is now under full steam and will occupy much of our sports attention through the summer months and on into the extravaganza of the league playoffs and the World Series. Spring training is almost my favorite part of the baseball year, and the sunlit days I passed in Florida and Arizona this time around were exceptionally warming and hopeful, because of the presence on every side of a remarkable group of rising young pitchers and batters—just about the best rookie crop I can recall—whose various fortunes I will happily follow now in the box scores and daily doings of their teams. But even as I began to put these fresh names to memory—Jose Canseco, Bob Tewksbury, Pete Incaviglia, Wally Joyner, Will Clark, Bobby Witt, Dan Plesac, and the rest—and scribbled notes to myself about their unfamiliar mannerisms on the mound and in the batter's box, it occurred to me that there was a special reason for my optimism over the arrival of another freshman class of shining youngsters and for my pleasure in the evergreen renewals of still another baseball season: I hoped they would let me at last put aside my anger and confusion about the drug scandals that so

271

altered the game last year. Sometime during this past winter, I suddenly realized that I didn't want to think about cocaine in baseball anymore. Most of my friends felt the same way, and so did a lot of the players I talked to about the matter during spring training. "Let's get it *over* with," one of them said. "Let's get on with the game." And the fans, I think, were more upset about drugs than anyone else. Like them, I was sick to death of the whole matter, and badly wished that those afflicted and now notorious stars and journeyman players had stayed away from the stuff in the first place, thus sparing me many anxieties and second thoughts about the nature of our sports infatuation in this country—about the realities of celebrity and big money and repeated, on-demand extraordinary athletic performance—and about the inflexibility of our old wish to keep the world of sports (no matter how artificial and commercial and exploitative it has plainly become) as a place of moral certitude and preserved values. I was also bored and wearied by the statements of position coming from the baseball commissioner and the players' union, and from lawyers and agents and sports columnists and editorial writers and drug therapists, and by speculations about the proper forms of drug detection and punishment and medical support that the game should now accept and endorse.

As a baseball writer, however, I dutifully did my work and tried to pay attention. I began to keep a file of drug stories, with annotations and reminders, and I interviewed a good many players and front-office people about drugs. But at the same time another part of me—the fan side—still felt aggrieved and bitter about the whole thing. None of this had anything much to do with *baseball*—the delectable and marvelously difficult old game that has brought me almost undiminished pleasure since I first began to take notice of it, more than fifty years ago. Like many other fans, of course, I could recall a previous clash of ideas and feelings—between baseball as I wanted it to be and baseball as it now inescapably and unhappily seemed to be in reality—during the seven-week baseball strike that brought the game to a halt during the summer of 1981. The same malaise had also afflicted me, in a creeping, fungoid fashion, during the gross inflation of salaries that followed the arrival of free agency for players in 1976, and raised the average major-league stipend from about forty-five thousand dollars in 1975 to the present four hundred and thirty thousand dollars—a swing that has taken these young athletes from the economic and social level of barkeepers and small farmers and veterinarians, say, to that of rock performers and Wall Street lawyers and corporate C.E.O.s. Now the presence of *drugs* in still another baseball crisis seemed almost too much. For the first time, I felt that I might be on the edge of turning away from baseball altogether, and consigning it in my mind to the inner forgettery, where I have tucked away so many other lost amenities and sweet, once-certain surroundings and institutions that most middle-class, middle-aged Americans have learned to do without. It was this horrid possibility— no more baseball for me, or else baseball seen with a distant, half-cynical, chilled attention—that shook me out of my self-pity, and forced me at last to try to sort out and set down some of the difficulties and angry conflicts that surround the matter, and even to venture some speculations about what has happened and why we feel so bad about it. Thinking about drugs and sports just now is probably not such a bad idea, in any case, because sooner or later the baseball owners and the Players Association (the major-leaguers' union) will compromise their differences and agree on a new drug program for the major leagues—and at that moment, of course, we fans will start to forget about the whole business as quickly as possible.

News about drug abuse turned up elsewhere in the media over this past winter: first when it was learned that some of the players for the New England Patriots, of the National Football League, who surprisingly played their way into the Super Bowl in January (and were there unmercifully demolished by the Chicago Bears), had been known by their coach to be struggling with drug problems during the regular season (the story was far less sensational in its details and implications than was first suggested in the Boston press); and then when Michael Ray Richardson, a star guard with the New Jersey Nets, was incapacitated for a third time by his severe drug addiction and, under the rules of the National Basketball Association, was banned for life from play—a private tragedy that saddened and silenced everyone in the sport. Drugs are an inescapable presence in *all* sports, it seems, and I suspect that the whole mysterious, titillating, and scary subject is more on our minds than we care to admit. The widespread recent use of cocaine—research findings tell us that up to thirty percent of the eighteen-to-twenty-five-year-olds in our society have been at least one-time users of the drug—is a disturbing matter: no one can be quite certain who among his friends or colleagues or relatives may now be trying the stuff, or is about to. Many of us already know a few young men or women whose lives and careers have been permanently damaged by cocaine; certainly anyone who has been involved with the sports world can easily bring to mind a particular athlete whose wonderfully promising career was cut down by drug addiction. (For me, this will always be Mike Norris, the angular and elegant right-handed pitcher—he had a killing, over-the-top screwball—with the A's, who went twenty-two and nine with the young Oaklands in 1980, and deserved but did not win the American League's Cy Young Award for his work that summer. I can still see the unique little flourish of his trailing leg as he finished his delivery, and his comical, hotdog mannerisms on the mound, and recall the charm and intelligence of his interviews. Injuries set him back after that season, but cocaine and alcohol finished the job, as he himself has admitted.) Cocaine addiction is a miserable illness, and there are peripheral risks to the innocent as well, who can conceivably fall victim to accidents at the hands of drug-affected vehicle drivers or pilots or surgeons. Work performance may be diminished in less critical places and professions, and the flow of enormous sums of money into the criminal substratum (where illicit dealers receive not only our cash but our tacit approval, since they are essential to the processes of the habit) inflicts cynicism and other psychic bruises on our society. Nothing much about cocaine use is known *for certain*, however, and the highly publicized trials of two accused drug dealers in Pittsburgh last September—when seven players, all but one of them still active in the majors, testified that they and many other players (seventeen were named) had been in-season cocaine users in the late nineteen-seventies and early eighties—provided a sudden focus for much free-floating concern. Previously, more than a dozen individual players—including established regulars like Tim Raines, Claudell Washington, Alan Wiggins, Steve Howe, and the aforementioned Mike Norris—had admitted to difficulties with the drug in recent years and had undergone therapy (and sometimes suspension by their clubs) while they attempted to deal with their problems. Four members of the Kansas City Royals—Willie Wilson, Vida Blue, Willie Aikens, and Jerry Martin—had even served jail terms for cocaine offenses. But the news from Pittsburgh was different, for it seemed to confirm some long-standing rumors about the prevalence of cocaine in the sport, and the September parade of stiff-faced testifying players (with some very familiar figures among them: Dale Berra, Dave Parker, Keith Hernandez), sent a seismic wave of dismay through the baseball world.

A bare four days after the Pittsburgh debacle, Commissioner

Peter Ueberroth, whose understanding of the public-relations process is regarded with awe in the business world, came forward with a proposal, presented in dramatic fashion at simultaneous pre-game club-house meetings around the leagues, that all major-leaguers should forthwith sign individual pledges to agree to a system of compulsory urine-testing for drugs, so that the good name of baseball could be restored "for us, our children, and for the generations to come." Mr. Ueberroth, who took office as commissioner in October of 1984, had come to baseball with a reputation as a swift, self-assured problem-solver. His achievements as president of the Los Angeles Olympic Organizing Committee had been dazzling, ultimately winning him *Time*'s accolade as 1984's Man of the Year. In that post, he had supervised a system of compulsory drug testing of Olympic competitors, although the screenings were not primarily for cocaine or marijuana but for performance-boosting amphetamines, steroids, and the like, and the athletes involved, of course, were amateurs. On taking over as baseball commissioner, he stated that the drug problem stood at the top of his agenda, and in the spring of 1985 he imposed a system of compulsory urine-testing for all minor-league players and for front-office workers throughout the sport (neither group has a union); he has since claimed that minor-league testing has been an unqualified success, although precise data about it have been hard to come by. Since Mr. Ueberroth did not present his sudden September testing plan to the Players Association, which had been a party to all such past discussions, he could not have been much surprised when the players balked, insisting that these matters should be resolved through their union. A charge of unfair labor practice in connection with this substantial issue has been filed by the Players Association, and a verdict is expected very soon. There were expressions of cynicism, and even bitterness, from many players about the Commissioner's motives in going public with his testing proposal directly after the Pittsburgh trials, since the whole tangled issue of drug abuse and drug testing had been a matter of intense study by the owners and the union for several years. Discussions between the two sides had resulted in a Joint Drug Agreement, signed in May 1984, which provided an essentially voluntary system of diagnosis, treatment, and rehabilitation for drug abusers, with many provisos—up to but not including compulsory testing—designed to involve even recalcitrant players in extended therapy without immediate penalty and with accompanying guarantees of privacy. The program, to be sure, had not been much used and was generally seen to be a tentative beginning to sorting out an obdurately difficult combination of social and medical and corporate issues, but the owners, in any case, announced during the World Series last fall that they were unanimously withdrawing from the Joint Drug Agreement, and they have since made it plain that their strategy would be secure compulsory urine-testing from each player as part of his next contract. The Commissioner, I should add, has said that he regrets the owners' impetuosity in throwing away the Joint Drug Agreement, but it is hard for me to believe that he was not consulted about the matter, or that his advice, if presented, would not have had more effect. Drug testing, we must conclude, had been suddenly perceived by the owners as a dramatic and politically useful simplification of an intractably complex private vice. (Mr. Ueberroth has also raised the spectre of cocaine-afflicted players' being blackmailed by their underworld suppliers and presumably forced to throw games at the behest of crooked gamblers, but this scare seems to have expired from unlikelihood; fixing the 1919 World Series required the mob to bribe seven or eight doltish, vastly underpaid members of the Chicago White Sox, and even then the trick almost misfired.)

The arguments against compulsory testing, some of which will be presented below, are of considerable weight, and they were much discussed among the players at the end of last season and over the winter. (I should explain that my own sampling of player opinion was always a narrow one, never encompassing more than three or four players on any one club, but the players I did consult always tried to offer a fair estimate of what others in their clubhouse believed. Most of the opinions summarized here, whether from players or from front-office people and executives, and even owners, must be unattributed, since individuals on both sides requested anonymity because of the pending grievance hearing—the Big Case, as it is sometimes called.) Players on different clubs, including several player representatives, who correspond roughly to shop stewards in the Players Association, told me that about half of their teammates had no objection to compulsory urine-testing—in fact, many of them were eager to see the plan in operation, so that the whole distracting issue could be forgotten and they could get on with their work—and others agreed with the notion that testing was a valid way for baseball to begin to set its house in order. A few of the players who had tried cocaine and run into difficulties with it

(Rod Scurry, now of the Yankees, for one) said that compulsory testing was the only weapon that might deter habitual offenders. Players on the other side of the question, however, were vehement in their opposition to testing; most of *them* saw testing as a violation of their privacy, and a good many also saw it as an unsubtle scheme by the owners to drive a wedge between the players and their union. These fears were not unfounded, one would conclude, for by the time spring training came around about five hundred of the major-league players (of the one thousand and forty on the winter rosters) had agreed to testing clauses in their new contracts. In many cases (it's hard to say how many, since contract negotiations are kept private), an offer of more money in return for testing, and a threat of less money without testing, swung the balance. Compulsory testing seems to have carried the day, at least for the moment, and it is my belief that this conclusion to the issue has become very popular with the fans, not just because it appears to enhance, or even guarantee, the purity of the sport but also because it slightly but clearly demeans the players (who must produce a urine sample on demand, in the presence of a drug cop), and thus punishes them all for letting us down so badly, for damaging our dreams about the game.

Penalties for the cocaine users who had testified or had been named at the Pittsburgh trials were announced by the Commissioner at the beginning of the spring-training season. After private interviews with all the players involved, he divided them into three categories, with accompanying degrees of severity in their punishment. For seven prime offenders—including Joaquin Andujar, Dave Parker, and Keith Hernandez—he decreed a year's suspension from the game, with the accompanying provision that the suspension would be lifted in return for a fine of ten percent of their salaries, plus two hundred hours' service in community programs to combat drug abuse, and compulsory drug testing for the remainder of their careers. Lesser penalties—sixty days' suspension or five-percent fines, fifty hours of community service, and compulsory testing—were imposed on four other players, and testing alone on the remaining ten. There may be some cogency to the Commissioner's expressed belief that this disposition of the very difficult matter of punishment might be of use in combatting drug abuse in and outside the game; and his determination of the cases—to judge by fans and friends I have heard from—has been popularly viewed as being fair and proper, although there remained a number of hard-line scribes and baseball executives who believe that the drug users, immunity or no immunity, should have been thrown out of the game for life, like the Chicago Black Sox. Mr. Ueberroth's tone toward the offenders has been regretful and conciliatory, but I have heard not a few coarse expressions of satisfaction from old-line coaches and front-office men, who surely speak for some of their employers in their belief that the wealthy, insufferably privileged young players of today have at last been cut down to size by the scandal, at least for the moment. There is a sense on the management side that the Players Association has lost some of its constituency over the issue of testing, and that, fairly or unfairly, the union is viewed by the public as having no plan or program of its own, and as standing stubbornly on the wrong side of the whole business.

• ◆ •

WHY NOT TEST? HERE ARE SOME REASONS PRESENTED TO ME BY players, by officers of the Players Association, by a handful of front-office people, and by doctors and lawyers and friends and fans I talked to over the winter. The arguments are set forth in no special order.

• Compulsory testing is a violation of personal privacy. The embarrassment of a compulsory urine test is not quite a constitutional issue, since the Fourth Amendment restrictions against unreasonable search and seizure apply only to measures imposed by the government, but testing clearly does harm to an individual's sense of self. Racehorses have their urine tested, to be sure, but, as one All-Star American League infielder put it to me last fall, "I am not a horse." Several of the more thoughtful front-office people I know explained to me this spring that compulsory testing is only a necessary small inconvenience, of exactly the same sort that we all accept when submitting ourselves to a metal detector at an airport—almost a convincing argument, I thought, until I began to envision lines of passengers at LaGuardia or O'Hare leading up to and into bathrooms occupied by waiting inspectors.

• It attaches a presumption of guilt to all the players. The easy little turnabout in our minds ("If they've done nothing wrong, they've got nothing to hide.") when we seize upon the quick fix of compulsory testing damages *us* in the end, for it demolishes an essential premise of a free society.

Urine-testing, up until now, has been an unreliable process, with a persistent error factor of from fifteen to twenty-five percent, divided equally between false negative and false positive results. Follow-up tests, in the case of positives, may correct a mistake, but they, too, require great care, and afford further possibilities of error and misdiagnosis. A more accurate means of urine-testing is available, but it is so expensive—up to five hundred dollars a test—as to make its everyday use unlikely.

· Urine-testing makes no distinction between the occasional recreational use of a drug and habitual or addictive use.

· Compulsory testing is a two-class system: lightly or forgivingly applied to star players, rigorously applied to everyone else. (Many black players believe that the system will be employed against them in discriminatory fashion.) Examples of this disparity are easy to find. When Dwight Gooden was presented with his new 1.32-million-dollar contract by the Mets this winter, it contained a compulsory-drug-testing clause; he demurred, and the matter was dropped without further ado. Mike Armstrong, a borderline member of the Yankee pitching staff, similarly refused, on principle, a drug-testing clause in his two-hundred-and-ninety-five-thousand-dollar contact, and eventually was forced to settle for thirty thousand dollars less in order to get it dropped.* Joel Youngblood, a veteran San Francisco outfielder who did not seem to fit into the Giants' plans for the coming season, was refused a three-year extension on his contract this winter unless he agreed to unspecified forms of drug testing; when he and his agent protested the vagueness of the terms in the testing clause, he was told to take his wares elsewhere. No one had suggested or implied that Youngblood might be a drug user, but he was

*Less than a year after this was written, Dwight Gooden failed a voluntary urine test and then missed two months of the 1987 season while he underwent treatment for cocaine abuse. He had been a sometime user of the drug, it turned out, going back to his high-school days. Some fans and writers and front-office people instantly claimed that Gooden's difficulties could have been headed off if compulsory testing had been adopted. Mets general manager Frank Cashen pointed out that if the old Joint Drug Agreement had still been in force, the club might have approached Gooden months before his use of the drug came to light.

forced to carry the issue to a labor-grievance procedure before the ban was dropped. Then he made the team.

- Compulsory drug testing in baseball has become a matter of public relations. Doctors and drug specialists I have consulted believe that, in practice, urine-testing is of limited use, and may even have a negative effect on therapy; the suggestion that it can help do away with the basic problem is illusory, and actually veils the stubborn nature of cocaine addiction and the difficulty of its cure.

- Compulsory testing in baseball, the national pastime, will become a symbolic, integral part of a national pattern of drug testing in industry and private business, in state and municipal governments, on newspapers, in schools, and so forth—part of a major alteration of our freedoms and priorities. This is a matter that has already produced very strong opinions on both sides. The recently presented findings of the President's Commission on Organized Crime recommended widespread testing in industry and compulsory testing of all federal employees, but this part of the report was immediately challenged by several members of the commission itself. The question of testing is being debated almost everywhere now, it seems (the National Football League is embroiled in much the same sort of wrangle as baseball), and may ultimately be resolved only in the courts. It should not come as an absolute surprise that proponents of a safer, more rigidly controlled society should turn up among the conservative businessmen and entrepreneurs who buy their way into sports franchises, and this larger issue—at its heart, an intergenerational conflict—has been visible just below the surface in the bitter labor and salary negotiations waged between the owners and the players over the past two decades. Regardless of our individual inclinations in this emotional subject, we should probably remind ourselves that if the practice of compulsory drug testing is accepted by all professional sports organizations, it will only be a matter of time—a very short time, in my view—before it is required of all college athletes, and very soon thereafter, surely, we will be asking high-school boys and girls to subject themselves to the same process if they wish to try out for a team.

◆ ◆ ◆

IF THERE IS ANY HOPE OR CERTAINTY TO BE FOUND IN THIS sorry business, it must be searched out somewhere beyond or to one side of our wishes for a restored "image" of the game, and also beyond or to one side of the assumptions by the Commissioner and the owners that the fans' feelings about the drug issue are clear enough to constitute some kind of mandate. Confusions and contradictions crop up everywhere, and probably within most of us as well. Last September 10th, in a crucial game against the Cardinals at Shea Stadium, when Keith Hernandez came up to bat for the first time after his Pittsburgh court appearance, he received a sustained standing ovation from fifty thousand home-town fans (he had to step out of the batter's box to compose himself), and no one who was there—as I was—and no one I have talked to since has quite been able to decipher the full meaning of that outburst of feeling. Maybe the fans were expressing forgiveness for Keith's transgressions. Maybe they were hailing his extraordinary season's performance, afield and at the plate, and saying that this outweighed all. Maybe they were saying "It's O.K., Keith—we understand," or maybe they were only saying "Let's play ball!" or "Let's go, *Mets*!" Perhaps they were expressing their belief that some corner had been turned, and that drugs in baseball was over and done with at last. I just don't know. I've heard in dugouts and pressrooms and clubhouses that the use of cocaine in the majors is much reduced from what it was four or five years ago, but no one knows how many recreational or habitual users there were or are in baseball—an amazing vacuum at the very center of the controversy. Physicians employed under the Joint Drug Agreement were preparing a confidential medical survey on this question, but the survey expired when the owners abandoned the agreement in October.

The need for symbolic victory seems to outweigh every other consideration or sensible procedure. Many people would agree that Commissioner Ueberroth had to invoke *some* form of penalty against the cocaine users whose names had surfaced at Pittsburgh, but, as it happened, his system of suspension and forgiveness came down hardest on some players—Hernandez, for one, and Lonnie Smith, of the Royals, for another—who had recognized their own addiction and had voluntarily taken the necessary steps to cure it; they had broken the law, to be sure, and had been guilty of great and self-destructive foolishness (Hernandez had also lied about his cocaine habit before he was called to testify under oath and under immunity), but their turnabout, surely, was exactly the sort of difficult self-rehabilitation that the clubs and the leagues would hold up as an example to other afflicted players. Complexities and ironies abound, and in the end we can only respond to some of them with a dismissive shrug—the gesture of our times. Amphetamines, which probably affect game performance more than cocaine, are still in use in many clubs (there aren't as many clubhouse jokes about greenies—which are now sometimes called "beans"—as there once were), but amphetamines, when prescribed, are legal. So is alcohol, and drinking, of course, is an ancient and celebrated companion to big-time sports—a seatmate at the games, so to speak—with infinitely more widespread and destructive consequences than drugs. It sounds naïve to point out that the Commissioner and the clubs, to the best of my knowledge, have never imposed suspensions or other penalties on players or managers who have had their licenses revoked for drunk driving.

Mr. Ueberroth, it must be added, has put forward no over-all program of his own for the treatment and rehabilitation of drug-afflicted players, which further reinforces the suspicion that the *appearance* of a drug-free sport is his prime objective. I don't mean to suggest that he is indifferent to the problem of addiction or unconcerned about the welfare of the players—only that his peculiar office is, of its nature, symbolic, paternal, and much given to enforced optimism. On Opening Day last month, he announced a more detailed plan for the compulsory testing of all major-leaguers, with accompanying assurances of full confidentiality in the process, and with no penalty for an initial positive finding for any player, but at almost the same moment it became clear that testing has been little more than a gesture or a symbol all along. Barry Rona, the executive director of the Player Relations Committee (an owners' group), said at a hearing before baseball's impartial arbitrator, Thomas Roberts, that for technical reasons drug tests could not be enforced upon the signers of non-guaranteed contracts (those whose terms do not apply if the player is dropped before the beginning of the regular season), which suggested that compulsory testing, if it ever did come, would apply only to the forty-three players who hold guaranteed contracts, plus the twenty-one under drug penalties imposed by the Commissioner: perhaps five percent of all major-leaguers. If this sounds baffling and anti-climactic, it is no wonder, for these alterations of stance were clearly intended to influence the outcome of the grievance procedure. The Players Association, for its part, has been relatively quiet, which suggests some confidence there about its fundamental argument that the drug-testing issue must be resolved, now as in the past, through collective bargaining. (The Association, it must be emphasized, has never flatly refused testing.) Whatever that verdict turns out to be, it seems clear that the owners and the Players Association will eventually have to agree upon an all-encompassing plan for drug education, therapy, and rehabilitation, which will be administered for the benefit of the players themselves, as individuals, rather than for any of the reasons that have inflamed and distracted us over the past year. The two sides were very close to an agreement about a week ago, but they have since receded from what looked like an ingenious solution to the bitterly divisive testing issue. If they do eventually come to terms, it will no doubt be over a plan very much like the Joint Drug Agreement, with some temporary acceptance of testing under limited conditions. (The Anti-Drug Program of the National Basketball Association, which has been in operation since September, 1983, empowers a single independent expert to determine whether there is reasonable cause to suspect that an individual player may be engaged in the use of illegal drugs, and this expert may then authorize the N.B.A. to test the player four times during a six-week period. Accommodations, in other words, are possible, and an accommodation, as I have said, will bring the two sides in baseball together once again.*

Several of the more progressive ball clubs—including the Baltimore Orioles, the Oakland A's, and the Milwaukee Brewers—have been working quietly on their own drug-rehabilitation programs while awaiting a resolution of the over-all testing issue. These antidrug plans have been in place for several years now, and form part of the teams' larger Employee Assistance Programs. During the past winter, twenty-two members of the Orioles' major-league roster agreed to a drug plan devised by an agent, Ron Shapiro, which will be administered by the Johns Hopkins Hospital and School of Medicine, and which appears

---

*My optimism was misplaced. The ruling on the grievance-procedure case (it was the Joel Youngblood dispute, previously described) came in July, and it upheld the Players Association's contention that since compulsory drug testing had never been subject to collective bargaining, it was a violation of the 1985 Basic Agreement between the player and the owners. Since the ruling, no progress has been made by the two sides toward the reestablishment of the Joint Drug Agreement, or something of its kind, which means that baseball has no over-all drug plan whatsoever. The whole matter will form part of the prodigiously difficult negotiations that will precede the signing (or non-signing) of the next Basic Agreement before the 1989 season.

to guarantee player privacy, for the club would not know which players were in treatment unless the treatment should require their absence from the field; it also calls for testing. This year, the A's were able to obtain drug-testing agreements from a majority of their players on an individual basis *after* their contracts had been signed; the documents had no relation to each other, that is. Sal Bando, who administers the Employee Assistance Program for the Brewers, told me that programs dealing with cocaine abuse in baseball should be aimed specifically at the player who is at the edge of making the shift from being a social user to being one with a more habitual problem; the true addict, he said, would always come into the program automatically, out of need. He also said that among the Milwaukee players who have recourse to the Employee Assistance Program, drug abuse is a much less common concern than everyday matters like stress, depression, divorce, child abuse, and alcohol.

Trust is what it comes down to, of course. Several players have told me that there are a handful of clubs with which they would readily sign drug-testing agreements, simply because they trusted the management there. The list was a small one, however, never exceeding five or six teams, and each of the players quickly added that he deeply suspected the ability or desire of most clubs to deal with their players in a non-punitive, consistent manner when it came to drugs. Some clubs have shown a degree of compassion toward a player who has admitted to cocaine trouble for the first time, only to turn pious and punitive if he runs into further difficulties. "They've taken a very hard line on drugs and testing, and you've got to ask what they were after, when we already had an industry-wide agreement that had a real chance to work," one American League player said. "They wanted the monkey on our backs. We have this emotional pressure from the fans, and then here comes the Commissioner telling people there's nothing that shows up in the sport that he can't handle. It's not right. The atmosphere is still very hostile."

One general manager, speaking privately to me a few weeks ago, said, "In our business, we've gone from hero worship down to finding any excuse to blame and bloody the players. We're cynical, and we tend to despise them, and we invite the public to join us in that. Something must be done to turn that around soon. It's the Steinbrenner style, and it can destroy us in the end." That same week, an official of the Players Association made almost the same point in conversation. "All our assumptions about fairness and innocence have been changed by the drug scare," he said. "This is an ugly place for the national pastime to find itself, especially if it's being done in the name of morality and of role models for our children. It always comes down to the same set of assumptions: the players should be better than the rest of us—they should set an example, toe the line, and all that, because they're lucky to be playing ball and because they're getting all that money. It's pathetic stuff, if you think about it, and it's got nothing to do with the realities of drug addiction. I see the Steinbrenner world view in this. It's angry, and it seems to infect us all in the end."

◆ ◆ ◆

WHAT WE FANS AND BYSTANDERS THINK ABOUT ALL THIS IS what counts, of course, because baseball belongs to us in the end, rather than to its transient and impatient owners, and because drug abuse in society and the image of professional sports are matters of our own making—images of ourselves. Most of my friends who are also fans seemed extremely upset with the players whenever the matter of drugs came up in conversation in recent months. Now and then, I ventured to suggest that baseball is simply another slice of American society, after all, and that since drugs are an everyday reality now it probably shouldn't surprise us much if they also turn up in baseball. Sometimes I went farther and pointed out that the large salaries now paid to major-league players, combined with their youth and their sudden celebrity, and with the unceasing pressures on them to perform at a very high level of success in a restricted, highly competitive line of work, would almost seem to guarantee some use of cocaine among their numbers. But most of my friends were unconvinced. "They've got it made," I kept hearing. "And what about their responsibility to the fans and to families? Kids are looking up to them, you know. They're meant to be models."

And here I would shut up, most of the time, for this cherished and wishful idea of athletes as heroes and exemplars seems to lie too deep in our emotions and memories to be dislodged or altered by argument. It is there, all right—I recognize it in myself, even after years of association with the young men (they are now much younger than I am) who play ball for a living—but I don't believe it means much. Most children I have known, including my own, have made the switch from hero worship of some ballplayer (or movie star or rock musician) to a more restrained and knowledgeable and accepting view of that individual almost overnight, with few visible signs of shock or loss. I can no longer remember the exact moment when I stopped thinking of Babe Ruth as a demigod, having somehow learned—I was ten or twelve years old—that he was much given to drinking and gluttony (I could see that he was fat) and prostitutes, but the news somehow made him more interesting to me, rather than less, and it did not impel me to emulate his disreputable habits or to turn on him because he had somehow let me down. Last year, I mentioned this matter of lost image to the peerless Kansas City relief pitcher Dan Quisenberry (I was preparing to write an article about him), and he recalled the moment when he first read Jim Bouton's "Ball Four," a funny, raucously debunking account of daily life with the New York Yankees (for whom Bouton pitched from 1962 to '68), which depicted the lordly champions as a band of hard-drinking, girl chasing boobs and overage adolescents. The book was roundly denounced by Commissioner Bowie Kuhn and the entire baseball establishment when it was published, in 1970. "I was about seventeen when I read 'Ball Four,' and all my friends and I *lived* for sports back then," Quisenberry said. "You could say I worshipped baseball, but when I read the book it only made the game and the players that much more exciting to me. I loved that book, but it didn't change me at all. I was a straight arrow back then, and I'm afraid I'm still a straight arrow today."

Last November, an acquaintance of mine came up to me at a party and produced a Polaroid photograph of his little daughter—I think she is about nine years old—dressed up in her Halloween costume. "She's Keith Hernandez," he said, and so she was, in perfect miniature: the blue-stripes Metsie home uniform, with Hernandez' No. 17 on the tunic; the interlocked "NY" on the cap, and the cap bill pulled low; the left-handed batting stance and the proudly upheld bat (it was painted papier-mâché); and a smudgy, painted-on Hernandez mustache. It was a captivating picture. "I just don't know what's going to happen to her when she grows up and hears about Keith and the cocaine," the father said. "She's a *total* fan of his. She's crazy about him. I don't know what I'll say."

I didn't know what to say, either, so I was startled when the same man came back over to me about half an hour later and said, "You know, I was thinking about what I said about Keith and Ada, and it just came to me that I'm crazy. It won't mean a thing to her when she finds out about Keith—I know that. She'll just grow up. I don't know why I've been so worried. She'll be fine.''

Yes. I think a great many of us have begun to see how deeply we want baseball players and other athletes to be better than we are. We may wish this now more than ever before, because other heroes—in politics, in our daily lives—seem to be in short supply. We cared most for ballplayers, of course, back when they really were heroes to us and when we wanted to *be* them, if we could. We know better than that now, surely, but because we still wish to keep baseball, our old game, in some special place in our affections and our imagination we want the players to remain the same, too—to be good at the game and good at life as well. Good at heart. This is an image, all right, and there is no damage in it as long as we remind ourselves from time to time that it is a dream or a wish and that we really *do* know better. Ballplayers are not much different from the rest of us, except for their unforgivable skills when it comes to playing ball, and there is a sudden releasing pleasure for us that accompanies the realization that we need no longer patronize them by making them into heroes, and that they are not all of a kind. Not by a long shot. If you talk to them and listen to them talk on almost any subject, you will get a range of response that is almost impossible to summarize, especially if they're talking about something like drugs in sports. "Of *course* we're divided on this issue," one team rep said to me this spring. "It's right that we should be, because there's nothing easy about it. We're just trying to make up our minds."

In Arizona this spring, I had a chance to talk with an old friend, Steve Garvey, the San Diego first baseman, who is baseball's acknowledged prince of straight arrows. We got around to drugs at one point, and he said, "I've known guys in baseball to get caught in drugs, and I could see how it happened, because this is such a tough game. I felt sorry for them, but I still think it's up to us players to do better than that, because of what we represent and who's watching us. That comes with the job and the good pay and the good life we've been given." Garvey takes this view somewhat farther in his recently published autobiography ("Garvey"), in which he says, "Baseball plays on its specialness to cultivate its position in the hearts and minds of the American people. We call ourselves the National Pastime and put ads on television dramatizing our importance as a tradition, even suggesting that going to games is the glue that keeps generations together. If we are going to tap those emotional veins to foster our own popularity, we in the game have an obligation to be clean—cleaner than the rest of society.''

No surprise there, perhaps, but the very next morning in Phoenix, I heard something rather different from Bruce Bochte, the Oakland A's first baseman. Bochte is an original. Three years ago, he took a sabbatical year off from baseball to live full time with his wife and two daughters in an economically and ecologically self-sufficient community on Whidbey Island, in Puget Sound. He is articulate and iconoclastic—but this sort of aside or explanation, it occurs to me, would not be necessary, or even acceptable, if he were employed in almost any other line of work. Bochte said, ''Drugs—well, you know, drugs are around. We're just in a life style and at a salary level where drugs are going to come onto the scene. Sometimes I think the problem has been exaggerated, but if you're in a business where you're going to play a hundred and sixty-two games, travel all across the country, stay up late, be away from home, and all that, then drugs will come with the territory. The situation should be addressed, but most of our reactions to it are exaggerated.

''So much of all this comes down to image, just the way it did during the strike, when so many people were upset about what was really just basic stuff—negotiating over bargaining rights and the rest. The money came into it later. Why couldn't people understand that? I couldn't figure this out for the longest time. I think it came down to image. The baseball player still represents the image of the American hero. But what's happened in our country? What is this country really like? The journey or destiny of the American people now is just to make money. We're brought up with that, and it's what everybody judges his performance on and sets his values by. We have an overpreoccupation with making money in this country. Well, we ballplayers just picked up on that. The twenty-six owners in baseball are mostly millionaires. We watch them, and we have to work for them, and we're around them and other high-powered people all the time, so we just began to emulate them. The public has begun to see something different about the American hero, about major-league ballplayers, that they don't like at all. Now if anybody asks me about our image I say, 'Yeah, that's what we're about. We're Americans, so we're making a lot of money. We're exploited, we see drugs coming into the scene, we have antagonistic relationships with the people we work for'—well, *I* don't, not here with the A's, but most players sure do—'because that's what the American scene is like.' I don't want us to go around making out that we're a bunch of good guys. We're just the American thing.

"We have to work at the causes of drug abuse, I know, but you have to look at the basics, too. You can't convince me that people who spend all their time and energy trying to maximize the profits of their business—making deals, working their butts off—are not doing damage to themselves and their families and other people they're involved with. It's an extremist mode of being. It's stressful, and if we ballplayers sometimes get into drugs—well, those people are into stress and alcohol and heart attacks. So who are they to say we're destroying America? There are different ways of destroying America, and they're doing it. I know this runs against the old pastoral view of baseball and what it's about, but it's what I believe."

I don't think I can entirely accept this harsh, almost despairing view of things, but I can't say that I wholly disagree with any part of it. It doesn't matter much, either way, because I am not offering Bruce Bochte as a role model or as an image of anything but himself. He's just another ballplayer.

TWELVE

Fortuity

MIDSUMMER 1986

T HE PRESS BOX AT WRIGLEY FIELD, IN CHICAGO, IS AN
extended narrow shed, two rows deep, that is precari-
ously bolted to the iron rafters just underneath the park's
second deck. To gain access, one must climb a steeply angled
ramp and clamber down a little starboard companionway,
guarded at its foot by a uniformed minion, and then proceed
giddily along a catwalk that hangs directly above the tiered,
circling rows of seats and spectators behind home plate. Seen
from this vantage point, the preoccupied fans below sometimes
suggest a huddled, uncomplaining horde of immigrants stuffed
into steerage on some endless voyage toward better luck—not
an inappropriate image if we remind ourselves that this famous
rustbucket, the good ship Cubbie, last dropped anchor in the
shining harbor of the World Series in 1945. The outward view
from the catwalk is felicitous and hopeful: the converging faraway left-field and left-bleacher sections complete the lines of
the ancient vessel that plows forever dead ahead into Waveland
and Sheffield Avenues, while the bleachers in center rise bravely
toward the prow of the great green scoreboard, topped by a
single lofty mast, its rigging aflutter with signal pennants (the
current standings, top to bottom, of the teams in the two National League divisions), which customarily tell of happier news

in other places. I visited the Friendly Confines on a Friday afternoon last July, just three days after the All-Star Game, which traditionally marks the equator of the baseball season; I was there not just to take in some daytime ball (there are no lights at the park) or to watch the Cubs engage the visiting San Francisco Giants over a midsummer weekend but also in search of a better understanding of some central processes of the game: luck or momentum or confidence, and their opposites—whatever it is that can unexpectedly make winning a habit for one club and losing such a curse for the other. I had chosen these two teams with care, as will shortly be seen, but the park was a break for me, too, because Wrigley Field always offers a fresh perspective on baseball: it is the *spécialité de la maison*.

I had skipped the All-Star Game itself (it was played at the Houston Astrodome this year, and won by the American League by a score of 3–2), but I did not grieve over my loss any more than I would have fretted about not getting a seat at the Emmy Awards or missing a Jerry Lewis telethon, which are also television promotions rather than sporting events. Like many other fans, I imagine, I employed the three-day All-Star break in the schedules to study the 1986 standings to date and to wonder about their strange configurations. In the National League East, the New York Mets, established before the season as solid favorites to win their division, had surpassed all expectations, bowling over their opponents in runaway-train fashion, and dominating both the standings and the National League team statistics. As a team, they led all comers in runs, home runs, runs batted in, and batting average, and had yet to be shut out in any game. This was a team effort, for once, since none of their players stood at the top of the list in any batting category, and their best-known sluggers—Keith Hernandez, Gary Carter, and Darryl Strawberry—were, in fact, experiencing slightly subpar years. The Mets also had the best pitching in the league, with a team earned-run average of 3.06; their four prime starters—Dwight Gooden, Ron Darling, Sid Fernandez, and Bob Ojeda (a left-hander picked up in a trade with the Red Sox over the winter)—had a combined record of 41–10, with twenty-one complete games. The Mets led the Montreal Expos, their nearest opponent in the National League East, by thirteen games; within a couple of weeks, they would widen the margin to sixteen games—a bigger lead than any of the three other first-place teams had established over the last-place clubs in their divisions. In the National League West, the Houston Astros (good pitching

and good defense; feeble batting and few fans) had been taking
turns at the top with the surprising Giants, last-place finishers a
year ago, while the Dodgers, sorely afflicted with injuries, floun-
dered along in the cellar, eight games back. The American
League West, habitually a rest home for most of the league's
losing teams, showed the California Angels holding a slim game-
and-a-half lead over the young Texas Rangers, with none of the
five other teams so far able to get its chin over the .500 bar. The
real news was the Red Sox, who were leading the second-place
Yankees in the mighty A.L. East by seven full games, mostly
on the strength of their pitching: a startling turn of events for a
club that has always specialized in winning by cannonade—the
four-hour, four-homer, 10–7 Fenway Park Special, with both
starting pitchers back in their street clothes by the middle of the
fifth. Roger Clemens, a powerful twenty-three-year-old right-
hander who sat out most of the 1985 season after a shoulder
operation, had accounted for this turnabout almost on his own,
winning his first fourteen decisions without a defeat; here at the
All-Star break, he stood at 15–2, with a league's-best E.R.A. of
2.48 and a hundred and forty-six strikeouts in his hundred and
forty-five innings pitched. On April 29th, he had fanned twenty
Seattle batters in a single game—the highest one-game total in
the history of the major leagues.

There were other happy surprises tucked in among the midterm
postings (including the wholly unexpected prosperity of the Cleveland Indians, who were more than holding their own in the savage
campaigning in the American League East), but the bad news
seemed far more absorbing. Just recently, the World Champion
Kansas City Royals had somehow lost eleven games in a row, with
their vastly admired corps of starting pitchers compiling an earned-
run average of 7.32 during that spell. Bret Saberhagen, the Cy
Young Award winner in his circuit last summer, had a 4–10 and
4.39 record, and was pitching so poorly that there was talk of
sending him to the bullpen for rest and cogitation.

If the Royals looked bad (fourth place and eight games below
.500), their World Series opponents, the Cardinals, were abysmal. Their 36–50 at the All-Star break had them a half game
out of the cellar and twenty-four games behind the Mets, and
they were batting .228 as a team. No one could explain what
had happened to the spirited and combative club that came so
close to winning the classic last fall, but their manager, Whitey
Herzog, was blunt about their season to date. "We're just a bad
club," he said late in May. "We're not deep in any department.

We're supposed to have a great defense, and we haven't played worth a damn.'' Asked if there was some remedy for his club's dismal showing, he said, ''Better players.'' When the schedule at last brought the Cards a day off at a point when they had lost eleven out of their last fourteen games, Herzog said the occasion called for a victory party.

The downside news was up in other places as well. Toronto's ace starter, Dave Stieb, was at 2–9 and 5.80 so far, and forty-one-year-old Steve Carlton, a lifetime three-hundred-and-eighteen-game winner, was given his unconditional release by the Phillies after surrendering twenty-five runs in twenty innings. (He was picked up by the Giants a few days later.) The Yankees lost a record ten straight games at Yankee Stadium, and the Oakland A's, who were believed to have a fair shot at a pennant this year in the American League West, set a team mark with fifteen consecutive losses on the road. Both Chicago managers lost their jobs, as did the Oakland and Seattle skippers; the deposed White Sox manager, Tony LaRussa, was instantly hired to manage the A's.

Midseason performances don't mean much by September, to be sure, but all this instability at the center of the sport was something to think about. The Mets are a pretty fair team on all counts, but the pace of their success so far seemed almost out of control: they weren't just good, they were imperious. What had happened to so many competent teams this year, I wondered, to make them go so flat? I recalled the pride and self-assurance and sense of accomplishment that only last October permeated the clubhouses of the Cards and the Royals and was equally apparent in the demeanor and conversation of their front-office people. Their teams had attained the heights on merit, these men seemed to be saying, and proved the corporate wisdom and foresight of the organizations that had produced them; success so plainly established almost looked like a guarantee of further success, even in the chancy world of competitive sports. The fatuity of such hopes, in the light of the 1986 season to date, suggested the anxiety and puzzlement and sense of quaky footing that must now infect every team in baseball.

Sports teams live on confidence; it is the air they must breathe if they are to survive at all. Each of the twenty-six major-league clubs spends millions of dollars every year on player development and on the signing of young talent; sizable further funds and thousands of hours of hard work go into scouting and planning trades and into long-range projections, all with the aim of putting a team on the field that will prove resolute in the face of adversity and opportunistic and aggressive when the chance to win presents itself. Quality, however, cannot be guaranteed, which is why the threats and petulant outbursts that George Steinbrenner directs at his Yankee players in times of trouble are so disliked by executives with a better sense of the game. "Maybe we'll surprise some folks" and "At least we'll be respectable" are what you hear from managers of potential fifth-place clubs, but when the season begins it always becomes plain that no one is ever quite ready for the heaven-sent pink glow of success that can suddenly envelop any team when everything—the starting pitching, the bullpen, timely hitting, sound defense, freedom from injury, and the breaks—is going your way, or contrariwise, ready for how bad a club, even a strong or famous one, can turn in the space of ten days. And no team, it seems, can even be sure of its own respectability when it is faced with more than its share of the vicissitudes of baseball: injuries, bad hops, bad calls, suddenly vapid pitching or hitting, trembly defense, and the unexpected and then unstoppable cascade of lost ballgames. Sandy Alderson, the able general manager of the Oakland A's, recently said to me, "If there's one thing I've learned in this game, it's that you can very seldom afford to smile. That's a sad statement, but the truth is that you never know which game may be your last win in a long while, or which day may turn out to be the high point of your season. If you've been going bad, you don't know if the game you've just lost is not yet your nadir or if it's going to be the last loss in a week. That old baseball saying about never letting yourself get too high or too low is a matter of self-preservation. You just never know."

I had never thought much about winning and losing as freestanding and presumably discussable elements of baseball, but now the idea came to me to travel about the leagues a little, here at mid-season, and talk to some players and managers and front-office people about good baseball luck and bad, watching some teams that had enjoyed the best of things in recent weeks take on opponents who had met with very little luck so far this year, and trying to learn from both sides how it felt to be hot or not, how much difference the manager makes, and how different crowds and owners and writers seemed to respond to hard times and high times. In the end, I might even have a better sense of what proportion of the game actually rests in the hands of the men who play it.

Luck always matters in baseball, and here I at once found some luck of my own in the schedules—the upcoming games at Wrigley Field, where the ebullient and onrushing Giants (they had just climbed into first place in the West again, and their nine-game margin over the .500 level represented their best grades in almost four years) would meet the better-established Cubs, who had been winners of the National League East a bare two years ago but were not skating in stately circles in the lower reaches of their division. Injuries did in the entire Cubs pitching rotation last year, but this year the Chicago pitching was the worst in the league. "Last year was an excuse year," a grizzled Cubs writer said to me later in the week. "This year—" He shrugged. "Well, Chicago is a Cubs town." A new manager, Gene Michael, had replaced Jim Frey in June, and Dallas Green, the Cubs' president and general manager, blamed his players for the ritual execution. "I'm not very happy about it," he told a reporter. "I told them in no uncertain terms that they had contributed in great part to it."

Directly after my weekend at Wrigley Field, I also discovered, I could repair to California in time to see the brilliant Red Sox, now at 56–31 for the year and seven games ahead of the pack, do battle with the miserable, last-place Oakland A's, whose season had gone down the drain during a stretch in which most of their pitchers were on the disabled list and they had dropped twenty-five out of thirty-one games; the club had likewise dispensed with a manager, the agreeable Jackie Moore, and had lately replaced him with the aforementioned Tony LaRussa. Looking at my plans, I felt a twinge of compassion for the battered losers of my planned mismatches, but baseball, I reminded myself, is not for the fainthearted.

◆ ◆ ◆

WRIGLEY FIELD LAY BECALMED IN FURNACELIKE DOLDRUMS AS the Giants and the Cubs took the field on Friday, but the natives, I noticed, were unaffected. With the temperature in the mid-nineties, the customary thirty thousand-plus Cubs fans threw themselves into the ancient environs for our uncrucial tilt, and the massed *descamisados* in the bleachers further tanned their pelts toward the prized North Side Gurkhatones of August. Drops of sweat from my brow formed paisley patterns on my scorecard, and between innings home-plate ump Jerry Crawford tottered back to a minuscule strip of shadow next to the backstop, where a ball girl tended him with elixirs and cold cloths. Perhaps sensing our need for a swift distraction from the weather, the Chicago starting pitcher, the tall right-hander Scott Sanderson, absolutely subdued the visitors in the course of his seven innings, striking out nine of the San Franciscos and giving up one hit, a double by Jeff Leonard, and a lone unearned run; his successor, the enormous flamethrower Lee Smith, was perfect, fanning three more Giants and preserving the 2–1 beauty. Sanderson's breaking ball, which an inordinate number of Giants took for called third strikes, bowing politely at the waist as it dipped across the corners, was the talk of both clubhouses. There wasn't much else to say, for great pitching is a silencer. The Giants, like all losing players in such circs, summed things up with a shrug and a wan smile: What are you going to do?

I had seen the Giants suffer an infinitely more painful loss earlier in the season, I now recalled. Back on May 30th, at Shea Stadium, the club had stood on the verge of a hard-earned one-run victory over the Mets in the bottom of the tenth inning. Then, with two out and two Mets aboard, Giants shortstop Jose Uribe and second baseman Rob Thompson somehow collided under a harmless infield fly; the ball popped loose and the winning run came in. A killing defeat, one felt, since it dropped the Giants three games behind the Astros and suddenly ran their string of losses to four straight, all on the road; last year, the Giants lost fifty-seven on the road, on the way to their last-place, worst-ever 62–100 finish. "Same old Giants," a San Francisco writer muttered as we waited for the Shea press-box elevator down to the clubhouses.

Only they weren't. That night, the Giants manager, Roger Craig, closed his clubhouse to exhort his young troops. That game was gone, he told them, and mourning or anger wouldn't bring it back or turn the score around. The team's young second-base combination had already won at least six games for the team with their gloves, so what had just happened only meant that they were 6–1 for the year. Tomorrow's game was the one that mattered now. And so forth. It worked—*something* worked. The Giants won the next day, knocking off Bob Ojeda; Rob Thompson was involved in four double plays for the afternoon and singled three times, and Uribe came through with a two-run double. The Giants won again the day after that, handing Ron Darling his first defeat of the year. The team then moved along to Montreal, swept two games there, and headed home with a suddenly satisfying 4–4 record for the road swing.

In Chicago, I talked to Giants catcher Bob Brenly about the turnaround. "That game in New York was the one that did it," he said. "You know, for any team there can come a day when you decide that this is going to be just another year, just like it was before. Losing can happen so fast. You lose a game, and you think, O.K., we're still all right. You lose the next day, and you think, Well, that was a tough one—no way we could have gone against the breaks there. Then you get blown out, say, and the day after that maybe you get beat 2–1, and before you know it it's five or six in a row and you've slid down a couple of places in the standings. But Roger prepared us for that sort of thing this year. We know we're a better team. We know we have that resiliency. Roger has done it—give him the credit. He's got guys bunting, doing the hit-and-run, guys hitting the ball to the right side of the infield who never bothered to learn that kind of ball. He's got *me* running, and I'm a catcher. Nobody's exempt, nobody's ahead on the ball club, and it's all from Roger. Call him a guru, call him a positive guy, call him a man—a grown-up human being. You know, almost every professional athlete has had one great coach in high school or college that he remembers and thinks of most highly. I had a high-school basketball coach back at Coshocton High named Bill Bowman, who always seemed like he could pull about ten percent more out of you than you thought you had. Well, that's the way Roger is for everybody in this room. We've talked about it. He reminds you of somebody important in your life. He makes you think winning is something you can be personally responsible for. The biggest difference is we're having fun. You can hear it in the air around here. I can hardly wait to get up in the morning and come to the ballpark. Last year was mostly just a personal thing, and I think that down feeling, that first bad day, came almost on Opening Day. Baseball is a team game, and once you lose that you've lost all concept. Some of our guys had a pretty good year in 1985, but I don't think they were enjoying it any. It all got washed away by the team. Roger wants it the other way now. I've never learned so much from one person.''

The one great coach that Roger Craig reminds me of is himself—a tall, engaging, noble-nosed North Carolinian who when last seen by me was accepting congratulations in the champagne-soaked Detroit Tigers clubhouse for his part in the making of that 1984 World Champion team. As pitching coach, he had brought the Detroit staff along from eleventh-best to best in the league in the space of two years, in considerable part through his teaching of the split-fingered fastball, a deadly little down-diver that he perfected some years ago while running a baseball school for teen-agers. Craig retired from baseball after the Tigers' triumph and went home to his horse ranch and his family in Southern California, but came back to take over as Giants manager in mid-September of last year, as part of a fresh regime headed by an incoming general manager, Al Rosen. Craig also had a previous two-year tenure as manager of the Padres, in 1978 and '79. This summer, he has been teaching the split-finger to anyone on the Giants staff who is interested—to Roger Mason and Mike Krukow and Mark Davis and Vida Blue (who has had trouble with it, because his fingers aren't very long), and even to Steve Carlton.

Whatever ballpark he is in, Craig is implored by the local writers to talk about his defeats as well as his successes—in particular, about the forty-six games he lost in two years while pitching for the newborn and disastrous New York Mets, near the close of his career. "Aw, I don't want to dwell on that story all the time," he said in the casbah of the Wrigley Field dugout early one afternoon. But then, because he's an obliging fellow, he talked about it just the same. He confirmed his most famous statistic, registered in 1963—eighteen consecutive mound losses, which tied an ancient mark. "I think the record still stands," he said now, "but maybe I'll pitch tomorrow and break it." He lost five games by the score of 1–0 in that stretch—also a record. "I kept telling the guys to go out and get me one run and we'd win," he told us. "Then, one time, I remember, it got to be about the fifth or sixth inning and I said, 'All right, just get me half a run!' You know, I always felt I pitched well those years. I got a raise at the end of both years, and I deserved it. I had twenty-seven complete games over those two seasons, and every game I started I expected to win."

Craig said he thought the Mets trauma had helped him as a manager. "I know all about the things that can make you lose, and all about the things that can help you win. A lot of my coaching is from that. If a guy gets on a losing streak on the mound or goes oh-for-four up at bat a few days, I can identify with that. He knows I've been there before him. But he also knows that I've been in five World Series and I got four winning World Series rings to show for it. At first, the guys on this club thought I was crazy when I said I could show them how to win, but now they've got the idea. If you've got some talent, you *can* win. Sure, we've lost some games, but I'm happier right now than I've ever been before in baseball." He paused, squinting in the sun. "Well, maybe you always say that. The first year I was with the Brooklyn Dodgers as a major-league pitcher, I didn't feel I could be any happier than that. But as an old man—I'm fifty-six—as an old man, right now

I'm very happy. I've got outstanding coaches and a fine young ball club, and that's all you can ask for.''

This summer in San Francisco, I've been told, you can some-times spot five or six Giants caps at the same time among the noonday crowds waiting for the lights to change on the corner of Kearny and Post Streets. Attendance at Candlestick Park (which will not be torn down or domed over in the near future, as had been much rumored in recent years) is up by a hundred and thirteen percent, and people at cocktail parties in Mill Val-ley or at dinner downtown at the Washington Square Bar & Grill sometimes refer to the Giants as ''the lads'' now, just as the sports columns do. Now and then, on the courts at the Berkeley Tennis Club, you can hear somebody out there yell ''Humm baby!'' when his partner pulls off a winning backhand shot down the alley. The expression comes from Roger Craig, and it means ''Great play!'' or ''Wow!'' or perhaps, as a noun, a pretty young woman across the street. Back in June, somebody took down the office-door sign at Candlestick that said ''NO. 33–CRAIG.'' Now it says ''HUMM BABY.''

◆ ◆ ◆

THE CUBS WERE LESS TALKATIVE, AND NO WONDER. DALLAS Green had recently suggested that he was prepared to dispense with almost anyone on his roster of well-paid underachievers (anyone but all-league second baseman Ryne Sandberg, one must assume, or the brilliant young shortstop Shawon Dunston, or perhaps Lee Smith), although there are cynics who claim he wouldn't find many takers, because of the lavish contracts that were given to the stars of '84. In any case, I had very little relish at the prospect of worming out losers' confessions in the Chi-cago clubhouse. Ron Cey, who had been riding the bench in recent weeks, probably because of his Rodinesque responses to hard-hit ground balls around third base, was polite but distant. Now thirty-eight years old, he had played nineteen hundred and fifty-three games at third base and hit three hundred and six home runs over ten full seasons with the Dodgers and three-plus with the Cubs, and he was not prepared to be forthcoming about unsuccess. ''You'd have to ask players who have been on teams that have been out of it a lot of years,'' he said stiffly. ''It's not a situation I'm familiar with—I don't qualify. I'm used to being up there in the midst of things. When you're in contention, you *contest*. It's what you're here for—why you exist as a professional. Now—well, not playing much and being with a team that's out of it, the way we are, is not an enviable position. I'm in a different place than I'm used to.''*

Forehandedly, I had arranged for further testimony about the Cubs from the best source possible—a fan. Cubs fans, by consensus, are the best in baseball. Year after year, in good times and (mostly) bad, they turn out in vociferous numbers, sustaining themselves with a heavenly ichor that combines loyalty, criticism, cheerfulness, durability, rage, beer, and hope, in exquisite proportions. The Cubs sold a million and a half tickets before Opening Day this year, and the sellout Saturday crowd on this second day of my trip would put them over the million mark in admissions on the second-earliest date in their long history. My companion at the game was a baseball pen pal of mine named Tim Shanahan, a young and friendly (it turned out) professor of education at the University of Illinois at Chicago. He grew up in Detroit and still sustains an ancient passion for the Tigers (''It's very, very unlikely that they'll ever end up playing the Cubs in the World Series,'' he said when I asked about his ultimate loyalty), and followed the Phillies closely when attending graduate school in Delaware. His attachment to the Cubs is of only six years' duration, which barely puts him on the waiting list for admission to the True Cubs Sodality, but he clearly belongs nevertheless. A few weeks earlier, he and his wife and two young daughters had turned up at Wrigley for a Sunday game, to find that the remaining tickets were only for standing room. ''My older daughter Erin is six, and she said that was fine with her,'' Shanahan said. ''She's been coming to games with us for years. But Meagan is three, and after my wife and I and the girls stood around outside the gate for about an hour we finally decided that it might be a little hard on her to be held in our arms for three hours at her very first game. *I* wouldn't have minded, of course, but—'' He was still thinking it over.

Shanahan and I had good seats in the deep stands just behind home, and, with the temperature back in the nineties, I did not respond when he suggested that we probably should have sat in the bleachers if I was in search of some *real* Cubs fans. We drank some beer, and he brought me up to date on the franchise gossip. The White Sox, who have been traditionally seen as

*Before my visit to Wrigley Field, the Chicago *Sun-Times* ran a story about Ron Cey that mentioned his age and declining mobility afield—and his insistence that he was still as good as ever out there. The headline went: ''WASHED UP? CEY: IT AIN'T SO.''

drawing most of their fans from within the city, were probably
moving out of Comiskey Park at last, he said; they were negotiating a move to the western suburb of Addison, if the financing
could be worked out for a new ballpark there. "The strange
thing is that most of the Cubs fans are from the suburbs, even
though Wrigley Field is a city ballpark," he said. "Most of the
White Sox fans cheer for the Cubs when the Cubs are in first
place, but Cubs fans never, never cheer for the White Sox. They
sort of don't notice them."

Wrigley Field seemed to have survived the great lights crisis,
Tim told me. After the winning 1984 season, the club had threatened to move the team elsewhere, so that it could conform with
the league's network-television contracts, which called for night
games in post-season play. The city and state ordinances forbid-
ding lights at Wrigley held firm under court testing, but now
Dallas Green was talking about adding twenty thousand new
seats to the park (which now holds thirty-eight thousand)—a
move that seemed certain to destroy its airy vistas and rural
ambience. It is reported that Green also wants the club to buy
up some of the cozy, tree-shaded blocks of ancient houses that
surround the field and convert them into parking lots. Shanahan
thought the lights controversy would be settled by compromise:
the lights would go in, but would be turned on for only fifteen
or twenty games during the regular season. "Nobody likes the
idea," he said, "but it may be the only way to keep Wrigley
Field. People care about this place."

The game began—the Giants' veteran ace Mike Krukow taking
on the Cubs' left-handed Steve Trout—and what Shanahan noticed
almost instantly was an innocuous fly ball out to left field struck
by the second Giant batter of the day, Rob Thompson. "Bad," he
announced. "Anything hit in the air like that against Trout means
he's going to get killed. And look at those flags." I looked, and
saw the pennants on the scoreboard and up on top of the upper
deck in right field beginning to stir and lift. They were pointing
away from us: local storm warnings for lakeside pitchers. Shanahan was wrong in one way, it turned out: the Giants didn't exactly
kill Trout as much as discourage him to death, finally dispatching
him in the third, when he got nobody out while giving up a passel
of singles, a walk, and a terminal double by the young power-
hitting third baseman, Chris Brown, which ran the score to 5–1,
San Francisco. But nothing is forever on windy days at Wrigley,
and the Cubs responded at once with four safe knocks, including
a home run by Gary Matthews that sailed five or six rows beyond

the ivy at left-center. "It's *Sandberg* that's the difference," Shanahan said, referring to Matthews' immediate predecessor in the lineup. "They've finally got him back where he belongs. He's got to bat second like this if we're going to score runs. It's vital to the whole thing."

This, I realized, was the long view—the experienced Cubsperson's caution—but there was no cynicism or artificiality in it that I could see. Tim nodded happily when Dunston and then Dave Martinez whacked windblown back-to-back homers in the fifth, with the Cubs scoring four more times and going ahead for good in the game, but when we sat down again he said, "I think all these pop-fly home runs in this park hurt the Cubs in the end. It's the reason we never seem to have any speed on the team, or any real defense. It's the same kind of team the Red Sox have always been, because of that wall at Fenway. Those big innings distract you from building a real ball team. I think we may have the best defensive stats in the league right now, but that's only because we're so slow in the infield that we never even get to the hard chances. It's an illusion."

Sandberg homered in the eighth, and Leon Durham bombed a triple into the ivy a moment or two later, and the Cubs won the thing by 11–6. I was happy for my new friend, but what I had discovered about him was that he was a baseball fan first and a Cubs fan—and a dedicated one—well after that. Maybe that was part of the secret about winning and losing—the fan's part. "What I love about Roger Craig is the way he's always in the game," Tim had said at one point. "He calls all the Giant pitchouts and pickoffs, you know. You remember how he used to do that when he was with the Tigers, I'm sure." I did remember, because he had reminded me. Then, a little later—an *instant* later—the Giant pitcher Krukow picked Sandberg off first on a move (I checked it later) signalled by Craig from the dugout. It took the Cubs out of an inning, but I noticed that Shanahan clapped for the slick move just the same. He was in the game, too.

◆ ◆ ◆

Now I BEGAN TO WORRY ABOUT THE GIANTS. THEIR DIVISION lead was gone—Houston had won again—and after the game Craig spoke urgently about the necessity of getting out of town with a split in the series. Matters looked even graver the next afternoon—a beautiful day, a bit cooler, with a noisy family crowd on hand for a Sunday picnic of baseball—when the Cubs went up by 4–1 in the third inning; two pitches by Giants starter Roger Mason bounced by Bob Brenly for passed balls in the three-run second (both split-finger specials, by the look of them), and further damage was avoided only by a nifty pitchout, wig-wagged by Craig, which allowed Brenly to cut down a base stealer with two Cubs on and no outs. Craig, in fact, was managing up a storm, at one point sending up a pinch-hitter for a batter in mid at-bat, with the count 3–1 (it didn't work); the day before, he had relieved one of his relievers in the middle of the count. What did work on this day for the Giants was a brilliant turn at the plate in the fourth by first baseman Harry Spilman, who ran the count to 3–2 against the Cubs' Dennis Eckersley and then fought off four outstanding sliders for fouls before Eckersley made a mistake, a fastball up, which Spilman hit into the right-field stands for a two-run homer. Spilman, an early-season pickup by the Giants after he was dropped by the Tigers, had been filling in elegantly for the injured and slumping rookie first baseman Will Clark, who had been sent down to Phoenix for rehabilitation. After the game, Spilman said, "That was probably the best at-bat I've ever had in the big leagues."

The Cubs were still up by a run when another Giants sub, Randy Kutcher, led off the eighth with a rocket to short, which Chicago shortstop Dunston fielded brilliantly and then horribly threw away, to put the tying run aboard. The Cubs infield defended in classic fashion against the inevitable upcoming bunt, but the batter, Robbie Thompson, pushed the ball beautifully to right, fast enough to get it past the pitcher and the onrushing first baseman, Durham, and short enough to allow the covering second baseman, Sandberg, no chance in the world to make a play. The bunt—a pearl of great price—went untouched, and a moment or two farther along Thompson outdid himself, pausing for an instant on the base path in order to hinder Durham's view of Leonard's weakly nubbed, lucky wrong-field infield bouncer to right. Durham lunged for the ball and barely missed it as it wobbled off into short right, and the game was tied, with Thompson on third; his run—he scored on a sacrifice fly by Brown, to put the Giants ahead—held up because Scott Garrelts, in from the pen, set down the six remaining Chicago batters in order, on fastballs that all measured in the mid-ninety-m.p.h. range. The Giants wound up with a 5–4 win and the split they had to have.

How you assessed such a game depended on which clubhouse you visited. Eckersley, who had pitched very well indeed—he struck out nine Giants—was bitter about the fact that manager

Gene Michael had allowed him to come up to bat in the seventh, with one out and a teammate on second, instead of wheeling in a pinch-hitter to try to deliver an insurance run. The loss ran Eckersley's record to 3–6 for the year, and the Cubs' to 38–50. "It's just frustrating," the Eck said. "I know everyone here feels the way I do, so why am I going to sit here and cry about it? It's just been a terrible year for all of us."

In the Giants' clubhouse, Roger Craig lit up his old-fashioned hook-stem pipe and blew a cloud of sweet smoke at the ceiling. "Humm baby," he said.

◆

The teams I found on the grassy field at the Oakland Coliseum at the outset of their three-game series had come through such different terrain in this baseball summer as to make them resemble the principals in some morality play about reward and punishment, good fortune and bad. The Red Sox, here in the midst of their longest road trip of the summer, had just lost three out of four games at the Seattle Kingdome but still held a comfortable six-game lead over the second-place Yankees. At their high-water mark, ten days earlier, the Sox had led the pack by eight games and—to employ the statistic by which most baseball people measure team success or the lack of it—stood twenty-six games above the .500 mark. They had the league's best pitcher in Clemens (then at 16–2) and the top batter in Wade Boggs (.365). The A's, in horrendous contrast, had slipped into the abyssal deep (a level at which the only light is provided by anglerfish and a few weirdly phosphorescent umpires), fifteen and a half games behind the West-leading Angels, but had lately managed a few feeble upward strokes under their new manager, LaRussa, and now stood thirteen and a half back although still dead last. Their only current celebrity was Jose Canseco, the enormous, thick-armed rookie slugger, who was leading the league with twenty-three homers and seventy-eight runs batted in. June held very different memories for the two teams. The Bosox had begun that month with feelings of great trepidation, having lost their most experienced starting pitcher, Bruce Hurst, who had just gone on the disabled list with a groin injury, at a time when they were already making do without the services of another strong starter, Al Nipper, who was recovering from a severe spike wound suffered in a collision at home plate two weeks before. The Sox came through June with a fairish 15–10 record for the month, but somehow increased their divisional lead from two and a half to eight games in the process. A five-game losing skid by the Yankees late in the month helped considerably, and so did Roger Clemens' six consecutive June wins—Nos. 9 through 14. The word "stopper," which is what Clemens is, doesn't just mean that the man out there on the mound keeps the other team from scoring; what he really stops is his own club's two-game and three-game losing streaks, which can suddenly become something much more damaging if not snipped short. The Bosox had swept a three-game series against the Yankees in mid-June and another three-game set against the Orioles at the end of the month, but that swoon by the Yankees was the kind of pure good fortune that all hot teams seem to experience, and even come to count on as being almost their due. Back in May, the Red Sox had beaten the Indians, 2–0, in a game at Cleveland that was called after six innings—called by *fog*. Later on, they beat Toronto when a Blue Jay pitcher walked in the winning run in the tenth, and then, in a July game, they completed a four-run twelfth-inning rally against the Angels when the California pitcher was called for a balk that brought in the winning run.

Oakland's moments were of a different nature: a series in Cleveland when the team blew leads of four runs, six runs, and three runs on successive days, losing all three games; a night in Kansas City when Rickey Peters, under the mistaken impression that the bases were loaded, trotted homeward after a base on balls and was tagged out to end the inning; a nine-run second inning by the Rangers at Arlington. This last was the low point, in the estimation of Bill King, the veteran A's television commentator. "It summed us up at that point," he told me. "It was a microcosm. Every play seemed a violation of some baseball principle. There were two misplayed line drives in the outfield, people failed to cover bases, and there was an inside-the-park home run. Another run scored while our pitcher was arguing with the first-base ump over a call and Canseco twisted his knee when his spikes caught on the wall padding in right field. Jackie Moore said it was the most embarrassing game in his baseball career. Three days later, Jackie was gone—no one blamed him for that one game, of course—and I think in a way he was almost relieved."

Bruce Bochte, the Oakland first baseman, said, "The month didn't feel like a collapse, because most of the time we kept playing just bad enough to lose. In a way, that's worse. It was like we were in a twilight zone. I guess the only regular player we didn't lose to injuries at some point was Alfredo"—Alfredo Griffin, the shortstop. "Even so, we should have played close to .500, and we didn't come close. It was an avalanche. When everything's going bad like that, you never think about baseball when you're away from the park. It isn't in your mind at all. It's harder to come to the park than it should be. You think you're tireder than you really are, and your injuries hurt more. When the game starts, the effort is there, but there's sort of a doubtful attitude. You're looking around almost in anticipation of what's going to go wrong."

Bochte and Sandy Alderson and most of the other A's agree that the most damaging stretch was a three-game series against the White Sox at Chicago early in the month, when two starting pitchers, Joaquin Andujar and Moose Haas, were disabled on successive days, at a time when the team was already trying to make do without its bullpen ace, Jay Howell, and its center fielder and team leader, Dwayne Murphy. Patchwork now became a daily necessity. Pitchers were wheeled in from the minors and, in some cases, wheeled back again; long relievers became starters; one starter, the young strikeout artist Jose Rijo, was tried in short relief—a mistake, everyone agreed later.

"After the injuries, things became very difficult," Alderson said. "The bad news seemed relentless. I remember one time when we were losing here and all the teams in our farm system lost, too, so we had an oh-for-seven day for the whole Oakland operation. But there was never any despair. You try to keep some distance in your mind at times like that, to be objective and keep your judgment, but in all our meetings here with our coaches and scouts and others in the organization we never concluded that there was something wrong with our system, that we'd made bad trades, or that any of our components—scouting, minor-league operations, or the major-league operation—were seriously flawed or at fault. Maybe there was a lack of team chemistry or a lack of effort—it's hard to judge—but when Tony got here he felt it was just a lack of talent. We'd lost too many players. At some point, it got out of control and something had to be done. You can't change twenty-five people, so we changed one—the manager."

Alderson didn't say so, but others on the Oakland club intimated that the crippling of the team which led to the deadly June losing streaks—nine in a row and the record fifteen straight losses on the road—probably delayed the firing of Jackie Moore, instead of hastening it. It seemed plainly unfair to dismiss a manager who was making do with a daily lineup half full of Class AAA ballplayers. Even before the downslide, however, there was a conviction that Moore had delegated too many responsibilities to his coaches; the pitching rotations and the decision about when to take a struggling pitcher out of a game were being made by pitching coach Wes Stock, and players had understandably begun to feel that there was no visible leadership or center of force on the club. (The new manager, Tony LaRussa, is more private and more intellectual than Moore—or than most major-league pilots, for that matter: he holds a law degree from Florida State University—but there is visible steel there as well. He had managed the White Sox for eight seasons, bringing them to a divisional pennant in 1983, and his departure from that club this summer is generally viewed as the result of a clash of personalities with the flamboyant new Chicago executive vice-president, Hawk Harrelson.) In any case, there is probably no proper time to fire a manager, if it must be done during the season. Jackie Moore's dismissal came just two days after the repellent and embarrassing rat episode (Dave Kingman, the brooding and misanthropic Oakland designated hitter, arranged to have a live rat delivered to Susan Fornoff, a beat writer from the Sacramento *Bee*, as a signal of his dislike of her presence in the clubhouse) and one day after the club at last broke its horrific fifteen-game road losing streak with a win over the Royals at Kansas City. LaRussa took charge after an interval when the club was directed by fill-in manager Jeff Newman, and by the time I arrived in Oakland the team had won six games and lost five under its new skipper.

Anybody can explain baseball, of course; the trick is to predict it. What happened now—what happened *of course*—was that the A's swept the series against the Red Sox, winning quite handily, in fact, only once falling behind in one of the games, by a lone early run. The A's also got the better of things in every department, including pitching (the Bosox never put together more than two hits in an inning in any of the contests); hitting (Carney Lansford, the Oakland third baseman, went eight for twelve, with two home runs); and defense (silky plays by Griffin and a marvelous 3–6–1 double play in a tight moment of the Tom Seaver-vs.-Joaquin Andujar middle game, which brought a sudden shout of pleasure from the Oakland crowd). The breaks had changed, too—a telling shift of ground. In the final game, Dusty Baker, the Oakland outfielder, made a full-length airborne dive to grab a drive by Bill Buckner inches above the grass in left center (''Last month, that's a triple,'' announced Bill Rigney, the senior Oakland baseball adviser, who was sitting with me); and in the bottom of the same stanza Tony Phillips' hard rap up the line bounced past Buckner at first base and into the right-field corner for a two-run double ("Last month, that's the other team at bat," said Rig). Baseball's inexorable cycle had swung the other way, and suddenly it was Boston's turn to play with a very short deck. Injuries and unexpected misfortunes had depleted the lineup; in the summer so far, the club had been forced to call up nine different minor-league replacements from its Pawtucket farm club. In the games I saw, Hurst and Nipper, each recently out of drydock (it was Hurst's first turn since his injury, and Nipper's sixth), were cruelly treated by the Oakland offense; they had been hurried back because of the absence of Oil Can Boyd, an 11–6 starter for the Red Sox, who was under suspension for various infractions and instabilities. The hard-hitting outfielders Tony Armas and Jim Rice were aching and unable to play at all in the Oakland games, and the bullpen was without stalwarts Sammy Stewart and Steve Crawford. Wade Boggs was aching with a lame back, and Buckner's bad ankles limited him to service as a designated hitter in the first two games. The customary D.H., Don Baylor, was filling in for Jim Rice in left field, where his feeble arm cost the Bosox an important run in the second game. By the time the series was over, the Red Sox lead was down to three games, and manager John McNamara was terse and careworn in his office. "We've got to show our character and just play our way through it," he murmured. "I don't know—maybe we're trying too hard." The day before, he had said, "Thank God we've got some leeway, but you can run out of leeway."

My own sympathies underwent something like a Nautilus workout during the games at the Coliseum, edging slowly away from the A's, whom I had so coldly selected as a laboratory animal for my research, and toward the gimpy Red Sox, and then settling firmly, or perhaps hysterically, upon myself. I am a Red Sox fan of good standing (an oxymoron if there ever was one), and those icy fingers up and down my spine, an odd unwillingness to consult the standings in the morning papers, and my sudden need to call up distant fellow-sufferers were symptoms I recalled all too well from previous foldo summers, such as 1978, when my Sox madly threw away a ten-game mid-July lead and ultimately fell before the Yankees in a beautiful and scarifying one-game playoff at the Fens. But Red Sox fans are no help at all at times like these. "It's all *over*!" sobbed a

Boston-bred colleague whom I now consulted, collect, coast-to-coast. "I *told* you this would happen. I knew it all along."

"We can play through this," I said stiffly. "Now is the time to show some class." I hung up.

• ◆ •

CHARACTER, TO TELL THE TRUTH, IS NOT A QUALITY THAT HAS been generally associated with Red Sox teams or the Red Sox clubhouse in recent years, but all that changed dramatically this summer—first when Don Baylor came over to the club from the Yankees (the teams traded designated hitters, with the left-handed Mike Easler going to the Yanks in an even-up swap for Baylor, who bats from the right side), and then when Tom Seaver joined the club in June, following a trade with the Chicago White Sox, where he had been pitching for the past two summers. Baylor, who is thirty-seven, has played for the A's, the Angels, the Orioles, the Yankees, and the Red Sox in the course of his illustrious fifteen years in the majors; he won a Most Valuable Player award in 1979, when he was with California. He is a longtime member of the executive committee of the Players Association. My presiding Baylor images are of his thunderous slides into second base against the double play; his crowding, obdurate stance up at bat, when his large and leaning left shoulder almost seems to obscure the pitcher's view of the plate; and the aura of magisterial calm that always seems to encircle his cubicle in a clubhouse. A prince of players.

"This game, for me, is not a play-for-yourself thing," he said before one of the Oakland games. "The exception is the hitter-versus-pitcher situation—when you're up at bat. That's when you're on your own. When a team is playing well, it's easy to be unselfish. Something intangible is being passed along. Winning is contagious—but losing can also be contagious. There are some selfish ballclubs—you can spot them after a while. Look at the Minnesota club; there are guys there who have great numbers year after year, but it doesn't mean much. The team may play good for a time and then you look up and they're out of it again. Playing against the Red Sox all this time, I got the impression that they were divided in a number of ways. They played for themselves a lot, and they weren't very close. You've heard that thing about twenty-five guys calling twenty-five cabs to take them back to the hotel after a game.

"When I got here, I told some of the pitchers they had to

throw inside more, and I said I'd be the first guy out of the dugout if anything happened—if anybody complained. I said they had the reputation of not doing that. You have to do that—move the batters off the plate—or else they're going to tattoo you off the wall. I know—I've been hit by pitches more than anybody in this league. There have been years when I got hit by more than fifteen or sixteen *teams*. But that pitcher has got to try to intimidate the batter just a little. Just one time can work. If he comes in on him in the second inning, let's say, the batter will still be thinking about it when he comes up in the ninth, when it counts. But if a team isn't in contention, if it isn't playing very well, the first thing you notice is that the pitcher has lost that kind of aggressiveness. He won't be thinking about it, and his E.R.A. will have gone up into the fours.''

I asked him how it felt to be on a club when everything was going right—when winning was the habit.

"Winning—well, everyone contributes," Baylor said. "You take the extra base, instead of playing it one base at a time. You take chances and they always seem to work. That kind of play just takes over, and the slowest guy on the team will suddenly think he's the fastest. I remember when I was with Oakland, a long time ago, and we came into Yankee Stadium to play the Yankees in a game that was on national TV. I stole second base, and as I came into the bag Thurman Munson's throw was off behind me toward the right-field side—he did that sometimes, with that sidearm throw—and out of the corner of my eye I saw that Mickey Rivers was playing in left center, with a long run to the ball. I got up and I knew I was going to try to score, and I did. I scored all the way from first base. Well, at that time Thurman was struggling with the bat as well as behind the plate, but he had *such* a determined way about him. When the season was over, he made a point of coming to me and thanking me for that one play I'd made, because it motivated him for the rest of the year, and in the end he was able to win an M.V.P. award for that 1976 season. From that day on, he played with a fire in his eye. So one play can turn a player or turn a team around, even if it's an example from the other side.

"You want to do well in this game, you know. You don't want to look bad—not in the major leagues. No one wants to be embarrassed. If you do well and the team is going good, it's a whole lot easier. You play for the team and not yourself. But if you happen to be going bad yourself and you can take a base on balls in front of somebody who's swinging the bat real well, that can be enough.

That will do it, maybe. You don't always want to be the man to hit an eight-run homer, because that doesn't happen. Even taking a base on balls can be a way of leading. Just lately, we've run into some rough spots, and we're looking to see who's going to lead us out of that. Everybody here wants to be that man."

◆

TOM SEAVER IS FORTY-ONE YEARS OLD NOW—IT'S HARD TO BE-lieve—and he has said that this, his twentieth major-league sea-son, may be his last. He is a different sort of pitcher from what he used to be—one who changes speeds and moves the ball around. Only a few times in a game do you see the hummer, thrown with that full-drop-down delivery, and even then the pitch is used as much for example as for effect—to set up the other stuff. In the game he pitched against the A's, he looked a bit rocky in the early going, giving up three runs on a walk and three hits in the first; then he steadied. He lost, 4–2, but he'd kept the Red Sox in the game, given them a chance to win if they could, which is the kind of outing he had promised when the trade was made. After the game, his opposing pitcher, An-dujar, said that he liked to work against Seaver because there was so much to learn from the experience—how to concentrate, how to take it easy and still bear down. "He's a professional out there, inside his head and outside," Joaquin said.

The next day, Tom said, "The most important thing for any club is to keep the entire season in perspective, to keep that in view at all times. You know there are going to be days when your club is down, but you can't let yourself be too affected by that. Otherwise, you'd be an emotional wreck at the end of the summer. You can't afford to lose a guy like that"—he gestured toward Jim Rice, across the clubhouse—"for any length of time and expect to be the same. But you can't win or lose it all in one day. You can't spend all your dollars at one sitting. If you've had a bad run, like this Oakland club just did, you still have to accept it. It's part of being a professional. You have to say to yourself, 'Well, today was the end of the down side, tomorrow is the beginning of the plus side.' I think there's been a notion on some of the clubs in the American League West that being good enough to win in their division is good enough. I can say with certainty that that's the way it was when I was on the White Sox. That attitude filters down from the front office to the players, and it makes you a mediocre club, no matter where you're playing. It's a huge mistake."

I asked him if it felt very different to be with a club that was in contention.

"My God, yes," Seaver said. "Everything you do has meaning. You're beyond your personal statistics, which is a real break for a professional. If you're ever in the position where you know that only your own numbers mean anything, you find that after a while that supply is drained, too. It's empty. On a contending team, even if a guy is hitting .212 or is 4–8 on the year—well, maybe those four games that the one guy contributed were the ones that put the club over the top. They have meaning. You take pride in what everyone is doing collectively, and that's a great feeling. It's an amazing phenomenon how winning and losing can become part of a clubhouse and will breed on themselves, feed on themselves."

I asked if he was aware of the trepidation that long-term Red Sox fans are so quick to feel when their club begins to sag a bit.

"I've heard of that," he said, "but I guess I didn't know it was so—so oppressing. But that negative is a compliment, really. They care. It might even be easier for fans like that to have their club in second place until late in the year, but I've never heard a *player* say that." He laughed—his old giggle. "Heck, no. No way!"

◆ ◆ ◆

THE OAKLANDS RESPONDED TO THEIR IMPROVING FORTUNES with tempered cheerfulness, each in his own fashion. Bochte said, "At this point, you have to forget about where you're going to finish and just try to get things back in order. You want to play one game well. Then it gets to be two good games in a row. Right now, we're trying to play a whole series of good games. You really have to play well for about a week before you know if you've pulled out of a real bad stretch."

Roy Eisenhardt, the Oakland president, said, "Winning is the condition that immediately precedes losing." Then he smiled and said, "The reverse is also true, which is the nice part."

Dwayne Murphy, the A's center fielder, denied Seaver's allegation about teams in the American League West. "I've never heard that on this club," he said. "And I'd have heard it if it was going around. Nobody wants to play .500 ball for a career. What you do hear when you're going bad is some people beginning to blame others. They're pointing fingers. It's always wrong, because one man can't do it for you—can't make you win and can't lose it for you. It's a team effort, either way." He paused—he is a quiet man, and speaks very softly—and I had to lean closer to hear what came next: "But I don't know the other side, really. I've never been on a real winning club, except in '81, when we got to those playoffs in the short season. I tell you, I'm dying to find out what it's like to win." He paused again and then repeated himself, even more quietly. "I'm dying to be there."

Tony LaRussa said, "There are clubs that have some success in the early part of the season and think that's where their club is going to end up, but this isn't always the case. There are clubs that have lost for a while and think that's it—it's over. But there are always those clubs that seem to be able to pick themselves up, no matter what they've done, because they have a history of doing well in the end. The Yankees. The Baltimore Orioles. To some degree, what we're all trying to do is extend the good side and cut down on the bad. It's difficult, but it isn't so hard that you just throw your hands in the air and say it can't be done. You try to do some little things. You want to make sure that the club is together—that you do things together. A little togetherness. You'd be surprised how often you'll notice that a winning club has the habit of going to places together on the road. They're at the same watering holes. On a losing club, guys are sort of embarrassed to be seen together. Playing better ball can make *such* a quick difference. It's so much more fun. I've been watching the Giants this year, because Roger Craig has his guys convinced of that. There may be a few people in baseball who are as good as Roger Craig, but none who are better. None. He's also got his coaches and players playing one game at a time, which is the whole trick. Back in 1982, the White Sox made a real strong comeback at the middle of the season. We'd won fifteen out of eighteen and put ourselves two and a half or three games out of first place. Then the nineteenth came along—it was against the Rangers, a road game. I wasn't there, because my first daughter was being born, and Charlie Lau had the club. We were down 1-0 in the top of the ninth, and we got two two-out hits—Squires and LeFlore—and that tied it up, 1-1. In the tenth or eleventh inning, we had a good two-run rally and took the lead, but in the bottom of the inning Dave Hostetler hit a three-run homer for them, and we lost it. Later, I heard a lot of people say, 'Oh, wasn't that a shame—that was the night the White Sox lost the pennant.' Bullshit. Sure you get your heart broken in this game. But what happened after that game was that this real depressed, we-lost-it atmosphere took over. We hadn't learned to handle that. What's worse than losing in extra innings? What's worse is carrying it over and losing two or three more. It's a million times worse. That's what you want to be afraid of.

"I think fear of not coming through can be a real motivator, no matter where you are or who you're up against. Right now, we're playing the Red Sox three games and then the Blue Jays three games, and I'm worried to death. What you have to do is try. I'm scared to death that between now and October we'll only be ordinary. If I do a job, we should at least be decent."

◆ ◆ ◆

I TOOK IN PARTS OF THE OAKLAND-BOSTON GAMES IN ROY EISEN-hardt's private box, behind first base, which offered a perfect view of the action below and of the pleasant, sun-drenched park (two of the games were afternoon affairs) and of the pains of major-league ownership. Eisenhardt, who is in his forties, is lean and athletic, and I sometimes have the impression that he would enjoy baseball more if he could be in uniform and out on the field himself. He watches a game with more intensity than anyone else I know, and I noticed now that he seemed almost wary about his team's improved fortunes and its suddenly brisk and efficient brand of play. He responded warmly to good news and surprises—a stolen base by Dave Kingman; another sparkling stop by Griffin, far behind second base; a pinch-hit single by Canseco, who had been struggling at the plate in recent games—but then he would resume his grave and abstracted view of the events before us. It had been a difficult summer for the Oakland club, which had begun the season with such high hopes but had seen most of the good news and most of the luck fall on the Giants, who are the perennial Bay rivals of the A's for a baseball audience that may not be quite large enough or dedi-cated enough to sustain two major-league clubs. Since purchas-ing the club, in 1980, the Haas family, which owns Levi Strauss, has made large investments in the refurbishing of the Oakland team and ballpark, and in the essential minor-league chain and scouting system, but the expected accompanying resuscitation of the team's fortunes on the field has been frustratingly slow in coming, as we have seen, and fans have not turned out in suf-ficient numbers to prevent a flow of red ink. The A's have cut back by trading away some high-salary stars, like Rickey Hen-derson (who went to the Yankees in 1985 in return for five younger prospects), but the club lost five and a half million dollars last year, and it seems clear that the rewards of good will and good works alone cannot be expected to keep the current owners in baseball forever. Over the last couple of years, there have been sporadic rumors that the club might be sold and moved to another city, but shortly before my visit the A's concluded an agreement with the city of Oakland to extend their lease on the Oakland Coliseum through the year 2000. In return, the club received a five-year low-interest loan of fifteen million dollars, a larger share of the Coliseum food-and-beverage revenues, and a promise that local business and industrial concerns would be recruited to take on a share of the A's losses; the agreement also includes an escape clause that would permit the club's departure by 1991, if revenue and attendance figures go below certain minimum levels.

Eisenhardt is a friend of mine, and I worried about him when the news turned bad for the A's this summer, because his complex appreciation of baseball and his concern for its future deserve better returns, to my way of thinking. Losing is always painful, as we have seen, but what Eisenhardt was forced to watch from his box this summer may have been something far more costly and difficult to accept than a few failed rallies and lost ballgames. When I talked to him between innings, he did not seem embittered by the team's poor record to date, but he told me that he had been startled by some hostile reactions in the sporting press (''The A's stink'' was the way a mid-June column in the San Francisco *Chronicle* began, and it went on to blame Eisenhardt and Alderson personally for the club's ''complete inability to develop young pitchers or to keep the ones they have in working order'') and by some vindictive, almost wildly angry letters from A's fans.

''Losing is a lightning rod for frustrations, many of which have nothing at all to do with sports,'' Eisenhardt said at one point. ''I don't think this bitterness is anything new, but its level is rising. People everywhere have highly polarized emotions just now, and they express them directly and often inappropriately. I think high player salaries have something to do with it, because there's always an accompanying and absolutely unjustified expectation of success. Television presents this stream of winning players and winning teams, which leads to artificially heightened expectations and an artificial, monolithic view of the world. A majority of the teams in baseball are losing money, and sometimes I'm not sure the game can survive the fans' unremitting demands for success. That's inconsistent with the genetic nature of baseball—what it's really like. I worry about it, because so many young people are coming to baseball through television. That's inescapable, but it leads to inattention and anger. If your team isn't winning, you turn off the set or switch to one of the eighty other channels. You don't stay with things."

I suggested that a winning team might make a very large difference in the response of the A's fans.

"Of course it would," he said. "And our fans deserve it. But no team wins forever, and nowadays no team even seems able to repeat as a winner. It's important for fans to be able to use professional sports as an outlet for their hopes and frustrations, but it would be better if we could keep that in proportion. You see that sort of balance at the Cubs' games, and it's beautiful. For some reason, there's a different perspective at Wrigley Field—a clearer understanding of failure as a consistent part of baseball. Because ball teams play every day, the chances for failure are always high, but the Cubs fans somehow understand that. It's a higher level of baseball culture. I think that's the model we should be striving for."

◆ ◆ ◆

JUST AFTER THE A'S HAD WON THE THIRD GAME AGAINST THE Red Sox, completing their unexpected sweep, I ran into Sandy Alderson in a corridor outside the A's clubhouse. Rock music came floating out of the locker room, along with the raucous, unmistakable sounds of young men who have just won a game. I said to Alderson that I had heard some of the Boston writers in the press box talking about their team's injuries and wondering how the Sox could be expected to win when there were so many substitutes and rookies—names like Romine, Stenhouse, Romero, and Tarver—in their lineup just now.

"That's exactly what we went through," Alderson said. "We still are—look at Dave Stewart, who pitched such a great game for us today. He's 3–0 as a starter now, but he was just a pickup for us. The Phillies had released him, but we knew he'd had major-league experience and we signed him up in May to play at Tacoma. Then we had all those injuries, and we brought him up. The same goes for Doug Bair. It's a matter of economics as well as necessity. Very few teams can afford to keep a full line of experienced major-league players on hand these days. We're all playing with twenty-four-man rosters this year, to save money, but you'll see a lot of clubs looking around and then picking up experienced older players when they need them. Like the Cards, who did so well when they signed Cedeno during the season last year. The Royals did the same with Steve Farr, and just the other day the Angels picked up Vern Ruhle. Only the Yankees can afford to keep all those high-salary veteran players around—people like Claudell Washington and Al Holland.''

"And look at the troubles the Yankees are having," I said.

He shrugged—not quite resignedly, I noticed. "You never know," he said. "In this game, whether you're a player or a manager or a coach or in the front office, there are just so many things you can control. After that, it's just fortuity. You may have an injury or a whole bunch of injuries. You may have a bad hop, a terrible call by an umpire, a ball that just goes through—whatever. Or a whole *bunch* of them. All this constitutes thirty or thirty-five or maybe even forty percent of the game. Nobody will ever accept that in the end, and so somebody is always held accountable for the result—for who wins and who loses. In a way, that's a good thing. If there wasn't that accountability, you'd have to ask 'So what the hell am I doing here?,' because then anybody could roll the dice—you or me or some child. These accidental events are important, because you always have to make some response to them—change the pitcher out there, make a trade, change the manager, throw away the uniform. In some cases, you decide to do nothing. You have to come to some rational judgment, no matter how irrational things have begun to look. It's what keeps you in the game.''

◆ ◆ ◆

SINCE I GOT HOME FROM OAKLAND, THE FOUR CLUBS I CAME TO know and care about on my little tour have not fared very differently, except for the Giants, who were swept by the Cardinals on their next stop and now trail the Houston Astros by a discouraging seven and a half games in the National League West. There was a prolonged brawl on the field in the second game at Busch Stadium, and photographs of the scene show Roger Craig still in the thick of things, as usual: this time, he was trying to tear Whitey Herzog's head off. The split-fingered fastball didn't help Steve Carlton, by the way, who won but one game for the Giants; early in August, he announced his retirement from baseball—but he reëmerged almost instantly as a member of the White Sox' pitching corps. Gods are inexplicable.

Nothing happened to the Cubs.

The Red Sox' lead was a mere four games on their return

home, but then they received back-to-back pitching master-pieces from Bruce Hurst and Tom Seaver and suddenly began to feel much better. Oil Can Boyd was back in action, too. The last time I looked (about twenty minutes ago, at this writing), the Sox led the Yankees by five and a half games, the Blue Jays by six and a half, and the Tigers by seven. September in the A.L. East will be *something*.

The A's continued their winning ways after the Boston games, sweeping the Blue Jays as well, and suddenly climbed into fifth place. Then they hit the skids again, losing four in a row, and slipped back into the cellar. Then they got better: by the middle of the month, their 18–9 record since the All-Star break was the second best in the league. They are as likely to end up in third place as in the cellar (often a capacious apartment in the A.L. West), which is to say that respectability—something better than Tony LaRussa's inner fears, something better than embarrass-ment—seems within reach.* Some of their recent encounters have presented a greater variety of adventure and disaster than the horrors of June. In a home game against the Mariners, Oak-land relief pitcher Fernando Arroyo (another late pickup) walked in the tying run in the ninth inning; then he walked in the win-ner. The next night, with the score again tied, the A's put their first two runners aboard in the bottom of the ninth, and Carney Lansford lined into a triple play. Then they won the game on the first pitch of their half of the tenth, which Mike Davis whacked for a homer. Nothing *to* it.

Before my trip, I would not have given my attention to such trifling melodramas, but these days, I notice, I watch or listen for the Boston scores and Oakland scores with almost equal hopes and trepidation. One evening in Maine (I was on vaca-tion), I asked my host at dinner if he'd heard the Oakland score from the night before—the A's had played the Twins in Minne-apolis, but my local Down East morning paper, which goes to bed with the chickens, had reported the results in typical fash-ion: "Oakland at Minneapolis (n)"—and he looked at me in a startled way and said, "But the A's are in last place, aren't they? They're a terrible team this year." He grinned. "Just terrible."

He said this with conviction, and I suddenly understood that he

---

*The A's finished the season in a tie (with Kansas City) for third place, sixteen games behind the division-winning Angels. Under LaRussa, the team compiled a 45–34 record and moved up from their season low of twenty-four games below .500 to ten below at the end.

found pleasure in the pronouncement. Nothing much else was established as yet in the baseball season (except for the Mets), but he knew one thing for a certainty: the A's were terrible.

The next morning, I discovered that the Twins had beaten the A's by 8–0, and as I studied the box score in the paper and tried to squeeze more news out of it than it could convey, I murmured to myself. "Oh, if the A's would only—"

Then I stopped. Would only *what*? I thought about it for a moment or two, and then it came to me that what I badly seemed to want for a team I cared about was an end to bad luck, an end to bad news—no more fortuity, to use Sandy Alderson's word. I wanted the exact opposite of what my friend had seen as established: I wanted good news forever. Then—within an instant, I think—I perceived something I hadn't quite understood about baseball before. Alderson had said that thirty or forty percent of the game was beyond his control or the manager's or the players' control. But I am a fan, and my lot is far worse, for everything in baseball is beyond my control; for me every part of the game is just fortuity. Because I am a fan, all I can do is care, and what I wish for, almost every day of the summer, is for things to go well—to go *perfectly*—for the teams and the players I most care about: for the Red Sox, for the A's now, for the Mets, for the Giants, for Tom Seaver and Keith Hernandez and Roy Eisenhardt and Don Baylor and Wade Boggs and Carney Lansford and Tim Shanahan and Darryl Strawberry and Roger Craig and many, many others. I think every true fan wants no less. We wish for this seriously, every day of the season, but at the same time I think we don't want it at all. We want our teams to be losers as well as winners; we must have bad luck as well as good, terrible defeats and disappointments as well as victories and thrilling surprises. We must have them, for if it were otherwise, if we could control more of the game or all of the game and make it do our bidding, we would have been granted a wish—no more losing!—that we would badly want to give back within a week. We would have lost baseball, in fact, and then we would have to look around, without much hope, for something else to care about in such a particular and arduous fashion.

THIRTEEN

◆ ◆ ◆

Not So, Boston

FALL 1986

YES, IT WAS. YES, WE DID. YES, THAT WAS THE WAY IT was, really and truly . . . The baseball events of this October—the Mets' vivid comeback victory over the Boston Red Sox in seven games, and the previous elimination of the Houston Astros and the California Angels in the hazardous six-game and seven-game (respectively) league championship playoffs—will not be quickly forgotten, but disbelief is a present danger. Sporting memory is selective and unreliable, with a house tilt toward hyperbole. In inner replay, the running catch, the timely home run become incomparable, and our view of them grows larger and clearer as they recede in time, putting us all into a front-row box seat in the end, while the rest of that game and that day—the fly-ball outs, the four-hop grounders, the fouls into the stands, the botched double play, the sleepy innings, the failed rally, the crush at the concession stand, the jam in the parking lot—are miraculously leached away. This happens so often and so easily that we may not be prepared for its opposite: a set of games and innings and plays and turnabouts that, for once, not only matched but exceeded our baseball expectations, to the point where we may be asking ourselves now if all this really did come to pass at the end of the 1986 season and if it was all right for us to get so excited about it, so hopeful

and then so heartbroken or struck with pleasure. To which let it
be said again: Yes, it did. Yes, it was. Yes, absolutely. What
matters now, perhaps, is for each of us to make an effort to hold
on to these games, for almost certainly we won't see their like
again soon—or care quite as much if we do.

Purists are saying that the postseason baseball this year was
not of a particularly high quality. In the World Series, the first
five games were played out without a vestige of a rally, or even
of a retied score; that is, the first team to bring home a run won
the game. Each of the first four games, moreover, was lost by
the home team: not much fun for the fans. One of the games
turned on an egregious muff of a routine ground ball, and another produced the decisive event (it turned out) on the third
pitch of the evening—a home run by the Mets' Lenny Dykstra.
Neither of the pennant winners' famous and dominant young
starters, Dwight Gooden and Roger Clemens, won a game in
the Series. In the playoffs, the Angels committed three errors in
one inning in the abysmal second game, and gave up two and
then seven unearned runs in their last two games. In that same
series, a plunked batsman figured significantly in the outcome
of the critical fourth game—and again in the fifth. The Astros,
over in the other league, contributed to their own downfall with
an errant pickoff throw in the twelfth inning of their penultimate
game, and with a butchered fly ball, a throwing error, and two
wild pitches in the sixteenth inning of the finale.

No matter. These games, although slipshod and human in
their details, were of a different order from the sport we thought
we knew—"too fairy-tale-ish," in the words of one Mets pitcher.
As the long eliminations ran down, the events on the field sometimes seemed out of control—not the plays or the players but
the game itself, the baseball. The World Series became the focus
of mass hopes and private wells of emotion, not just because of
the rival kinships and constituencies of the Red Sox and the
Mets, of Boston and New York (Athens and Sparta, in the words
of Peter Gammons in *Sports Illustrated*), but because of a cumulative fan sense of intensity and gratitude that grew around
them near their amazing end, by which time the strongest feeling
seemed to be a wish that there should not be a loser. But probably that was a second wish, after we knew how it did end, and
maybe not one that is felt much to this day in New England. In
mid-October, however, caring had become an affliction. More
and more, we fans wanted each game to go our way, to come
out right, to end the right way—our way—but again and again,

it seemed, that wish was thwarted or knocked aside, and we would find ourselves tangled in a different set of baseball difficulties and possibilities, and pulling for *that* to end right somehow. We wanted to be released, and until the very end the games refused to do that; the baseball wouldn't let us up. And if we were sometimes sorry for ourselves, because of these wearying repeated pains and disappointments and upsets, I think we felt worse about the players and the managers (sometimes the managers most of all), because they, too, were so clearly entwined in something they couldn't handle, couldn't control or defeat, in spite of all their efforts and experience and skill.

"Come on," we fans said again and again, addressing the team or the score or the situation. "Come *on*!" In the end, that cry didn't seem to be directed at anything except the sport itself, which twisted and wrung us, day after day, to the point where we wanted the games over with and this strange trial ended, even while we laughed and smiled at each other and wanted it to go on forever. "Wasn't that wonderful!" we cried. "My God, wasn't that terrific?" And "Did you *see* that? I couldn't bear it! Wasn't it awful!" And then "I just can't *take* it anymore. It's too much."

No poll or instrument can determine whether such paroxysms of fan feeling were felt in more distant parts, away from the big-city narcissism of Mets-mania or from the peat fires of devotion and doubt of the Red Sox faithful, but it is my guess that every fan was affected by these games to some degree. It's hard to be sure—and here a bias must be confessed. As readers of these reports may know by now, I am a baseball fan as well as a baseball writer (most scribes, however grizzled and game-worn, are fans at heart, although they love to deny it), and although I am capable of an infatuated interest in almost any accomplished or klutzy nine that I happen to watch over a span of four or five games, the true objects of my affection down the years have been the Mets and the Red Sox. I have written almost as many words about these two clubs as I have put down about the twenty-four other major-league teams combined. I have publicly exulted in their triumphs (the World Series captured by the boyish Mets in 1969; the wholly unexpected pennant in 1973, after the Mets went into first place in the National League East and reached the .500 level on the same evening in mid-September; the autumn weeks in 1967 when the Red Sox' Carl Yastrzemski seemed to have taken a pennant and a Series into his own hands; the sudden, scintillant glory of Game Six of the 1975 World Series), and I have put forth nostrums and philosophies to explain their much more frequent disasters and stretches of ineptitude. It did not occur to me that an October might arrive when my two true teams would come face to face in a World Series, and that I would have to discover and then declare an ultimate loyalty. The odds against two particular teams' meeting in a World Series in any given year are so extreme (a hundred and sixty-seven to one against, in fact) that I felt safe in moonily wishing for this dream date: when it came closer, during this year's pennant races and then again late in the playoffs, I became hopeful and irritable, exalted and apprehensive, for I didn't know—had no idea at all—which outcome would delight me if they did play, and which would break my heart. In dreams begin responsibilities, damn it.

Twenty postseason ballgames (the same total was rung up last year, when the league championships were first expanded from a three-out-of-five game playoff to the full four-out-of-seven format that governs the World Series) are too many to keep in mind, even with the help of line scores and summations, and at this late date it may be possible to recapture some trace of these vivid and engrossing baseball doings and to glimpse the men on the field in their moments of duress and extremity only by concentrating on a handful of particular games, with perhaps more of our attention going to the league championships than to the World Series itself, for there is little doubt in my mind that the earlier events surpassed the classic. This was the possibility foreseen and deplored by so many baseball people (including this one) when the expansion of the playoffs was first proposed, but after it happened it didn't seem to make any difference. An exceptional set of games, wherever it may come, enhances our appreciation of the richness and surprises of the pastime, and there is a carryover of involvements and good feeling that burnishes the next game we see, and the one after that. Baseball is cumulative, and rewards the stayer.

What will not be set forth here is much news of the regular league seasons—two thousand one hundred and two games (three late-season dates were cancelled by natural causes, and there was one tie that was never untied) that will now vanish by magical elision, since they did not produce a vestige of a pennant race in any division. Lost in this process is a proper full appreciation of some players who enjoyed remarkable seasons while toiling for clubs that did not make the finals. Mike Schmidt, for instance, at the age of thirty-seven, led his league in homers (he had thirty-seven) for the eighth time and in runs batted in (a hundred and nineteen) for the fifth, and later was voted his third Most Valuable Player award. Don Mattingly, who failed for the second year in a row to beat out Wade Boggs as the American League batting champion (.352 to Boggs' .357), nonetheless put together an altogether brilliant year at the plate, becoming the first American League player to surpass thirty homers, a hundred runs batted in, and two hundred and thirty hits in a single season; his two hundred and thirty-eight hits were the most ever by a Yankee batter. His teammate, the relief wizard Dave Righetti, accounted for an all-time-record forty-six saves; and their skipper, Lou Piniella, beat perhaps even longer odds when he was rehired to manage the Yankees for another year. Fernando Valenzuela, of the Dodgers, won twenty games for the first time (he was 21–11 at the end), and so did his fellow-countryman Teddy Higuera (20–11), for the Brewers; the two Mexicans were the talk of the All-Star Game, when they went head to head in three blazing middle innings. The Indians, of all people, came up with a genuine star in their third-year outfielder-slugger Joe Carter (.302, twenty-nine home runs, two hundred hits, and a hundred and twenty-one runs batted in); his nearest rival in the last category was Oakland's rookie bombardier Jose Canseco, who had thirty-three homers and was perhaps the best of a notable freshman class in the American League that also included the Rangers' Pete Incaviglia, the Mariners' Danny Tartabull, and the Angels' Wally Joyner.

The real news around the leagues, however, was the manner in which the four divisional winners entirely suppressed the opposition throughout the summer. The calendar is conclusive. The Mets took over the top of their division for good on April 23rd, the Red Sox on May 15th, the Angels on July 7th, and the laggard Astros on July 21st. The Mets' four starting pitchers— Dwight Gooden, Ron Darling, Bob Ojeda, and Sid Fernandez— had a combined record of forty-one wins and ten losses at the midseason All-Star-Game break, by which time the club led its nearest pursuer, the Expos, by thirteen games. Its ultimate 108–54 won-lost record for the season tied the modern National League level set by the 1975 Reds (the 1954 Indians went 111–43, to establish the modern American League and major-league mark, but it should perhaps be noted that the Mets' .667 winning *percentage* is less remarkable. Twenty-six previous clubs, most of which date back to the one-hundred-fifty-four-game schedules in effect prior to the league expansions in the early sixties, surpassed that win-two-lose-one ratio, including Frank Chance's stone-age 1906 Cubs, who finished up at 116–36, or .763; the thunderous 1927 Yankees, with 110–44, or .714; and even the 1942 Dodgers, whose 104–50, .675 season only won them second place, two full games behind the Cardinals). The Mets' home attendance total of 2,762,417 was the best ever for any New York team in any sport. In retrospect, the Red Sox' one important (or perhaps only symbolically important) game of the summer seems to have been a series opener at Yankee Stadium on June 16th, when Roger Clemens bested Ron Guidry in a 10–1 blowout and ran his record to 12–0 for the season to that date; it was Guidry's sixth loss in a row. The injury-depleted Sox sagged a bit during a swing west in late July, but stood firm against all comers thereafter (to the amazement of their care-worn, wary fans and many of their writers), running their lead from three and a half games to ten in the first twelve days of September.

Nobody finished like the Astros, however. Pitching and defense was their game—or let's just say pitching. On September 23rd, in Houston, rookie left-hander Jim Deshaies struck out the first eight Dodgers of the evening and shut out the visitors, 4–0, on two hits. The following night, Nolan Ryan gave up no hits to the Giants in the first six innings, and wound up with a 6–0 two-hitter, and the night after *that* Mike Scott beat the same team with a 2–0, no-hit game that clinched the Astros' divisional pennant in the National League West. The absence of a race or of any sort of rival to these top four teams did not deter fans from coming out to the games this summer; 47,500,347 turned up in all, which was a new record, and, for the first time ever, no club drew fewer than a million in its own park. The pennant races were a success in another way as well, for they produced divisional winners that, for once, really were the best four teams in baseball. The championships promised well, and that promise was kept.

The Mets' runaway, I think, was responsible to a considerable degree for all the speculation around New York about Dwight Gooden. "What's the matter with Doc?" became a handy sub-stitute for talk about the onrushing Expos or Cardinals or Phillies, who never onrushed at all. If we are to undertake a brief exploration of Gooden's year, it should start with the under-standing that by most pitchers' standards there was nothing at all wrong with Dwight in 1986, when he finished with a 17–6 record, an earned-run average of 2.84, and two hundred stri-

keouts in two hundred and fifty innings pitched. These are wonderful figures by almost any standard except Gooden's own. His
performance in 1985, when, in his second season in the majors,
he was 24-4 and 1.53, with two hundred and sixty-eight strikeouts, allowed him to walk away with the Cy Young Award in
his league, along with the consensus opinion that this was the
finest young pitcher to turn up in baseball since Bob Feller. A
good many well-respected (by me, at least) baseball sages are
of the opinion that Gooden's somewhat diminished record this
year is perfectly in line for a great young hurler (he has just
turned twenty-two) who is on the way to a Hall of Fame career.
Tim McCarver, the Mets' perceptive television announcer, has
stated his belief that no pitcher, including Dwight Gooden himself, will again put together anything like Doc's summer of '85,
and that it is unfair to expect him to duplicate something unique
in the annals of the sport. For all that, Gooden's at times disappointing performance this year—he was more disappointed
than anyone else, for he is a hardworking professional, and very
mature in his approach to his tasks—is worth speculating about,
since it tells us so much about the rigors of his job. I think we
can put aside some of the simpler, one-shot or cheap-shot explanations—an ankle he sprained in the middle of the winter last
year (which never bothered him for a day of the season, he and
his coaches insist), rumors of drug abuse (no proof of any sort),
and some difficulties in his private life—and just think about
pitching.* One theory, much enunciated in the pressrooms during the playoffs and the World Series, arose from the premise
that experienced major-league hitters learn in time to stop
swinging at great fastballs up near the ceiling of the strike zone,
or just above it—which is the path of Doc's heater—and that the
umpires, for their part, become more stubborn about calling that
same high strike in a second season. If that is the case, the umps
(and the hitters, too) must have held a series of extensive long-
distance conference calls along about June 10th of this season
to settle on their new strategy, for it was not until Doc's thirteenth start of the year, on June 13th, that his year began to look
much different from the one that preceded it. After Gooden's
first twelve starts of this season, his record stood at 8-2 (there

---

*The news about Gooden's difficulties with cocaine, which came to light in the early
spring of 1987, damages this advice, of course, but it is still difficult to say whether
Gooden's addiction (he was a social or occasional user, according to his physicians)
affected his work in 1986.

were two no-decision games), with a 2.11 earned-run average, seventy-one strikeouts, and six complete games, including four shutouts. He was less of a pitcher after that, with no shutouts in his remaining twenty-one starts (there were eight no-decisions), a 9–4 record, and an earned-run average of 3.29. No injury or sudden stratagem by the opposition explains this. For me, the answer may be found in Doc's strikeout totals. Let's take a look at his three major-league seasons to date:

	GAMES	WON-LOST	E.R.A.	INNINGS	STRIKE-OUTS	WALKS
1984	31	17–9	2.60	218	276	73
1985	35	24–4	1.53	276.2	268	69
1986	33	17–6	2.84	250	200	80

The 1984 total of two hundred and seventy-six strikeouts led every other pitcher in the majors, and translated out to an astounding 11.39 strikeouts per nine innings pitched. Along the way, Gooden had fifteen ten-strikeout-or-better games, thus giving birth to Shea Stadium's "K Man" placards. In September of that season, Dwight threw two sixteen-strikeout games in succession.

What was happening, I should say at long last, was that Doc was simply trying to become a better major-league pitcher. Outs, not strikeouts, are what count, and Gooden, who is intelligent, has clearly been persuaded that retiring the side on six or eight pitches, with no strikeouts, is easier on an arm and on a career than taking fifteen or sixteen pitches to fan the side. In spring training this year, I saw Gooden working assiduously at a new pitch—an off-speed, high-to-low breaking ball—to add to his famous fastball and its lethal curveball counterpart. He fell in love with the new delivery, as young pitchers do when they find a beautiful toy, and for a time he had success with it in the regular season. The K's went down, as we have seen, but his performance and his success ratio were just about as before. In midseason, though, he ran into unexpected difficulties, and there were several games in which I saw him begin to struggle as never before. He would miss—just miss—with a cut fastball or an off-speed breaking ball, and fall behind in the count, and when he then came back to the fastball and its companion he often couldn't quite find the strike zone. The heater would be up a bit, or wouldn't seem to have much movement on it even when it was in the black. He began walking batters, sometimes five, or even six, in a game (unheard of, for him), and after May 6th there were no more shutouts. He had some excellent games along the way (a four-hitter and a two-hitter in September), but he wasn't the same: he was a little less.

In the postseason games (to look ahead a bit), Gooden pitched powerfully in his two starts in the playoffs, and his loss in his only decision was on an unearned run; in the Series, he gave up six runs in five innings in Game Two (he was the loser), and was taken out in the fifth inning of Game Five, by which time he had given up four runs and nine hits. He was deeply troubled by this last outing, and so were his teammates and his manager. But never mind the results for the moment. To me, Dwight Gooden in this game looked like a different pitcher altogether, just as he had in some stretches in midseason. The beautiful flow and freedom of his delivery weren't there, even when he did throw the fastball for a strike. He didn't seem to be finishing his motion in quite the same place as he did last year, with his body twisted over to the left and the fingers of his pitching hand almost down by his left shoe. He was straighter away on the mound, somehow.

My guess about Dwight is that he slightly altered his pitching motion (his mechanics, in the parlance) this summer in the course of mastering his new off-speed delivery, and then found he couldn't always get back the stuff and the great control that were there, game after game after game, last year. He said he was squeezing the ball too hard at times, he said he had problems with his location. Whatever it was, he wasn't all of a piece out there, which is what great pitchers look like and the way they feel themselves to be when things are going right for them. Bob Boone, the Angels catcher, told me that it had probably taken young Mike Witt an extra season or two to get his pitching act together, because Witt is so tall. (He is six-seven.) "His checkpoints are farther apart," Boone said, with a smile. Gooden's checkpoints (this foot, that shoulder, the turn on the rubber, the microsecond when the arm starts forward, and so on) may have drifted apart by a fraction or two this summer, because of the very different motion and rhythm involved in throwing an off-speed delivery. Now he will have to get them together again.

After Gooden's departure in Game Four, Marty Barrett, the Red Sox second baseman, said, "I feel Dwight's mechanics are a little off. I went against him in spring training when he had that great year last year, and he was more straight up and over the top then. Now it's almost like he's throwing over and moving across his body." One of the Mets regulars said to me, "If Marty Barrett says anything like that, you can believe it. Anything from Barrett is like a message from Western Union. I think that's what happened to Doc, and it made it a tough year for him. But we all have tough years. Now he'll just have to go out there and get it back. Don't bet against him."

Game Three,
National League Championship Series

It came on a chilly gray afternoon at Shea Stadium, and by the end of the second inning the Mets were in heavy weather of their own making, down by 4–0 to the Astro left-handed starter Bob Knepper. These N.L. playoffs, it will be recalled, had opened at the Astrodome with a dominant, almost suffocating 1–0 shutout performance by the Astros' big, sleepy-faced right-hander Mike Scott, who had struck out fourteen Mets batters with his darting split-fingered fastball and high heater, thus nullifying a strong effort by Dwight Gooden. The visitors had evened matters the next day, when the Mets, blown away by Nolan Ryan in his first trip down their batting order, jumped on him for five quick runs on their second look, to win 5–1, behind their left-handed off-speed precisionist Bob Ojeda. But here at Shea the sudden four-run Houston lead looked serious, for Knepper, a ten-year veteran with exquisite control, had defeated the Mets three times during the regular season, and we knew that Scott, the best pitcher in the National League this year, would be back for the Astros the very next day. Watching these glum proceedings from my press seat in deep left field (the foul pole actually blocked my view of the mound), I was afflicted by grumpiness and self-pity. The night before, at home by my television set, I had watched the Red Sox drop a 5–3 game to the Angels out in Anaheim, to slip behind in *their* playoffs by two games to one. My dream was already coming apart, and here at my sixth game in five days (two up at Fenway Park and three via television) I felt baseballed out. Ron Darling, the Mets' starter, had composed himself after two egregious innings (five hits, a base on balls to the No. 8 batter, two stolen bases, a wild pitch, and a two-run homer by second baseman Bill Doran), but the Mets in their dugout—as viewed unsteadily through my binoculars—looked glum and wintry, with their arms crossed and their paws buried in the pockets or the armpits of their shiny blue warmup jackets. In among them I could pick out Wally Backman and Lenny Dykstra, the Mets' dandy two-cylinder self-starting machine that had figured in so many uprisings this summer; Dykstra bats from the left side and Backman is a switch hitter who does much better against right-handers, and so both were sitting out Knepper. ("I don't care how fiery you are," Mets manager Davey Johnson said about Dykstra before the game. "It's on-base average that counts.") The Shea multitudes made imploring noises from time to time, but they, too, looked muffled and apprehensive. Nothing doing.

Kevin Mitchell led off the Mets' sixth with a single over third, and Keith Hernandez followed with a modest fly ball that dropped into short center field for another hit—nothing *much*, except that Craig Reynolds, the Astro shortstop, now booted a grounder by Gary Carter (a double-play ball, in fact), sending Mitchell home, and Darryl Strawberry lofted Knepper's next pitch into the first deck in right field, to tie the game. I revived instantly, but also briefly, for the Mets now handed back the gift run—a walk (Rick Aguilera was pitching for the home side by now), a throwing error by Ray Knight, and an infield out—and very soon thereafter had to deal with Charlie Kerfeld, the Astros' lumpy, menacing right-handed rookie flamethrower, who blew out the candle in the eighth on a handful of pitches. Kerfeld is a hotdog—all shades, chaw, belly, and heat out there—and when he somehow reached behind his back to spear Carter's hard one-hop grounder to the mound, he pointed at Gary as he ran up the line, relishing the moment before he threw him out.

I had improved my seat by a section or two during the afternoon, scrounging the places of no-show reporters closer to the action, but at the end of the eighth I decamped for the interview room, just beyond the Mets clubhouse in the nether corridors of the park—a way to beat the crowds, and a pretty good vantage point from which to watch the last few outs of a game, by means of a giant television monitor. Panting, but certain of my long wisdom in these matters, I attained my goal, to find the room virtually deserted: somebody had forgotten to set up the monitor. And so it happened that I got to see not the longest game-winning home run of my life but certainly the smallest—the sudden two-run, bottom-of-the-ninth smash to right by Lenny Dykstra that I watched, huddling with similarly misplaced media friends, via a palm-size Sony Watchman TV set that one foresighted reporter had brought along to the game. Peering like

microbiologists, we watched the mini-replays and filled in the
missing details. Backman, pinch-hitting, had dropped a leadoff
bunt down the first-base line and made a skidding slide into the
bag around an attempted tag by first baseman Glenn Davis; then
he had motored along to second on a passed ball. The Houston
pitcher was the Astros' short-relief specialist Dave Smith, who
had been wheeled in by manager Hal Lanier to wrap things up,
thus expunging Kerfeld. Now a postage-stamp-size Backman,
seen in black-and-white slow-motion replay, flung up his arms
as he watched Dykstra's homer sail into the Mets' bullpen and
then began his jumping, backward-running dance toward third,
while the rest of the Mets streamed onto the field to celebrate
the 6–5 victory and their sudden lead in the playoffs. Dykstra,
it should be explained, had come into the game in the seventh,
when he fanned against Knepper. Davey Johnson was proud of
this maneuver (he likes to have his pair of deuces in there late
in a game), and explained that he had guessed—guessed right,
it turned out—that Knepper would shortly be done for the day,
leaving Dykstra still in there to swing against a right-hander his
next licks.

Dykstra is a pistol. In this, his first full season, he not only
had won the job in center field (moving Mookie Wilson to left,
on most days, and permitting the club to drop the increasingly
ineffective George Foster) but had quickly emplaced his engaging and brattish mannerisms in our mass Shea consciousness—
his odd preliminary forward lean in the batter's box, with bat
held upright, as if to conk a burglar; the facial twitches, winces,
and squinchings as he prepares for the pitch, and, before that,
the peculiar, delicate twiddling of a gloved fingertip along his
brow; the joyful little double jump and hand pop as he comes
to a dusty stop beyond first with another base hit; and, contrariwise, his disbelieving, Rumpelstiltskin stamp of rage when a
pitcher has caught a corner against him for strike three. Here in
the interview room, Lenny was all cool and charisma—a guest
on some late-night talk show. He said that the only other time
he had hit a winning home run in the bottom of the ninth was
in Strat-O-Matic (a board game), against his kid brother, Kevin.

In the clubhouses, I heard more talk about Strawberry's home
run than about Dykstra's. Strawberry had suffered through a
ghastly midsummer batting slump (he was booed horrendously
by the upper-deck critics at Shea, where he went 0 for August),
and had looked particularly helpless against left-handed pitching. The three-run homer struck off Knepper meant something,

then—something beyond this game. Keith Hernandez said, "Baseball is a constant learning experience. Nothing happens very quickly for most hitters, and you have to remind yourself that Darryl is still only twenty-four years old. He's played four years in the majors, but he's still a baby. It isn't often that a Gehrig or a Mattingly comes along, who can do it all at the plate right away. When I first came up, the Matlacks and Koosmans and Carltons of this league—all those left-handers—gave me fits. Jim Rooker just killed me at the plate. You have to be patient and try to learn to adjust, and Darryl is still learning."

What happened on this afternoon (and again in the fifth game of the playoff, when Straw whacked another telling homer against the Astros) did not quite turn Strawberry's year around, for he batted only .208 in the World Series, with six strikeouts and a lone, superfluous home run and run batted in on his very last at-bat. He is an enigma and a challenge, perhaps to himself as much as to us and to his club, and his style (those thick, long young arms; the looping, easeful swing; the long-loping catch in right-center field that ends with a casual heavenward reach to suck in the ball, with the gesture of somebody taking down a hat from a top shelf) is always so effortless that it looks magical when it succeeds and indolent when it fails. Each year, we wait for the performance that will lift his numbers (.259 this year, with twenty-seven homers and ninety-three runs batted in) to the next level, which is superstardom; each year, that once-certain goal seems a little farther away.

Here in the clubhouse, Strawberry said that Knepper had been throwing him breaking balls all afternoon (he'd nubbed one down the third-base line in the fifth, for a thirty-foot single), and he had guessed fastball the next time up—guessed right, that is. The batting and first-base coach Bill Robinson said, "When Darryl got on base after that little hit, I said 'That's the way to beat on that ball!' and he told me maybe that at-bat would make him stay in the next time up. And that's what he did do—he kept his right side in on that swing and didn't pull off the ball. I tell them all, '*Guess fastball.*' You can adjust to a curveball, a knuckleball, a slider, or a change off the fastball, but it's tough to guess a curveball, a knuckleball, a slider, or a change and then hit the fastball. I believe most pitchers will throw the fastball six out of ten times. So six out of ten times I'm sitting on dead red and knowing I still have a chance on the others. If Knepper throws me a good slider or something outside that's nasty, I'm not going to hit it anyway. You can count the good breaking-ball hitters in this league on the fingers of one hand—well, the fingers of *two* hands. We're all fastball hitters in the end.''

Game Five,
American League Championship Series

Home in fine fettle after the Mets' sudden resurrection that Saturday, I had a drink and some dinner, and took my ease in front of the set, where my Red Sox, out in the late sunshine at Anaheim Stadium, played resolute, patient ball in their almost boring Game Four, eventually dispatching the ancient and wily Don Sutton in the seventh inning. (I should explain that the two sets of playoffs never exactly overlapped in their progression, thanks to the vagaries of the network schedulers.) The Sox' 3–0 lead midway through the ninth looked safe as houses, for their pitcher was Roger Clemens, their soon-to-be winner of both the Cy Young and the Most Valuable Player awards in his league; he had gone 24–4 for the season, after winning his first fourteen decisions in a row, and had also established a new all-time record by striking out twenty batters in an April game against the Seattle Mariners. So far in this game, Clemens had simply brushed aside the Angels, allowing no one to reach third base; three more outs would bring the teams even in their playoff, at two games apiece. But in fact Clemens was running out of gas, and after a leadoff home run by Doug DeCinces in the ninth and one-out singles by Dick Schofield and Bob Boone he was abruptly gone. His successor, the young fastballer Calvin Schiraldi, suffered a nasty shock when a well-hit but catchable fly by Gary Pettis became a run-scoring double because Jim Rice lost the ball in the lights. With the score now 3–2, and with the bases loaded after an intentional pass, Schiraldi fanned Bobby Grich and went to two strikes and one ball on Brian Downing, but then hit him on the thigh with his overreaching next pitch (''Oh, *no!*'' I cried, badly startling the snoozing terrier at my feet as I sailed up out of my chair, to the invisible balletic accompaniment of three or four million Sox fans to the north and east of me—along with *their* dogs, I suppose), to force in the tying run. The Angels won it in the eleventh (oh, yes), bringing exquisite joy to their rooters but ruin to my overcrowded baseball day.

Game Five, played out lengthily at Anaheim the next afternoon, has already taken its place on the little list of Absolute

All-Timers, and I must assume that its immoderate events are known by heart by even the most casual followers of the pastime. The Angels pitched their main man, Mike Witt, a spidery right-hander with an exceptional curveball, which he throws in two variant modes; he had eaten up the Red Sox batters in the playoff opener, retiring the first seventeen in a row. Now he survived a two-run homer by Rich Gedman in the early going and was still in command as the ninth began, with his club ahead by 5-2, three outs away from a pennant. The last two California runs had come in when Dave Henderson, the second Boston center fielder of the day (he had entered the game after Tony Armas twisted an ankle), made a fine running catch of Grich's deep drive, only to have the momentum of his effort carry the ball up over the top of the center-field wall and, appallingly, out of his glove for a home run. In the ninth, Witt gave up a single to Bill Buckner, fanned Rice, and then threw a pretty good breaking ball, down and away, to Don Baylor, who reached out and drove it over the left-field fence: a sobering moment there in Southern California.* Dwight Evans popped up for the second out, though, and manager Gene Mauch called in a left-hander, Gary Lucas, to pitch to the left-side batter Gedman, in search of one more out and a championship. The tactic, arguably logical (and arguably the only appropriate occasion for "arguably" ever to see print), since Gedman had ripped Witt for a homer, a double, and a single for the day, didn't work, because Lucas plunked Gedman on the hand with his first pitch, thereby setting up the next confrontation, between Dave Henderson and the Angels' less than imperious right-handed relief stopper Donnie Moore, who had thrown well in his most recent appearance. With the crowd putting up an insupportable din, with the ushers arrayed along the baselines and police stuffing the dugouts and bullpens, with the Angels up on their topmost dugout step for the pennant spring and the huggings and the champagne, Henderson worked the count to two and two, fouled off two fastballs, and then hit the next delivery—a forkball, perhaps—into the left-field seats.

Silence and disbelief out there. Exultation on the opposite coast. The Angels, it will be recalled, quickly made up the new one-run deficit in their half of the ninth, and even had the next

---

*Baylor's home run, which I watched again and again in taped replay during the winter, ranks as Feat of the Month in this feat-filled October. Witt's pitch broke sharply away over the farthermost part of the strike zone, and Baylor not only got his bat on it but somehow muscled the ball over the opposite-side fence.

winning run—the pennant-winner once again—poised at third base when DeCinces popped to short right field and Grich lined out softly to the pitcher. These extended melodramatics had settled nothing so far (Al Michaels, the exemplary ABC television play-by-play man, summed things up along about here by saying, "If you're just tuning in, too bad"), but now it suddenly seemed clear that the Red Sox *would* win, although that took a couple of innings: a hit batsman (it was Baylor), a single, an unplayable bunt by Gedman, and the winning sacrifice fly to center—by Henderson, of course. Schiraldi came in at the end and got the save. The Angels repacked their gear and de-iced the champagne (I guess) and returned to Boston, where they lost their last two games of the year, 10–4 and 8–1. "I don't think we ever should have had to come back here," Donnie Moore said when it was all over.

My eagle-eye view of Game Five was not nearly as clear as I have depicted it, since duty forced me to leave my TV set in the middle of the ninth that evening and head back to Shea for the fourth Mets-Astros affray, and I picked up most of the amazing and extended events in Anaheim over my car radio while tooling along on the Grand Central Parkway. Taking pity on his old man, my son taped the action on our VCR, and when I got home very late that night (the Mets had lost again to Mike Scott, just as I had feared) I played the last three innings over for myself, and, sure enough, the Red Sox won, 7–6, in eleven innings. It was the first time all month I didn't have to keep score.

I thought back on this game many times after the Red Sox had won their championship and the Angels had packed up and gone home for the winter, but with a good deal less than pure pleasure. These last-moment reprieves and reversals are so anguishing for the losing players and coaches (and the fans, too, to be sure) that one's thoughts return to them unbidden, long after the winners' celebrations have been forgotten. Players in the winning clubhouse always look like boys (and not just because they are behaving like infants), while the ones in the other clubhouse resemble veteran combat soldiers who have barely survived some dreadful firefight. They look worse after a playoff defeat than after the World Series, because the losing team in a championship elimination has won nothing at all; it has become a trivia question. Even the Red Sox players, I noticed later on, talked about their narrow escape in Game Five with dire, near-funereal images. "We were on our deathbed," Roger Clemens said. "The heartbeat meter was on a straight line." John Mc-

Namara, who has a whispery, monsignorlike habit of speech, said to me, "We were dead and buried. When Henderson went to two strikes and the police were all set to go, I looked over and saw Reggie taking off his glasses in their dugout, getting ready for the celebration. That's how close we were."

I feel bad about the Angels, who were a team made up of some distinguished, or very well-known, older players—Don Sutton, Reggie Jackson, Doug DeCinces, Bob Boone, Brian Downing, George Hendrick, Rick Burleson, and Bobby Grich (Sutton and Jackson are in their forties, and the others in their upper thirties)—who fitted well with younger stars like Dick Schofield, Gary Pettis, Mike Witt, Kirk McCaskill, and the splendid rookie first baseman Wally Joyner. (He missed all but the first game of the playoffs with a leg infection.) I see that I have just referred to the Angels in the past tense, which is understandable, for this particular Angels team has ceased to exist. Grich has already retired, Jackson is a free agent—with no assurance that anyone will pick him up for next season—and so are Downing, Boone, and DeCinces, and management has been extremely quiet about which of the other expensive old-timers we will see in Anaheim next summer. I feel sorry for Gene Autry, the seventy-nine-year-old president and chairman of the board, who is revered in the game (he is known as the Cowboy) and has owned the still pennantless team ever since its inception, as an expansion club, in 1961.

I even feel bad about the Angels fans. There is a popular dumb theory here in the East that there is no such thing as a California Angels fan, and that those two-and-a-half-million-attendance totals at Anaheim Stadium, year after year, are made up of moonlighting sunbathers and foot-weary families resting up from Disneyland. This is parochial nonsense, of course, and it's about time we old-franchise inheritors admitted the Angelvolk to the ranks of the true sufferers—the flagellants, the hay-in-the-hair believers, the sungazers, the Indians-worshippers, the Cubs coo-coos, the Twins-keepers, the Red Sox Calvinists: the *fans*. I have heard from a few of them by mail. One pen pal, a professor of Byzantine history from Canoga Park, California, sent me a five-page single-spaced typed letter delineating his pains and his heroes down the years, starting in 1961, when the Angels played at the Pacific Coast League Wrigley Field, in Los Angeles, and won seventy games in their very first season. "Now we know that rooting for the Angels is just like rooting for the Red Sox," he wrote. "One does it guardedly, always looking over one's shoulder.'' Another Angels correspondent, a medical-journal editor who lives in San Francisco, sent along his scorecards for the A.L. playoff games this fall—beautifully detailed, meticulously executed, pitch-by-pitch delineations of the seven games, which concluded with a gigantic, smudgy execration of Gene Mauch scrawled across the bottom of the seventh-game scorecard: the last Angels loss of the year. My correspondent apologized for this in a covering note: ''I'm sorry—I was very upset. I still am.''

I feel bad about Gene Mauch, too—*everybody* feels bad about Mauch by now—who has managed in the majors for twenty-five years without ever setting foot in the World Series, although he had come excruciatingly close before this. In 1964, his Phillies led the National League (this was before divisional play) by six and a half games with two weeks to go, and then lost ten of their last twelve games and, on the last day, the pennant. Four years ago, his Angels led the Milwaukee Brewers in the five-game American League playoffs by two games to one but lost—an outcome so painful that Mauch moved up to the front office for a couple of seasons, and took up the managerial burdens again only last year. He is a dour, unapologetic baseball chancellor (a former colleague of his told me that he'd never heard Mauch ask an opinion or invite a discussion about any move he had made, on or off the field), who has acquired a sharply divided body of passionate loyalists and dedicated doubters in the press boxes and front offices of the game. He has also been second-guessed as much as anyone in his hard profession, but this, I have come to believe, is due not so much to his hard-shell exterior or to his reputation for over-managing as to a deep wish, however unconscious, among other managers and players and watchers of the game to prove that baseball really is more tractable, more manageable in its results, more amenable to tactics and patience and clear thinking, than it seems to have been for him. All of us—even us fans—want the game to be kinder to us than it has been to Gene Mauch, and we are terribly anxious to find how that could be made to happen. No group of games in recent memory had produced anything like the second-guessing of managers that one heard at these two championships, but this is explained, to my way of thinking, by the fact that five of the thirteen games were settled in the ninth inning or later—in the ninth, tenth, eleventh, twelfth, and sixteenth, to be precise— and that prolonging reties were also produced, twice in a ninth inning and once in a fourteenth.

Mauch's moves during Boston's ninth inning of that fifth game, when the three-run Angels lead was converted to a one-run deficit, will be a Gettysburg for tactical thinkers for years to come. An old friend of mine who has managed extensively in both leagues was in Anaheim that afternoon, and later on I asked him what it was like when it all began to come apart for the Angels out there, and what he would have done in the same circumstances.

"When Baylor hit his home run, the game still didn't have that feeling of doom," he said. "You thought, All right, you don't win 5–2, you win 5–4. There were so many different directions Gene could have gone—he just chose the one that didn't work. Gedman looked like the problem, because he'd gone three for three against Witt. But for me, the one to worry about, the key batter, is the *next* guy, the right-handed hitter Henderson, and I'm not too worried about him, because my very best right-handed pitcher—my best pitcher of all—is still in the game. Mike Witt, I mean. He's just struck out Rice and popped up Evans, so he can't be all that tired. If he loses Gedman somehow, he just needs to get Henderson out, and if he can't do *that*, then we don't deserve the pennant. And Henderson would have a whole lot more trouble against him than against a Donnie Moore.

"We know that Gene went to Lucas, and Lucas came in and hit Gedman. Gene's move could have worked, but I think *the wrong man hit Gedman*. If Witt hits him, it's a very different story. With Witt on the mound and Gedman coming up to bat and all eager for that next rip at my pitcher, I would have walked out to Witt and said, "Look, the *next* batter is the one you want. Don't worry about Mr. Gedman. Hit him on the hip with your first pitch, and if you miss go back and hit him with the next one. Then go after Henderson and we're out of this and into the World Series.'

"You know, when Donnie Moore came in after Lucas, I had the same little feeling I'd had back in Milwaukee when Gene's Angels got so close in '82: Now, *wait* a minute: this is ours, but it isn't quite ours yet—let's not gather the bats. And then it all happened again. The fans took it hard, but I think they felt, Well, O.K., we still just need one of the two games back in Boston. But you only had to look at the players' faces to know that it had gotten away from them and it might never come back. Once that phoenix gets out of the ashes, he wants to fly."

My friend the manager told me that he felt terrible about Gene

Mauch. "He's been in this place for so long, and he won't give in to it and he won't walk away from it. This one's going to be very tough for him. He gets within one pitch and one run of the Series, but all those 'one's are still there for him. I know Gene, and I know all the cigarettes that have been smoked and the drinks that have been drunk and the miles that have been paced over this kind of thing, down the years. He'll pay that price to get there, but now I don't know if it will ever happen for him. How do you go on?''

Game Six,
National League Championship Series

I wasn't there, and had to pick up most of its extended, convoluted, and startling events in bits and pieces—by television and cab radio and word of mouth and television again—and then put them together in my head at last with the help of another tape made for me by the Mets screamers at my house. I was in Boston for the American League finale, and the Mets and Astros, as we know, had moved back to the Astrodome. The day before, I had seen the Mets go one up in their playoffs, in a makeup afternoon game at Shea (the thing had been rained out the night before), in which Nolan Ryan and Dwight Gooden pitched each other to a 1–1 standstill over the regulation distance. Ryan, who is thirty-nine years old, fanned twelve Mets and threw a two-hitter, but one of the two was a home run by Strawberry. Ryan left after nine innings and Gooden after ten, and the Mets won in the twelfth, when Gary Carter rapped a run-scoring single past Kerfeld's rump, which Charlie this time did *not* grab behind his back, although he tried. The Astros were sore about an umpire's out call at first base, which had cost them a run back in the second inning, but nothing could be done about it, of course.

I took in most of Game Six the next afternoon by television in my Boston hotel room—not much sport, to tell the truth, for the Mets instantly fell behind by three runs in the first inning, and could do nothing at all against Bob Knepper over their initial eight. It's embarrassing to curse and groan and shout *"C'mon!"* twenty or thirty times in an empty hotel room, but yelling and jumping up and down on the bed—which is what I did during Dykstra's pinch-hit triple, Mookie's single, Keith's double, and Ray Knight's game-tying sac, all in the Mets ninth—is perfectly all right, of course. And here, perhaps, we should pause for statistical confirmation of the kind of baseball week that it had turned out to be. Somebody along about here had noticed or discovered that in the six hundred and forty-two postseason games played prior to 1986 no team had ever made up a deficit of more than two runs in its final chance at bat. Now it had happened three times in five days.*

Darkness had fallen on the Public Garden by the time the Mets got all even, and I was overdue at Fenway Park. Four or five times, I turned off the set, grabbed my game gear, and headed for the door, only to come back and click on again for another out or two. (I didn't know it at the time, but millions of Mets fans in New York were in the same pickle; baseball had burst its seams and was wild in the streets.) The Mets scratched out a run at last in the fourteenth, against Aurelio Lopez (possibly a leftover character actor from a Cisco Kid movie), and that was good enough for me: the Mets had it in hand for sure. I doused the game and headed out to keep my other date, and so missed Billy Hatcher's gargantuan solo home run into the left-field foul-pole screen, which retied things in the bottom half. The sixteenth did wrap it up at very long last, but my patchwork impressions of its events (snatches over somebody's radio just ahead of me on the outside staircase at Fenway Park, and then glimpses on a TV monitor at the back of the overstuffed rooftop press-room while several scribe friends tried to catch me up, viva voce, at the same time) have required subsequent firming up by tape. The Mets' three runs in the top half of the sixteenth and the Astros' gallant but insufficient answering pair in the bottom are still thrilling, of course, but the fatigue and bad nerves of the principals make you jittery, even in replay. Strawberry's mighty-swing semi-bloop fly became a double when the Houston center fielder, Hatcher, got a very late start in for the ball, and a throwing error by right fielder Kevin Bass and two wild pitches helped the Mets almost as much as Knight's single and then Dykstra's. Jesse Orosco (who won three games in the play-offs) was so arm-weary by the uttermost end that fastballs became an impossibility for him; one last, expiring sinker fanned Bass, with the tying run at second, and that was the pennant. A

---

*Bobby Thomson's miracle ninth-inning, three-run homer in 1951, which put down the Dodgers and won the pennant for the Giants, has not been overlooked here. The two clubs had finished their seasons in a tie, and the homer came in the final game of a two-out-of-three playoff. This was an extension of the season, in short, and batting and pitching records in the games were included in the 1951 league statistics.

moment or two earlier, Davey Johnson (he told some of us about this back in New York), with the enormous, domed-in roarings of the Houston multitudes cascading and reverberating around him, noticed that his nearest companion in the Mets' dugout, pitching coach Mel Stottlemyre, looked a tad nervous. Davey leaned closer and said, "Come on, Mel, you knew this had to come down to one run in the end. It's that kind of game."

What I missed by not being in Houston that day may have been less than what I missed by not being in New York. The pennant-clinching celebrations in Boston were happy indeed (about a four on the Roger Scale), but the excruciating prolongation and eventual exultation of the Mets' Game Six were something altogether different—a great public event, on the order of a blackout or an armistice. The game began at 3:06, New York time, and ended at 7:48, and in that stretch millions of Mets fans in and around New York, caught between their day-watch of the game and some other place they had to be, found themselves suspended in baseball's clockless limbo, in a vast, mobile party of anxious watching and listening and sudden release. Sports can bring no greater reward than this, I think. In time, I—like many others, I imagine—began to collect Game Six stories: where folks had been that night, and what they had seen and heard and done during the long game's journey into night. There was no rush hour in New York that evening, I kept hearing: so many office workers stayed in their offices to follow the game that the buses and avenues in midtown looked half empty. Subway riders on the I.R.T. platform at Grand Central heard the score and the inning over the train announcer's loudspeaker. A man I know who was in bed with the flu or something said that he rose to a sitting position during the Mets' rally in the ninth, and then left his bed and paced the floor; when it was all over, he got up and got dressed and was cured. Another man, a film editor—not at all a fan—was running around the Central Park Reservoir when a strange, all-surrounding noise stopped him in his tracks. It came from everywhere around the Park, he said, and it wasn't a shout or a roar but something closer to a sudden great murmuring of the city: the Mets had won.

Men and women on commuter trains followed the news by Panasonic or Sony, clustering around each radio set for the count and the pitch, and calling the outs and the base runners to the others in their car. At the Hartsdale platform, in Westchester, a woman with a Walkman, having said goodbye to other alighting commuters as they hurried off to their car radios, started up a stairway and then stopped and cried "Oh!" Her companions from the train stared up at her, stricken, and she said, "Gary got thrown out, stealing." There were portables and radios at Lincoln Center, too, where the ticket holders at the Metropolitan Opera's performance of "The Marriage of Figaro" reluctantly gave the game up at seven-thirty and went in and took their seats for the overture. After a moment or two, a man in the orchestra section sprang up and disappeared through a side exit; he slipped back in a few minutes later (he'd found someone in the cloakroom with a radio, he subsequently explained) and, resuming his seat at the beginning of Figaro and Susanna's opening duet, turned and signalled, "Seven-four in the sixteenth!" on his fingers to the rows around him, and then did a thumbs-up to show he meant the Mets. A newspaperman heading back home to New York stopped off in an airport bar at Boston's Logan Airport, where the game was on, and fell into Mets conversation there with a woman who turned out to be a Merrill Lynch investment broker; they missed the three-o'clock, the four-o'clock, and the five-o'clock Eastern shuttles, somehow tore themselves away for the six-o'clock—and discovered that the game was still on when they deplaned at La Guardia. A colleague of mine who lives in New Jersey said that while going home he'd followed the game by stages over a spontaneous electronic relay network that had sprung up along the way—a TV set in the fire station on Forty-third Street, a wino's radio in Grace Plaza, a big TV in the window of a video store on Sixth Avenue, some kids with a boom box in the doorway of a Spanish deli, and then a crowd-encircled gray stretch limo parked in Herald Square, with its doors open and the windows rolled down and, within, a flickering tiny television set turned to the game. Radios on his PATH train went blank during the journey under the Hudson but they came back to life in the Hoboken station, where he changed to a New Jersey Transit train, and where the Astros retied the game in the fourteenth. A frightful communications disaster—the long tunnel just before the Meadowlands—was averted when his train, a rolling grandstand, unexpectedly ground to a halt ("Signal difficulties," a conductor announced), and stood right there through the top of the sixteenth, when the Mets scored three and service resumed.

Writer friends wrote me about the game, too. A woman's letter began, "My friend Sandy came over to my place for the game with a quart of beer and some snacks—he doesn't have a color TV set. Sandy and I had been to a couple of games at Shea

together, and I assumed it would be just about the same, but this
was more like the time we'd been to see the movie 'Dawn of the
Dead'—he kept turning his face away from the screen in dread.
I kept up a casual, chatty, reassuring act, saying comforting
things like 'It's all right now. Ojeda is totally in command,' but
then there was this one terrifying closeup of Knepper out on the
mound—eyes burning and steam coming out of his ears. A real
image from a horror movie. As the game went on, I realized
that I was living it through the Mets pitchers, maybe because
the pitcher's motions can give you that trancelike feeling of security. Just about all I was aware of late in the game was
McDowell's right leg coming down and that little bow-legged
hop he takes after every pitch, over and over. As long as I kept
seeing that, I knew we'd be all right.''

An art critic who lives in the East Village wrote, ''At our
apartment during the late innings of Game Six were my wife
Brooke, our daughter Ada, myself, two dinner guests, and two
people who had dropped in on short notice and then stayed
around. One of the guests was Nell, a film director we like a
lot, even though she's one of those people who can't believe that
anyone of your intelligence actually cares about baseball. One
of the drop-ins, an Australian poet named John, knew nothing—
nothing!— about baseball but took a benign attitude, asking
polite, wonderfully dumb questions about the game. The other
drop-in was Aldo, our neighborhood cop on the beat, a Mets
fan and a friend. Aldo was in full cop gear, and voices crackled
from his walkie-talkie: cops out there talking about the game.

''Nell is one of those people who don't know any policemen
and who can't believe that you do. She looked at Aldo for a
while and then said, 'Excuse me, but what are you doing here?'
I had to explain that it was all right, he was here for the game.

''I don't remember it all, but of course I do remember the
growing delirium—like trying to explain to John what a foul ball
was and how to throw a slider, and Nell becoming more and
more agitated, and Brooke assuming her old rally posture in a
particular doorway we have, and then, at the very end, all the
whooping and hollering and inaccurate high-fiving, and some
wild hugging. Nell was leaning out the window shrieking with
joy.''

Game Five, World Series

This was less than a classic, perhaps, but there was spirit and pleasure in it. The home-team Red Sox ravished their Fenway supporters with a 4–2 win, behind their mettlesome left-hander Bruce Hurst, and defeated Dwight Gooden for the second time in the process. This was the Sox' high-water mark (it turned out later), putting them ahead by three games to two, but it also felt like the first game in which the Series competition was fully joined. The Bostons, it will be recalled, had won the Series opener down at Shea, with a splendid 1–0 effort by Hurst against Ron Darling, in which the only run had come in on an error by Mets second baseman Tim Teufel. A promised Gooden-Clemens thriller the next day came to nothing when the Sox won by 9–3, doing away with Dwight almost without effort; Clemens, for his part, was wild, and was gone in the fifth inning. This was Dwight Evans' great game: a mighty two-run homer that caromed off a tent marquee out beyond left-center field, and then a lovely sliding, twisting catch against Dykstra in right. Up in Boston, the Mets, now in a jam, rebounded strongly, with four first-inning runs against Oil Can Boyd in Game Three; Dykstra's leadoff home run set the tone, all right, but the central figure of the evening may have been the Mets' lithe left-hander Bobby Ojeda, a member of the Red Sox pitching corps last year, who nibbled the corners authoritatively ("You don't live in one place in this ballpark," he said later) in the course of his 7–1 outing, and became the first left-hander to win a postseason game at Fenway Park since Hippo Vaughn turned the trick for the Cubs in 1918. Those two quick losses to the Red Sox in the early games meant that Davey Johnson would be overdrawn at the pitching bank in the ensuing games, but he got even at last in Game Four, when Ron Darling shut down the Sox for seven innings (he gave up no earned runs at all in his first two outings), and the Mets roughed up Al Nipper et al. with twelve hits, including two homers by Gary Carter. (A missing figure in the Red Sox pitching rotation was Tom Seaver, who suffered a knee-cartilage tear in September and was forced to sit out all the postseason games: hard news for Sox fans—and for Mets fans, too, I believe.)

Hurst's work here in Game Five was the kind of pitcher's outing that I have most come to admire over the years—a masterful ten-hitter, if that is possible. This was his fourth start in postseason play, and although he was not nearly as strong as he had looked during his gemlike shutout at Shea, he used what he had and kept matters in check, scattering small hits through the innings and down the lineup, and racking up ground-ball outs in discouraging (to the Mets) clusters with his forkball. ("IT HURSTS SO GOOD," one Fenway fan banner said.) The pitch, which disconcertingly breaks down and away from right-handed batters, sets up the rest of his repertoire—a curve and a sneaky-quick fastball—and although Hurst resolutely refers to it as a forkball, it is in fact the ever-popular new split-fingered fastball (*sort* of a forkball), which Hurst learned in 1984. He didn't actually have enough confidence to use the pitch in a game until late June last year, at a time when he had been exiled to the Red Sox bullpen, but it revived his career wonderfully, transforming him from a journeyman 33–40 lifetime pitcher (in five and a half seasons) to a 22–14 winner in the subsequent going. Hurst missed seven weeks this summer with a groin injury, but he deconvalesced rapidly, wrapping up his season's work by going 5–0 and 1.07 in his last five starts, which won him a league accolade as Pitcher of the Month in September. Despite all this, I think we should be wary about making too much of one particular delivery, for pitching is harder than that. Hurst, it should be noticed, belongs to the exclusive Fenway Lefties Finishing School, which numbers two other polished and extremely successful southpaw practitioners among its graduates: Bob Ojeda and John Tudor, who pitched the Cardinals to a pennant last year with a tremendous 21–8, 1.93 summer and then won three games in postseason play. Ojeda, for his part, had an 18–5 record with the Mets this year, which was the best won-lost percentage compiled by any of the Mets' celebrated starters; it was the best in the league, in fact. Previously, Ojeda had toiled for six summers in Fenway Park, and Tudor for five. The uniting characteristics of the three Wallmasters are control, extreme confidence, and a willingness to come inside. At Fenway Park, the inside pitch to a right-handed hitter is what it's all about, for it discourages him from leaning out over the plate in the hope of something he can rap onto or over the Green Monster, and requires him, in fact, to compete with the man on the mound for his—the pitcher's—part of the plate and for his sector of the ballpark, which is to say outside, and to right or right-center: a mismatch. The inside pitch, it should be added, is mostly thrown in the early innings, to plant the *idea* of it in the batter's head, but is then eschewed in the late going, when weariness is more likely to result in a tiny, fatal mistake. Actually, it doesn't have to be thrown for a strike in order to have its effect, and unless you are a Clemens or someone of that order, it's probably a much better pitch, all in all, if it's a ball. "What Ojeda does, over and over, is one of the beauties of the game," Keith Hernandez said at one point in the Series. "When you miss, you've got to miss where it doesn't hurt you. That's what pitching is all about." For his part, Hurst, who throws over the top and finishes his delivery with a stylish little uptailed kick of his back leg, works with great cheerfulness and energy, and here in Game Five he finished this evening's work with a flourish, fanning Dykstra for the last out of the game, with Mets runners on first and third. "BRUCE!" the fans yowled. "BRUUUUCE!"

It was a great night at the Fens. A gusty wind blew across the old premises (left to right, for the most part), and a couple of advertising balloons out beyond the wall bucked and dived in the breeze, tearing at their tethers. The long cries from the outermost fan sectors (the oddly slanting aisles out there looked like ski trails dividing the bleacher escarpments) came in wind-blown gusts, suddenly louder or fainter. The wind got into the game, too, knocking down one long drive by Henderson in the second (it was poorly played by Strawberry) and another by Jim Rice in the fifth, which sailed away from Dykstra and caromed off the top railing of the Sox' bullpen—triples, both of them, and runs thereafter. It was the kind of game in which each player on the home team (in that beautiful whiter-than-white home uniform, with navy sweatshirt sleeves, red stirrups, the curved, classical block-letter "RED SOX" across the chest, and a narrow piping of red around the neck and down the shirtfront) seems to impress his own special mode or mannerism on your memory: Rich Gedman's lariatlike swirl of the bat over his head as he swings through a pitch; Rice's double cut with the bat when he misses—swish-*swish*—with the backward retrieving swing suggesting a man trying to kill a snake; Boggs' way of dropping his head almost onto the bat as he stays down in midswing; Buckner (with that faro-dealer's mustache and piratical daubings of anti-glare black on his cheeks) holding the bat in his extended right hand and, it seems, aiming it at the pitcher's eyes as he stands into the box for an at-bat. And so on. Almost everyone out there, it seemed—every one of the good guys, that is—had his moment in the game to celebrate and be put aside in recollection by the fans: Hendu's triple and double, Marty Barrett's walk and single and double (he batted .433 for the Series), a beautiful play by Boggs on Kevin Mitchell's tough grounder in the second, and, best of all, Billy Buck's painful and comical hobbling gallop around third and in to the plate in the third inning to bring home the second run of the game on a single by Evans. Buckner can barely run (can barely play) at all, because of his sore back and his injury-raddled ankles; it takes him two hours to ice and wrap his legs before he can take the field. He had torn an Achilles tendon in the September 29th game and was playing in this one only on courage and painkillers and with the help of protective high-top boots. No one wanted to laugh at his journey home after Evans bounced the ball up the middle, but you couldn't help yourself. He looked like Walter Brennan coming home—all elbows and splayed-out, achy feet, with his mouth gaping open with the effort, and his head thrown back in pain and hope and ridiculous deceleration. When he got there, beating the throw after all, he flumped belly-first onto the plate and lay there for a second, panting in triumph, and, piece by piece, got up a hero.

This was the last home game of the year for the Red Sox, and when it was over the fans stayed in the stands for a time (John Kiley gave them "McNamara's Band" on the organ again and again), clustering thickly around the home dugout and calling out for Hurst and Billy Buckner and the others, and shouting "We're Number One!" and waving their white Red Sox painters' caps in exuberance. There had been great anxiety about this game, because of the Mets' sudden revival in Games Three and Four, but now the Sox were moving down to New York for one more win, with a rested Clemens going on Saturday and with Hurst ready again, if needed, on Sunday, and I don't think anyone there at the end that night really thought it might not happen. There is great sadness in this, in retrospect, since the team's eventual loss (and the horrendous way of it, on each of the last two days) has brought back the old miasmal Boston baseball doubt and despair—the Bermuda low that has hung over this park and this team perhaps since the day in 1920 when owner Harry Frazee sold a good young outfielder named Babe Ruth to the Yankees, two seasons after Ruth, then a pitcher, had helped bring the Sox their last (to this day) World Championship. Once again, New England's fans have been sent into the winter with the dour nourishment of second-best to sustain them: Indian pudding. If they wish, they may once again ponder the wisdom of George Bernard Shaw's opinion that there are two tragedies in this world: one is never getting what you want, and the other is getting it—a dictum they would love to put to the test someday.

But enough of this. Glooming in print about the dire fate of the Sox and their oppressed devotees has become such a popular art form that it verges on a new Hellenistic age of mannered excess. Everyone east of the Hudson with a Selectric or a word processor has had his or her say, it seems (the *Globe* actually published a special twenty-four-page section entitled "Literati on the Red Sox" before the Series, with essays by George Will, John Updike, Bart Giamatti—the new National League president, but for all that a Boston fan through and through—Stephen King, Doris Kearns Goodwin, and other worthies), and one begins to see at last that the true function of the Red Sox may be not to win but to provide New England authors with a theme, now that guilt and whaling have gone out of style. I would put forward a different theory about this year's loss and how it may be taken by the fans. As one may surmise from the *Globe*'s special section, the Red Sox have become chic: Pulitzer Prize winners and readers of the *New York Review of Books* hold season tickets behind first base, and the dropped "Geddy" and "Dewey" and "Roger" and "the Can" clang along with the sounds of cutlery and grants chat at the Harvard Faculty Club. The other, and perhaps older, fan constituency at Fenway Park has not always been as happy and philosophical about the Sox. The failures of the seventies and early eighties were taken hard by the Boston sports crowd (the men and women who care as much about the Celtics and the Patriots and the Bruins as they do about the Sox), and the departure of Carlton Fisk, Rick Burleson, Freddy Lynn, and Luis Tiant, and the retirement (at long last) of Yastrzemski, left a very bitter taste, and so did the team's persistent, almost stubborn unsuccess in this decade. (It finished fifth, fourth, and sixth in the American League East in the three years before this one, an average nineteen games behind the leader.) The ugly "Choke Sox" label was much heard, and the team's ancient, stubbornly held style of play, characterized by insufficient pitching, insufficient or nonexistent speed, a million ground-ball double plays (by the Sox, I mean), and an almost religious belief in the long ball, had become a byword in the game, a "pahk your cah" joke around the league. Nothing could change this, it seemed. But this year it changed: a baseball miracle. This year, the Red Sox not only won their division and the American League playoffs and, very nearly, the World Series, but became a different sort of team, to themselves above all.

Nineteen-eighty-six turned around for the Red Sox because of Roger Clemens (and perhaps because of Schiraldi's sudden mid-season arrival as a bullpen stopper), but a more significant alteration was one of attitude—a turnabout that began when Don Baylor came over from the Yankees and almost immediately became the team leader, something the Sox had been lacking for as long as anyone could remember. He told the young pitchers that they had to pitch inside if the team was to win; he persuaded the batters to take the extra base, to look for ways to get on base in the late innings (like getting hit with pitches, for instance: a Baylor specialty), to find that little edge—the one play or moment or lucky hop—that turns games around. Tom Seaver came aboard in June, and deepened this same aura with his maturity, his ease, and his sense of humor and proportion. The Sox grew up this summer: you could see it on the field—in Jim Rice choking up on the bat by an inch or so when he got to two strikes (this for the first time ever) and stroking the ball to right-center now and then, so that though his homers went down by seven (to twenty), his batting average improved by thirty-three points and his hits by forty-one—and in the results. The players spoke of it themselves. ''We have more character,'' they said, and ''We're going to win''—words unheard by this writer from any Boston club of the past.

What fans think about their team is subtle and hard to pin down, but I am convinced that everything was changed this year by one game—by that stubborn and lucky and altogether astounding Red Sox return from near-defeat in the fifth game out at Anaheim, when they came back from extinction and a three-run deficit in the ninth inning and won by 7–6. It almost carried the month, and it is startling to notice, in retrospect, that the Red Sox actually won five games in a row right in the middle of the postseason—the last three of their championship playoffs and the first two of the World Series. There is no prize for this, of course, but no other team in October played quite so well for quite so long. In its killing last-minute details, their loss to the Mets in Game Six (they fell after holding a two-run lead in the tenth inning, with no one on base for the Mets) was so close to what the Angels had experienced that their fans—even the most deep-dark and uncompromising among the bleacherites, I think—must have seen the connection, and at last sensed the difficulties of this game and how much luck and character and resolve it takes to be a winner in the end. History and the ghost of Sox teams past had nothing to do with it. The Choke

Sox died in Anaheim, and this losing Red Sox team will be regarded in quite a different way in New England this winter. It will be loved.

Game Six, World Series

The Mets are not loved—not away from New York, that is. When the teams moved up to the Hub, with the Mets behind by two games to none, there was a happy little rush of historical revisionism as sportswriters and baseball thinkers hurried forward to kick the New York nine. Tim Horgan, a columnist with the Boston *Herald*, wrote, "Personally, I don't think anything west of Dedham can be as marvelous as the Mets are supposed to be. I wouldn't even be surprised if the Mets are what's known as a media myth, if only because New York City is the world capital of media myths." Bryant Gumbel, on NBC's "Today" show, called the Mets arrogant, and ran a tape of Keith Hernandez' bad throw on a bunt play in Game Two, calling it "a hotdog play." Sparky Anderson, the Tigers manager, declared over the radio that the Indians, the traditional doormats of his American League division, put a better nine on the field than the Mets, and a newspaper clip from the heartland (if San Diego is in the heart of America) that subsequently came my way contained references to "this swaggering band of mercenaries" and "a swaying forest of high fives and taunting braggadocio." Much of this subsided when the Mets quickly drew even in the games, and much of it has nothing to do with baseball, of course; what one tends to forget is that there is nothing that unites America more swiftly or happily than bad news in Gotham or a losing New York team. Some of these reflections warmed me, inwardly and arrogantly, as Game Six began, for I was perched in a splendid upper-deck-grandstand seat directly above home plate, where, in company with my small family and the Mets' mighty fan family, I gazed about at the dazzlement of the ballpark floodlights, the electric-green field below, and the encircling golden twinkle of beautiful (by night) Queens, and heard and felt, deep in my belly, the pistol-shot sounds of clapping, the cresting waves of "LETSGOMETS! LETSGOMETS! LETSGOMETS!," and long, taunting calls—"Dew-eee! DEW-EEEE!" and "Rog-errr! ROG-ERRRR!"—directed at some of the Bosox below: payback for what the Fenway fans had given Darryl Strawberry in the last game in Boston. And then a parachutist came sailing down out of the outer darkness and into the bowl of light and noise—a descending roar, of all things—of Shea. "GO METS," his banner said as he lightly came to rest a few steps away from Bob Ojeda in mid-infield and, encumbered with minions, went cheerfully off to jail and notoriety. We laughed and forgot him. I was home.

Game Six must be given here in extreme précis—not a bad idea, since its non-stop events and reversals and mistakes and stunners blur into unlikelihood even when examined on a scorecard. I sometimes make postgame additions to my own scorecard in red ink, circling key plays and instants to refresh my recollection, and adding comments on matters I may have overlooked or misjudged at the time. My card of Game Six looks like a third grader's valentine, with scarlet exclamation points, arrows, stars, question marks, and "Wow!"'s scrawled thickly across the double page. A double arrow connects Boggs, up on top, to Spike Owen, down below, in the Boston second—a dazzling little hit (by Wade)-and-run (by Spike) that set up Boston's second score of the game. Two red circles are squeezed into Jim Rice's box in the Boston seventh—one around the "E5" denoting Ray Knight's wild peg that put Rice on first and sent Marty Barrett around to third, and the other around the "7-2" that ended the inning, two outs and one run later, when Mookie Wilson threw out Jim at the plate. A descendant arrow and low-flying exclamation points mark Clemens' departure from the game after the seventh (the Red Sox were ahead by 3-2, but Roger, after a hundred and thirty-one pitches, had worked up a blister on his pitching hand), and an up-bound red dart and "MAZZ PH" pointing at the same part of the column denote Lee Mazzilli's instant single against Schiraldi, while the black dot in the middle of the box is the Mazzilli run that tied the score. But nothing can make this sprawling, clamorous game become orderly, I see now, and, of course, no shorthand can convey the vast, encircling, supplicating sounds of that night, or the sense of encroaching danger on the field, or the anxiety that gnawed at the Mets hordes in the stands as their season ran down, it seemed certain, to the wrong ending.

The Red Sox scored twice in the top of the tenth inning, on a home run by Dave Henderson ("Hendu!" is my crimson comment) and a double and a single by the top of the order—Boggs and then Barrett—all struck against Rick Aguilera, the fourth Mets pitcher of the night. Call it the morning, for it was past midnight when the Sox took the field in the bottom half, leading by 5–3. Three outs were needed for Boston's championship, and two of them were tucked away at once. Keith Hernandez, having flied out to center for the second out, left the dugout and walked into Davey Johnson's office in the clubhouse to watch the end; he said later that this was the first instant when he felt that the Mets might not win. I had moved down to the main press box, ready for a dash to the clubhouses, and now I noticed that a few Mets fans had given up and were sadly coming along the main aisles down below me, headed for home. My companion just to my right in the press box, the *News'* Red Foley, is a man of few words, but now he removed his cigar from his mouth and pointed at the departing fans below. "O ye of little faith," he said.

It happened slowly but all at once, it seemed later. Gary Carter singled. Kevin Mitchell, who was batting for Aguilera, singled to center. Ray Knight fouled off two sinkers, putting the Red Sox one strike away. (Much later, somebody counted up and discovered that there were *thirteen* pitches in this inning that could have been turned into the last Mets out of all.) "Ah, New England," I jotted in my notebook, just before Knight bopped a little single to right-center, scoring Carter and sending Mitchell to third—and my notebook note suddenly took on quite a different meaning. It was along about here, I suspect, that my friend Allan, who is a genius palindromist, may have taken his eyes away from his set (he was watching at home) for an instant to write down a message that had been forming within him: "Not so, Boston"—the awful truth, no matter how you look at it.

Schiraldi departed, and Bob Stanley came on to pitch. (This was the Steamer's moment to save what had been an unhappy 6–6 and 4.37 season for him, in which his work as the Sox' prime right-handed stopper had received increasingly unfavorable reviews from the Fenway bleacher critics; part of me was pulling for him here, but the game was out of my hands—and evidently out of his as well.) Mookie Wilson, batting left-handed, ran the count to two-and-two, fouled off two more pitches, and then jumped away, jackknifing in midair, to avoid a thigh-high wild pitch that brought Mitchell flying in from third, to tie it. Wilson fouled off two more pitches in this at-bat of a lifetime and then tapped a little bouncer down toward first, close to the baseline, that hopped once, hopped twice, and then slipped under Buckner's glove and on into short right field (he turned and stared after it in disbelief), and Knight thundered in from around third base. He jumped on home plate with both feet—jumped

so hard that he twisted his back, he said later—and then disappeared under an avalanche of Mets.

The post mortems were nearly unbearable. "This is the
worst," Bob Stanley said.

"I'm exhausted," Ray Knight said. "My legs are trem-
bling."

"As close as we came . . ." whispered John McNamara.
"As close as we came, I can only associate it with California."

"It's baseball," said Dave Henderson. "It's baseball, and
we've got to live with it."

Questions were asked—they always are after major accidents—and some of them must be asked again, for this game
will be replayed, in retrospect, for years to come.

Q: Why didn't Davey Johnson double-switch when he brought
in Jesse Orosco to get the last out of the eighth inning? Without
an accompanying substitute at some other slot in the order, Jesse
was forced to depart for a pinch-hitter an instant later, in the
Mets' half, thus requiring Johnson to wheel in Aguilera, who
was a much less certain quantity on the mound, and who quickly
gave up the two runs that so nearly finished off the Mets. A: I
still don't know, for Davey is a master at the double switch—a
textbook maneuver in National League tactics, since there is no
designated hitter—and a bit later on he made a much more ques-
tionable switch, which removed Darryl Strawberry from the
game. It came out all right in the end, but I think Davey just
forgot.

Q: Why didn't McNamara pinch-hit for the creaking Buckner
in the tenth, when another run could have nailed down the Mets
for sure? And, having decided against this, why didn't he at
least put the much more mobile Stapleton in to play first base in
the bottom half—perhaps to gobble up Wilson's grounder and
make the flip to the pitcher? More specifically, why didn't he
pinch-hit Baylor, his designated hitter, who batted in the No. 5
slot throughout the regular season and in the playoffs but rode
the bench (no D.H.) almost to the end during the games played
at Shea? A: Johnny Mack has defended himself strongly against
both of these second-guesses, citing Buckner's excellent bat (a
.267 year, with eighteen home runs and a hundred and two runs
batted in) and Buckner's glove ("He has good hands," he said),
in that order. His answer to the Baylor puzzle is to say that Baylor
never pinch-hits when the Red Sox are ahead—sound strategy,
one can see, until a game arrives when they might suddenly fall
behind at the end. McNamara also claims that Stapleton nor-

mally substitutes for Buckner at first base only if there has been
an earlier occasion to insert him as a pinch-*runner* for Buckner;
this is mostly true (it wasn't the case in Game Five), but the fact
remains that Stapleton was playing first base in the final inning
of all three games that the Sox did win. My strong guess is that
McNamara is not beyond sentiment. He knew the torments that
Buckner had gone through to stay in the lineup throughout the
season, and the contributions he had made to bring the club to
this shining doorstep (he had mounted a seventeen-game hitting
streak in mid-September, and at one stretch drove in twenty runs
in a span of eight games) and he wanted him out there with the
rest of the varsity when the Sox seemed certain to step over it at
last.

◆ ◆ ◆

WE NEED NOT LINGER LONG ON GAME SEVEN, IN WHICH THE
Mets came back from a 3–0 second-inning deficit and won going
away (as turf writers say), 8–5. It was another great game, I
suppose, but even noble vintages can become a surfeit after
enough bottles have been sampled. A one-day rainout allowed
us to come down a little from the sixth game and its astounding
ending, but then we came to the last day of all, and the sense of
that—a whole season rushing to a decision now—seized us and
wrung us with almost every pitch once play resumed. Ron Darling, who had given up no earned runs in the Series so far,
surrendered three in the second inning (Evans and Gedman
whacked home runs on successive pitches) and was gone in the
fourth. Hurst, for his part, permitted only a lone single in five
full innings, but ran dry in the sixth, when the Mets evened the
game. They had specialized in this sleeping-dragon style of play
all through the championship season, and this last time around
they showed us once again how dangerous they really were: nine
hits and eight runs in their last three innings of the year. Somehow, the anguish of the Red Sox mattered more than the Mets'
caperings at the very end, because it was plain by now that it
could have just as easily gone the other way. In the Boston clubhouse, Al Nipper, who was badly battered during his very brief
appearance in the New York eighth, sat at his locker with his
back turned and his head buried in his hands. Dennis Boyd,
who had not been called on in the Sox' extremity, rocked forward and back on his chair, shaking his head in disbelief. Friends
of mine said later that they had been riveted by a postgame

television closeup of Wade Boggs sitting alone in the dugout with tears streaming down his face, and a couple of them who are not fans asked me how it was possible for grown men to weep about something as trivial as a game. I tried to tell them about the extraordinary heights of concentration and intensity that are required to play baseball at this level, even for a single trifling game in midseason, but I don't think they believed me. Then I remembered a different moment on television—something I saw a couple of years ago on a trip abroad, when the captain of the Australian cricket team was interviewed over the BBC just after his eleven (I *think*) had lost a protracted test match to the West Indies. I listened to the young man's sad recapitulations with predictable American amusement—until I suddenly noticed that there were tears in his eyes. He was crying over *cricket*! I suppose we should all try to find something better or worse to shed tears for than a game, no matter how hard it has been played, but perhaps it is not such a bad thing to see that men can cry at all.

The acute moment in Game Seven was produced in the Mets' sixth, when Keith Hernandez came up to bat against Hurst with the bases loaded and one out and the Red Sox still ahead by 3–0. Anyone who does know baseball understood that this was the arrangement—this particular batter and this precise set of circumstances—that the Mets wanted most and the Red Sox least at the end of their long adventures. It was the moment that only baseball—with its slow, serial, one-thing-and-then-another siftings and sortings—can produce from time to time, and its outcome is often critical even when reëxamined weeks later. I think the Red Sox would have won this game if they had got Hernandez out. As it was, he took a strike from Hurst (a beautiful, dipping off-speed breaking ball) and then rocketed the next pitch (a fastball, a bit up) to deep left-center for a single and the Mets' first two runs and the beginning of their championship comeback. I'm not sure that anyone remembered at the time, but we should remember now that Hernandez, then a member of the Cardinals, hit a crucial two-run single up the middle in the sixth inning of the seventh game of the 1982 World Series, to start that team on its way to a comeback 6–3 victory over the Milwaukee Brewers.

Many fans think of Gary Carter as the quintessential Mets player, while some may see Lenny Dykstra or Wally Backman or Dwight Gooden, or even Ray Knight (who won the Series M.V.P. award), or perhaps Mookie Wilson in that role (Metshaters despise them all, for their exuberance, their high-fives, their cap-waving encores, their vast publicity, their money, and their winning so often: winning is the worst mannerism of all), but for me the Mets are Keith Hernandez. His game-long, season-long intensity; his classic at-bats, during which the contest between batter and pitcher seems to be written out on some invisible blackboard, with the theorems and formulas being erased and rewritten as the count progresses; his style at the plate, with the bat held high (he is mostly bare-armed), and his pure, mannerism-free cuts at the ball; and, above all, his demeanor afield—I would rather watch these, I think, than the actions of any other player in the game today. Watching him at work around first base—he is sure to earn his ninth consecutive Gold Glove for his performance at the position—you begin to pick up the little moves and glances and touches that show what he is concerned about at that instant, what dangers and possibilities are on his mind. Holding a base runner close, with a right-handed pull hitter up at bat, he crouches with his left foot planted on the baseline and toeing to right—a sprinter's start, no less—and he moves off so quickly with the pitch that he and the runner appear to be tied together, one mass zipping along the base path. When there's a left-handed batter in the box under the same circumstances, Keith leaves his post just as quickly once the pitcher lets fly, but this time with a crablike backward scuttle, quicker than a skater. He makes the tough 3–6 peg down to second look easy and elegant, and he attacks bunts with such assurance that he sometimes scoops up the ball on the third-base side of the invisible pitcher-to-home line (I have seen only two or three other first basemen pull this off even once; Ferris Fain, of the late-nineteen-forties Athletics, was one of them) and then gets off his throw with the same motion. If you make yourself notice where Hernandez has stationed himself on the field, you will sometimes get a sudden sense of what is really going on down there. Wade Boggs, the best hitter in baseball, usually raps the ball up the middle or to left, even though he is a left-handed swinger, but his failure to pull even one pitch up the line to right in the course of the World Series allowed Hernandez to play him more and more into the hole as the Series went on, and contributed to Boggs' problems at the plate in these games. Even one pulled foul would have altered his positioning, Keith said after the Series ended; he was amazed that Boggs hadn't attacked him in this way.

Hernandez is probably not an exceptionally gifted athlete, but

his baseball intelligence is remarkable. Other Mets players say
that he always seems to be two or three pitches ahead of the
enemy pitcher and catcher, and that he almost seems to know
the other team's coaches' signals without looking, because he
understands where they are in their heads and what they hope
to do next. He shares all this with his teammates (keep count in
a game of the number of different players he says something to
in the course of a few innings), and the younger players on the
club, including Darryl Strawberry, will tell you that Keith's
counsel and patience and knowledge of the game and its ways
have made them better ballplayers, and winners. All this comes
at a price, which one may guess at when watching Hernandez
chain-smoke and put away beers (there is a postgame ice bucket
at his feet by his locker) in the clubhouse as he talks and comes
down after the game. The talk is a season-long seminar that
Mets writers attend, day after day, taking notes and exchanging
glances as they write. The man is in the game.

Davey Johnson also has some baseball smarts, and in this last
game he showed us, if we needed showing, how far ahead he
had been all along. Sid Fernandez, the Mets' dumpling left-
handed strikeout pitcher—their fourth starter this year, and during some stretches their best—came into the game in the fourth
inning, with the Mets down by 3–0, and stopped the Sox dead
in their tracks: a base on balls and then seven outs in succession,
with four strikeouts. "That did it," Keith said afterward. "When
Sid was in there, we began to feel that we might win this game
after all. He was the necessary hero." Johnson had passed over
Fernandez as a starter in the Series (he is streaky and emotional), but he had brought him along, all right. Fernandez had
pitched a shaky one-third of an inning in Game Two, surrendering three hits and a run late in a losing cause; in Game Five,
which the Mets also lost, he had pitched four shutout innings,
with five strikeouts. He was Series-tested by the end, and he
became Johnson's last and best move.

The Sox, for their part, mounted a courageous rally in their
eighth inning, when three successive solid blows accounted for
two runs and closed the score to 6–5 before Orosco came in and
shot them down for good. By this time, the Mets hitters had
done away with Schiraldi and were loose in the Boston bullpen—
John McNamara's worst dream come true. Strawberry's homer
and the cascade of Mets runs at the end released the fans at last,
and their celebrations during the final outs of the year—the
packed thousands together chanting, roaring out the Freddie

Mercury rock chorus "We will, we will . . . ROCK YOU!" while pointing together at the Boston bench—were terrific fun. There was a great city party there at Shea, and then all over town, which went on into the parade and the ticker tape (it's computer paper now) the following afternoon, but when it was all over I think that most of us, perhaps all of us, realized that the victory celebration didn't come up to the wonderful, endless sixteen innings of Game Six, back during the playoffs. As one friend of mine said later, "For me, that night was the whole thing. Whatever there was to win had been won."

There was a surprise for me, there at the end. I am a Mets fan. I had no idea how this private Series would come out, but when the Mets almost lost the next-to-last game of the Series I suddenly realized that my pain and foreboding were even deeper than what I had felt when the Red Sox came to the very brink out in Anaheim. I suppose most of my old Red Sox friends will attack me for perfidy, and perhaps accuse me of front-running and other failures of character, but there is no help for it. I don't think much has been lost, to tell the truth. I will root and suffer for the Sox and the Mets next summer and the summers after that, and if they ever come up against each other again in the World Series—well, who knows? Ask me again in a hundred and sixty-seven years.

FOURTEEN

◆ ◆ ◆

The Arms Talks

SPRING 1987

THE LESSER WONDERS OF BASEBALL—THE SACRIFICE FLY, the three-six-three double play, the wrong-side hit-and-run bouncer through a vacated infield sector, the right-field-to-third-base peg that cuts down a lead runner, the extended turn at bat against an obdurate pitcher that ends with a crucial single squiggled through the middle—are most appreciated by the experienced fan, who may in time also come to understand that expertise is the best defense against partisanship. This game can break your heart. No other sport elucidates failure so plainly (no other sport comes close), or presents it in such painful and unexpected variety. My favorite team, the Mets, won a World Championship last fall, but the pleasure of that drained away much more quickly than I thought it would, and now, in company with their millions of other fans, I am stuck with the increased anxieties and diminished pleasures of a possible repeat performance. The 1986 league championships and World Series produced so many excruciations and twists of the knife that these, I suspect, are now remembered more vividly than anything else: the Mets' and Astros' day-into-night sixth game, which brought the Mets their pennant after sixteen innings of nearly insupportable tension and ennui; the fifth game of the American League playoff, when the California Angels,

359

three outs away from their first World Series, surrendered four
runs in the Boston ninth on a pair of home runs and a hit batsman, and eventually lost both game and championship; and, of
course, Game Six of the World Series, in which the Mets, trailing in the tenth by two runs, came down to their last out of the
year with nobody on base, and then—I still don't believe it—
beat the Red Sox on three singles, a wild pitch, and an ugly little
error, and went on to take the last game as well. Hundreds of
thousands of TV spectators must have fallen in love with baseball in the course of watching these soap operas, but during the
winter I sometimes wondered how many of those newborn fans
would stay with the game once they perceived its slower and
less melodramatic midsummer flow, and whether (if they were
Mets rooters) they were giving thought to the lingering, inexorably recalled off-season sufferings of the worthy (and, together,
much more numerous) fans of the Astros and the Angels and
the Red Sox, some of whom or all of whom may have to wait
for many seasons—decades, perhaps—before they find better
luck and a shot at redress. There are easy days and lesser rewards for every fan, of course, but losing, rather than winning,
is what baseball is about, and why, in the end, it is a game for
adults.

Spring training is meant to bring surcease to such dour no-
tions. There are young faces and fresh arms, the northbound
sun is delicious, and the games, which mean nothing, are
apprehension-free. This year, as is my custom, I toured the March
camps in Arizona and Florida and tasted these old pleasures,
but restoration came slowly. Some old friends and familiar faces
were missing. Tom Seaver was gone, after twenty major-league
seasons; he required a knee operation last fall, to repair an injury
that kept him from pitching for the Red Sox in the playoffs and
the World Series, and no team had invited him to camp this
year. Absent as well were the free agents who had been closed
out of the sport, at least for the time being, by the owners'
apparently concerted plan to avoid competitive bidding for the
services of any player who had chosen to take his chance in the
marketplace this year rather than sign up again. By the time
the season opened, a couple of dozen teams with an ostensible
interest in winning a pennant had found no use at all for the likes
of Tim Raines, Bob Boone, Ron Guidry, Rich Gedman, Bob
Horner, Lonnie Smith, and Doyle Alexander. According to the
rules governing such matters, these men would be free to rejoin
their original clubs on May 1st, possibly chastened by the

knowledge that they weren't worth as much as they (and we) thought they were. Raines, by the way, has been a lifetime .305 hitter for the Montreal Expos, with four hundred and sixty-one stolen bases. A teammate and fellow free agent of his, André Dawson—who has batted .280 over eleven years, with two hundred and twenty-five home runs—was so disgusted with the freeze-out that he instructed his agent to accept any offer that the Chicago Cubs wished to make him, and signed on for five hundred thousand dollars (with some further incentives contingent upon his durability), which was five hundred and forty-seven thousand dollars less than his previous year's stipend. Just recently, Bob Horner, of the Braves, went off to play for the Yakult Swallows, in Japan. Earlier, Lance Parrish, a fixture behind the plate for the Tigers over the past decade, signed with the Phillies, in the only unblemished deal of its kind this year. A batterymate of his, the Detroit ace Jack Morris, who has won more games in this decade than any other pitcher, gave up on free agency even before the bidding season began, in January, when he and his lawyer discovered that no other team was interested in his wares; he took the Tigers to salary arbitration instead, and won a salary raise to a million eight hundred and fifty thousand dollars. Both Raines and the Red Sox' Gedman, by the further way, also agreed this spring to accept less money than they had been offered by their previous clubs, but when they did, the teams with whom they were negotiating inexplicably withdrew or altered their perhaps less than serious offers. I take no pleasure in these ironies, but the owners, I am convinced, don't give a damn about what we fans feel; they wish us to believe that the free agents and the rest of the players are paid far too much and should be taught a lesson—a lesson in economics, I suppose. I sympathize with the owners' wish to lower their payrolls and balance their books, but what they are doing looks to me like an unfunny coincidence, of Thoreau's trout-in-the-milk variety. The matter is now in the hands of an arbitrator, who will rule on a grievance plea on this issue brought last year by the Players Association. Lawyers tell me that collusion is hard to prove and almost impossible to police, even if a finding of conspiracy is made, but what is all too plain is that this is the weather pattern that may bring baseball to another strike two years hence, when the present agreement concludes.

I did find a scattering of rookies to admire, but not nearly as many as last spring, in the great vintage year of '86, when I had my first, awed look at the Angels' Wally Joyner, the Rangers'

Pete Incaviglia (an even better Texas youngster, Ruben Sierra, didn't join the club until midseason), the Giants' Will Clark, and the Athletics' ("the A's" has undergone official unabbreviation) Jose Canseco. This year's sprouts appear to have a little less ability and, for a change, a lot less size. Joey Cora, the Padres' new second baseman, and Luis Polonia, a future Oakland outfielder, are both five feet eight inches tall, and Casey Candaele (it's pronounced "Candell"), a young backup infielder for Montreal, goes five-nine; all three are switch hitters, and exude the glitter and élan of players who show us the best of themselves at every instant. I was at Winter Haven one afternoon when Candaele made some slick plays afield and went four for five against the Red Sox' pitchers, with a home run and three runs batted in. ("Who *was* that little guy at second base?" Boston manager John McNamara asked the writers when the game was over.) Jose Canseco (six feet three inches) has gained twenty pounds since last spring, when he was listed at two hundred and ten—all muscle, by the look of him, and most of that in his arms, which now resemble pipeline sections. Last spring, I saw him waft several pitches into distant sectors of Arizona real estate (he went on to hit thirty-three home runs and bat in a hundred and seventeen runs, and was voted the American League's rookie of the year), but this time around I arrived a day too late for a memorable pair of home runs he hit against the Cubs at their home park, in Mesa. Joe Rudi, now an Oakland coach, told me that the first of these blows, which sailed over his head in the visitors' bullpen, in left field, was easily the longest homer he had ever seen; the next one, on about the same arc and flight plan, was a bit longer. Canseco didn't oblige me with any homers this year, but he startled me in other ways. He kept hitting rocketlike singles through the infield, he bunted once for a base hit and a run batted in, and he struck out only twice in the twelve at-bats I saw. He may be a ballplayer as well as a legend.

Back in Florida, I spent much of my time with the Red Sox and the Mets, as might be expected, but I noticed that my baseball holiday was less fun as the season got closer and the teams got better. The Bostons had resumed the sour, withdrawn misanthropy that had made up such a traditional part of their team psyche before last summer (Jim Rice and Don Baylor were not speaking, I was told), and anxiety over Roger Clemens' absence (he was holding out—nothing to do with free agency—and agreed to a new two-year and perhaps two-million-dollar contract only a day or two after the new season began) seemed to haunt their doings on the field. The Mets were more cheerful and optimistic, as is their nature, but their vast attendant media corps added an air of frazzled, election-year foolishness to their comings and goings; one morning, I counted fourteen writers encircling Keith Hernandez as he talked about Darryl Strawberry's brief, petulant walkout when he was fined for missing practice. All this, to be sure, was before the very bad news came about Dwight Gooden's cocaine troubles, and his departure from baseball while he embarked upon a course of drug rehabilitation that may keep him off the field for months, and perhaps for a full season. The pain and sadness we feel about this are off to one side of baseball, I think—or should be—but there is a sense of loss that reminds us of the kind of wishful hero worship that every real fan has within him or her, even in middle age; we think we have outgrown it, but in truth we can hardly wait for the next shy and shining, extraordinarily talented young man to come along and make the game thrilling for us once again. Doc will return to baseball, I'm sure, and I hope he will be as good as or better than before, but it will be a little while, I think, before I will be able to love a ballplayer in quite that way again—to make him a man and myself a boy. To be fair about it, we should remind ourselves that the players have not agreed to these ancient but unwritten conditions of our affiliation, and may not understand them at all. Addiction in any form is a mystery.

◆ ◆ ◆

TRYING TO LEARN THE GAME, AS I HAVE SUGGESTED, PROTECTS us from its overattachments and repeated buffetings, and for me, as the years go by, this has become almost the best part of baseball. This spring and last spring, I passed many hours in the company of coaches and managers and players—older players, for the most part—as I tried to learn a bit more about pitching. I wasn't so much concerned with strategy—where the ball is pitched, and with what intention, to different batters in different game situations (the heart of the game, in fact)—for that art is better pursued during the regular season, when each pitch matters. Rather, I wanted to learn for certain how the different pitches are thrown and why; how the ball is held and what happens to it in flight and which styles in pitching and pitchers' thinking are undergoing alteration. (In the course of these talks, I often found myself moving a ball this way and that in my right hand—I pitch and write righty—while some pitcher or coach tried to arrange my fingers around it in different ways, and I would suggest to readers who wish to accompany me closely over the ensuing paragraphs that they might do well to hunt around the house for an old baseball and keep it close by as a teaching aid.)

Early on, I found out about—or was confirmed in my guesses about—an amazing revolution in pitching style and theory that has been in progress for more than a dozen years now. Pete Rose put it well (Pete puts *everything* well) in Tampa a year ago. "The two biggest changes I've noticed in baseball in my twenty-three-year career are, first and obviously, the much bigger salaries and, second, the maturity of big-league pitchers today," he said. "There's a reason for this, which is that in every class and level of baseball today there is a pitching coach. It didn't used to be that way when I was coming up. I don't think the pitchers are faster than they used to be, but I think they're better. By the time a pitcher is twenty or twenty-one years old now, he's very comfortable throwing 2–0 changeups and 3–1 curveballs. We've gotten used to that, but it's something real different. When I first came up, most of the relievers were freak-ball pitchers, who threw screwballs or knuckleballs or forkballs or palmballs. Now the hardest throwers—I'm only talking National League, because that's where I've been—the hardest throwers are in the bullpen. Gooden is an exception. Most of the other burners—Gossage, Lee Smith, Jeff Reardon, Ted Power, Niedenfuer—are coming out of the pen." Ted Power, it should be noted, was moved into the Reds' starting rotation last summer—a move made by the Reds' manager, Pete Rose. "I mean, the top relievers are smokers, and most of the starters are the other way," he went on. "More and more, the starters in this league pitch backward—2–0 breaking balls and changeups, and 0–2 fastballs. They don't give in to you. It's a good way to pitch, if you can do it, because you can win that way."

Steve Garvey, the first-base perennial—he is thirty-eight years old and is now in his nineteenth season in the majors—agreed with Pete Rose right down the line, and said as well that the advent of the new split-finger fastball (which we will examine in more detail shortly) has brought a fresh dimension of difficulty for the batter. He thinks that the batter who tends to go with a pitch and rap it up the middle of the diamond—a hitter like his Padre teammate Tony Gwynn, for example—will have more success against the new pitch than someone who likes to pull the ball. Garvey told me that the swift arrival of very talented relievers in a game also adds to the batter's burdens. "The second guy to pitch now is as good as a fifth starter," he said, "and that's pretty decent." The man up at bat gets to see three and maybe four pitchers pitch in the same game, he noted, each with a different style and size and delivery point, and batting averages in both leagues are drooping as a result. Garvey feels that the old respectable, upper-level .280-to-.295 hitter is being forced down into mediocrity merely by much better pitchers and tougher pitches.

"Basically, we're all fastball hitters," Garvey said. "If we couldn't hit the fastball, we wouldn't be here. But if you have to look at breaking balls all the time you're only as good as your ability to adjust. It's a whole different game. When I came up, there was more of that pure challenge from the starting pitchers. Seaver threw hard, Jerry Koosman threw hard. Bob Gibson threw, I mean, *hard*. Fergie Jenkins threw hard and had that good slider away. Jerry Reuss and Steve Carlton threw hard when they were together on the Cardinals in the seventies. So did Candelaria, when he came along, and that same Pirates team had Terry Forster and Goose Gossage coming out of the bullpen. Hard throwers. The 2–0 breaking ball used to be a special trait of the American League, because they had smaller ballparks and it's harder to hit the breaking ball out. But now, because of free agency, the National League has a lot of American League pitchers in it, and even with our bigger ballparks the whole pitching staff is saying, 'Why don't we do it that way, too, instead of being the hardball league?' It's tougher on hitters every day."

Joe Rudi told me that when he first came up the slider was a relatively new pitch and he had to deal with the new masters of the genre, like Jim Lonborg. "Now it's this split-finger fastball," he said. "It seems like the pitchers are always getting ahead. The real change, to me, is that middle-innings relief specialist—the long man. You hear pitching coaches talking about your rookies, and they'll say, 'This guy is going to be a real good middle-innings pitcher.' That's something new. What it really means is you never get that fourth at-bat against a great pitcher. I used to have to face Jim Palmer in maybe three or four games a year, and the first two or three at-bats against him were tough, believe me. But the fourth time up I thought maybe I had a chance. Nowadays, that pitcher is out of the game by then and you're looking at a sinker-baller like Quisenberry or a Jay Howell throwing gas. That good last at-bat is gone.''

Doug DeCinces, the California third baseman, said he almost missed the old challenge of waiting for a guaranteed fastball (''sitting dead fastball,'' in baseballese) on a 3–1 count, but not if the pitcher was Goose Gossage. He said, ''You didn't want *that* every day, but Goose sure liked it. It was 'Here it is, what are you going to do about it?' You knew that before you stepped in there. But I wouldn't say that the hard throwers are all the same. I mean, they're not dumb. I remember when I was younger I was with the Orioles, and Nolan Ryan threw a no-hitter against us at Anaheim Stadium one day. He struck out Bobby Grich on a 3–2 changeup for the last out of the game. He made Bobby look so bad it was pathetic. I mean, everybody in the park knew that with a 3–2 count it had to be a fastball coming. Only it wasn't.''

There were echoes and variations on these themes everywhere. In Mesa, Herm Starrette, the Cubs' pitching coach (he has held the same post with the Braves, the Giants, the Phillies, and the Brewers), said, ''There's no doubt in my mind that pitchers are better than they used to be. They know more things.'' Starrette is kindly and gently pedagogic in manner; he wears outsized spectacles and reminds you a little of a small-town insurance man. ''I think a starting pitcher in the big leagues has to have three pitches he can get over the plate in any situation, and now the man who comes in and relieves him is just about as good,'' he went on. ''You don't follow a starter with a reliever who has the same kind of delivery. It's like dancing with somebody—if you shift to a partner with a different sense of rhythm, it takes a time around the floor to get used to it. It's not easy for the batter to pick up the change—from left-hander to right-hander, or a new release point of the pitcher's hand, or whatever—and by the time he does the game is about over. Then here comes Lee Smith, who's throwing ninety-per or better, and now he's got a slider to go with it, and that hard sinker, too. It's unfair. I think pitchers are the smartest people on the field. They've got to know every batter and understand every situation in the game. If a guy wins twenty games, he's real smart. If he doesn't—well, he's proved it: he's not so smart.'' He laughed.

◆ ◆ ◆

HOTDOG: NOTHING IS EASY IN BASEBALL, OF COURSE, EVEN FOR the pitchers. In Phoenix Stadium last spring, Bill Rigney and my teen-age son, John Henry, and I watched from behind home plate while Oakland's Joaquin Andujar worked in a little B-game against the Indians one day. It was about ten-thirty in the morning—a time of day when a ballgame feels like a special treat, like a children's birthday party—and the desert sunlight was putting a fresh-paint sheen on the empty rows of reserved-seat stands around us. Four or five scouts sat together on little metal chairs in a box-seat section down behind the screen, and now and then one of them would pick up a coffee container from between his feet and sip at it and put it down again. There were about thirty fans in the rest of the park, and the only unhappy folks in view may have been Andujar, out on the mound, and Rig, just to my right, who were equally unimpressed with the pitching just then. Andujar, a combustible 21–12 pitcher with the Cardinals the year before, had been acquired in a trade over the winter and was expected to add some zing to the lacklustre Oakland pitching corps. Rigney, a former manager of the Giants and the Twins and the Angels, is the chief baseball adviser to the Athletics, and now he exchanged a couple of sharp glances with me as Andujar kicked unhappily at the rubber and stared around at a couple of Cleveland base runners he had put aboard on a walk and then a single that was hit off an unimpressive 3–1 pitch. A white-haired, mahogany-tan gent with a cigar came along the aisle and sat down behind us and put his arms up on the back of our row of seats. "You see it, don't you, Rig?" he said instantly in a deep, mahogany-colored voice. "The whole key to Joaquin is that front knee. If he don't pick it up in his motion and bring it right up 'long-side the back leg, it opens him up too soon. There—he just did it again. He throws three-quarters that way, and when he's three-quarters the goddam ball gets up, and his slider just goes *shh-shh-shh*. When he gets tired, he does that all the time, and his sidearm is horseshit. He's got to tuck in that front knee—just that much more gives him time to get up on top of the ball. . . . Like *that*—he did it that time."

Our new companion was Hub Kittle, a legendary erstwhile pitching coach with the Cardinals. Now seventy, he had become a travelling instructor in the Cards' farm system and a part-time scout. He was dressed in several eye-shattering shades of Cardinals red, with a thong tie and a turquoise tie clasp. Rig introduced us, and Kittle buried my hand in his, but his eyes stayed on the field.

"Oops—there's that little forker I taught him," he said. "But that forearm has got to come down, *down* onto his goddam knee. He's so quick you don't see where he's going wrong." He curled his right hand into a spyglass and peered through it with one eye. "Close out the batter, close out the hitter and the ump, and then you can see him," he muttered. "I had him at Houston and down in the Dominican for five years, and I know you got to stay on his goddam ass. 'O.K., now,' you say to him. 'O.K. ¡Bien! ¡Arriba! ¡Bueno!' You keep on his case so the *brujo* don't get him—the witch doctor. He gets in those spells out there."

Andujar gave up a little single, which scored a run, and then the home-plate ump—the woman umpire Pam Postema—called a balk when he tried to pick off the runner at first.

"Oh-oh," Kittle said. "Now he's pissed. See him stompin' around out there. He's talking to himself again." Kittle half rose and shouted something in Spanish to Andujar. "Go full circle!" he roared. "Keep the ball down, *hombre*!"

Joaquin, struck dumb, stared around the stadium in confusion—I think for a moment he looked straight up at the sky. Then he spotted Kittle and waved his glove. The next two pitches were good breaking balls, and then he struck out the batter with a fastball to end the half inning.

"There," said Kittle. "That's the *pistola*. He's still got it."

"I think you should have been part of the deal," Rig said. "This man"—he grabbed Kittle by the knee—"this man and I played together on the Spokane Hawks in 1938," he went on, to John Henry and me. "He was a pitcher, and I was a kid shortstop. That was a B League, and it was my first professional team. Wes Schulmerich was finishing up his career there." He shook his head. "Nineteen thirty-eight . . ."

◆ ◆ ◆

THE SPLIT-FINGER FASTBALL IS BASEBALL'S RUBIK'S CUBE of the eighties—a gimmick, a supertoy, a conversation piece, and a source of sudden fame and success for its inventor. It is thrown at various speeds and with a slightly varying grip on the ball, but in its classic mode it looks like a middling-good fastball that suddenly changes its mind and ducks under the batter's swing just as it crosses the plate. The pitch isn't exactly new—nothing in baseball is exactly new. A progenitor, the forkball, was grasped in much the same fashion, between the pitcher's forefinger and middle finger, but tucked more deeply into the hand, which took off spin and speed—a "slip-pitch," in the parlance.

Elroy Face, a reliever with the Pirates, was its great practitioner in the nineteen-fifties and sixties, and he put together an amazing 18–1 won-and-lost record (all in relief) with it in 1959. Bruce Sutter—like Face, a right-handed relief specialist—came along with the first so-called split-finger fastball a decade ago while with the Cubs, and has employed it (and very little else by way of repertoire) to run up a lifetime National League record of two hundred and eighty-six saves, with a Cy Young Award in 1979; he later moved along to the Cardinals and is now with the Braves and in temporary eclipse, owing to a sore arm. The Sutter pitch seemed not only unhittable but patented, for no one else in the game has quite been able to match his way of combining the forkball grip with a mid-delivery upward thrust of the thumb from beneath, which imparted a deadly little diving motion to the ball in flight. Here matters rested until 1984, when Roger Craig, a pitching coach with the Tigers, imparted his own variant of the s.-f. fb. to several members of the Detroit mound staff, with instant effect. Craig went into retirement after that season (he has since unretired, of course, and manages the Giants), but he is an affable and enthusiastic gent, who loves to talk and teach pitching. He is tall and pink-cheeked, with a noble schnoz; as most fans know, he has endured every variety of fortune on the mound. Callers at his home near San Diego that first winter of retirement included a good many opportunistic pitchers and pitching coaches from both leagues who were anxious to get their hands on the dingus. Most prominent among them—now, not then—was Mike Scott, a large but as yet unimpressive pitcher with the Houston Astros (the Mets had traded him away after 1982, at a time when his lifetime record stood at 14–27); he spent a week with Craig and came home armed with Excalibur. With the new pitch, he went 18–8 in 1985 and 18–10 last year, when he won a Cy Young Award after leading the majors with three hundred and six strikeouts and a 2.22 earned-run average. He capped his regular-season work with a no-hitter against the Giants, clinching the Astros' divisional pennant, and then zipped off sixteen consecutive scoreless innings while winning his two starts in the championship series against the Mets, to whom he surrendered but one run over all. Indeed, the other great "what if" of this past winter (along with second-guessing the way the Red Sox played the tenth inning of Game Six in the World Series) is the speculation about the Mets' fate in the playoffs if they had been forced to face Scott for a third time, in a seventh and deciding game.

"The split-finger is mostly a changeup," Keith Hernandez told me in St. Petersburg. "It can be thrown in different ways, so you can say it's really a three-speed changeup, with the fork-ball action as the other half of it. Scott can make it run in or out, but when he throws it inside to me he throws it *hard*. It has so much velocity on it that it's a real fastball for him, plus it goes down. It just drops off the table. Sutter's was the best until this one, but Scott has perfected it. He has tremendous command over the pitch—he never makes a mistake." (Mike Scott, it should be added, might not agree with this generous appraisal, for Hernandez hits him better than anyone else in the league: .377 lifetime, according to the *Elias Baseball Analyst*.)

Roger Craig told me that both Scott and Morris throw the split-finger at eighty-five miles an hour or better—faster than anyone else, although Scott Garrelts, a fireballing reliever on Craig's Giants, is now approaching that level. "Jack has his fingers up higher on the ball than Mike does," Craig said. "Mike's got the ball as far out in his hand as you can get it. He throws it about sixty or seventy percent of the time now, and there was a stretch at the end of last year when he was just unhittable. The pitch was a phantom—you'd swing and it wasn't there." (A good many batters in the National League are convinced that Mike Scott also imparts another sort of witchcraft to the baseball, by scuffing it in some secret fashion, in contravention of the rules. Steve Garvey told me that retrieved balls Scott has thrown often show a patch of lightly cut concentric circles on one of the white sectors—something that might be done with an artificially roughened part of his glove or palm. Garvey made a little sidewise gesture with his hand. "That's all it moves," he said, smiling. "It's enough.")

Craig—to get back into the sunshine here—said that the best thing about the split-finger is that it can be thrown at so many different speeds. "It depends on where you've got it in your fingers, on how you cock your wrist—on a whole lot of things," he said. "But the ultimate is when it comes out off the tips of your fingers—they just slip down along the ball on the outside of the seams—and the ball *tumbles*. That's the great one, because it's the opposite spin from the fastball. People keep telling me it isn't really a fastball, but I keep saying it is, because I want that pitcher to throw it with a fastball motion. Dan Petry, back with the Tigers, used to let up on it, because it was in the back of his mind that it was an off-speed pitch, but that's wrong. Here—gimme a ball, somebody."

We were sitting out on a bullpen bench in left field on a shining morning in Scottsdale—Craig and I and one of the Giants' beat writers. Craig has large, pale, supernally clean hands—Grandpa hands, if Grandpa is a dentist—and when he got a ball he curled his long forefinger and middle finger around it at the point where the red seams come closest together. ''I start with my fingers together like this, and I say 'fastball' . . . 'fastball' . . . 'fastball' ''—he waggled his wrist and fingers downward again and again—''but I have them go this way each time: just a bit wider apart. By the time you're out here''—the fingers were outside the seams now, on the white, slippery parts of the ball—''you're throwing the split-finger. There's a stage where it acts sort of like a knuckleball, but it'll come. You've started.''

Craig told us that he'd discovered the pitch back in 1982, while he was coaching fifteen- and sixteen-year-old boys in California. He takes great pleasure in the fact that several older or middle-level professionals have saved their careers with the pitch (Milt Wilcox, a righty with the Tigers, was one), and that subvarsity high-school and college pitchers have made the team with it. Superior pitchers sometimes resist it, by contrast. ''Jack Morris thinks he's the greatest pitcher who ever lived,'' Craig said. ''He has that great confidence. He insisted he didn't need it, even though he was getting killed with his changeup. So I said, 'Do me a favor. Pitch one game and don't throw a change—throw the split-finger instead.' He did it, and it was a two-hitter against the Orioles.''

When Craig arrived at Candlestick Park in September of 1985, as the Giants' new manager, he took all the pitchers out of the bullpen on his second day and asked for a volunteer who had never essayed the split-finger. Mark Davis, a left-hander, came forward, and Craig sent the rest of the staff down to stand behind the catcher. ''Well, in about twenty, twenty-five pitches he was throwing it,'' Roger said, ''and all my other pitchers were thinkin', Well, if he can do it, *I* can do it. That way, I didn't have to go out and try to convince them one by one.'' Everybody on the Giants throws the pitch now, and one of Craig's starters, Mike Krukow, went 20–9 with it last year—his best year ever. Craig hasn't counted, but he believes that thirty or forty percent of the pitchers in the National League have the pitch by now, or are working on it. Five of the Dodgers' staff—Welch, Hershiser, Niedenfuer, Young, and Leary—employ the pitch, and the American League is beginning to catch up. Gene Mauch, the

Angels' pilot, told Craig this spring that all his pitchers would be working on it this year.

I suggested to Roger that he should have registered the split-finger, so that he could charge a royalty every time it's thrown in a game, and his face lit up. "*That* would be nice, wouldn't it?" he said. "Just kick back and stay home, and take on a few private pupils now and then. That would be all right! But I've stopped teaching it to other teams. About ten pitching coaches called me up last winter and asked if they could come out and pick it up, but I said no. And there was this one general manager who called me up and said he'd send me and my wife to Hawaii, all expenses paid, if I'd take on his pitching coach and teach it to him. It's too late, though—I already showed it to too many guys. Dumb old me."

Not everybody, in truth, picks up the split-finger quickly or easily, and not all split-fingers are quite the same. Ron Darling, the Mets' young right-hander, mastered the delivery last summer, after a long struggle, and when he did, it became what he had needed all along—a finishing pitch, to make him a finished pitcher. (He was 15–6, with a 2.81 E.R.A., for the year, along with a hatful of strong no-decision outings.) He has never talked to Roger Craig, and, in fact, his split-finger started out as a forkball taught to him by pitching coach Al Jackson at the Mets' Tidewater farm club in 1983. But Darling, who has small hands, could never open his fingers enough to grasp the ball in the deep forkball grip, so it became a split-finger delivery instead. (Craig told me that some pitchers he knew had even gone to bed at night with a ball strapped between their fingers, in an attempt to widen their grip.) Darling had very little luck with the pitch at first, but kept at it because of Jack Morris's example—especially after Morris pitched a no-hitter against the White Sox at the beginning of the 1984 season.

"The whole idea about pitching—one of the basics of the art—is that you've got to show the batter a strike that isn't a strike," Darling said. "More than half—much more than half—of all the split-fingers that guys throw are balls. They drop right out of the strike zone. That's a problem, because you might have a great split-finger that moves a lot, and the batter is going to lay off it if he sees any kind of funny spin. So you have to throw it for a nice strike now and then. Hitters adjust, you know. Most of the time, you're going to throw the pitch when you're ahead in the count. But sometimes I throw it when I'm behind, too. All you have to do is make it look like a fastball for at least half the distance. A lot of times last year, I'd try to get a strike with a fastball and *then* throw a split-finger strike. If it does get over— and this began to happen for me for the first time last year—it rocks the world, because then here comes another split-finger and the bottom drops out, but the guy still has to swing. He has no other choice. Nobody can afford not to swing at that pitch— unless he's Keith Hernandez. Umpires don't call third strikes on Keith.''

• ◆ •

K FOR KOUFAX: EACH YEAR, I NOTICE, ONE PARTICULAR OLD player's name pops up again and again in baseball conversations. I don't understand it. This year, it was Sandy Koufax. Roger Craig told me that he and Koufax were among the old Dodgers who had turned up at Vero Beach for a thirtieth reunion of the 1955 Brooklyn World Champions, and that Sandy immediately began asking him how to throw the new split-finger pitch. The next afternoon, he summoned Craig over to watch him working off a mound. ''Well, first of all, Sandy was throwing the fastball at around eighty-five miles an hour,'' Craig said. ''He was in great shape, as usual, and he just did it naturally—no effort at all. I couldn't get over it. He was working on the split-finger, of course, though, and already he had it down pretty good. You know how long *his* fingers are. Sandy was pretty excited, and after a while he told me he was going to unretire and get back into the game as a pitcher again. I said, 'Jesus Christ, man, you can't do *that*! You're fifty years old!' But I thought he really meant it for a while, and so did Buzzie Bavasi and some of the others who heard him. I guess somebody talked him out of it in the end, but I almost wish they hadn't. Wouldn't that've been something!''

At Winter Haven, Eddie Kasko, the Red Sox' director of scouting (and a former manager of the Bosox), was talking about Sandy, too. He had a couple of friends from Massachusetts in tow—fans down to watch the Sox in training—and at one point he told us about a day back in the early nineteen-sixties, when he was an infielder with the Reds, and he and Whitey Lockman and Ed Bailey were sitting together on the bench, watching Koufax in action for the visiting Dodgers.

''Sandy is just chewing us up out there, putting down the batters in rows with that tremendous fastball,'' Kasko said, ''but Ed Bailey keeps saying, 'Well, he don't look like nothing special to me. That pitch isn't much. I wish they'd give me just one crack at him.' Ed loved to pinch-hit, you know—he thought there wasn't anybody he couldn't hit. Well, a little later we're way behind in the game, and Hutch sends Bailey up to bat against Sandy, and it's one, two, three strikes, you're out. Eddie swings three times and doesn't come within a foot of the ball. He walks back to the dugout and sits down, and after a while I give Whitey a little nudge and I say, 'Well, Ed, what do you think now?' And Bailey turns around, all red in the face, and says, 'He's *too straight*!' Whitey says, 'Yes—and so is a .30-.30.' ''

◆ ◆ ◆

BOTH LEAGUES RANG UP STRIKEOUT RECORDS LAST YEAR—a phenomenon attributable at least in part to the split-finger—and what one makes of this depends on whether one thinks like a batter or like a pitcher. Roger Craig smiled when I asked him about it and said, "I can't call it bad." Hernandez said, "What I'm concerned with is that the sixties brought us the slider, and now here's the eighties and this pitch. What's going to happen in the nineteen-nineties? What's going to happen to us hitters? The slider was a much harder pitch to hit than the curveball, and in the end they had to change the strike zone in order to even things out a little. The only thing on our side now is that the hanging split-finger is a great pitch to hit. It's just sitting up there on a tee for you."

The change that Hernandez alluded to—a historic proceeding in baseball, which has rarely altered its essential rules and ancient dimensions—came just after the season of 1968, when the two leagues showed a combined batting average of .236. Carl Yastrzemski won the A.L. batting title with an average of .301 that year, and in the same summer a rookie pitcher—the Mets' Jerry Koosman—accounted for seven shutouts, Bob Gibson achieved an earned-run average of 1.12 (a modern record), and Gaylord Perry and Ray Washburn threw no-hitters on consecutive days in the same ballpark. The batters were dying. The remedy, put into effect the following year, was to cut down the strike zone by a couple of inches, top and bottom, and to shave the pitching mounds from fifteen inches to ten inches above field level. Offensive statistics picked up almost at once (National League hitters batted .253 last year, and those in the A.L. .262), but many contemporary hitters believe that their eventual return to form was mostly because the batters began to recognize the slider a little sooner and to attack it with more success. I have also heard them say that the same thing will happen after they've seen the split-finger pitch more often. They may be whistling in the dark. For one thing, most pitchers who have mastered Craig's Little Jiffy say that they don't know exactly where the pitch is going to end up once it has been launched; in this respect, at least, it resembles the knuckleball to some degree. We'll see.

I asked Marty Barrett (of the Red Sox) and then Wally Backman (of the Mets) how many split-finger pitches each of them sees, and what they told me suggests that the pitch is much less employed, or less trusted, in the A.L. Both Barrett and Backman are bantam-size contact hitters (well, Barrett has a bit of power: he hit thirty-nine doubles last year) who bat second in power-laden lineups, which means that pitchers tend to work them with extreme care. Barrett told me that he didn't run into many split-finger pitches, perhaps because the pitchers were afraid that they'd get behind in the count and end up walking him. "I think the pitch is for bigger guys, who aren't as selective and will probably go to swinging at pitches that end up being balls," he said. "I get more fastballs. If Jim Rice got the pitches I get, he'd hit seventy home runs."

I told Backman what Marty had said, and he was surprised. He said he saw the pitch often. To be sure, if the leadoff man got on base just ahead of him he wouldn't be served many breaking balls, but whenever the Mets were behind late in a game the whole lineup would probably see the split-finger. "A lot of times, the split-finger is a ball," he said, "but even if you know that, it's hard to lay off it sometimes. I just think there are more guys in our league who are throwing the thing."

A further ingredient in the shifting batter-vs.-pitcher wars is the indisputable evidence that in the past four or five years, the umpires in both leagues have responded to the breaking-ball and sinkerball epidemic by lowering the strike zone. There was no plan to this; it just happened. The high fastball—the old Koufax or Seaver hummer that crossed the plate at the level of the batter's armpits, which is still the official ceiling of the strike zone—would probably be called a ball today, and umps today are also calling a lot of strikes on pitches that cross below the knee-level demarcation. Contemporary umpires are handing out quick warnings on brushback or knockdown pitches as well, and as a result the batters feel free to take a better toehold up at the plate and swing hard at low pitches away—"diving at the ball," in the new jargon. As I mentioned in a previous chapter, Don

Drysdale, the old Los Angeles intimidator, has said that modern-day batters are less wary when up at bat, and he and some other thoughtful baseball people warn that one of these days somebody is going to get beaned by an inadvertent high, inside pitch. On the other hand, it is the lower strike zone that also makes the batters so vulnerable to the split-finger's skulking little ways, because so few of them will trust the umpire to call a ball on a pitch that ends up below the strike zone.

To return to the slider, there is very little agreement about its origins but unanimity about the fact that it is easy to throw and hard to hit. Bill Rigney says that it caught on in the National League in the early fifties, after Don Newcombe's sudden flowering with the Dodgers. "Erskine and Branca had those big old wide-breaking curveballs, but then suddenly here was Newk with his hard pitch," he told me. "It only broke about *this* much, but it was a bear. It just took over the league. It was easier to control than a curveball—you could throw it for strikes—and the batters hated it. I remember riding in the team bus before the 1948 All-Star Game, and Ted Williams was asking us, 'What's this new thing over in your league—this slider?' Well, he found out about it, too. A lot of batters used to put it down, you know—they called it a nickel curve—but they still couldn't hit it."

The slider is admired but mistrusted, for the evidence seems clear that it can destroy a pitcher's arm. The Dodgers discourage its instruction in their minor-league clubs, and a great many baseball people think it can permanently damage kid pitchers who begin to fool with it at the Little League and Pony League levels. "I like the slider," Herm Starrette told me, "but I'd teach it last to a young pitcher, if at all. It's a great pitch to throw when you're behind in the count and want to throw some kind of breaking ball. But it will hurt your arm unless it's thrown properly. I teach the loose-wrist slider—the Steve Carlton pitch. It has a shorter, quicker break, and it moves downward. The stiff-wrist slider is what you call the cut fastball. It's a flat slider."

Pitchers say that the standard slider is thrown overhand, with the forefinger and the middle finger slightly off center on the ball, and that the proper wrist action gives the ball the same spiral imparted to a passed football. The fingers are off center on the cut fastball, too, but the pitch, launched with a full fastball motion, results in a brusque, twisting action of the elbow and forearm that shortens the delivery—and, in time, a career.

"Right-handed pitchers can do better with the cut fastball

against a left-handed hitter than against a right-handed hitter, because for the right-handed hitter the ball comes in on the same plane as the fastball, and you have a chance to get more wood on it,'' Starrette went on. "But if your slider breaks across and *down* to a right-handed batter, you've got a chance he'll miss it or bump the ball on the top half for a ground-ball out. If you're a right-hander facing a left-handed batter . . . well, most left-handed batters are low-ball hitters, so if you throw the stiff-wrist slider—that cut fastball—up and in, you can get by with it, because it's on the small part of the bat, in on the fists. And that's why pitchers go back to it, even if it's dangerous for them. Anything that works will be used, you know.''

The slow or sudden ruin of an arm and a livelihood is on every pitcher's mind, and examples of crippled careers are to be found on all sides, although fans and pitchers alike prefer not to notice them. Steve Garvey believes that the near-epidemic of torn rotator cuffs (it is the section of muscle that encircles the arm in the same fashion, and at approximately the same site, as the seam that attaches a shirt-sleeve to a shirt) arises from pitchers' trying to throw too many different deliveries, and from overthrowing in crucial game situations. "You see a lot of guys who used to throw hard who have lost a few miles an hour on their fastball after a couple of years,'' he said. "Then they go to other stuff, to compensate, and they get into trouble. Stress comes into it more than it used to, because there's so much more money to be made in the game. The desire to win in important situations has gone way up.''

Craig, for his part, claims that his split-finger special will be kinder to pitchers in the end, for it is thrown with a full, easy fastball motion. "Hell, you can hurt your arm throwin' a pebble or a rock, or flyin' a damn kite,'' he said at one point, "but there's less chance of it this way.'' Other coaches and managers (Sparky Anderson is among them) are dubious, and say that we'll have to wait and see about the long-range effects of the split-finger. One pitcher showed me that if you repeatedly split your throwing fingers apart you will feel a twinge in your upper forearm, and said that he does exercises to compensate. *Any* overhand pitching motion is probably unnatural, for that matter. Joe Rudi believes that the spitball (still illegal, and still in the game, of course, because it works so well) is the most dangerous delivery of all. "You're gripping the ball off the seams, which is to say your fingertips have very little resistance, nothing to pull down against,'' he said. "When that part of the ball is wet, the ball suddenly comes flying out of there, and there's nothing left—no resistance at all. Your arm accelerates exactly at the point when it's begun to decelerate, and that's a great way to blow it out for good. It's like when you go to pick up a bag of groceries, only there's nothing in the bag. You go *oops*—and you've thrown out your back. I don't let the outfielders on my team throw the ball any kind of a funny way, even when they're fooling around in practice. A lot of young players have no idea how vulnerable the arm really is. It's a delicate mechanism.''

In 1980, by the way, a wonderful young Oakland pitching staff, featuring Mike Norris, Rick Langford, Matt Keough, Brian Kingman, and Steve McCatty, led the American League in complete games (by a mile) and earned-run average, but after three years all but McCatty were gone, with their careers in tatters. One popular theory for the debacle was that Billy Martin and his pitching coach, Art Fowler, allowed the youngsters to stay too long in too many games (the A's had almost nothing in the way of a bullpen), but another theory claimed, or whispered, that Fowler had taught the kids the spitball. It's hard to be sure.

◆ ◆ ◆

SCROOGIE: THE FIRST SCREWBALL PITCHER I EVER SAW WAS CARL Hubbell, the great—the word fits here—Giants left-hander of the nineteen-thirties, who, along with Joe DiMaggio, became my earliest baseball hero. I recall the thrilling moment at the Polo Grounds when my father pointed out to me that Hubbell's left arm turned the wrong way around when it was at rest—with the palm facing out, that is—as a result of his throwing the screwball so often and so well. (The ball is delivered with the hand and wrist rotating in an unnatural direction—to the right for a left-hander, to the left for a right-hander—and the pitch breaks wrong, too. It's what pitchers call ''turning it over.'') I couldn't get over Hubbell's hand; it was like meeting a gladiator who bore scars inflicted at the Colosseum. Since then, I have talked with Hubbell a few times—he's a thin, stooped elderly gent who lives in Mesa, Arizona—and whenever I do I can't help stealing a glance at his left hand: it still faces the wrong way. The prime screwballer of our time is Fernando Valenzuela, of the Dodgers. His pitching arm looks perfectly normal so far, I'm sorry to say.

Last summer, I ran into Warren Spahn, the old Boston Hall of Famer, in the visiting-team dugout at Fenway Park. He was there for an Old Timers' Game—he's a regular at these events—

and he was wearing an old Braves uniform, with that tomahawk across the chest; he played twenty years for the Braves, eight of them in Boston ("Spahn and Sain and pray for rain") and the rest in Milwaukee, and his lifetime three hundred and sixty-three victories are still the most compiled by any left-hander. Spahn, a leathery, wiry, infallibly cheerful man, was sitting with some of the Texas Rangers (they would play the Bosox that afternoon, once the exhibition innings were over), and in no time he had begun teaching his famous sinker-screwball delivery to another left-hander—the veteran Mickey Mahler, who was trying to stick with the Rangers as a middle-innings relief man.

"Look, it's easy," Spahnie said. "You just do this." His left thumb and forefinger were making a circle, with the three other fingers pointing up, exactly as if he were flashing the "O.K." sign to someone nearby. The ball was tucked comfortably up against the circle, without being held by it, and the other fingers stayed up and apart, keeping only a loose grip on the pill. Thrown that way, he said, the ball departed naturally off the inside, or little-finger side, of the middle finger, and would then sink and break to the left as it crossed the plate. "There's nothing to it," he said optimistically. "Just let her go, and remember to keep your hand up so it stays inside your elbow. Throw it like that, and you turn it over naturally—a nice, easy movement, and the arm follows through on the same track." He made the motion a few times, still sitting down, and it certainly *looked* easy—easy but impossible.

Spahn went off to join some other uniformed geezers, and I asked Mahler if he intended to work on the pitch, now that he'd had it from the Master.

"Oh, I don't think so," he said. "I'm trying to learn the screwball from our pitching coach, and this would mess me up for sure." He seemed uncomfortable, and after a couple of minutes he told me that a little earlier he and Spahn had been standing near the stands and some kids there had asked him, Mickey Mahler, for his autograph. "They asked me—not Warren Spahn," he said. "Can you *believe* that?" He was embarrassed.

◆ ◆ ◆

I DON'T LIKE TO SEE YOUNG PITCHERS GET THEIR HEARTS BROken in spring-training games, but it's much worse when it happens to somebody you know and remember and care about—to a veteran, I mean. In Winter Haven, the starting pitcher for the

Tigers one afternoon was Frank Tanana, a thirty-three-year-old lefty with fourteen years' service in the majors. Like many fans, I remembered him as a slender, dazzling left-hander when he first came up with the Angels. He led the league then with two hundred and sixty-nine strikeouts in 1975, and went 19–10 the next year, and the year after *that* his 2.54 earned-run average was the best in the league. (A scout told me once that as a teen-ager Tanana had played in a high-school league in and around his native Detroit, where two strikes on a batter retired him and three balls meant a walk. "Nobody touched him there—it was just a mismatch," the scout said. "Everybody got home for supper early that spring.") But Tanana went down with a rotator injury in 1979 (his pitching motion was across the body—a dangerous habit for a fastballer), and he was a different sort of pitcher after that. He lost eighteen games for the Rangers in 1982, but then he began to do better. He is smart, and he knows the corners, and he has become a master at changing speeds. Over the last four years, he won forty-six games and lost forty-seven while toiling for the Rangers and then the Tigers, but there was more arm trouble last year. Against the Red Sox, in his outing at Winter Haven, he gave up ten runs on eleven hits, and couldn't quite get the last out in the third inning. When he left, he raised his cap to the Boston fans just before he disappeared into the dugout, and got a nice little hand in return. I hated it.

The Sox' opponents the next afternoon were the Montreal Expos, a team that has systematically stripped itself of most of its expensive stars and is engaged in filling out its roster with youngsters and retreads. Len Barker threw three pretty fair middle innings for the visitors, giving up a lone run on three hits, but I felt edgy the whole time he was out there. A hulking, six-foot-four flinger with blazing speed, Barker had a brief time in the sun with the Indians at the beginning of this decade, when he led the American League in strikeouts two years running. Early in the 1981 season, in a game against the Blue Jays, he achieved the ultimate rarity, a perfect game: no hits, no walks, no runs, nobody on base. His occupational injuries began in 1983, and ultimately required extensive surgery on the elbow of his pitching arm, and he never had a successful or pain-free season after that. He moved along to Atlanta in time, and spent all of last summer with Indianapolis, a Class AAA minor-league team, but his most common address was the disabled list. He didn't make the team this year, it turned out; the Expos gave him his release just before the season started, and his career may

be at an end at last. Another rotator-cuff casualty, Bruce Berenyi, gave it a last try this spring with the Expos, but the pain
was too much, and he announced his retirement a few days after
camp opened; he had been with the Mets and, before that, the
Reds, but he never returned to form after shoulder surgery two
years ago. He was a hard thrower, too. Bob McClure, a left-
handed ten-year man who has worked mostly out of the bullpen,
hung on and made the Expos' opening-day roster—an exception
in this unhappy litany, for he has made do in the majors ever
since his rotator-cuff trauma in 1981. His spring wasn't exactly
carefree, however: just before the regular season began, he gave
up nine runs to the Yankees in two-thirds of an inning of work,
during a grisly 23–7 blowout at Fort Lauderdale.

Earlier, when I was out in Arizona, the Athletics had announced that Moose Haas, a prime starter for them last year
until he was side-lined by bursitis, was suffering from a pulled
muscle in the rotator cuff of his pitching shoulder and would be
unable to start the season. And then, a bare day or two before
the season began, Pete Vuckovich announced his retirement
from baseball, thus terminating a distinguished eleven-year career that included a Cy Young Award in 1982, when he put
together an 18–6 season for the Brewers, which helped take them
into the playoffs and the World Series that fall. A torn rotator
cuff got him the following spring. I was in the Brewers' camp
at Sun City the day it was announced, and I well remember the
waves of dismay that went through the clubhouse that afternoon—dismay but perhaps not surprise, for it was known that
Vukey had pitched in great pain during the final stages of the
pennant race the year before. In late September, two days after
receiving a cortisone shot in his shoulder, he somehow went
eleven full innings against the Red Sox, throwing a hundred and
seventy-three pitches, and won the game. (I reported on this
unhappy business at the time.) Vuckovich underwent extensive
shoulder surgery early in 1984 and sat out the entire season. He
was never sound again, but he just wouldn't give up. As scarcely
needs saying, he is a man of enormous determination, pride,
and stubbornness. The Brewers demoted him a year ago, but he
refused to report to the minors; then he changed his mind and
went to Vancouver after all, when he threw well enough (a 1.26
E.R.A. in six games) to be invited back to the Brewers again in
September. Now it's over for him.

Vuckovich and Haas and McClure were on the same Brewer
pitching staff in the early eighties, and so was Jim Slaton, who

also suffered a rotator-cuff injury but eventually recovered. So was Rollie Fingers, the slim, flamboyant relief pitcher who won his Cy Young in 1981 but could not pitch for the team in the playoffs or the World Series in 1982, because of an injury to his forearm that forced his retirement three sad seasons later. And so on. I don't think we should draw any particular conclusions about the Milwaukee club of that time, beyond its famous combativeness and pride, but the point I am getting at here is that all the pitchers just mentioned, with the exception of Berenyi, came up in, and mostly pitched on, American League clubs. To go back a bit, we should also remind ourselves that the 1980 Cy Young Award winner in the American League—Steve Stone, who won twenty-five games and lost seven for the Orioles—was forced into retirement by elbow miseries after but one more summer's work. When three successive Cy Young winners in the same league—Stone, Fingers, and Vuckovich—together arrive at a point when none of them is able to throw a pitch in combat, the award suddenly begins to take on the meaning of a Purple Heart.

Tony Kubek, the NBC baseball commentator, often points out that the designated-hitter artifice, which was adopted by the league in 1973, allows a manager to stay with his starting pitcher for as long as he seems to be pitching effectively, even though his team may be behind in the game, and, furthermore, that A.L. pitchers have to make a larger number of high-level, high-strain pitches per game, because they are facing an additional dangerous bat in the lineup in the person of the designated hitter. Kubek remembers asking Catfish Hunter about the D.H. rule when it was first enacted (Hunter pitched in the A.L. exclusively), and the Cat said, "Well, it's going to make me a lot more money, and it's going to shorten my career by about two years"—a dazzling prognostication, it turned out, for Hunter's number of games won, complete games, and innings pitched suddenly rose after 1973 (he led the league in all three categories in 1975) and then almost as quickly dwindled, when arm miseries overtook him. By 1979, he was down to 2–9 with the Yankees, and by the next year he was gone, at the age of thirty-three.

Steve Garvey, another thoughtful mikado of the pastime, is also convinced that the designated-hitter rule has been a stroke of very bad fortune for the A.L. pitchers. "Because there's no pinch-hitter, the good starting pitchers stay in the game longer and run into more of those stressful late-inning situations—a men-on-base, close-game crisis, where they'll be throwing that much harder just when their arms are getting tired and are most vulnerable,'' he said. ''There are very few easy batters in big-league lineups now, and in the American League, of course, the pitcher never gets to pitch to the other pitcher. There's no rest for him, I mean. Count up the good American League starters we've lost these past few years and see. It's not a situation you want to think about.''

Perhaps we should think about David Bush instead. Last year, in the midst of spring training in Arizona, David felt some minor and then not so minor twinges of pain in his right shoulder, and finally consulted Mark Letendre, the Giants' new trainer, who had just ascended to the post. Letendre poked and pulled and then diagnosed a mild rotator-cuff injury (''My first rotator cuff!'' he exclaimed to Bush), and suggested anti-inflammatory drugs and rest. Bush, who is a veteran baseball-beat writer with the San Francisco *Chronicle*, refused to baby himself, and did not miss a single deadline (''I'll play through pain,'' he said stoutly), and there is some hope that he may have made a complete recovery. When I inquired about the possible source of the injury, David finally confessed that it might have happened when he heaved his wife's clothesbag up on his shoulder the morning she was flying back to the Bay after a conjugal visit to Scottsdale. Lesly Bush, a stylish lady, does not travel light.

◆ ◆ ◆

THE HOOK: NEW FANS ALWAYS WANT TO KNOW WHAT THE MANager is saying to his pitcher when he goes to the mound to take him out of a game. The answer is: Nothing much. There are four or five new baseball books out every week, it seems, and soon, I don't doubt, there will be an anthology of pre-shower epigrams. In Scottsdale, I saw a thin Athletics right-hander named Stan Kyles give up a walk and single in the fifth inning. Then he walked three batters in a row—walking himself to Tacoma, in effect. Eventually, manager Tony LaRussa showed mercy and got him out of there, and when the game was over I asked LaRussa what he'd said to Kyles. ''I said it looked like he'd run into a moving target today,'' Tony said.

Bill Rigney told me once that one day in his first summer as a major-league manager he went out to the mound in the Polo Grounds to yank a veteran Giants relief man named Windy McCall, who had got nobody at all out during his brief stint that

day. Rig said, "I walked out there and I said 'How are you?'
and McCall said 'Great. How the hell are *you*?' So I never asked
that question again."

◆ ◆ ◆

I TOOK A DRIVE ACROSS THE DESERT TO VISIT THE INDIANS IN
Tucson—in particular, to watch their two new genuine stars: Joe
Carter, who rapped twenty-nine home runs last year and led
both leagues with a hundred and twenty-one runs batted in; and
Cory Snyder, the phenom sophomore, who, by sudden consen-
sus, is said to have the best outfielder's arm in the majors. The
Indians are trying to deal with an unaccustomed emotion—
hope—and may make a real run at the leaders in the American
League East. The most hopeful Indian of them all, I found—by
far the most cheerful pitcher I talked to this spring—was Tom
Candiotti, a youthful-looking, almost anonymous twenty-nine-
year-old right-hander, who had been informed the day before by
Tribe manager Pat Corrales that he would be the team's opening-
day pitcher. A year ago, Candiotti was invited to Tucson for a
look-see by the Indians, in spite of his most ordinary seven-year
prior career, passed mostly in the bushy lower levels of the
Milwaukee organization. He had a scattered 6–6 record while
up with the Brewers, but had spent all of the previous, 1985
season in the minors; three years before that, he sat out an entire
season after undergoing elbow reconstruction. Cleveland wanted
to look at him because of some gaping vacancies on its own
pitching staff and because Candiotti had experienced some recent success while throwing a knuckleball in a winter league in
Puerto Rico. His early adventures with the flutterball in the
American League last summer were a bit scary—he was 3–6 by
mid-June—but he finished up with an admirable 16–12 record,
including seventeen complete games. Only scriptwriters fashion
turnabouts like that, but Candiotti's help had come from a more
reliable source—Phil Niekro, a forty-eight-year-old knuckleball
grand master (only four other men in baseball history were still
active players at his age), whom the Indians picked up on waiv-
ers when the Yankees released him just before the 1986 season
got under way. Niekro had won his three-hundredth game at the
end of the previous season, and he went 11–11 for the Tribe last
year, his twenty-third in the majors; Candiotti and everyone else
on the club gave him much of the credit for the younger man's
wonderful record as well.

"Knucksie is my guru," Candiotti told me. (Knucksie is Niekro: sorry.) "He coached me during every game and in between. Last year—early last year—I was trying to throw the knuckleball hard all the time. It was a nasty pitch but tough to control, so I was always in trouble—3-0, 2-1. He said, 'Listen, that's not the way to do it. First of all, you *want* the batter to swing at it. You don't want to go 3-2 all day. So take a little off it, make it look tempting to the batter as it comes up to the plate.' I did that, and after a while I began to get a little more movement on my slower knuckler. I haven't come close to mastering anything yet, the way he has, but I'm better."

The knuckleball looks particularly tempting if you are a lizard or a frog. It is thrown not off the knuckles but off the fingertips—off the fingernails, to be precise—which renders the ball spinless and willful. It meanders plateward in a leisurely, mothlike flight pattern, often darting prettily downward or off to one side as it nears the strike zone, which results in some late and awkward-looking flailings by the batter, sudden belly flops into the dust by the catcher, and, not uncommonly, a passed ball or a wild pitch. It is the inelegance of the thing that makes it so unpopular with most managers, I believe (some of them call it "the bug"), but some distinguished and wonderfully extended careers have been fashioned by wily Merlins such as Wilbur Wood, who had two twenty-four-victory seasons in the course of his seventeen-year tenure (mostly with the White Sox) in the nineteen-sixties and seventies; Charlie Hough, of the Rangers, now in his eighteenth year in the big time; and, of course, Hoyt Wilhelm, who went into the Hall of Fame after twenty-one years of knuckling, with a record—let's say "all-time" this once: with an all-time-record one thousand and seventy game appearances. The pitch, in short, is unthreatening to a pitcher's arm, and I have often wondered why it isn't practiced and admired more widely.

Candiotti, an agreeable fellow, told me that Niekro had emphasized that it was absolutely necessary for a knuckleballer to field his position well and to learn how to hold the runners close (Niekro's pickoff move is legendary), since the bug is unhurried in its flight and tends to spin weirdly when nubbed along the ground. "The pitch takes its time, you know," Tom said. I asked how much time, and he said that his knuckleball had been timed between forty-eight and seventy-one miles per hour last year. "Seventy-one is *slow*, you understand," he said. "You just can't believe how easy on your arm this pitch feels. Knucksie keeps telling me that I'll go through a lot of frustrating days with the knuckleball, and sometimes you'll get racked up. But the thing to do is stay with it."

Niekro pitched against the Giants that afternoon in beautiful little Hi Corbett Field, and tried his damnedest to stay with the pitch. It was a bright, windy afternoon (the knuckleball becomes even more flighty in a breeze, or else refuses to perform at all), and Phil gave up four runs, including a couple of walks and two doubles, in his three-inning outing. The pitch seemed to arrive at the plate in stages, at the approximate pace of a sightseeing bus.

Niekro, whom I found in the Indians' empty clubhouse after his stint, was not much cast down. "I haven't thrown a real knuckleball all this spring training," he said. "It's too dry here, and the wind keeps blowing. I can't sweat. Just can't get it right. If the knuckleball ain't there, I'm a mass of confusion. I can't defend myself with a fastball or a slider, like other pitchers. It seems like it takes me a little longer to find it each spring."

He sounded like a man who had been going through his pockets in search of a misplaced key or parking-lot stub, and it came to me that I had sometimes had this same impression when listening to Dan Quisenberry, the Kansas City sidearm sinkerballer, talk about *his* odd little money pitch. Niekro said that this feeling around for the perfect knuckleball—this sense of search—was a year-round thing with him. "You've got to sleep with it and think about it all the time. It's a twenty-four-hour pattern," he said. "The margin for error is so slight, and it can be such a little-bitty thing—your release point, the ballpark, your fingernails, the ball you've just gotten from the umpire. If anything is a fraction off, you might not have a thing out there." He crooked his fingers and waggled his wrist. "It's hunt and peck, all year long."

Niekro is lean and gray-haired, with an easy manner and a sleepy sort of smile. Watching him take off his spikes and his elastic sock supporters and the rest, and tuck his gear into his square-top travel bag (the club was going on a road trip the next day), I was reminded of an old-time travelling salesman repacking his sample case. Niekro is unhurried and precise in everything he does. I have never seen a neater ballplayer. Something else about him surprises you, too, but you can't quite figure it out at first: he is a grownup.

He told me that helping Candiotti had been a treat for him, because the young man had exactly the right makeup for the job. "He knows his limitations," he said. "He changes pitches better than I did when I was his age. I used to go: Bang—here's a knuckleball. Bang—here's another. He's really pitching: Go at one speed, go at another. Take a little off. Throw one knuckler to set up another one. But he's sort of like me, at that. I won my first game in the big leagues at the age of twenty-six, and he won his at the age of twenty-five. So he's right on track.''

Niekro's lifetime record is an herb garden of statistics—three twenty-game-or-better winning seasons, two years when he *lost* twenty games (he combined the two in 1979, when he won twenty-one games for the Braves and lost twenty), and a 17-4 record in the summer of his forty-fourth year: the best percentage in the league that season. He has thrown a no-hitter, he has struck out four batters in a single inning, and he has thrown four wild pitches in one inning and six in one game. Almost any day now, he and his brother Joe, who is a starting pitcher for the Yankees, will set another record when they surpass Gaylord and Jim Perry's lifetime total of five hundred and twenty-nine victories by pitcher brothers. Joe, who also throws the knuckler, is forty-two, and has won two hundred and fourteen games.

"I learned my knuckleball from my daddy," Phil said, "but Joe was a different kind of pitcher at first. He had a three-quarter mediocre curveball, a fastball, and a slider, and he was just getting by in the major leagues. I think he was on his way down when he said, 'Oh, hell—all right,' and he went into his back pocket and began throwing the knuckleball, too. It took him three or four years to make the transition, but once he got it he was as good a pitcher with the knuckleball for eight or nine years as there'd ever been in baseball.''

I asked Niekro if he was ever tempted to giggle when one of his pitches danced away from a batter for strike three.

"Oh, no—you can't do that," he said. "I won't ever laugh at him, but I'll laugh with him sometimes, if I see he's laughing over it. We'll have a little fun out there." He gave me a glance, and said, "You know, there's lots of guys can throw the damn knuckler for fun. It ain't all that hard to pick up. But here's a game: You're out on the mound, here's the strike zone, and there's a man standing there with a bat in his hand. It's a 3-2 count, there's a man on third base, or maybe the bases are loaded, and now you've got to throw the knuckleball over the plate on pitch after pitch after pitch—because he's sure as hell going to foul some of them off. You just go back to it and throw it for another strike, and that's not fun. That's a little different.''

Niekro got up and pulled off his sweatshirt. He is trim and

narrow, and his body doesn't show his years. He is famous for never doing conditioning sprints, never running at all, and when I mentioned this he smiled and said, "I've never run the ball across the plate yet." An old joke. "I stretch and I do just about ever'thing else," he said, "but I don't do weights. It's just that much more muscle to tighten up when you've finished for the day. Maybe those big boys can throw the ball harder, but when the game's over you see them iced down from their wrists to their hips. I never ice. Well, maybe I did about four times in my career, but I can't exactly remember the last time. Maybe I'm getting old."

◆ ◆ ◆

GRUMPY: SOME OF US WERE EATING OUR COLD-CUTS LUNCH off paper plates in the Cardinals' pressroom before a Cards–Blue Jays game in Al Lang Stadium, when I noticed that the small, snub-nosed man sitting next to me was Birdie Tebbetts, the old-time Tiger catcher; he also managed the Reds, the Braves, and the Indians. Tebbetts is seventy-four years old, and scouts for the Indians. He listened to our conversation about pitches and pitchers, and muttered, "Sometimes I watch one of these young pitchers we've got, and I tell my club, 'This man needs another pitch. By which I mean a strike.'"

◆ ◆ ◆

THERE IS A LOT TO THIS GAME. AS MY TRIP BEGAN TO RUN OUT, I realized how many aspects of pitching I hadn't gone into yet, or hadn't asked enough about—what it takes to break in as a major-league pitcher, and how great a part luck plays in the kind of pitching roster and the kind of club a rookie is headed for, for instance. Pete Rose said that it was often easier for a young-ster to make it up to the majors in the middle of a season, if the chance came, because his control would be better than it was in the spring. What about bum steers—poor advice from a pitching coach, or the wrong advice for that particular pitcher? Charlie Leibrandt, a first-rate left-hander with the Royals, told me that the Cincinnati coaches had insisted that he was a power pitcher, a fastballer, when he tried to catch on with the Reds some years ago, because they were a team that specialized in big hard throwers. He had four scattered, so-so seasons with the team, then went back down to the minors, and when he came back, with the Royals, it was as a breaking-ball, control sort of pitcher, and he felt at home at last. "I remember being on the mound at Riverfront Stadium and hearing the ball popping over the sidelines while the relief pitchers warmed up to come in for me," he said cheerfully. "I was about to be gone again, and somebody in the dugout would be yelling 'Throw strikes!' and I'd think, Oh, *strikes*—so *that's* what you want! Why didn't you say so?" I also wanted to talk with the Mets about how they bring along *their* young pitchers, because they seem to be so good at it. And someday I want to sit down with a first-class control pitcher and go over a video of a game he has just pitched, and make him tell me why he chose each pitch to each.batter, in every situation, and how it related to what patterns he had thrown before that.

The business of strength came up a lot in my conversations, I noticed—which pitchers lasted, and why, and whether young pitchers today were in better shape than their predecessors twenty or thirty years ago. Almost everybody said yes, they *were* in better shape today, and probably stronger, too. Aerobics and weight work and a much better understanding of nutrition came into that, of course, and so did plain genetics; ballplayers are all noticeably bigger and taller than they used to be—you can see it. But I heard some interesting opinions to the contrary.

Jim Kaat, the deep-chested left-hander who pitched twenty-five years in the majors (he is one of the few players at any position who have performed in the big leagues in four calendar decades), told me that he'd been wondering about the decline of the fastball pitchers—the burners—and about why so many pitchers of his generation, like Gaylord Perry, Nolan Ryan, and Phil Niekro, had lasted so long. "One of my theories is that we did a lot of work by hand when we were kids," he said. "Mowed the lawn, washed the car, shovelled snow, and walked. I used to walk everywhere." (Kaat grew up in Zeeland, Michigan, on the western edge of the Michigan peninsula.) "Now you see kids who haven't logged as many sandlot innings as I did, and when they come into baseball you don't know how big they're going to be. When I was eighteen, my body was developed."

Mel Stottlemyre, the old Yankee wizard who is now the pitching coach for the Mets, said, "There's no doubt that there are fewer good arms than there used to be. For one thing, a lot of young pitchers start throwing breaking balls when they're too young, and they don't develop their bodies the way they could have. That's going to take a toll. I think there's less plain throwing than there used to be—just throwing the ball back and forth with your neighbor or your brother. There are more things for kids to do now, so they end up not playing catch. You see kids in Little League who aren't strong enough to pitch at all, hardly, and there they are, throwing breaking balls. There's nothing I hate worse than to see a Little Leaguer with his arm in ice—but I've seen that a lot.'' (Mel Stottlemyre's twenty-one-year-old son Todd, by the way—or perhaps *not* by the way—is a pitcher with the Toronto organization; he is still a year or two away from the majors but is considered one of the great young prospects in the country.)

Other pitching people I talked to did not quite agree. Dave Duncan, the pitching coach for the Athletics, said, ''I'm sorry, but I just don't go along with that idea about the old days. Oh, young players and pitchers may have lost some of that sandlot toughness, but baseball is taught so much better now, with all that work on body strengthening and conditioning, that I think skill and muscular development are way ahead of what they were when I first came along.''

I put this question to Tex Hughson, the commanding old Red Sox righty of the nineteen-forties—he is seventy-one now, but still long and cowboy-lean; he used to raise quarter horses near San Marcos, Texas—and at first he went along with Duncan and that group. He was sure that young players at the college and minor-league levels were far stronger and better developed than they had been in his time. But then I mentioned what Jim Kaat had said—what I think of as the Walk-to-School Factor—and he did a turnabout. ''Why, that's so,'' he said cheerfully. ''Course it is. I walked to school every day—three miles on a gravel road in Kyle, Texas, throwin' rocks the whole way. Maybe I picked up some control that way, and developed my arm. Chunked at everything. But if it was bad weather my mother would drive us in our old Model A Ford.'' And I'd heard somewhere that Roger Clemens also walked three miles to school—it's always three miles, never two or three and a half—when he was a kid.

I didn't know what to think, but in time it came to me that, of course, it is mental toughness that matters most of all to a pitcher: nobody would disagree about that. I was strengthened in this conviction by a talk I had with Bob Ojeda, the left-hander picked up by the Mets in a trade with the Red Sox, who played such a sizable part in his team's triumphs last summer and last fall. Ojeda is midsize and tightly put together. His uniform fits him perfectly—not a rumple or a wrinkle on the man or his clothes. He looks dry-cleaned.

When I asked how he would describe himself, he said that he was a man who had to work at his work—think ahead of the hitters, concentrate on control, and come inside on the batters. This last can be a long lesson for lefties at Fenway Park, where Ojeda first came to full command, because of its horribly proximate left-field wall. He told me that he had talked to Roger Craig over the winter (not about the split-finger, for Ojeda already possessed a peerless changeup, which he throws by choking the ball back in his hand), and Craig had said to him at one point, "You're a *pitcher*."

"That meant a lot to me," Bobby O. said. "If I hadn't learned some things over the years, I wouldn't be here. When I say I'm a pitcher, I'm thinking of guys like Mike Flanagan and Scott McGregor, of the Orioles. I always tried to watch how they worked, how they set up the hitters. Or Steve Carlton, if he was on TV. I remembered how they pitched in certain situations, how they changed from what they'd done before, because of what the game situation was—man on first, men on first and second, and the rest. To me, it doesn't matter if you strike out ten guys in a game. But if you've got the bases loaded and nobody out, and then you get your first strikeout and then a ground ball, how big was that strikeout? That's the kind of stat players notice. Tommy John sometimes gives up six, seven, eight hits in a game, but only one run, and that is the number that counts."

I told Ojeda that his victory over the Astros in the second game of the playoffs had been the sort of game I enjoy most—a first-class ten-hitter—and he grinned. "That's right—it was," he said. "There are always days when every ground ball is going to find a hole. Days when you have to reach back a little. It all comes down to how many runs you give up. I look at the runs—not whether they're earned or not. You look in the paper, and if you've lost it'll say 'Larry Ojeda.' " ("Larry" for "loser," as in a line score or box score: "L: Ojeda.") "A run is a run, and you try to prevent those. There's *so* much strategy that goes into that. Each day is different. Each day, you're a different pitcher. Consistency is the thing, even if it's one of those scuffle days. When I've started, I've been very consistent, and that's something I'm proud of. I led the league in quality starts last year—you know, pitching into the seventh inning while giving up three runs or less. That means something to me."

He said that breaking into a new league, with unknown batters, hadn't been especially difficult for him. "I was as new to them as they were to me," he said. He doesn't believe in extended studies of the opposing team's batters before the game. "I see them up at bat—where they are in the box, how they stand—and it clicks into place: Oh, yeah—you're *that* one. It's the situation that matters more than the batter—there's always the situation. Maybe this particular batter doesn't like to pop people in—maybe he bats .300 but only has fifty runs batted in. Then, there are the guys who bat .260 unless there are men on base. Then they're much, much tougher up at the plate. Those are the guys I respect."

Like who, I asked, and Ojeda said, "I don't want to name them—I don't want to *think* about them—but I know who they are, and they know who they are. No, there really are some great, famous hitters that I don't mind seeing up at bat in certain situations, because I know those are the situations they don't like."

Ojeda relishes being on a World Champion team. "I can't get over what we did last fall," he said seriously. "When you grow up in this sport, all you hear is people talking about what they're going to do if they ever get into a World Series. But that's just talk—we went out and did it. I like the chance to do things. It's 'This *happened*,' and then there's no more talk. Back when I was a kid, I had those dreams of playing in a World Series someday, but so what? Every player in this clubhouse and every player in all the twenty-five other camps right now had those same dreams. But those other guys don't know how they'd do, and we know. To get there *and then win it*—that's the thing. Because who knows if you'll ever have another shot? If I'd still been with the Red Sox—If you'd gotten there and then you didn't win it, if you'd made some bad mistakes like some of their guys did—*major mistakes!*—and then you began to think you'd never get that chance back, because you'd never be there again . . . I don't think I could stand that."

◆ ◆ ◆

TWO DAYS AFTER THIS, I FOUND MYSELF IN THE VISITING-TEAM dugout at Al Lang Stadium, in St. Pete, where, surrounded by Pirates, I watched a steady downpour of rain and waited for the game to be called, as, indeed, it shortly was. I didn't care, I decided. My trip was almost over and I was feeling a little baseballed out, and I was pretty sure there wasn't much more about pitching that I could pick up on this particular afternoon. Sitting on the bench just to my left was Syd Thrift, the Pittsburgh general manager, and after a few moments' conversation we simultaneously recalled that we had both been at Ypsilanti, Michigan, for a college doubleheader on an afternoon in May, 1976, and had watched Bob Owchinko pitch the first game for Eastern Michigan University, and Bob Welch, then a college junior, pitch the second. I had gone there in the company of a scout named Ray Scarborough, whom I was preparing to write an article about, and Thrift, a friend of Scarborough's, was there scouting for the A's. "*That* was a day!" Thrift said now, for both Owchinko and Welch, of course, had later matriculated as long-term major-league pitchers.

Thrift and I chatted about the Pirates a little, and then (he had been holding a baseball in his hands and turning it slowly this way and that) he said, "How many times do you think a ball rotates between the time it leaves a pitcher's hand and the time it crosses the plate? A fastball, let's say."

I was startled, for Thrift could not have known that I had been thinking about pitches and pitchers all month.

"I have no idea," I said. "A lot, I guess. Fifty rotations?"

"That's what everybody thinks," Thrift said with relish. "Everybody is way too high. It turns over only fourteen to sixteen times in that space, which is amazing, because your eyes tell you something quite different. We had no notion until we did those measurements back at the academy in about 1970. We had cameras set up, and on a background screen we marked off the distance from the mound to the plate into four fifteen-foot segments, but even then we couldn't figure out those rotations until somebody came up with the idea of painting half the ball black. Then we could see it."

I remembered now that Syd Thrift had been the founding director of the Kansas City Royals' Baseball Academy, in Sarasota—a long-since-defunct institution where rookies could be trained in fundamentals, away from the pressure of making a particular team, and where the first time-motion studies of the sport were essayed. One of the academy's significant experiments had been to make a precise definition of the proper lead off first for a good base-stealer, and to take stopwatch measurements of the time it took for him to make it down to second, in comparison with the optimum elapsed time between a pitcher's release, the catcher's reception of the pitch, and his best peg down to second base. These conclusions correctly predicted the arrival into the game of the ninety-to-a-hundred-stolen-base specialists—the Rickey Henderson–Tim Raines fliers of the nineteen-eighties.

Thrift next asked me if I knew which pitch was quicker—the two-seam or the four-seam fastball. These are baseball definitions deriving from the appearance of the ball when it is held in different positions in the pitcher's hand; there is in fact only one stitched seam on a ball. With the two-seamer, the ball is held with the forefinger and middle finger together on top of a seam at the point where the tips of the fingers touch, at right angles, the narrowest alley of white on the ball. With the four-seamer, the fingers are held at a forty-five-degree angle off this position, with the fingers now up on the seam that forms the wider, horseshoe sector of white. Rotating the ball out from under the fingers will produce two spinning seams in the first mode and (amazing!) four in the other.

I told Syd that I'd been given conflicting answers to this question, but that I'd always somehow assumed that the two-seamer was the faster pitch, because it looked as if the ball would encounter less wind resistance that way.

"Well, it's the four-seamer," he said. "The four-seam fastball is approximately four miles an hour faster than the two-seam, when thrown by the same pitcher, and it's because of just the thing you mentioned. What happens—isn't this *interesting*—what happens is that those four seams set up a molecular mass underneath the ball that sustains it just a little in flight. There's less turbulence in flight, so it gets there sooner."

Thrift is a sizable man, with a buttery Virginia accent, and when he talks his big, intelligent face lights up with his fervor for his subject. "The second thing," he went on, "is that that same thrown pitch falls approximately twenty-one inches between the time it leaves the pitcher's hand and the time it crosses the plate. That's at eighty-five miles an hour, and it's with the four-seam pitch. The two-seam pitch falls twenty-four inches. That three-inch difference is about the width of a baseball. At first, I just didn't believe this, because a lot of the time the fastball just looks straight, doesn't it? But it's only straight laterally. It always falls."

He told me that he had once asked Ted Williams if he swung at all pitches the same, and Ted had said no—if the pitch was across the seams he'd swing at the middle of the ball, but if it was a two-seamer he'd swing at the bottom of the ball. If he hit two ground balls in a row against two-seam pitches, on the next time up he would swing at an imaginary ball just under the real one. "You can see that difference in pitches, you know," Thrift said to me. "If you're not too far back in the stands, you'll notice that the four-seamer looks a little smaller in flight, and the two-seamer looks more white as it's comin' in."

He said that whenever he receives a report about a new pitching prospect and his velocity, he always asks the scout how the kid was throwing the ball. "If he's doing eighty-eight on the gun and he's throwing two-seamers, we know we can get him up in the nineties with the four. Isn't that something? So many of the scouts say this boy is throwin' straight or this boy has a rising fastball, and I say there's no such thing. The rising fastball is an impossibility in physics."*

"But what about Sandy Koufax?" I said at once. "I saw that pitch again and again, and it *rose*. Everybody knew that."

"I saw it, too," Thrift said, "but it was an optical illusion. The batter was only swinging at where he thought the ball was going to end up—a batter has to make up his mind about a pitch in the first eight to fifteen feet after it leaves the pitcher's hand, you know. We measured *that*, too. But if that fastball of Sandy's was well up in the nineties it probably fell only seven inches instead of fourteen, so the batter would miss it by seven inches or more. No wonder it looked as if it was rising."

In Thrift's estimation, these findings are of more use to a batter than to a pitcher. He believes that the batters need all the

---

*This statement by Syd Thrift aroused extended retorts from various quarters, including the Jet Propulsion Laboratory at Cal Tech. A physicist there, Tom Yunck, reminded me in a letter that anyone who has thrown a wiffleball or a Ping-Pong ball with a sharp downward flip of the fingers (as I have) will see in an instant that a rising fastball is not an impossibility. A spinning ball (including sliders and curveballs and the rest) causes air to flow around it asymmetrically, and if the air over the top of a fastball is moving faster than the air beneath it as the result of backspin, lift will ensue—the same lift that causes an airliner (or a Sikorsky helicopter, Mr. Yunck adds) to rise. But no one is quite prepared to say that a major-league pitcher can throw the four-seamer with sufficient speed and backspin to make a five ounce-plus baseball move upward. Mr. Yunck admits this would be tough, but he believes that a few pitchers may be equal to the task; John Garver—he is cited just ahead—by contrast, very much doubts it. Incomplete investigations of his seem to suggest that a one-hundred-and-fifty-m.p.h. fastball would be required in order to achieve a perceptible rise, but he quickly adds that calculations of the necessary degree of spin are not at hand. I believe Syd Thrift meant to say that a rising fastball is an impossibility in physics *until we find a rookie pitcher who is fifty percent faster than anyone we've seen out there to date.* He is a famous optimist as well as a famous scout, and I don't think we should bet against him.

help they can get right now, and he thinks that baseball is badly in need of another research laboratory along the lines of the old academy. If so, it is clear that he should be invited back to be its Oppenheimer, its Wernher von Braun. Sitting with me in the damp little dugout, he went on at length about the researchers he had brought into the Baseball Academy to conduct those pioneering studies—a Youngstown, Ohio, inventor and physicist named John Garver, and a retired banker from Chicago named John Nash Ott, who had done pioneering studies on the effect of light on plants and animals. He told me that most baseball people had doubted and discarded their discoveries at first. Some years after the academy closed down, he recalled, he had been driving in South Carolina, on his way to scout a game at The Citadel. He had the radio on, and suddenly he heard a program about Igor Sikorsky, the helicopter inventor and developer, and about a special interest of his, the physics of a thrown baseball. His findings were exactly the same ones that Ott and Garver and Syd Thrift had come up with. "Isn't that great!" Thrift exclaimed. "I tell you, I was so excited I had to pull my car over to the side of the road and think about it. I was thrilled."

We sat together watching the rain fall on the soggy field and the puddles forming on the infield tarp, and Syd said, "Well, here comes another season, and nobody knows what's going to happen. Nobody can say for sure. We can study and study and make plans for our team and for the season, but what we don't know is always there. It's the best part of the game."

FIFTEEN

• ◆ •

Up at the Hall

HERE WE ARE, AND HERE IT ALL IS FOR US: ALREADY too much to remember. Here's a meerschaum pipe presented to Cy Young by his Red Sox teammates after his perfect game in 1904. Here are Shoeless Joe Jackson's shoes. Here's a life-size statue of Ted Williams, beautifully done in basswood; Ted is just finishing his swing, and his eyes are following the flight of the ball, into the right-field stands again. Here is John McGraw's little black mitt, from the days when he played third base for the old Orioles: a blob of licorice, by the looks of it, or perhaps a small flattened animal, dead on the highway. Here's a ball signed by seventeen-year-old Willie McCovey and his teammates on the 1955 Class D Sandersville (Georgia) club—Stretch's first address in organized ball—and over *here* is a ball from a June 14, 1870, game between Cincinnati and the Brooklyn Atlantics; Brooklyn won, snapping the Red Stockings' astounding winning streak of two full years. Babe Ruth, in a floor-to-ceiling photomural, sits behind the wheel of an open touring car, with his manager, little Miller Huggins, almost hidden beside him. The Babe is wearing driving gauntlets, a cap, a fur-collared coat, and a sullen, assured look: Out of the way, world! Let's hum a song or two (from the sheet music for "Home Run Bill" or "The Marquard Glide"

397

or "That Baseball Rag") while we think about some intrepid barnstormers of the game: the Chicago White Sox arrayed in front of the Egyptian Pyramids in 1889; King George V (in a derby) gravely inspecting a visiting American exhibition squad (in uniforms and spikes) in 1913; and shipboard high jinks by the members of a 1931 team headed for Japan (Mickey Cochrane is sporting white-and-tan wingtips). The 1935 Negro League Pittsburgh Crawfords were travellers, too; their blurry team photograph has them lined up, in smiles and baggy uniforms, in front of their dusty, streamlined team bus. Over here are some all-time minor-league records for us to think about: Ron Necciai pitched a no-hitter for the Appalachian League's Bristol Twins in 1952 and struck out all twenty-seven batters in the process; and Joe Wilhoit hit safely in sixty-nine consecutive games for the Wichita Wolves in 1919. Wilhoit was on his way down by then, after four undistinguished wartime seasons with four different big-league clubs, but Necciai's feat won him an immediate starting spot with the Pittsburgh Pirates—and a lifetime one-season 1–6 record in the majors, with a 7.08 earned-run average. Hard lines, but another kid made more of *his* chances after hitting safely in sixty-one consecutive games with the San Francisco Seals in 1933: Joe DiMaggio.

Enough. Come sit down and take a load off—let's sit here on these old green ballpark seats and watch this movie tape. I think it's—Yes, it *is*:

COSTELLO: Now, wait. What's the name of the first baseman?
ABBOTT: No, What's the name of the second baseman.
COSTELLO: I don't know.
ABBOTT: He's the third baseman.
COSTELLO: Let's start over.
ABBOTT: O.K. Who's on first.
COSTELLO: I'm asking *you* what's the name of the first baseman.
ABBOTT: What's the name of the second baseman.
COSTELLO: I don't know.
ABBOTT: He's on third . . .

What about bats? Pete Rose had a nearly knobless bat, with six separate strips of tape on the handle—or at least that's what he swung when he rapped out his four-thousandth hit (he was with the Expos then), against the Phillies, in 1984. Probably he wouldn't have done so well with Babe Ruth's thick-waisted model, or with Home Run Baker's mighty mace. Maybe weight isn't what matters: here's Jim Bottomley's modest-looking bat lying on its side in a case—the bat he used in a September 16, 1924, game, when he went six for six against the Dodgers (Sunny Jim played for the Cardinals, of course) and batted in twelve runs. I won't forget *that*, I'm sure, but here in the World Series section (there is a cutout silhouette of Joe Rudi making that beautiful catch up against the wall in 1974: I was there!) some text tells us that the Tigers batted .455 against the Padres' starting pitchers in the 1984 Series—and how in the world could I have forgotten that, now that I know forever that Cy Young's 1954 Ohio license plate was "C-511-Y" Cy won five hundred and eleven games, lifetime) and that Mrs. Lou Gehrig's New York plate for 1942 (Lou had died the year before) was "1-LG"?

◆ ◆ ◆

THIS CLOTTED FLOW IS AN INADEQUATE REPRESENTATION OF the National Baseball Hall of Fame and Museum in Cooperstown, but it is perhaps a good tissue sample of one man's brain taken after a couple of hours in the marvelous place. What has been left out so far is the fans themselves—dozens and scores and hundreds of them, arrayed throughout the four floors of the modest Georgian edifice on any summer afternoon, with wives (or husbands) and kids and grandfathers and toddlers in tow, and all of them talking baseball a mile a minute: "Pop, look at *this*! Here's Roger Clemens' cap and his gloves and his shoes he wore on the day he struck out all those guys last year—you know, that twenty-strikeout game?" and "Ralph Kiner led the National League in home runs his first *seven* years running— how do you like that, honey!" and "Alison! Alison-n-n! Has anybody seen Alison?" I have done some museum time in my day—if I had to compare the Hall with any other museum in the world it would be the Victoria and Albert, in London—but I can't recollect a more willing and enthusiastic culture-crawl anywhere. It took me a little while to dope this out, and the answer, it became clear, is geographical. The Hall of Fame draws a quarter of a million visitors every year—a total that cannot be fashioned out of drop-in locals from Cooperstown (pop. 2,300), plus a handful of idle music lovers, up for the nearby Glimmerglass Opera summer season, and a few busloads of kids from day camps scattered along adjoining Otsego Lake. (There are other tourist attractions in town as well: the Farmer's Museum and Fenimore House, the latter of which displays some furnishings of the eponymous and tireless non-Cleveland Indian publicist James Fenimore Cooper.) Cooperstown is an inviting little village, with flowering window baskets set out in front of its dignified old brickfront stores, but it isn't near anyplace else, unless you count Cobleskill or Cazenovia. From New York City, it's three hours up the New York Thruway and another hour out west of Albany before you hit the winding back-country road that takes you thirty miles to the lake and the town. Folks who come to the Hall are pilgrims, then; they want to be there, and most of the visitors I talked to during a couple of recent stays told me they had planned their trip more than a year before. This place is a shrine.

I had resisted it, all these years, for just that reason. I've been a baseball fan all my life—starting long before the Hall of Fame opened, in 1939—but lately when each summer came along I realized once again that I preferred to stay with the new season, close to the heat and fuss and noise and news of the games, rather than pay my respects to baseball's past. Cooperstown seemed too far away, in any case, and I secretly suspected that I wouldn't like it. I was afraid I'd be bored—a dumb idea for a baseball fan, if you think about it. By mid-June this year, however, up-close baseball had begun to lose its flavor for me. The World Champion Mets—*my* Mets—had lost most of their dashing pitching staff to injuries and other unhappy circumstances, and the team fell victim to bad nerves and bickering as it slipped farther behind in the standings. The Red Sox, who also held my fealty, were even worse off: twelve games behind and already out of the race, it seemed—a terrible letdown after their championship season of 1986. Spoiled and sulky, I suddenly remembered Cooperstown one afternoon in late June, and within an hour had extemporized a northward expedition with Charles, a colleague of mine and a fellow-Soxperson, and his ten-year-old Soxson, Ben—perfect companions, it turned out. We cheated a little by flying up from LaGuardia on a Catskill Airways commuter hop to Oneonta, where we rented a car and instantly resumed our colloquy (it was too noisy in the plane to talk about baseball or anything else), which went on uninterrupted through two soggy days and four meals and three bottom-to-top sojourns in the Hall of Fame; an essential trip, we decided, maybe even for Yankee fans.

◆ ◆ ◆

LIKE OTHER SHRINES, PERHAPS, THE BASEBALL HALL OF FAME is founded on a fantasy—the highly dubious possibility that baseball was "invented" in Cooperstown by a local youth, Abner Doubleday, while he was fooling around with some friends in a pasture one day in the summer of 1839. In 1905, a committee of baseball panjandrums and politicos, the Mills Commission, forgathered to determine the origins of the national pastime, and after three years of deliberation it bestowed the garland on Doubleday, who had not done damage to his cause by growing up to become a major general and fight in the Mexican and Civil Wars. (He himself never laid claim to the baseball invention.) The commission, we might note, was invented at a time when organized professional baseball was not quite thirty years old and the modern, two-league era (and the first World Series) was only three years old. Teddy Roosevelt was in office, in a time of glowing national self-assurance, and the Mills Commission reacted with alacrity to a letter from one Abner Graves, a mining engineer who had grown up in Cooperstown and swore he had been on hand on the day when nineteen-year-old Abner Doubleday scratched out the first diamond in the dust of a Cooperstown pasture, put bases at three angles, and added a pitcher and a catcher for good measure. Subsequent and more cautious baseball historians have agreed that the American game almost surely evolved out of a British boys' amusement called rounders, and that the true father of baseball was Alexander Cartwright, a young engineer and draftsman and volunteer fireman, who first marked off the crucial ninety feet between the bases and formulated the pretty and sensible arrangement of nine innings to a game and nine men to a side; his team, the New York Knickerbockers, came into being in Hoboken in 1845, and their sort of baseball—"The New York Game"—became the sport we know today. The Cooperstown chimera persisted, however, and was wonderfully transfused by the 1934 discovery of a tattered homemade baseball among the effects of the aforementioned Graves, in Fly Creek, New York, three miles west of Cooperstown. The ball—soon ennobled as The Doubleday Baseball—was purchased for five dollars by Stephen C. Clark, a Cooperstown millionaire who had established a fortune with the Singer Sewing Machine Company. The ancient pill became the centerpiece of Clark's small private collection of baseball memorabilia and, very soon thereafter, of the National Baseball Museum—an idea happily seized upon and pushed forward by Ford C. Frick, the president of the National League, and by

other gamekeepers of the era, including Commissioner Kene-
saw Mountain Landis. The museum opened its doors on June
12, 1939. It is providential, I think, that the Hall has no official
connection with organized baseball, although Commissioner
Peter Ueberroth and his predecessor, Bowie Kuhn, are both on
the Hall's current board of directors, as are the two league presidents and a couple of team owners. The Hall is also financially
independent, making do nicely on its gate receipts (admission
is five dollars for adults, two for kids), donations, and the revenues derived from an overflowing and popular souvenir shop.
The place seems to belong to the fans.

The Doubleday Baseball, the touchstone of the sport, is on
view in the Cooperstown Room of the H. of F.: a small dark
sphere, stuffed with cloth, which looks a good deal like some
artifact—possibly a pair of rolled-up socks—exhumed from a
Danish peat bog. Near its niche, on the same wall of the Cooperstown Room, there is an eloquent and unapologetic establish-
ing text (it was written by Carl Lundquist, a long-term early
publicist) that disarms and pleases in equal measure:

> Abner Doubleday, who started baseball in Farmer Phinney's
> Cooperstown pasture, is not enshrined in the Hall of Fame. How-
> ever, it is known that as a youth he played in the pasture and that a
> homemade ball, found in a trunk, belonged to him. Of such facts
> are legends made. As a Civil War general, Doubleday performed
> deeds of valor that earned him a place in history; but in the hearts
> of those who love baseball he is remembered as the lad in the pas-
> ture where the game was invented. Only cynics would need to know
> more.

The journey that even the most distant fan must endure to arrive
at the Hall of Fame is but a few steps compared to the passage
required of its members—one hundred and ninety-nine retired
major-league players, players from the defunct Negro Leagues,
old umpires, old managers, baseball pioneers, celebrated bygone executives—whose bronze plaques, each with inscribed
name and feats and features, line the wall of the Hall of Fame
Gallery and form the centerpiece and raison d'être of the pan-
theon. Elections consist of an annual polling of four hundred
members of the Baseball Writers' Association of America, and
to be selected for the Hall a player must be named on seventy-
five percent of the ballots. To be eligible for the ballot, the
candidate must have put in at least ten years' service in the
majors, plus a five-year waiting period following retirement. A

backup system permits election by the Committee on Veterans, an august eighteen-man body (baronial old players, executives, and writers, including Stan Musial, Roy Campanella, Monte Irvin, Gabe Paul, and Shirley Povich) that selects notables of the distant and not so distant past who have somehow been passed over by the B.B.W.A.; a subcommittee picks players from the Negro Leagues, which went out of business in the early fifties. (Eleven Negro League players have been elected to date.) In the early days of the Hall, the Veterans Committee was the more active body, since it had to deal with the claims and statistics of many hundreds of old-timers, dating back into the nineteenth century, while the writers were voting on players most of them had actually seen on the field. One hundred and twenty-six plaques in the Hall (ninety of them depicting players) are attributable to the Veterans Committee, but a more accurate view of the workings of the present system emerges when one sorts out the fifty-four living players now in the Hall, sixteen of whom ascended by way of the Veterans Committee and thirty-eight by way of the writers' poll.

Election of the immortals began even before the Hall was completed, and by Dedication Day four years' balloting had produced twenty-five members—senior gods, if you will. One of the riveting exhibits at the Hall is a formal photograph of the living inductees (there were eleven of them, and ten are in the picture) who came to Cooperstown that sunny June afternoon in 1939. Connie Mack, spare and erect and fatherly in a dark suit and high collar, sits next to Babe Ruth in the front row; the Babe, moon-faced and gone to beef, has an open collar above his double-breasted suit, and his crossed left leg reveals that his socks have been rolled down to shoe-top level. Tris Speaker, playing short center field as usual, stands directly behind Ruth, and Honus Wagner and Walter Johnson, with their famous country sweetness perfectly visible, occupy the corners. As you study the photograph (never a quick process, no matter how many times you have seen it), your gaze stops at the other men's faces, one by one, as recollection of their deeds and their flair for the game comes flooding back: Eddie Collins, Grover Cleveland Alexander, Nap Lajoie, Cy Young (pipe in hand), and George Sisler—old warriors squinting in the sun, comfortable at last. The one man missing is Ty Cobb. He had car trouble on the road and missed the photo opportunity by ten minutes—late for the first time in his life.

The Hall of Fame Gallery—part Parthenon, part bus termi-

nal—is a long hall, windowed at the far end, with dark columns
that set off the raised and illuminated galleries, left and right,
in which the plaques are arrayed. You want to resist the place, but
you can't—or at least *I* couldn't. I am an old cosmopolitan, and
I live in a city where wonders are thrust at you every day,
but not many gala openings have produced the skipped heartbeat, the prickle down the neck, the interior lampglow of pleasure that I felt every time I walked into this room. Others there
felt the same way—I heard them, every time—and I noticed,
too, that the bronze memorials, which are hung in double rows
within alcoves, elicit a neighborly flow of baseball talk and baseball recollection among the strangers standing together before
them. The familiar plaques—the immortal's likeness, in framed
bas-relief, supra, with accompanying decorative bats and laurel
spray, and the ennobling text and stats below—start on the right,
as you enter, and proceed by years and order of election down
that wall and then, doubling back, up the left side of the room.
The early texts tend to be short: Jove needs few encomiums. Ty
Cobb's five lines read, "Led American League in batting twelve
times and created or equalled more major-league records than
any other player. Retired with 4,191 major-league hits." Babe
Ruth: "Greatest drawing card in history of baseball. Holder of
many home-run and other batting records. Gathered 714 home
runs in addition to fifteen in World Series." That "gathered"
is felicitous, but all the texts—almost fifty years of them now—
have a nice ring to them: a touch of Westminster Abbey, a whiff
of the press box. Christy Mathewson (he died young, in 1925)
was among the first five players voted into the Hall, and the
shining raised lines on his plaque sound the trumpets, all right:
"Greatest of all the great pitchers in the 20th century's first
quarter, pitched 3 shut-outs in 1905 World Series. First pitcher
of the century ever to win 30 games in 3 successive years. Won
37 games in 1908. 'Matty was master of them all.' "

The early likenesses on the plaques (no one seems to know
the name of the first sculptor)* show an assurance and zest that
lift them above the heroic genre. Different (and sometimes indifferent) talents have worked the portraits in subsequent years,
but no matter: fine art isn't quite the point here. Ted Williams,

*A few weeks after the publication of this story in the *New Yorker*, I received a letter
from Benjamin and Philip Bayman, who identified the sculptor of the early plaques
(from 1939 through 1959) as their father, the late Leo Bayman, of New York. Leo
Bayman's distinctive contribution to the Hall is now part of the archives.

who waltzed into the Hall in 1966 (his first year of eligibility, of course), so disliked the looks of his plaque that he persuaded the Hall to have another one struck off and hung in its place. This one missed him, too, but you overlook that when you notice that his nose and the brim of his cap have been worn to brightness by the affectionate touches of his fans. ("I'm a *saint*, you mean?" he said when I told him about this not long ago, and he gave one of his bearlike huffs of pleasure.) In time, my visits to the Gallery became random cruises from alcove to alcove, until I would be brought to a stop by a likeness, a name, a juxtaposition, or a thunderous line or two of stats. I found Casey Stengel, Burleigh Grimes, Larry MacPhail, Hank Aaron, Rube Waddell. Amos Rusie (The Hoosier Thunderbolt) adjoined Addie Joss, my father's favorite pitcher. Here was Freddie Lindstrom. ("As youngest player [he was eighteen] in World Series history, he tied record with four hits in game in 1924.") And here, all in a cluster, were Yogi Berra, Josh Gibson, Sandy Koufax ("Sanford Koufax . . . Set all-time records with 4 no-hitters in 4 years, capped by 1965 perfect game, and by capturing earned-run title five seasons in a row"), Buck Leonard, and Early Wynn. Hack Wilson's plaque showed his determined jaw but stopped just above the place where he became interesting: his mighty shoulders and thick, short body (he was five feet six), which powered fifty-six homers and a record one hundred and ninety R.B.I.s in 1930. I found Roberto Clemente (". . . rifle-armed defensive star set N.L. mark by pacing outfielders in assists five years") and Eppa Rixey (but why did they delete his nickname: Eppa *Jephtha* Rixey?). I looked up Johnny Mize and learned something I had forgotten about the Big Cat, if indeed, I'd ever known it ("Keen-eyed slugger . . . set major-loop records by hitting three homers in a game six times"). The plaques of this year's Hall of Famers—Catfish Hunter, Billy Williams, and Ray Dandridge (another star from the Negro Leagues)— were not yet in place, of course, and after I looked at the bare wall that awaited them I moved along into an empty alcove and thought about the faces that would be hung up there in bronze over the next few summers: Willie Stargell, Johnny Bench, Carl Yastrzemski, Gaylord Perry, Rod Carew, Jim Palmer, Pete Rose . . . I could almost see the plaques already, and I pretty well knew what the lines on them would say, but these longtime favorites of mine would be altered, in quite, thrilling fashion.

Men embronzed have a certified look to them, as if they had always belonged here, but for many of them the selection process has been far from peaceful. Great stars usually jump into the Hall on their very first year of eligibility—in the past decade, these have included Willie Mays, Bob Gibson, Frank Robinson, Brooks Robinson, and Willie McCovey. But Juan Marichal had to wait three years before garnering the requisite seventy-five percent of the writers' ballots, and Don Drysdale waited out ten. Looking back, we detect other excruciations, some of them (but perhaps not all of them) inexplicable. Charlie Gehringer didn't pass muster until his fifth ballot; Gabby Hartnett waited nine years and Lou Boudreau thirteen. Ralph Kiner made it on his thirteenth try, and Ducky Medwick on his fifteenth, and last, year of eligibility. Candidates who fall shy after fifteen Baseball Writers' ballots must survive three further years in limbo before their names and feats can be taken up by the Veterans Committee—twenty-three years after their retirement from the game. Johnny Mize, whose apotheosis was decreed twenty-eight years after he had hung up his spikes, told me that he was grateful for the honor, but confessed that he had lost interest in the process along the way; he had been particularly unhappy whenever he saw his name slip lower in the writers' estimation because of some arriviste youngster on the ballot. Jack Lang, of the *News*, who, in his capacity as the near-perennial secretary-treasurer of the B.B.W.A., supervises the voting (he himself was voted into the writers' section of the Hall at this year's induction), told me that many newly eligible stars experience an early ground swell of support and then tail off in ensuing ballots. Columnists and owners and fan clubs have been known to campaign intensively for favorites (Joe Sewell, a stubby little shortstop with the Indians in the nineteen-twenties, and Bob Lemon, the big Cleveland right-hander, inspired an inundation of letters before being admitted), but the process can backfire. Phil Rizzuto, the Yankee shortstop, has become the Harold Stassen of the Hall in recent years, and Lang believes that the sort of electioneering for the Scooter conducted by George Steinbrenner and by segments of the New York media helped bring about the defiant selection of another diminutive shortstop from the same town and the same era: Pee Wee Reese. The committees have considerable power, when you come to think about it, and one must assume that the writers are more reliable today than they were at times in the past: twenty-three B.B.W.A. voters left Willie Mays' name off their ballots altogether when he first came up for consideration, in 1979. He survived this knockdown pitch and made it home that first year just the same. Lang is uneasy when asked to speculate for long about such matters, and so is another good gray baseball friend of mine, Seymour Siwoff, the chief flamekeeper at the Elias Sports Bureau. He and I had a telephone conversation about the vagueness of the statistics emanating from the old Negro Leagues, and he said, "The numbers just aren't there, so we have to rely on what the guys who played with him say about a player we're thinking about for the Hall. But I don't worry about it. When a man is in, he's in, and we should be happy for him. We need the Hall, is how I see it. You gotta have that romance."

◆ ◆ ◆

MUSEUMS WEAR YOU DOWN, AND BEN AND CHARLES AND I TOOK time off from the Hall whenever the bats and stats and babies and souvenir Astro key rings and genuine Cubs Christmas-tree balls began to swim and blur in our heads. We visited Doubleday Field, the lovely old brick-grandstand ballpark (it's owned by the village) where an annual exhibition game between two big-league teams is played during Induction Weekend; a local high-school team and a semi-pro club play here, too, but the field was sopping on the morning we got there, and the only players on it were some robins busily working the base paths. Ben took a shot at an adjoining baseball range, and his father and I watched him swing like Yaz, like Wade Boggs, and now perhaps like Mickey Mantle and Tris Speaker and Joe D. as well. Mostly, though, we used our time away from the Hall to talk about the Hall. Ben's favorite feature was the I.B.M. Major League Leaders computer stations, where you could punch in the names of players (nine hundred and twenty-two of them) in more than eleven hundred categories, and doodle them around on the screen. "I didn't know all that much about Ty Cobb before this," he said at lunch one day. "I'd read about him in books, but I didn't pay much attention, because he was such a rat. But he was great—I have to admit it." Charles was fond of a second-floor nook given over to the old Boston Beaneater teams and their near-prehistoric stars, like Jimmy Collins, Kid Nichols, King Kelly, Hughie Duffy, and Billy Hamilton, who had battled Ned Hanlon's Orioles for dominance of the National League at the end of the last century. A splendid photomural of the Beaneater fans shows a thousand derbies. "I think there was a song way back then called 'Slide, Kelly, Slide,'" Charles said, "and when I was a kid there was a 'Slide, Kelly, Slide' ride at Whalom Park, in Fitchburg, Massachusetts. I'll bet it's still there.''

All three of us loved the basement in the Hall, and we kept going back there. It was a catchall—a *basement*—full of leftovers and old board games and stuff: Abner Doubleday's campaign trunk; a Hillerich & Bradsby batmaking lathe; an awesome red iron pitching machine (circa 1942) on rubber wheels—a farm implement, you would guess—which fired balls plateward with a mighty rubber band, after a black paddle had flipped up to alert the batter just before the *twangg!* In another sector we found an assemblage of slotted All-Time Leaders boards—lists of the individual lifetime standings in hits, doubles, runs batted in, and so forth; it reminded you of the lobby of a high-school gym. The names Aaron and Cobb and Musial ran across the offensive boards like bright threads in a tapestry. The lists were up to the minute, with Reggie Jackson's five hundred and fifty-five home runs, putting him sixth on the Home Runs roster, eighteen back of Harmon Killebrew and nineteen up on Mickey Mantle. Nearby, I lingered over a little exhibit about the handful of perfect games that the sport has produced in its long history, from John Richmond's 1–0 victory over Cleveland for the Worcester Ruby Legs, on June 12, 1880, down to Mike Witt's perfecto on September 30, 1984, when his Angels beat the Rangers by the same score. (Catfish Hunter had a perfect game to his credit, too: Oakland 4–Twins zip, in 1968.) These had been quick entertainments. Cy Young whipped the Athletics in an hour and twenty-five minutes in 1904, and Sandy Koufax needed only eighteen additional minutes to wrap up his famous outing (Dodgers 1–Cubs 0) in 1965. There have been only eleven perfect, nobody-on-base-at-all games in big-league play, if you count Don Larsen's win over the Dodgers in the 1956 World Series, and *don't* count Harvey Haddix's twelve perfect innings for the Pirates against the Braves in 1959. (He lost the no-hitter, and the game, in the thirteenth.) John Montgomery Ward, pitching for the Providence Grays against the Buffalo Bisons, pulled off the second perfect game in the National League only five days after Richmond's feat, and the *next* perfect game in that league came along eighty-four years later: Jim Bunning and the Phillies over the Mets, 6–0, on June 21, 1964. You can't beat baseball.

Now and then, I sensed a fleeting wish that the Hall were less optimistic and decorous. I think I would have enjoyed a visit to Cliché Corner, in a sector devoted to baseball and the language, and perhaps a downside exhibit—Boot Hall, let's say—of celebrated gaffes of the sport: Merkle's Boner, Snodgrass's Muff, and so forth, right on down to Bill Buckner's through-the-wickets error in Game Six of the Series last year. Sometimes you wonder if the Hall isn't excessively preoccupied with the past, but the charge doesn't quite hold up. The Great Moments display that catches your eye the moment you walk in has Joe Dimaggio's fifty-six-game hitting streak and Johnny Vander Meer's successive no-hitters in 1938 and Babe Ruth's sixty homers (and Roger Maris's sixty-one), and so on, but Roger Clemens is up there, too, striking out those twenty batters (they were Mariners) on April 29th last year. The sport is ongoing and indivisible, and the Hall's Baseball Today room downstairs has every single Topps Bubble Gum card for 1987 *and* the bats wielded by Marvell Wynne, Tony Gwynn, and John Kruk when they led off the Padres' first inning against the Giants on April 13th this year with a first-ever three home runs in succession. "I wouldn't give up my bat if I'd done something like that," Ben said on inspecting this wonder. "I'd sell it. No—I'd *keep* it."

The Hall, in any case, wouldn't have bought Ben's bat; it doesn't buy stuff. Aside from a few objects on loan, all twenty-three or twenty-four thousand artifacts on view or tucked away in Curator William T. Spencer's workroom have been acquired by gift—often a solicited gift, to be sure. The regularly incoming flood of baseball memorabilia and baseball junk is so heavy that a staff committee, which includes Director Howard C. Talbot, Jr., Associate Director William J. Guilfoile, and Registrar Peter Clark, who are the worthies most responsible for the imagination and wit and good sense evident in the present Hall, meets every Friday to decide what to accept and (mostly) what to turn down. Dozens of putative Babe Ruth home-run balls are offered by mail, and so, too, are "authentic" Babe Ruth bats, including innumerable samples of a Louisville Slugger model, once turned out by the hundreds, with the Babe's imprinted signature on the barrel. The committee is slow to reject, however, for slim leads often yield treasures. A hesitant letter about a box full of clothes belonging to "somebody named Bender" that turned up in an attic in Washington, D.C., three years ago eventually produced Chief Bender's dazzling white 1914 Athletics uniform, which is now to be seen in the General History sector on the second floor, next to a dandy photo of the Chippewa fireballer. Players are prime sources, of course, and some—Hank Aaron among them—have almost emptied their lockers for the Hall, possibly on the theory that immortality can always be improved a little.

Bill Guilfoile has spent a lifetime in baseball. (He writes the texts for the current plaques, among other things.) Before he came to Cooperstown, in 1979, he was assistant to the general manager and director of public relations for the Pirates, and I suspect that he may be responsible for the acquisition of the life-size wax statue of Roberto Clemente that now stands just outside his office door. This mysterious-looking effigy used to live in a back room at Three Rivers Stadium, in Pittsburgh, and one day—this was long before Clemente's untimely death in a plane crash—Pirate trainer Tony Bartirome and pitcher Jim Rooker spirited the thing down to the clubhouse and laid it out on the trainer's table, and turned off most of the lights. Then they told team physician Dr. Joe Finegold that Clemente had just fainted on the field, during batting practice. Dr. Finegold—or so the story goes—hurried in, took one appalled look, and felt for a pulse.

If I have slighted Mr. Guilfoile and his colleagues here, the National Baseball Library, which adjoins and is part of the Hall itself, must suffer a similar inadequate dismissal. I did pay a brief visit to the library, where the director, Tom Heitz, shrugged and laughed when I asked him to tell me about the four or five million newspaper documents, the hundred and twenty-five thousand photographs, the fifteen thousand-odd baseball books, the old radio-broadcast tapes, and so forth, that are in his care. The library is the custodian of the famous John Tattersall Collection of early-to-recent box scores, and Heitz told me that game information and biographical material about eighty-five percent of all the men who have ever played the game, at any professional level, was readily at hand. He permitted me to leaf through the files of that day's letters and applications to visit the stacks (ten thousand or so scholars consult the library every year), and I found queries from someone who wanted a photograph of the 1934 World Series; from someone who needed the box scores of games he had attended in 1934, 1961, and 1965 (there's a lot of this, Heitz said); from someone who wanted the name of every pitcher who had ever struck out ten or more batters in a single game (not feasible to sort out, Heitz said); an extensive communication from a Belgian scholar, Léon Van-vière, who is the world's No. 1 expert on baseball references in stamps; a letter from Bill Marshall, a scholar at the University of Kentucky, who is preparing a work on the mid-America, lower-minors Kitty, Bluegrass, Ohio State, and Appalachian Leagues; and two or three letters asking for information about a family member or ancestor who claimed or was said to have played professional ball once. Almost a quarter of such heroes, Heitz told me, turn out to be phantoms. But, like Bill Guilfoile, he is cautious. A woman who called up the library a few months ago was found to be a relative to Ted Welch, who pitched in three games for the St. Louis Terries, in the old Federal League, in 1914 (Won 0–Lost 0; E.R.A. 6.00). The library knew nothing else about him—not even his birthplace—but a research questionnaire was mailed off, and Heitz expects that Ted Welch will have an extra agate line or two in the next edition of the *Baseball Encyclopedia*.

Before I said goodbye, I asked Heitz if his staff could dredge up the box score of a game played in the spring of 1930, in which Lefty Gomez, pitching his first big-league game, beat the White Sox at Yankee Stadium. I was pretty sure about that much, because I was there that day (I was nine years old), and because I had talked with Gomez about the game a few years back. The box score came to me in the mail two days later, and the first thing I noticed when I looked it over was that there were five future Hall of Famers on the field that day, including both pitchers: Red Faber and Lefty Gomez. Lefty fanned the side in the first inning (there was a little game summary attached to the box score), and the Yankees went on to win, 4–1.

◆ ◆ ◆

I HADN'T PLANNED TO GO BACK TO COOPERSTOWN AT ONCE, but when Induction Weekend came along, late in July, I couldn't stay away. I was a little nervous about too much pomp and oratory, but what I encountered was a jolly family party of baseball. Twenty-five Hall of Fame members came back, to welcome the inductees—Hunter, Williams, and Dandridge—and so did their wives and (in many cases) children and grandchildren, and so did neighbors, brothers and sisters, and old teammates. Mary Rice, the widow of Hall of Fame outfielder Sam Rice, of the old Washington Senators, came back, as usual (Sam died in 1974), and so did her daughter Christine and her granddaughter Kimberly; this was Kimberly's nineteenth reunion at Cooperstown. Hall of Famer Happy Chandler—former commissioner, former Kentucky governor, former Kentucky senator—turned up, still hale and handshaking at eighty-nine, and so did Willie

Mays, Ralph Kiner, Bill Dickey, Robin Roberts, the Splendid Splinter (more a tree now), Campy, Cool Papa, Country, Pee Wee, the Big Cat, Stan the Man, and more. The noble, Doric-columned old Otesaga Hotel, whose lawns ran down to the glistening Otsego waters, took us all in (my wife and me included), and, hanging out in and around its lobby, bars, deep verandas, and restaurants, you heard baseball and nothing else for three steaming, cheerful summer days and nights. The fans were there, too, though at a distance—eight to ten thousand of them, heavily familied as well. The Hall had set up a long, airy tent down by the lakefront for three extended autograph sessions—all comers on the first and third days, kids only on the second—and the waiting lines were so long that they had to be mercifully truncated; the foresighted early arrivals had camped out all night to hold their places. I sought no autographs (one small girl in a Mariners T-shirt asked for *my* signature, somehow under the impression that I was Billy Williams), but I happily stuck around, and there in Cooperstown, encircled by great souls and heroes of the pastime, I bathed in a Ganges of baseball:

Johnny Mize (*at seventy-four, he is melon-faced and massively calm—unchanged*): These batters today are so nervous. You look at Winfield and he's *duh, duh, dah-duh* at the plate. They're doing a dance up there. I'd always walk into the box, drop my bat down, get my feet right, and then I'd be on base or out of there. . . . My worst day was when I got traded to the Giants and I knew I'd have to hit in the Polo Grounds all year, with that five-hundred-foot center field. It was four hundred and twenty-two feet to right-center, where I liked to hit the ball. Bill Terry hit straightaway and he batted .400 in the Polo Grounds before I got there, and to me that's .500, easy, in any other park.

Ray Dandridge (*square and squatty, with bowed legs and broad, large hands; he wore a snowy white cap by day and an engaging smile at all times; seventy-three years old, possibly older*): I played shortstop and second base, but third base was my real position. I played with the Detroit Stars in 1933, then in Newark—the Newark Dodgers that turned into the Newark Eagles. I played all year round, mostly for fifteen dollars a week. Went to Puerto Rico, and it was fifteen dollars a week; went to Cuba, fifteen dollars a week; Venezuela and Santo Domingo and Mexico, fifteen dollars a week. I played seven years in Mexico and made some more money there in the end. We won the championship for Mexico City. . . . I'm a place-hitter—hit the ball to all fields. I'm a Stan Musial man. I loved to see that man hit. He's my idol, because I hit like him—or he hit like me.

Monte Irvin (*played in the Negro Leagues and then for seven years with the Giants and, briefly, the Cubs; he batted .458 in the 1951 World Series; tall and dignified*): Ray Dandrige played third base with style and class. He had the quickest hands—I never saw anybody come in and sweep up the swinging bunt the way he could do it. He's in a class with Brooks Robinson. . . . If the major leagues had integrated ten years earlier, you'd have seen the great Negro League stars in their prime—Satchel, Buck Leonard, Josh Gibson. We had some sure Hall of Fame pitchers you probably never heard of—Roy Partlow, Raymond Brown, and Leon Day. Leon is here this weekend, you should talk to him . . . Back then, you had to go easy at the beginning with your team, because there'd likely be an old-timer holding down your spot. He'd say, "Boy, this position belongs to *me*—go play somewhere else." So you learned to play all over the place.

Ted Williams (*no description needed; he talked about hitting, of all things*): The man who made that statue of me noticed something most people never did: I shortened up on the bat. I knew I was smarter than ninety-nine percent of the other hitters—not mentally but baseballically. I said to myself, "The quicker I am, the longer I can wait. The longer I can wait, the less I'm likely to get fooled. So how can I be quick? Don't get too heavy a bat. Don't swing from the end of the bat. And with two strikes don't try to pull the ball all the time. And *get a good pitch to hit*." That's all there is to it! When I was first in the Pacific Coast League, I went to see Lefty O'Doul, because I was a student of hitting. I talked to him one afternoon—he was with the Seals—when he was sitting on the grass out in center field, taking some sun. He said, "Kid, don't let anybody ever change you." And that's when I thought, Boy, I must be pretty good!

Ernie Banks (*still narrow as a slat at fifty-six; still talking, here to Ted Williams, in the next chair in the autographing tent*): You should be a Rhodes Scholar, Ted—baseball's never had one. We need a Rhodes Scholar, because this game takes brains. You even *look* smart, so you could have done it. You and me, we're the same kind of players. We like people who focus on the task, not the results. It's not the gold, it's the getting.

Billy Williams (*eavesdropping from the next chair in line*): Oh, no. Not again. I was Ernie's roommate, so I heard this stuff for sixteen years. But I'm all right. I'll survive it.

Joe Sewell (*eighty-eight years old, and probably an inch or two under his listed height of five feet back with the Indians in the twenties; struck out only three times in 1930 and again in 1932, and only a hundred and fourteen times lifetime, in more than seven thousand at-bats; wears thick glasses now and carried nine pens and pencils in his shirt pocket*): I have the bat at home that I used for fourteen years. The same bat. It weighs forty ounces. I never cracked it, because I knew how to swing the right way. I took good care of it—worked on it every single day. I rubbed it with a chicken bone and a plug of tobacco, and then I'd roll it up and down with a smooth bottle. The bat was your tool, so you took care of it. They wanted that bat up here at the Hall, but I'm keeping it.

Catfish Hunter (*at forty-one, he is the second-youngest player—second to Koufax—ever to attain the Hall; he looks even better than he did when he was out there painting the corners*): I don't miss the game, because I'm still in it, coaching my boys. One son, Todd, I coached up from Little League right on through Legion ball. Now he's graduating, so I'm going back to wait for my son Paul, who'll be ready for Little League in a couple of years. I'm a Little League groundskeeper right now. Some parents think Little League pressure is too much for kids, but you got to get used to pressure sometime if you're going to want to play . . . My wife and my three kids are here. My three sisters will be here tomorrow, and three of my four brothers, and *their* kids. There's two busloads and ten or twenty carloads of folks coming from North Carolina, so my home town—there's twenty-five hundred inhabitants, same as when I was a kid—will be not at home tomorrow.

Leon Day (*he is not young—he must be in his late seventies—but is broad, low, and still powerful-looking, with long arms; sunny disposition; many believe he will be the next player from the Negro Leagues to attain the Hall*): With the Newark Eagles, we played every day it didn't rain. Played all kinds of teams, in the league and out of the league. One Fourth of July, we played at Bay Ridge Parkway, in Brooklyn, in the morning—I think it was the Bushwicks that game. Then we played a league double-header in the afternoon at Ebbets Field—the Dodgers were away on the road. Then we played another game someplace that night. The same pitcher, a fellow named Jackman, started all four games. He got knocked out of the box each time, but he'd say "Gimme the ball, I can beat these guys," so he ended up losing four games on the same day. . . . I had the reputation of being

the kind of pitcher who'd knock you down if you'd got a hit off
of me, but I wouldn't always do it on the first pitch. Maybe I'd
throw you a knuckleball instead. Then a curveball. Then a nice
change of pace. You'd start to think, Good, he forgot about that
hit, and right then—*whap*—down you'd go. (*Laughs delight-
edly.*)

◆ ◆ ◆

EACH OF THE HALL OF FAMERS HAD HIS OWN ROUND TABLE AT
the banquet that night, and the Lefty Gomez party made room
for me and my wife. I had brought along my old 1930 box
score—I had to read it to Gomez, who had forgotten his reading
glasses—and he thanked me and said, "My God, I was six feet
two and I weighed a hundred and forty-nine pounds that year.
I was a *ghost.*" He looked around the crowded, cheerful room
and said, "When I was a kid in the game, the older players
would talk about all the famous guys that had once played with
them or against them, but I never listened. I just wasn't interested. Now that's all I ever do."

I sat next to a delightful daughter of Lefty's who told me that
she was Vernona Lois Gomez (Lefty is Vernon) and that the
name had been selected after her parents had held personal con-
sultations with the editor of a "Your Baby's Name" feature in
the Boston *Post.* I asked her what the runner-up handle had
been. "Juanita," she said.

Then I looked across the table at her slim and radiant mother,
and a buried line or two of five-decades-old sports-page chatter
came paddling up out of my memory: "The Gay Castilian [Lefty
Gomez, in the sports parlance of that day], accompanied by his
fiancée, Broadway's beautiful June O'Dea . . ."

"Is your mother the beautiful June O'Dea?" I asked Vernona.

"She certainly is," she said.

A little later, the B.J.O'D. told me that she and Lefty had met
in a night club, the Woodmansten Inn, up in the Bronx, and that
he had been absolutely tongue-tied that first evening. "We were
engaged in two weeks, but we didn't get married for two years,"
she said. "I was playing in 'Of Thee I Sing' by then. We had a
one-night honeymoon in Atlantic City, and the next morning he
said, 'So long, sweetheart, I'm going to spring training,' and I
didn't lay eyes on him for six weeks. That was fifty-four years
ago, so I guess you could say we worked it out."

When the gala party moved over to the Hall for dessert and drinks, there were crowds of fans jammed together on the sidewalk and beside the front steps there, waiting to cheer for the old stars as they came in; it reminded you a little of the mobs at the Oscar awards, in Los Angeles, but without the kitsch and the craziness. The players had the museum to themselves that night; the Catfish Hunters just about wiped out the souvenir shop single-handed.

I chatted with Warren Spahn in the Gallery, and at one point he made a little gesture toward the party and the plaques and said, "There's such a *feeling* to this place. I go to Washington a lot—I was there last week—and I always get a thrill when I see the Capitol or visit the Congress. I feel the same way here. It's awe. I look around and I see all these men who played the game so well—great players, you know—and did it for peanuts, because they loved to play. I'm lucky to be part of something like that. I'll be back next year. I always come back."

When my wife and I left—it was after eleven o'clock—it happened that we walked out of the Hall directly behind Cool Papa Bell, who went carefully down the steps on the arm of his daughter. He is eighty-four now. There were still some fans outside, waiting in the warm summer night, and when they saw who it was they came forward and gave him a terrific round of applause, and Cool Papa shifted his cane to the other hand and waved to them in reply.

The induction ceremonies the next day were more of the same, really: it was as if the party had gone on into the following afternoon. The weather gave us a break at last, and there was a gusty fresh breeze moving in the thick, tall trees in Cooper Park, where the thousands of sitting and standing fans almost engulfed the handsome verdigris-green statue of James Fenimore Cooper. Up on the steps of the library, the Hall of Famers were introduced, one by one. Ted Williams was wearing a bright-green blazer. Willie Mays—or maybe Roy Campanella—got the biggest hand. The sun shone, and the speeches and encomiums were sweet and boring and almost not too long. The Commissioner reminded us that Catfish Hunter had played for both Charlie Finley and George Steinbrenner (they were both there, down front with the V.I.P.s), which was enough in itself, he said, to put a man into the Hall of Fame. Jack Lang was teary, and Jack Buck (the voice of the Cardinals, who received the Ford C. Frick Award for his long career in baseball broadcasting) was lengthily grateful. Each of the inductees introduced all the members of his family after he received his plaque, and then delivered an acceptance address. Hunter told us about his long-ago contract negotiations with the Yankees; and Billy Williams, who had memorized and also copyrighted his speech, said it was high time that baseball became fully integrated by giving blacks and other minorities a chance at jobs in the front office and as managers. This day, he said, was "the most precious thing in my life." Ray Dandridge was the best: "The only thing I ever wanted to do was to put one foot into the major leagues, but they didn't want it," he told us. "Now I can thank each and every veteran on the committee for allowing me to smell the roses . . . I love baseball, and today it looks like baseball loves me."

◆ ◆ ◆

THERE IS A BASKETBALL HALL OF FAME IN SPRINGFIELD, MASsachusetts; a College Football Hall of Fame in Kings Island, Ohio; a Professional Football Hall of Fame in Canton, Ohio; a Bowling Hall of Fame in St. Louis, but I don't think they are quite the same as the Baseball Hall of Fame. I'd be surprised if they worked the same way. These thoughts came to me back in June, during the evening of the two-day visit that Charles and Ben and I made to Cooperstown. It was a muggy night, with some thundershowers, and after dinner the three of us gathered in the living room of the handsome old inn where we were staying and sat with some other guests there and watched a ballgame on television—a "Monday Night Baseball" game in Oakland between the Kansas City Royals and the Oakland Athletics. Ben went off to bed after a couple of innings, but Charles and I stayed to the end. It was a good game, because the Athletics hung tough and beat Bret Saberhagen, the Royals' ace, whose record coming into the game was an amazing 12-1 for the 1987 season. Reggie Jackson, who had been having a discouraging sort of summer so far—he is retiring at the end of this year—whacked a home run (No. 556, lifetime) in the second inning, and Charles and I instantly remarked to each other that somebody would have to change the digits beside his name in the basement of the Hall the next morning. Reggie will make the Hall of Fame easily, probably on the first ballot.

I began thinking about the other players in the game we were watching, and I decided that George Brett had a good shot at the Hall, too, with his lifetime .314 batting average to date and ·

that wonderful .390 season a few years ago. I wouldn't bet against Saberhagen, either, although it's much too early to tell, and no one in the world could say yet what kind of slugger the Oakland first baseman, Mark McGwire, might turn out to be. Already he had twenty-two homers in this, his first full season; he has been all the rage this year, but, of course, he is only a rookie.

With two outs in the eighth inning and the Royals trailing by 2–1, Dan Quisenberry came in to pitch for Kansas City, with a man on base. He fell behind on the count and then came in a hair too high with a breaking pitch, and Tony Phillips hit the ball over the right-field fence, to put the game out of reach. Quisenberry is a submarine relief specialist, with an odd, looping delivery, and his total of two hundred and thirty-six official saves is already the fourth best in baseball history. I spent some time with him two years ago while preparing an article about him; he was then on his way to his fourth consecutive Fireman of the Year award in his league. I thought at the time that he might be headed for the Hall of Fame, but he has gone into a sharp decline in the past two seasons—no one quite knows why— and I don't think anyone gives him much of a chance for Cooperstown now. I have suffered for him last year and this year (we are friends), and I was unhappy about his difficulties, but Quis himself had reminded me—even then, at the peak of his powers and success—that relief pitching is tricky and unpredictable, and that baseball, of course, is always tough to figure in advance. "The great ones are the ones who get it up year after year," he said.

Most of us fans fall in love with baseball when we are children, and those who come aboard as adults often do so in a rush of affection and attachment to a local team that has begun to win. These infatuations are ferociously battered and eroded by various forces—by the schlocky macho posturing and gossip and exaggerations of the media; by the failure of many players to live up to our expectations for them, both on the field and off the field; and, most of all, by the wearisome, heartbreaking difficulty of the sport, which inexorably throws down last years's champions, exposes rookie marvels as disappointing journeymen, and turns lithe young stars into straining old men, all in a very short space of time. Baseball is absorbing and sometimes thrilling, but it is also unrelenting; it is rarely pure fun for any of us, players or fans, for very long. Except at Cooperstown. The artifacts and exhibits in the Hall remind us, vividly and with feeling, of our hopes for bygone seasons and teams and players. Memories are jogged, even jolted; colors become brighter, and we laugh or sigh, remembering good times gone by. But the Hall of Famers themselves, with their plaques and pictures and citations, are the heart of something larger, for they tell us that there exists a handful of baseball players—it comes out to a bit over one percent of the thirteen thousand-odd men who have ever played major-league ball—who really did come close to our expectations. They played so well and so long, succeeding eventually at this almost impossible game, that we can think of them as something more useful than gods or heroes. We know they are there, tucked away up-country and in the back of our minds: old men, and younger ones on the way, who prove and sustain the elegance of our baseball dreams.

About the Author

ROGER ANGELL is the author of *The Stone Arbor*, *A Day in the Life of Roger Angell*, *The Summer Game*, *Five Seasons*, and *Late Innings*. He is senior fiction editor of *The New Yorker* and lives in New York with his wife and son.